# *Real*ising Systems Thinking: Knowledge and Action in Management Science

# Contemporary Systems Thinking

**Series Editor:** Robert L. Flood
Monash University
Australia

COMMUNITY OPERATIONAL RESEARCH
OR and Systems Thinking for Community Development
Gerald Midgley and Alejandro Ochoa-Arias

CRITICAL SYSTEMIC PRAXIS FOR SOIL AND
ENVIRONMENTAL JUSTICE
Participatory Policy Design and Governance for a Global Age
Janet McIntyre-Mills

GUIDED EVOLUTION OF SOCIETY
A Systems View
Bela H. Banathy

METADECISIONS
Rehabilitating Epistemology
John P. van Gigch

PROCESSES AND BOUNDARIES OF THE MIND
Extending the Limit Line
Yair Neuman

REALISING SYSTEMS THINKING
Knowledge and Action in Management Science
John Mingers

SOCIOPOLITICAL ECOLOGY
Human Systems and Ecological Fields
Frederick L. Bates

SYSTEMIC INTERVENTION
Philosophy, Methodology, and Practice
Gerald Midgley

A Continuation Order Plan is available for this series. A continuation order will bring delivery of each new volume immediately upon pulibcation. Volumes are billed only upon actual shipment. For further information please contact the publisher.

# *Real*ising Systems Thinking: Knowledge and Action in Management Science

John Mingers

 Springer

John Mingers
University of Kent
Canterbury, UK

Library of Congress Cataloging-in-Publication Data


ISBN-10: 0-387-28188-6 (HB)  ISBN-10: 0-387-29841-X (e-book)
ISBN-13: 978-0387-28188-9 (HB)

Printed in the United States of America.        Printed on acid-free paper.


9 8 7 6 5 4 3 2 1                    SPIN 11400066

springeronline.com

Dedicated to my family—Julie, Laura and Emma

# Table of Contents

# Chapter 1: Introduction

## *1.1 Introduction*

Systems thinking and the systems movement have been enormously productive and innovative since they emerged through developments in biology and information technology in the 1930s[1]. To highlight a few of the major contributions:

- Von Bertalanffy's (1971) first conscious articulation of general systems theory.

- Cybernetics as developed by Weiner (Weiner 1948), Ashby (1956), Bateson (1973) and others, and then applied to management by Stafford Beer (1966).

- The living systems approach to biology developed by Miller (1978).

- C West Churchman's (1968; 1971) ideas on dialectical systems further developed by Ulrich (1994).

- Ackoff and Emery's (1972) theory of purposeful systems.

- Hard systems engineering (Hall 1962).

- Checkland's (1981; 1990) reorientation of the discipline with the development of soft systems.

- Maturana and Varela's (1980; 1987) enormously influential theories of autopoiesis and cognition.

- Social systems theory developed, for instance, by Buckley (1967), Luhmann (1995), Habermas (1984; 1987) and Giddens (1984).

- Jackson (2000), Flood (1991), Midgley (2000) and Mingers' (1997) investigations of critical systems thinking and most recently multimethodology.

- Developments in chaos and complexity theory particularly at Santa Fe (Kaufmann 1995).

---

[1] I do of course recognise that systemic thinking has occurred throughout human history. Checkland (1981). but we can trace the current developments to the specific origins discussed above.

Taken together these works demonstrate both the coherence and the value of the underlying ideas and the huge range of disciplines within which they can be applied—from biology and neuroscience through to practical interventions in the organisational world.

I have been working and publishing in the systems field for over twenty-five years and my contributions have also been wide-ranging. My personal background was basically scientific. My first degree was in Management Sciences and I specialised in operational research (OR) and computing. At the time, OR was a relatively new subject and I engaged wholeheartedly with its underlying premise—OR was the science of rational action. In order to make a decision about some course of action, define the objective (usually assumed to be minimising costs or maximising profits); collect relevant data; build mathematical or computer models of the various options; and choose the optimal one. This seemed to my scientific mind eminently sensible, and I embarked on a career in information systems (or systems analysis as it was then called) and OR with several large companies confident that the power of computer-based modelling would solve all problems.

Sadly, I was in for a rude awakening. Whilst there were some occasions where a fairly standard technique such as mathematical programming was genuinely helpful to a manager, I soon discovered that real-world organisations were not easily and tidily fitted into mathematical models—they had social and political dimensions which were not touched by the OR techniques I had learnt. There were interpersonal problems of dealing with people—communicating with them, gaining their confidence, understanding what they were really wanting (to the extent they themselves knew), and convincing them of one's proposals. There was the discovery that neither managers, nor for that matter myself, spent a lot of time single-mindedly "maximising profits" or "minimising costs." Rather we had a whole range of organisational and personal goals that, in reality, we pursued but which I could not formally model, or even acknowledge. There was the embarrassment of relying on data that turned out to be patchy, often impossible to measure, and as much a reflection of its own processes of production as a reflection of "objective" reality (Mingers 1989).

Most importantly (and shockingly) I discovered the politics of organisational life. The projects that never got started because certain people refused to co-operate or provide information; the projects that were eagerly welcomed because they could be used by one department against another; and the antagonism towards us, and indeed attempts at sabotage, when our studies threatened the power position of particular groups. These "extraneous factors," that were never mentioned in OR or IT books or courses, seemed to have more influence over the success or otherwise of my work than anything I might do with my formal knowledge.

These experiences led me to systems thinking, as it promised a holistic approach that might have the potential to bring quantitative approaches together with the social and personal aspects of organisations that I had experienced. I decided to return to academia and joined (in 1976) virtually the only postgraduate systems course in the

UK, that at Lancaster. This was much more fortunate than I realised for this was the time when soft systems methodology (SSM, although not yet christened) was being developed by Peter Checkland and others who had had very similar experiences to myself.

For myself, I became convinced that here was a genuine attempt to deal with the actual reality of organisational life, but one which employed a rationality very different from that of traditional science. By the end of my Masters I was wholly converted to SSM as embodying a new way of thinking about interventions in organisations, and I looked back on operational research and its abstract mathematical formalisms as virtually useless for dealing with real-world problems. It was at this time that I came across several of the other streams of ideas that will be woven together into this book—the writings of Maturana and Varela on autopoiesis, Jürgen Habermas on critical theory, and Roy Bhaskar on critical realism.

However, having embraced SSM and its phenomenological underpinnings whole-heartedly I began to discover the limitations of such a philosophy. If you follow this path to its logical conclusion then you end up in a solipsistic pit from which it is difficult to escape. Every theory becomes simply another viewpoint or Weltanschauung, another interpretation of the world, no better or worse than any other. There can be no external social world that enables or constrains us, indeed no world at all that is more than a construction of the observer as Checkland himself argued:

'{we} need to remind ourselves that we have no access to what the world *is*, to ontology, only to descriptions of the world, ... that is to say, to epistemology. ... Thus, systems thinking is only an epistemology, a particular way of describing the world. It does not tell us what the world *is*. Hence, strictly speaking, we should never say of something in the world: "It is a system," only: "It may be described as a system." ... The important feature of paradigm II {soft systems} as compared with paradigm I {hard systems} is that *it transfers systemicity from the world to the process of enquiry into the world.*' (Checkland 1983, p. 671)

This recognition, not just on my part, led to the development of a "third way"— *critical* systems thinking—drawing in the main on the work of German sociologist Jürgen Habermas (1974; 1978). The main tenets of critical systems as it developed were two fold:

1.  To critique both positivism and interpretivism thus demonstrating that whilst both had a degree of validity in particular circumstances neither had a sole claim to truth and so other approach(es) were necessary. At the time this was seen as Habermasian critical theory; now I would argue that it is critical realism.

2.  To critique the inequitable and repressive conditions prevailing in society in order to bring about a fairer and more rational one.

Once interpretivism and then critical theory had entered the scene, several other philosophical positions were also proposed. For instance, postmodernism (Ciborra 1998; Robinson, Hall et al. 1998; Greenhill 2001) and actor-network theory (Walsham 1997), as well as a whole variety of systems and OR methodologies (Mingers 2000c). This led to further research developing a pluralist approach to combining methods and paradigms together (Mingers and Gill 1997) known as multimethodology. In parallel with work on practical OR methodology I also pursued my interests in autopoiesis, phenomenology, information theory, social theory, critical realism and research methodology.

At first sight such a diversity of areas might appear disparate and unrelated but, to me at least, there have always been underlying themes and implicit, if not always explicit, connections. Indeed, for me there is actually a coherent path from the most fundamental work on philosophical issues of ontology and epistemology through specific domains of knowledge about the nature of information and meaning, human communication, and social interaction right up to the implications of these theoretical developments for action and intervention in real-world affairs. It is the purpose of this book to lay out this path from knowledge to action and make clear the interactions and connections between these varied fields.

## *1.2 Structure of the Book*

The underlying structure of the thought behind this book can best be understood from Table 1.

This is divided into three main sections—Foundations, Knowledge and Action. These are to be seen as intimately linked.

The underlying philosophy upon which everything else rests is known as critical realism (CR) as developed primarily by Roy Bhaskar, whose main features are:

- This philosophy maintains a basically realist stance towards the world—there are independent objects of knowledge, and we can gain reliable knowledge of them, whilst at the same time recognising that knowledge, especially in the social science, is always fallible and culturally, spatially, and historical relative.

- In accepting ontologically the existence of a plurality of different types of objects or structures—material, social and conceptual—with different properties it accepts the need for a variety of methodologies. It thus provides critiques of both pure hard and soft systems thinking, or empiricism and interpretivism if these terms are preferred, and instead leads towards the combination of a rich variety of research and action methods.

- It embodies a *critical* perspective towards science and society, denying dichotomies between knowledge and action or facts and values

## Table 1.1. Overview of the Book

| Chapter | Contents |
|---|---|
| 1. Introduction | Background to the ideas in the book |
| **Foundations** | |
| 2. Philosophical Foundations—Critical Realism | An overview of the philosophy of critical realism and its relevance for management science |
| 3. Living Systems—Autopoiesis | A review of Maturana and Varela's theory of autopoiesis and of cognition. This provides an underpinning for much of the rest of the book. |
| 4. Observing Systems—the Question of Boundaries | Fundamental to the systems approach is the question of system boundaries. This is a contentious issue and yet is seldom discussed explicitly. This chapter addresses the fundamental questions raised by the process of observing systems. It also shows the importance of boundaries and constraints in interventions in a later chapter. |
| **Knowledge** | |
| 5. Cognising Systems—Information and Meaning | The issue of the nature of information and its relation to meaning has never been successfully resolved within information systems. This chapter proposes a solution based on autopoiesis, critical theory and the work of Dretske. |
| 6. Knowledge and Truth | This chapter draws on the earlier ones on critical realism and the nature of information to develop a multi-faceted view of knowledge and truth. It leads into discussion of knowledge management. |
| 7. Communication and Social Interaction | This chapter moves up from the level of the embodied individual to that of social interaction and the social group. It will draw on Luhmann's theory of autopoietic communication as well as Habermas's theory of communicative action. |
| 8. Social Systems | This chapter moves up a level again to consider the nature of social systems. It too draws on earlier chapters, especially those on critical realism, autopoiesis, and Luhmann's work. It develops a characterisation of social systems that synthesises the theories of Bhaskar and Giddens. |
| **Action: Research and Intervention** | |
| 9. Theory of Multimethodology | The final chapters move back to the practical world of management science. What are the implications of the theory so far developed for research and practical interventions? Here the main proposals are multimethodology and multi-method research … |
| 10. Process of Multimethodology—Critical Pluralism | and the importance of boundaries and constraint in undertaking critically-inspired work |

Although Bhaskar's work tends not to make explicit mention of the systems literature it is fundamentally systemic. In the early CR theory the primary systemic motifs were the ontological designation of structures and mechanisms that had powers or tendencies, the operation and interaction of which generated actual events; and the emphasis on ontological stratification and emergent powers. These concepts can be translated almost directly into the language of systems thinking: systems forming wholes with emergent properties, structure and process, and systemic structure and interaction generating observed behaviour.

With the development of dialectical critical realism and the specification of the MELD schema in (Bhaskar 1993), the systemic concepts become even more explicit. The prime moment (1M) includes the concepts mentioned above of structure, generative mechanisms and emergence. The second edge (2E) brings in change and temporality. The key concept of *absence*, although not a central feature of systems thinking, is certainly compatible with ideas of goal seeking through error-controlled feedback (removing an absence of equilibrium), and different causal processes cancelling each other out, leading to an absence of change. The third level (3L) is clearly central with its emphasis on totality, holistic causality, and recursive embeddings (nested hierarchies in systems terms). The fourth dimension (4D) brings in the realm of agency, embodiment, reflexivity and social transformation, all of which are concerns especially of second-order, soft systems thinking. Bhaskar also emphasises that in the social world systems are always open and cannot be closed as in a laboratory. Finally, Bhaskar explicitly draws on the concept of autopoiesis as a key feature of the process of knowledge production, emergence and social reproduction itself.

The next foundation is the theory of autopoiesis. As Maturana has said, "everything said is said by an observer" and that applies to this book as much as anything else. For me, Maturana and Varela have produced an answer to one of the most profound questions—what is the nature of life or, at least, living systems? They have gone on to consider the implications of autopoiesis for thinking, languaging and observing. Autopoietic systems are systems that continually produce or create themselves in closed circular processes of production (a paradigm example is a single-celled organism such as amoeba). They have no other purpose, and if the dynamic circularity is interrupted then they disintegrate. Evolution has led to multicellular organisms and ultimately to humans whose distinguishing characteristic is a complex nervous system that enable them to use language and be observers.

Whilst not accepting all their conclusions, concepts such as organisational closure, structure-determinism, and structural coupling inform much of the theorising in later chapters. Autopoiesis has also been explicitly taken up within social theory by Luhmann whose work will be discussed in Chapters 7 and 8.

The third foundation is the crucial question of system's boundaries. This is a much neglected area the importance of which has become more apparent to me. Whilst Checkland's soft systems and Maturana's second-order cybernetics have both raised fundamental questions about the existence and identification of systems in the world they have not dealt explicitly with the nature of system boundaries. Yet, in fact, the two are inseparable, for decisions about the nature of and location of a system's boundary are identical to decisions about its existence. If a system exists (in any sense) then it will have a boundary, and the drawing of the boundary will determine the identity of the system.

After these three foundational chapters, the book moves to a section I have called "Knowledge," as it covers specific knowledge, or at least theories, that I have developed. These chapters have a partly hierarchical relation as they move from individual cognition through group communication to social systems.

The first (Chapter 5) is concerned with a question of great importance for information systems, that is what exactly is "information"? And how, if at all, does information differ from data or meaning? If a message carries information is that distinct from its meaning or from the data? Maturana has claimed that because of the closed nature of the nervous system no interactions are inherently informative and information must be a purely metaphorical as opposed to operational concept. On the other hand Checkland argues that information equals data plus meaning making it intrinsically subjective. In developing my own theory I also brought in the work of Dretske (1981) Luhmann (1990b) and Habermas (1979) and came to a view that information does, in fact, exist objectively as the propositional content of signs although we humans could only ever access it after a conversion process into *meaning*. This led into an enactive and embodied view of the process of cognition which fits well with Merleau-Ponty (1962) and Varela (1991).

The question of information leads quite naturally into a consideration of knowledge (Chapter 6). If, for example, information has to be true to be information (as Dretske argues) does that also make it knowledge? Or, is knowledge different from or wider than just information? In this chapter I develop a multi-faceted view of knowledge and truth drawing both on critical realism and the model of information and meaning from the previous chapter. I argue that there are at least four substantively different forms of knowledge—propositional, experiential, performative, and epistemological. These differ in terms of the objects of knowledge, the source of knowledge, the form of representation and their relation to various conceptions of truth. This variety has strong implications for the development of knowledge management within information systems.

Chapter 7 also develops from the material in Chapter 5 on information and meaning. Information was defined as the propositional content of signs and was seen to be converted by humans into meaning through a process of digitalisation. This process is developed in more detail where it is seen to be largely unconscious and embodied in opposition to the Cartesian view of a split between mind and body. Reference is made here to the work of Merleau-Ponty (1963) and Varela (1991). For humans, much of their information comes from interaction with other people rather than simple perception of the world and this leads to a consideration of the nature of communication, initially reciprocal interactions between two people, and then moving on to the level of the social group or network. These sections draw on

Luhmann's theory of society as communication (itself based on autopoiesis) and Maturana's theory of the social organisation.

Part II concludes with a chapter on social systems. This largely revolves around the deep question as to whether or not social systems, however they may be defined, can be said, in themselves, to be autopoietic. Or, put another way, can we characterise social systems in such a way that can can be seen to be self-bounding and self-constructing? This chapter proceeds with a detailed discussion of the social theories of Luhmann, Giddens and Bhaskar.

Moving to Part III we are concerned with action, that is, deliberate and purposeful activity intended to increase our understanding of particular real-world situations and thereby bring about desirable change. Within the book this is grounded within the areas of operational research (OR), information systems, and systems practice (what I shall generally refer to as management science) but the implications apply much more widely to any domains in which conscious change is being engineered, for instance education, development, or environmentalism.

Part I: Foundations

# Chapter 2: Philosophical Foundations: Critical Realism

## 2.1 Introduction and Context

Over the last four hundred years science has been incredibly successful in generating knowledge about the world and producing the vast array of technology that now shapes every minute of our lives. It is not surprising therefore that (natural) scientific knowledge came to be seen as the only valid form of knowledge. Modern-day science began in the days of the Enlightenment with the then novel idea that we could gain knowledge and understanding not from tradition or religious dogma or subjective contemplation but by observing and experimenting with the natural world itself. The origin of knowledge was to be *empirical* rather than metaphysical leading ultimately to the philosophies of empiricism and positivism that reached their apogee in the early twentieth century.

For empiricism the source of all knowledge must be empirical—i.e., open to the senses and able to be observed by others. That which cannot be observed, directly or indirectly through instruments, ultimately cannot exist. The logical positivists insisted that observations should be quantifiable and expressible mathematically, and that discussion of anything else was actually meaningless. Social science also wanted to emulate natural science with the work of Compte and Durkheim in sociology and Skinner's behaviourism in psychology.

Management science (including operational research (OR) and information systems (IS)) and systems thinking had their roots in this era. OR began in the Second World War when scientific methods were used to analyse military operations such as the size of convoys, the use of radar and depth charging (Trefethen 1995). These methods emphasised the collection and analysis of data, and building mathematical and simulation models to test out hypotheses. After the war OR groups were established in large organisations and in government with the intention of scientifically improving societal processes. The systems approach also began in the 1930s with the biologist von Bertalanffy (1971) developing the idea of general systems theory applying across all disciplines, and Weiner (1948) and Ashby (1956) recognising the importance of feedback and communications processes which they termed cybernetics (Heims 1993).

However, empiricism and especially positivism were then subjected to major critiques by philosophers (e.g., Popper (1972)), psychologists and sociologists and virtually all their major tenets were discredited to some degree. Within natural science a degree of support was established around what was known as the hypothetico-deductive model but social science became strongly split into what were seen as mutually incompatible paradigms (Kuhn 1970; Burrell and Morgan 1979). The main rupture was between functionalists who followed a broadly positivist approach and interpretivists who claimed that the meaning-based nature of the social world made it inherently unavailable to external observation and measurement.

These developments were paralleled within management science and systems with the emergence of "soft" systems and OR, and second-order cybernetics (Checkland 1985; Eden 1993; Hayles 1999).

The pendulum swung fully away from positivism with the emergence of extreme anti-realist and anti-rationalist positions such as postmodernism (Rosenau 1992) and constructivism (Von Glasersfeld 1984). These, in various ways, denied the taken-for-granted assumptions of modernism: that there was an external world about which we could discover knowledge; that there were general standards of rationality such as true/false, good/bad or right/wrong; or that, especially in the social world, there was an underlying order or theory to be discovered rather than simply superficial surface happenings. Again, these positions were echoed, albeit somewhat mutedly, within the practically-oriented disciplines of management science (Hassard and Parker 1993; Taket and White 1993; Coyne 1995; Robinson, Hall et al. 1998).

It is against this background that we can examine the development and contribution of critical realism as a significant philosophy of science able to underpin the management science disciplines.

## 2.2 Philosophical Problems within Management Science

As management science developed it was dominated by an empiricist philosophy that led it to see quantitative modelling and statistical analysis as the main legitimate type of research method. Within other fields of management (and indeed management science outside the United States) interpretive or constructivist philosophies also became legitimised, employing a range of non-quantitative methods. In some cases, e.g., information systems or operational research, this has led to divisive debates over "hard" and "soft."

This chapter argues for a reorientation of the fundamentals of management science in terms of both underlying philosophy and related methodology. In particular, it suggests that critical realism provides an underpinning that resolves many issues as well as fitting in with management science's distinctive approach. It will also be argued in Chapters 9 and 10 that *multimethodology* (the combination of a plurality of intervention or research methods) is an appropriate and complementary methodology. These arguments illustrate the intimate connection between theory, especially philosophy, and research methods. Current approaches such as positivism and interpretivism embody particular theories and assumptions about the nature of the natural and social worlds and this conditions the type of research methods and methodology that they utilize. So too does critical realism but in a way that enables it to build on important insights from differing paradigms whilst bringing forward its own distinctive tenets.

Management science, taken broadly, has been based in a strongly positivist, quantitative paradigm although more recently softer, interpretive methodologies have been gaining credibility. For example, surveys of the information systems literature

(Orlikowski and Baroudi 1991; Cheon, Grover et al. 1993; Walsham 1995; Nandhakumar and Jones 1997) agree that the majority of information systems research that is published, especially in N. American oriented journals, is generally of a positivist nature and, more specifically, relies on some form of statistical analysis and modelling. Mingers' (2003b) survey concluded that nearly 50% of empirical research published in the top IS journals employed observation, experiments, surveys or simulations and would thus involved some sort of statistical analysis. When positivistic case study research was included this proportion rose to 75% (over 90% in the case of the top journal Information Systems Research).

Despite this positivistic hegemony, alternative research approaches have been proposed and to some extent employed (Nissen, Klein et al. 1991; Galliers 1992; Goles and Hirschheim 2000; Mingers and Willcocks 2004). These generally come from an interpretive or subjectivist perspective (Myers 1994; Avison and Myers 1995; Harvey and Myers 1995) although there is also work within the critical tradition (Ngwenyama and Lee 1997; Klein and Huynh 2004). Interpretive researchers tend to be very critical of positivism, and statistical analysis in particular, on the grounds that the social world is inherently different to the material world and is in essence a human social construction not able to be quantified and captured in statistical models. However, this often leads to a strongly anti-realist position that tends to deny the existence of any forms of external social structures.

Similarly, the history of operational research can be seen (Mingers 1992; Mingers 2000a) to embody a range of alternative philosophical viewpoints. There is the traditional positivist or empiricist viewpoint with various flavours—inductivist, deductivist, falsificationist (Dery, Landry et al. 1993); a wider view of science as craft, developed by Ravetz (1971) and debated by Miser (1991; 1996), Keys (1991), and Ormerod (1996a; 1996c); various types of constructivist, interpretive or post-modern stances that to a greater or lesser extent deny the possibility of an observer-independent reality (Bryant 1993; White 1994; Brocklesby and Cummings 1996; Tsoukas and Papoulias 1996; White and Taket 1996; Brocklesby 1997); or the social studies of science argument that successful science is actually the result of a political and social process (Keys 1997; Keys 1998).

There has been a range of reactions to this plurality of philosophical approaches. Imperialists argue for the dominance of one particular paradigm (usually positivism), either on epistemological grounds (that it is the correct way to generate knowledge) or in the belief that it is necessary to create a strong discipline (Pfeffer 1993; Benbasat and Weber 1996). Isolationists tend to accept the arguments of Burrell and Morgan (1979) that there are distinctively different paradigms within a discipline and that these are generally incommensurable—i.e., they cannot be directly compared with each other because they are based on radically different assumptions. From this perspective, research should develop separately within each paradigm (Parker and McHugh 1991; Deetz 1996). Finally pluralists accept, and indeed welcome, a diversity of paradigms and research methods. Within this group we can distinguish between those who welcome diversity for its own sake (Van Maanen 1995; Van Maanen 1995); those who see different methods as being more or less appropriate for particular research questions or situations (Landry and Banville 1992; Robey 1996); and those who argue that research should strive to be trans-paradigmatic, routinely combining philosophically distinct research methods (Jackson 1999; Goles and Hirschheim 2000; Midgley 2000; Mingers 2001a). Management science is not unique in respect of this diversity—most social sciences, for example, organisation theory, sociology, or geography, are equally split.

However, what is often not recognized is that there are significant problems within the underlying philosophies, of science and social science, themselves. Positivism has been extensively critiqued and the resulting consensus around a weak empiricist position (known as hypothetico-deductivism) leads to an impoverished view of (realist) ontology and causality. Within the social sciences extreme constructivist and post modern positions have undermined even the most basic tenets of science and rationality.

This chapter considers a particular philosophy of science—*critical realism*—as a way of resolving or dissolving most of these issues, and providing a consistent and coherent underpinning philosophy for management science. The next section discusses the problems with the philosophy of science, particularly as they inhibit a realist (although not "naïve" realist) approach. Later sections develop critical realism and shows how it addresses these problems.

## 2.3 Problems in the Philosophy of Natural Science

In general, a *realist* understanding of science takes the view that certain types of entities—be they objects, forces, social structures, or ideas—exist in the world, largely independent of human beings; and that we can gain reliable, although not perfect, knowledge of them. However, from as long ago as the eighteenth century Hume (1967) and Berkeley (1995) undermined such a view by denying fundamental tenets like the existence of a physical world, causal necessity, or unobservable entities. Berkeley argued that we only actually know objects through our ideas and perceptions of them and that, therefore, is all we can actually take to exist. Thus, to be is to be perceived. Hume was highly sceptical of several basic notions such as causality, unobservable entities, and induction. With regard to causality, he says we often see one event regularly followed by another and we believe that event A (e.g., swing a bat) causes event B (a ball moving). However, all we can actually observe is the constant conjunction of the two events. Our belief that A *causes* B is simply that—a psychological belief. There is nothing more to causality than a regular succession of events. Hume is similarly sceptical about induction—the idea that witnessing an event occur many times (e.g., the sun rising) warrants us claiming it will always happen. These views, particularly that of Humean causality, underlie empiricism and have serious anti-realist implications.

During the twentieth century, "naïve realism" continued to be under constant attack from empiricism (which restricts science to mathematical formulations of empirical regularities) on the one hand and the many different forms of conventionalism or constructivism (that deny the existence of a world independent of human thought and perception) on the other.

## Empiricism

In very broad terms, empiricism refers to those philosophies that see science as explaining events that can be empirically observed. That which is not manifest and capable of observation must be non-scientific or even, in the extreme case of the Vienna Circle philosophers, literally meaningless. Events are expected to display regularities or patterns that can be explained as being particular instances of universal laws of the form "given certain conditions, whenever event X occurs then event Y will occur." Science is seen as the systematic observation of event regularities, the description of these regularities in the form of universal laws, and the prediction of particular outcomes from the laws.

*Logical empiricism* was developed during the 1920s by a group known as the Vienna Circle (e.g., Schlick (1979), Neurath (1987)) who aimed to specify a truly scientific conception of knowledge and the world. Their main tenets were:

- Scientific knowledge must rest ultimately on that which is empirically open to the senses. This meant that any scientific propositions must be able to be empirically verified, and that anything unable to be directly or indirectly observed must be non-scientific or even meaningless.

- Empirical observations must then be reformulated into some strict mathematical or logical language (following the work of Frege (1952) and Russell (Whitehead and Russell 1925)), generally expressed in terms of universal laws.

- There must be a unity of method across all sciences, thus social science and history must also be formulated in such a way.

These propositions rested on particular fundamental assumptions: i) the idea that observation and perception were unproblematic—simply providing a mirror on nature; ii) the Humean (1967) principle that the observation of one event following another (e.g., one ball hitting another) did not enable us to prove some underlying causal mechanism—all that we can claim are "constant conjunctions of events"; iii) the principle of induction—that *universal* laws could be derived from a set of *particular* observations accompanied by the deduction of predictions from the laws.

This view of science was extensively critiqued. The idea of pure, objective perception and observation was exploded by psychologists (Piaget; Gregory 1972), sociologists (Cicourel 1973) and philosophers (Hansen 1958; Merleau-Ponty 1962; Popper 1972). They showed, theoretically and experimentally, that the brain was not simply a blank slate on which the external world imposed itself, but rather perception and conceptualisation was an active construction of the nervous system. Hesse (1974), Popper (1972), Wittgenstein (1958), and Kuhn (1970) showed that observational terms, i.e., the language we use to describe our observations, were not an atomistic picturing of reality but part of a pre-given linguistic structure—in short that all observation was theory-dependent. And Popper (1959; 1969), based on Hume, rejected the possibility of induction and verification replacing it with deduction and falsification.

In response to these criticisms there developed the "deductive-nomological (D-N)" or "hypothetico-deductive" method centred around the work of Hempel (1965) and Popper. Science was still seen to be based fundamentally on empirical observations, although recognising their theory-dependence. From such observations theories were generated and expressed in terms of universal (nomological) laws ("covering laws"). Explanation, or prediction, then consisted of the logical deduction of particular events given some antecedent conditions and a set of laws. It was accepted that the laws might only be expressed in terms of statistical probabilities, and that they could not be *proved* to be true inductively. Some people maintained a confirmationist view that empirical evidence could provide support for a theory while Popper developed the falsificationist approach that negative observations could definitely refute a theory. On this view, science should constantly aim to reject poor theories rather support or confirm good theories. Hume's view of causation was still largely accepted. There was still general scepticism about the ontological status of theoretical concepts that could not be observed fairly directly leading to debates about the legitimacy of "theoretical entities." Perceptibility was the criterion for existence.

The D-N approach also suffers from a range of problems, some of which will be explained in the next section on conventionalist alternatives. But, to highlight a few:

- Falsificationism, certainly in simple form, does not stand up—does a failed experiment falsify an underlying theory, or simply the experiment itself and its supplementary theories? Theories often need to be developed despite initial failures, not just abandoned. Does not falsificationism implicitly rely on induction—i.e., moving from particular instances (of failure) to the general statement that it will always fail?

- The covering law model and especially Humean causality was very impoverished simply providing a description of *what* happened in highly constrained experimental conditions, with no explanation of *why* it happened, or sometimes did not; and with no mechanism for the generation of new theories or putatively real entities. This is particularly problematic from a realist point of view as it restricts "reality" to the domain of empirically observable events and prohibits underlying generative mechanisms.

- It did not correspond, in many ways, with the actual practices of scientists and could not therefore satisfactorily explain the *de facto* success of science.

- The proposal that the social world was in essence no different from the natural world simply could not be sustained.

## Conventionalism

Problems with the empiricist view of science centre on the impossibility of pure, unmediated observation of empirical "facts." So, the term conventionalism covers a wide range of philosophies that all emphasise the inevitable dependence of scientific theories on human perception, conceptualization and judgement.

The first position, *pragmatism,* derives from philosophers such as Dewey (1938) and Peirce (1878) and has been developed most radically (and perhaps somewhat illegitimately) by Rorty (1980; 1989). At a general level pragmatism is a view about the purpose of science—that it is essentially a practical activity aimed at producing useful knowledge rather than understanding the true nature of the world. Thus, Peirce developed a pragmatist theory of meaning such that the meaning of a concept was specified purely in terms of the actual practical effects that it would have; and a consensus theory of truth as that which would come to be believed by a community of scientists in the long term, rather than as correspondence to reality (Habermas 1978). Dewey saw knowledge and truth as the outcome of processes that successfully resolved problematic situations.

The second position on the nature of science comes from those who study the actual practices of scientists and find that they do not correspond to the standard philosophical theories. This becomes more than mere description when it is used to critique the possibility of particular philosophical prescriptions. Kuhn's (1970; 1977) identification of major paradigms of thought throughout science is so well known as to need little exposition. The general idea is a development of the theory-dependence of observation—at any one time there is a broad, underlying theoretical conceptualization (e.g., Einsteinian physics) that is unquestioned within "normal" scientific activity. This paradigm informs all actual experimentation which is simply puzzle-solving within the paradigm. The failure of particular experiments does not refute, or even question, the basic paradigm. Only in periods of "revolutionary" science, when there are many anomalies, do paradigms actually become questioned or compete.

This view leads to a much greater recognition of the social and psychological nature of scientific activity. A paradigm develops through consensus within a social community of scientists through many practical mechanisms such as learned societies, journals, or funding bodies. Individual scientists come to accept the underlying assumptions concerning research practice, theoretical validity, and core values as they become members of the community. Theoretical innovations that challenge the paradigm are generally rejected without serious consideration.

The basic idea of paradigms replacing each other over time has developed, particularly within social science, to the idea of there being competing paradigms existent at the same time (e.g., positivist, interpretive and critical). This is often combined with the claim that paradigms are incommensurable (although Kuhn himself did not agree with this (Kuhn 1977)). That is, each paradigm is so all-inclusive in defining its ontological and epistemological presuppositions that it is literally not possible to actually compare them—each defines its own "reality." Clearly, the Kuhnian view has major relativistic implications for empiricism since it points out the constructed, conventional nature of scientific theorizing, and makes truth not correspondence to some external reality but that which is accepted by a scientific community at a particular point in time. The incommensurability thesis is even more undermining since in makes it impossible to judge between paradigms or even assert that a later paradigm is actually superior to an earlier one.

The third viewpoint, the sociology of scientific knowledge (SSK), can be seen as an intensification of Kuhn's study of the actual practice of science. It investigates the way in which scientific and technological knowledge comes to be constructed and accepted within a scientific community (Bloor 1976; Barnes 1977 ; Knorr-Cetina and Mulkay 1983; Collins 1985; Bijker, Hughes et al. 1987; Latour 1987; Woolgar 1988). The most radical theories from this perspective (e.g., Bloor) argues that in fact science is no different to other forms of purposeful social activity and actually has no greater claim to truth.

## The Relationship between Natural and Social Science

So far, the discussion has centred around the nature of natural science on the assumption that this was most relevant to management science, but in recent years there has been persuasive arguments that since IS is conducted within social organisations, social science is also of relevance (Boland 1991; Orlikowski and Baroudi 1991; Galliers 1992; Myers 1994; Avison and Myers 1995). This then brings into the picture major philosophical debates concerning the nature of social science in relation to natural science that can only be sketched here (for overviews see Giddens (1976), Burrell and Morgan (1979), Keat and Urry (1981), Outhwaite (1987).

Broadly, there are three possible positions:

- The *naturalist* view that there is one general approach to science that applies to all domains. Within this category, positivists hold that for anything to be scientific it must follow the canons of positivism/empiricism and thus be based on universal generalizations from empirical observations (Giddens 1974). This was in fact accepted by early sociologists such as Comte and, despite much criticism, continues in areas such as empirical and functionalist sociology and much IS research. Critical realists, on the other hand, maintain a modified naturalism that is non-positivist and that accepts there are some differences between the natural and social worlds.

- The antithesis is the view that the social world is intrinsically different to the natural world, being constituted through language and meaning, and thus involves entirely different hermeneutic (Bleicher 1980), phenomenological (Schutz 1972), or social constructivist (Gergen 1999) approaches. The argument here would be the idealist one that ontologically social objects do not exist in the way physical ones do (i.e., as subject independent), and that epistemologically there is no possibility of facts or observations that are independent of actors, cultures or social practices. Both Habermas (1978) and Giddens (1976) fall in this category.

- The most radical position denies the possibility of objective or scientific knowledge at all, in either domain. Arguments here come from the strong sociology of knowledge program discussed above; post-structuralists such as Foucault (1980) who point out the extent to which even our most basic categories such as male/female are socially constructed, and the inevitable intertwining of knowledge and power; and more generally post modernists (Best and Kellner 1991) who attempt to undermine even the most basic categories of modernist rationality such as distinctions between truth and falsity, better or worse, or the existence of external reality.

## 2.4 An Introduction to Critical Realism

Critical realism has been developing for some years (Bhaskar 1978; Bhaskar 1979; Keat and Urry 1981; Bhaskar 1986; Bhaskar 1993) in response to the fundamental difficulty of maintaining a realist position in the face of the criticisms, outlined above, of an empirical and naturalist view of science. Its original aims (which this chapter will concentrate on) were:

- To re-establish a realist view of *being* in the ontological domain whilst accepting the relativism of knowledge as socially and historically conditioned in the epistemological domain (Bhaskar 1978). In other words, to establish that there is an independently existing world of objectives and structures that are causally active, giving rise to the actual events that do and do not occur. But at the same time, to accept the criticisms of naive realism and to recognise that our observations and knowledge can never be pure and unmediated, but are relative to our time period and culture.

- To argue for a critical naturalism in social science (Bhaskar 1979). That is, to maintain that the same general process of science is applicable in both the natural and social domains but to accept that the particular characteristics of the social world place inevitable limits on that process.

Originally Bhaskar referred to his work as either "transcendental realism" or "critical naturalism," reflecting these two aims, but these became contracted to "critical realism." In later work (Bhaskar 1993; Bhaskar 1994) the use of the qualifier "critical" related also to critical social theory (Habermas 1974; Habermas 1978), and he put forward the argument that no social theory can be purely descriptive, it must be evaluative, and thus there can be no split between facts and values. And, following from this, the view that social theory is inevitably transformative, providing an explanatory critique that logically entails action (Archer, Bhaskar et al. 1998, Part III).

Critical realism is becoming influential in a range of disciplines—geography (Pratt 1995; Yeung 1997), economics (Lawson 1997; Fleetwood 1999), organisation theory (Marsden 1993; Reed 1997; Tsang and Kwan 1999; Ackroyd and Fleetwood 2000; Reed 2001), sociology (Layder 1994; Archer 1995; New 1995; Sayer 1997), international relations (Wright 1999), Marxism (Brown, Fleetwood et al. 2002) and research methods in general (Sayer 1992; Layder 1993).

## 2.4.1 Arguments Establishing an Independent Ontological Domain

The first step is to put forward arguments that establish the existence of an ontological domain separate from the activities and cognitions of human beings.

Bhaskar's (Archer, Bhaskar et al. 1998, p. 23) starting point is to argue, specifically against empiricism and positivism, that science is not just a matter of recording constant conjunctions of observable events but is about objects, entities and structures that exist (even though perhaps unobservable) and generate or give rise to the events that we do observe. The form of the argument is a *transcendental* (this follows a broadly Kantian interpretation of "transcendental") one. That is, it begins with some accepted happening or occurrence and asks what must the world be like for this to occur or to be intelligible? In this case, what is accepted by both empiricism and many forms of idealism is that we do have perceptual experience of the world, and that science is carried out through experimental activity in which scientists bring about particular outcomes.

The argument is that neither empiricism nor idealism can successfully explain these occurrences, and that they necessitate some form of realist ontology. With regard to perception, we can note that as human beings we have to learn (as babies) to perceive things and events; that our perceptions can change or be mistaken (e.g., visual illusions); and that scientists, for example, have to be trained to make observations correctly. These all imply that there must be a domain of events that are independent of our perceptions of them—what Bhaskar calls an *intransitive* domain. And, indeed, that these events would exist whether or not they were observed or whether or not there were even observers. Thus, there is a domain of actual events only a (small) subset of which are perceived and become empirical experiences. That which is not experienced is not known but that does not mean to say that it does not exist. In other words, there is an infinity of events that do actually occur but are never empirically observed.

Moving on to experimental activity, this shows several things. We can note that the experimenter causes (i.e., brings about) the experimental conditions but does not cause the results, these depend upon the underlying causal laws or mechanisms that are operative at the time. The regularities that are expected may or may not occur and this depends partly on how well the experiment is carried out rather than on whether the presumed laws are or are not working. In fact, the occurrence of empirical regularities (i.e., constant conjunctions of events) in general is fairly rare—that is why the experiment is necessary to try to bring them about in the first place. The world is not full of constant conjunctions. But despite this, experimental results do in fact hold outside the experiment as is attested by the enormous success of our technology.

The implications of this are that causal laws (more precisely from a critical realist perspective causal *mechanisms*) must be different from and independent of the patterns of events they generate; and that the experimenter aims to produce a constant conjunction of events by *closing* what would otherwise be an open system. Thus the intelligibility and success of experimental activity demonstrates the existence of an intransitive domain of casual mechanisms separate from the events they generate. And the corrigibility of perception demonstrates the separation of events from particular experiences of them. This leads to a conceptual separation between a domain of causally operative structures or systems; the events that they generate; and those events that are empirically observed. Thus empiricism is doubly wrong in identifying causal laws with empirical regularities. It reduces underlying laws or mechanisms to actual events, and then events in general to experiences.

The argument can be expressed in terms of the mistake that both empiricism and strong forms of idealism or conventionalism make—that is, the *epistemic fallacy*. The essential mistake is in reducing the ontological domain of existence to the epistemological domain of knowledge—statements about being (i.e., what exists) are translated into ones about *our (human) knowledge* or experience of being. For the empiricist, that which cannot be experienced cannot be. For the conventionalist, limitations of our *knowledge* of being are taken to be limitations on being itself. In contrast, the realist asserts the primacy of ontology—the world would exist whether or not humans did.

The argument so far establishes that, given the successful occurrence of science there must be an intransitive world of events and causal laws, but what exactly are causal laws? Or, rather, what is it that causes or generates events given both the regularities that can be established in experiments, and the common absence of regularity outside? Equally, how can we assure ourselves that event regularities are based on necessary connections rather than simply coincidence? The answer is that there must be enduring entities, physical (e.g., atoms or organisms), social (e.g., the market or the family) or conceptual (e.g., categories or ideas) (Bhaskar 1997), observable or not, that have *powers* or *tendencies* to act in particular ways. The continual operation and interaction of these entities generates (i.e., causes), but is independent of, the flux of events.

Entities are structures, consisting of particular components that have certain properties or powers as a result of their structure. Thus gunpowder has the power to cause an explosion, a plane has the power to fly, a person has the power to compose music, a market has the power to generate wealth, and an inequitable distribution system the power to cause poverty. Entities may have powers without exercising them at a particular time (it may need an experiment or particular stimulus to trigger them), and powers may be exercised but not become manifest in events because of the countervailing operation of some other generative mechanism. The heart of this argument is that of a *causal* criterion for existence rather than a perceptual one. In other words, for an empiricist only that which can be perceived can exist, whereas for a realist having a causal effect on the world implies existence, regardless of perceptability.

## 2.4.2 Critical Realism and Natural Science

For Bhaskar, reality is both intransitive (existing independently of humans) and stratified—i.e., hierarchically ordered (Archer, Bhaskar et al. 1998, p. 41). The first form of stratification is between structures or mechanisms, the events that they generate, and the subset of events that are actually experienced. These are known as the domains of the *Real*, the *Actual*, and the *Empirical* (see Figure 2.1). The real contains mechanisms, events, and experiences—i.e., the whole of reality; the actual consists of events that do (or do not) occur and includes the empirical, those events that are observed or experienced. These distinctions arise from the transcendental arguments above—namely that we should not reduce all events to only those that are observed, and we should not reduce enduring causal mechanisms to events.

A second form of stratification is within the realm of objects themselves (Archer, Bhaskar et al. 1998, p. 66) where causal powers at one level (e.g., chemical reactions) can be seen as generated by those of a lower level (atomic valency). One strata is emergent from another (what Bhaskar terms "emergent powers materialism"). The picture of the real is thus one of a complex interaction between dynamic, open, stratified systems, both material and non-material, where particular structures give rise to certain causal powers, tendencies, or ways of acting often called by Bhaskar "generative mechanisms" (Bhaskar 1979, p. 170). Although the term "mechanism" sounds like a physical object, in fact Bhaskar uses the term to refer to the powers or properties of an object. For example, an airplane embodies the generative mechanism of the power to fly. The interaction of these generative mechanisms, where one often counterbalances another, causes the presence or absence of actual events.

Having established the intransitive *objects* of knowledge, we must recognize that the *production* of knowledge is very much the work of humans, and occurs in what we could call the *transitive* dimension (Bhaskar 1989 p. 18). Acknowledging the work of sociologists, the practice of science is a social process drawing on existing theories, results, anomalies and conjectures (the transitive objects of knowledge) to generate improved knowledge of science's intransitive objects. This distinction allows us to admit the *epistemic* relativity of science, the fact that knowledge is always historically and socially located, without losing the ontological dimension. We should also note that such epistemic relativity does not imply a corresponding *judgmental* relativity, i.e., that all views are equally valid and that there are no rational grounds for choosing between them.

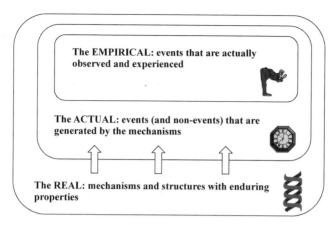

**Figure 2.1. The Real, the Actual, the Empirical.**

We can now characterise the realist method of science as one of *retroduction* (this is the same as "abduction" as developed by Peirce (Habermas 1978, p. 113) in contrast to induction and deduction) where we take some unexplained phenomenon and propose hypothetical mechanisms that, *if they existed*, would generate or cause that which is to be explained. So, we move from experiences in the empirical domain to possible structures in the real domain. This does not of itself prove that the mechanism exists, and we may have competing explanations, so the next step is to work towards eliminating some explanations and supporting others. Bhaskar summarises this as: Description, Retroduction, Elimination, and Identification (Bhaskar 1994, p. 24) (DREI). He also considers a variant for applied science that may be more relevant to OR/MS (RRREI):

**Resolution** of the event or phenomena to be explained into its component parts and their relations.

**Redescription** of the phenomena in a way that makes it theoretically significant, that is, that makes it relevant to the concepts or issues of some particular theory(ies).

**Retroduction**—the postulation of a hypothetical mechanism(s) or structure(s) that, *if they existed*, would generate the observed phenomenon. The structure could be physical, social or psychological, and may well not be directly observable except in terms of its effects (e.g., social structures).

**Elimination** of alternative explanations and attempts to demonstrate the existence of the mechanism by experimental activity or by the prediction of other phenomena or events.

**Identification** of the correct generative mechanism from those considered, and appropriate development to the theoretical base.

Of potentially even more relevance, although underdeveloped as yet, is a discussion (Bhaskar 1993, p. 260) of practical problem resolution (Diagnosis, Explanation, and Action to absent the problem), and attempting to change morals or norms (Description, Explanation, Transformation) that derive from and utilise RRREI. The key point is in going from surface observations (the empirical domain) to underlying explanatory structures (the real domain) and back again. See Section 9.2.2.

An obvious objection is how do we *know* that such hypothetical mechanisms actually do exist rather then being merely interesting ideas? At one level the answer is that we can never know for certain, since critical realism accepts that our knowledge is always ultimately fallible. More practically, however, the intransitivity of real structures means that they will always have the potential for effects that go beyond us, i.e., are out of our control, and the methodology means that we should aim to eliminate alternative explanations by testing in some way for their potential effects.

So, the main feature of a critical realist approach to science is a fundamental concern for *explanation* in terms of independent underlying causal or generative mechanisms which may in principle be unobservable. This is in contrast to the empiricist approach which limits itself to empirically measurable events and their abstraction into general laws; or the idealist approach that has difficulty accepting a causally efficacious ontological domain.

### 2.4.3 Critical Realism and Social Science

We now move to the second major argument of critical realism, that social science is essentially similar to natural science in its realist character albeit with modifications to reflect the particular nature of the social world. We can begin by asking what would rule out a realist approach to social science? The answer is that there are no intransitive objects for social science to investigate. Such an argument could come from the extreme constructivists (or superidealists as Bhaskar calls them) who would also apply it to the natural world; or from those, such as Checkland (1989), who would argue for the distinctive nature of social phenomena as being intrinsically meaningful and not existing independently of social actors. Space precludes a full discussion of this complex issue (see Bhaskar (1979); Outhwaite (1987); Bhaskar (1994); Archer (1995); New (1995); Bhaskar (1997); Archer; Bhaskar et al. (1998); Part III; King (1999a) but I will outline: i) the argument for intransitive social structures; ii) implications for the nature of societies; iii) the limits on naturalism that follow from i) and ii).

The primary argument (Bhaskar 1979 ch. 2) is against methodological individualists, such as Popper (1962) (and Margaret Thatcher who claimed that "society" does not exist!) who argue that all explanations can be couched in terms of an individual person's beliefs and actions. The first refutation concerns emergent properties—there are attributes that can be applied to people that concern physical features such as height, weight; there are attributes that we share with other animals such as pain or hunger; but there are many attributes, essentially human ones, that are unavoidably social, for example "bachelor," "banker," or "nun." These are only intelligible within the context of a social institution or practice (Searle 1996). The second argument is that many activities we undertake, most obviously perhaps language, must already exist and be available for people to learn and then use. As Wittgenstein (1958) argued, there can be no such thing as a private language—every time anyone has a conversation, uses a credit card, or waits for a train they are assuming the existence of a structured, intransitive domain of resources, concepts, practices, and relationships. The successful occurrence of social activities warrants the existence of causally efficacious, although unobservable, social structures.

Bhaskar (1979) does accept, however, that social phenomena are inherently different from material phenomena and that this does put limits on the nature of social science:

### Ontological

- Social structures do not exist independently of the activities they govern, or, put another way, they exist only in their effects or occurrences. Social structures enable social activities and through that activity are themselves reproduced or transformed. Thus, they are themselves the result of social activity. In contrast, the laws of the natural world are not affected by their own operation.

- Social structures do not exist independently of the agents conceptions of what they are doing. Thus agency always requires some degree of interpretation and understanding of the meaning of the actions undertaken, although this does not imply that agents cannot be mistaken, and it does not require that they be fully aware of the consequences of their activity. In contrast, natural phenomena are independent of our conceptions of them.

- Social structures are localised in both space and time, unlike natural laws or tendencies that are generally universal. They only hold in particular cultures or sub-cultures for finite periods of time.

### Epistemological

- Social systems are inherently interactive and open. Whilst the same is true for natural systems, it is the case that they can be artificially closed or controlled in the laboratory, and this indeed is the principal reason for experiments. This however is not (generally) possible in social systems. The main effect is that it is difficult to test theories since predicted effects may or may not occur depending on a multitude of factors. It focuses attention on a theory's explanatory rather than predictive power.

- The possibilities of measurement are very limited since intrinsically the phenomena are meaningful, and meanings cannot properly be measured and compared, only understood and described.

**Relational**

- Social science is itself a social practice and is, therefore, inherently self-referential. This means both that social science knowledge can itself affect the social world, and perhaps change it (e.g., the self-fulfilling prophesy); and that it is itself a social product and therefore will be shaped by the social conditions of its production. This does not make social science totally transitive—once an event has occurred, or some theory been produced, it becomes intransitive relative to possible explanations of it.

- I would draw a second conclusion from this, that social theories must be self-consistent in not contradicting their own premises since they are part of their own domain.

- All of the above place limits or constraints on the practice of social science, but do not make it different in principle from natural science. It is still driven by the existence of an intransitive domain of generative mechanisms; recognition of the epistemic (but not judgmental) relativity of knowledge; and a retroductive methodology that explains events by hypothesising underlying causal mechanisms.

## 2.5 Criticisms of Critical Realism

It is interesting that little has been written as a direct critique of critical realism especially within the philosophical literature. We may speculate that this is partly due to Bhaskar's disengagement from the philosophical establishment—he has never had a significant academic position always remaining independent; he writes books but rarely papers and so is not well established in the mainstream journals; and does not really engage in philosophical conferences and debates. His work has mainly been picked up in other disciplines, especially the social sciences, where the reception has usually been positive rather than critical. Indeed, even some of the critics discussed below (e.g., Chalmers and Callinicos) end up saying that despite their concern with particular arguments, they basically think CR is true!

The first point is the status of one of the main planks of CR—the transcendental argument for an independent, stratified ontological domain. This form of argument is the reverse of the traditional syllogism—it goes from the agreed occurrence of some phenomena (in this case scientific experimental activity) backward to an inference about what, therefore, the world must necessarily be like (independent stratified ontology):

"The intelligibility of experimental activity presupposes then the intransitivity and structured character of the objects of scientific knowledge, at least in so far as these are causal laws. And this presupposes in turn the possibility of a non-human world … and in particular of a non-empirical world" (Archer, Bhaskar et al. 1998, p. 26).

Doubt can be cast about the strength of this argument in several ways. It seems to rest very much on what is meant by "intelligible." If it simply means understandable or explainable then this seems quite a weak argument. Does it really imply the existence of an external world, or does it just imply that scientists have that belief, whether or not it is actually true? We could similarly argue that the intelligibility of religious activity implies the existence of God but presumably we would only wish to argue that it implies a *belief* in God on the part of religious people. In fact, does not the argument rest on the *success* of science rather than its intelligibility (Chalmers 1988)? In other words, it is not so much what scientists believe about what they are doing, but the fact that knowledge generated through experimental activity is found to hold outside the experimental situation as testified by the enormous developments of successful technology.

We might also question whether the premises about experimental activity are actually shared by competing positions or, indeed, an indubitable description of science anyway (Callinicos 1995). How do we know that there are not competing theories about scientific practice and that these offer different accounts that still make the activity intelligible? Here Bhaskar would probably argue that his is an *immanent critique.* That is, his arguments are always contextual and directed against particular positions, in this case empiricism and some forms of idealism, rather than being totally general. There may well be other views on the nature of experiments, e.g., from a postmodern perspective, but then the nature of the argument would be different.

Finally, we could object that even if we accept the premises, the nature of the conclusions depends very much on general scientific knowledge of the day. If a Greek or medieval philosopher attempted a similar argument they would come up with a very different picture of the nature of the world. I think this argument has to be accepted but is compatible with CR's wider acceptance of fallibility. Bhaskar accepts that knowledge is temporally relative and will change, and even accepts that CR itself is only "the best explanation so far"—"the transcendental consideration is not deployed in a philosophical vacuum: it is designed to situate, or replace, an existing theory; and may of course come, in time, to suffer a similar fate." (Bhaskar 1979, p. 6)

A second area of concern is the extent to which the theory of science is simply descriptive or actually normative, and the strength of its prescriptions. Many would agree that CR (Baert 1996), with its acceptance of unobservable entities, the role of metaphor and analogy, and the importance of explanation, is a much better description of the activities of actual (natural) scientists than empiricism or even Popperianism. To what extent, however, does it provide powerful normative procedures for natural science; and to what extent does it apply to the activities of social scientists?

Methodologically, the Description, Retroduction, Elimination and Identification formulation has several weaknesses. Given the acceptance of the subjectivity of the transitive domain and the theory dependence of observations, it seems unlikely that one can begin with objective and agreed descriptions of particular phenomena. The description will already be imbued with underlying theoretical concepts and in the social sciences will also be highly value laden[2]. This will clearly condition the forms of generative mechanisms that are postulated to explain the phenomenon and make any sort of comparison or contrast very difficult.

Retroduction itself is clearly an intuitive and creative process, rather than a logical one[3], and this is a necessary part of scientific endeavour, but it can result in a proliferation of possible explanations, some of which may well be untestable, or at least unrefutable. This places a lot of weight on the latter stages of elimination and identification but here CR runs into problems because of its critique of traditional empirical testing, verification, and induction. How is the scientist, especially the social scientist, ever going to be able to undertake testing that unambiguously rules out or rules in particular hypothetical mechanisms, particularly when such mechanisms may be unobservable, and their powers may be unactualised?

This is related to a third problem, the nature of truth within critical realism. While the basic orientation is towards a correspondence theory of truth, i.e., that knowledge in the transitive domain in some sense corresponds to its objects in the intransitive domain, the acceptance of epistemic relativity means that we can never prove or be certain that this is the case. This potentially brings in elements of a consensus theory of truth. Bhaskar himself recognises four dimensions of truth (Bhaskar 1994): *normative-fiduciary,* truth as that which is believed by a trustworthy source; a*dequating:* truth as based on evidence and justification rather than mere belief; *referential-expressive,* truth as corresponding to or at least being adequate to some intransitive object of knowledge; and *ontological/alethic,* the truth of things in themselves and their generative causes in the intransitive domain, i.e, no longer tied to language although expressible in language. The fourth aspect is clearly controversial (Groff 2000). We are thus left with a problem of precisely what criteria we can use to judge between competing explanations if not a clear view of truth.

A fourth area of criticism concerns that of naturalism—i.e., the extent to which an approach developed largely in relation to natural science can be applied to social science. Clearly Bhaskar recognises the fundamentally different nature of the social world and the limitations this places on science. But are not these limitations in fact so great that CR-type science is not possible? Giddens (1976) recognises that even natural science involves a transitive, hermeneutic domain but that social science involves a double hermeneutic in that the objects of knowledge are themselves intrinsically socially structured and human-dependent. If social "structures" are unobservable, and indeed only exist through people's activity; if social systems are open and not amenable to experiment; and social activities always rely to some

---

[2] A point Bhaskar clearly accepts.

[3] Indeed Peirce, who coined the term, called it basically guesswork.

extent on prior common sense or theoretical conceptualisation, then to what extent is it really possible to test competing explanations and identify "true" ones?

Coming from the opposite direction, King (1999b) argues against the realist notion of a causally effective social structure over and above the knowledgeable actions of individual agents. He suggests that Bhaskar's concept of social structure involves two contradictions (or "antinomies"). The first is that society is both dependent on individuals and is also independent of individuals. From Bhaskar's viewpoint this apparent contradiction is resolved through the idea of emergence. Society, as a separate ontological entity, emerges from but is separate to the activities of individuals. This allows for the development of a social theory with two separate types of entity—individuals and society—that interact with and mutually shape each other. King objects that such a view of society is a reification and that in fact

"The apparently structural and emergent aspects of society can be successfully accounted for by hermeneutic reference to individuals and their meaningful interactions with other individuals alone. ... Social reality is coextensive with the individuals involved and is neither more nor less than those individuals" (King 1999b, pp. 271–272).

The second antinomy is that social action is said to be always intentional, yet is also said to be non-intentional and materially caused. The point at issue is related to the previous one—to what extent should individual action be explained in terms of external social and material structures as opposed to simply the intentions of the individual? This is clearly a major debate within social theory and I can only refer the interested reader to the literature.[4]

The fifth area of debate I will discuss is the nature and extent of critical realism's claim to be "critical" not so much in the epistemological sense but in the political sense of bringing about change in society. The idea is that social science is not value-neutral description but inevitably explanatory critique of the status quo[5]. Social science concepts must always be evaluative or moralised, never purely descriptive. For instance, it is more correct to say "Two children were murdered" than "Two young humans ceased functioning" since it is a more precise and accurate description requiring a more specific explanation. Social science will always reveal examples of false beliefs, unmet needs, and unnecessary suffering; and will often be able to identify their structural causes. Other things being equal, it is then possible to condemn the causes and propose action to remove or absent them. We thus move from fact to values and from values to actions in support of a transformation of society.

---

[4] King (1999a), King (2000), Giddens (1984), and Archer (1995), Archer (2000).

[5] This is in direct opposition to positivism's insistence on a separation between fact and values.

Sayer (1997) accepts these arguments at a general level but points out the difficulty of enacting them in practice. In particular, it is not difficult to find many examples of false beliefs or suffering but doing something about them requires both a correct identification of their causes and specific changes that are both desirable and feasible, and do not generate new problems elsewhere. The world is now highly complex and incredibly inter-dependent. Particular events or problems will often have multiple interlocking structural causes which are very difficult to untangle, and possible changes will often have undesirable and unintended consequences, and have to contend with an increasing diversity of values and cultures.

Baert (1996) maintains that Bhaskar's social theory is actually much better at explaining why societies remain the same rather then why they are transformed. Certainly it is true that Bhaskar's transformational model of social action (TMSA) emphasises the way in which social actors necessarily draw on an already existing social structure and through their interactions reproduce it, and only potentially transform it[6]. Archer (1990; 1996; 1998) has addressed this point to some extent in her morphogenetic model which emphasises the independence of society from individual actors and therefore allows both reproduction and transformation through their mutual interaction. Baert also suggests that the TMSA model undervalues the extent to which social actors (not just social scientists) can develop their own discursive, theoretical knowledge of society and act on it to change rather than merely reproduce social structure.

Fine (2002) is particularly concerned with economics where there has been a significant attack on traditional theory, especially econometrics, from CR (Lawson 1996; Lawson 1997; Fleetwood 1999; Lawson 1999; Fleetwood 2001; Fleetwood 2002). Interestingly, rather than being a supporter of the status quo (in economics) Fine argues that CR is neither critical nor realist enough to have much effect. It is not critical enough because it has largely confined itself to critique at the level of methodology rather than substantive theory. Fine suggests that mainstream economists (and perhaps this can be extended to other disciplines) have no interest in methodology, or indeed realism or the real world. And, it is not realist enough in not having significant theoretical conceptions of core economic phenomena such as capital and capitalism. One could reply that Bhaskar has always maintained that the *philosophy* of CR is intended as a foundation for specific sciences, not as a replacement. So now perhaps is the time for critical realists within the disciplines to use it to generate more and better substantive theories and prove its worth in practice.

## 2.6 Conclusions

This chapter has made a case for the contribution of critical realism as an underlying philosophy for management science as a practical discipline. It has approached this

---

[6] There are indeed many similarities with Giddens' theory of structuration which is also criticised as being overly regulative.

by showing that critical realism addresses the unresolved problems within the philosophy of science, whether it be natural or social. In particular: the impoverished view of explanatory theory within empiricism; the major critiques of observer- and theory-independence that empiricism assumes; the logical problems of induction and falsificationism; the dislocation between natural and social science; and the radical anti-realist positions adopted by constructivists and postmodernists.

The main points to be taken from this chapter are:

- Ontologically, the strongly held claim that there does exist a world independent, to differing degrees, of human beings and that the underlying mechanisms generate the events we observe and experience.

- Epistemologically, the fact that we do not have pure, unmediated access to this world but that our knowledge must always be locally and historically relative. But in accepting epistemic relativism we do not thereby accept judgemental relativism—there are grounds for chosing between competing views.

- Methodologically, the retroductive approach of hypothesising generative mechanisms that would explain our experiences and then trying to confirm or deny their existence. This underwrites a pluralist view of research and intervention methods which will be explored more fully in Chapters 9 and 10.

# Chapter 3: Living Systems: Autopoiesis

## 3.1 The Essence of Autopoiesis

The fundamental question Maturana and Varela set out to answer is what distinguishes entities or systems which we would call living from other systems, apparently equally complex, which we would not? How, for example, should a Martian distinguish between a horse and a car and recognise one as living and the other as not? This is a similar but not identical question to that of Monod (1974, p19) who is concerned with distinguishing between natural and artificial systems.

This has always been a problem for biologists who have developed a variety of answers. First, vitalism (Bergson, 1911; Driesch, 1908) which held that there was some substance or force or principle, as yet unobserved, which must account for the peculiar characteristics of life. Then systems theory, with the development of concepts such as feedback, homeostasis and open systems, paved the way for explanations of the complex, goal-seeking behaviour of organisms in purely mechanistic terms (for example, Cannon, 1939; Priban, 1968). Whilst this was a significant advance, such mechanisms could equally well be built into simple machines which would never qualify as living organisms.

A third approach, the most common recently, is instead to specify a list of necessary characteristics which any living organism must have—for example, reproductive ability, information-processing capabilities, carbon-based chemistry, nucleic acids (see for example Millar, 1978; Bunge, 1979). The first difficulty with this approach is that it is entirely descriptive and not in any real sense explanatory. It works by observing those systems which are accepted as living and noting some of their common characteristics. However, this assumes precisely that which is in need of explanation—the distinction between the living and the non-living. The approach fails to define the characteristics particular to living systems alone, or to give any explanation as to how such characteristics might generate the observed phenomena. Second, there is inevitably always a lack of agreement about the contents of such lists. They will contain different characteristics; and it is difficult to prove that every feature in a list is really necessary or that the list is actually complete.

Maturana and Varela's work is based on a number of fundamental observations about the nature of living systems. They will be introduced briefly here, but discussed in more detail later.

i)   Somewhat in opposition to current trends which focus on species or the genes (Dawkins, 1978), Maturana and Varela pick out the single, biological individual (for instance, a single celled organism such as amoeba) as the central example of a living system. One essential feature of such living entities is their individual autonomy. Although they are part of organisms, populations and species, and are affected by their environment, individuals are bounded, self-defined entities.

ii) Living systems operate in an essentially mechanistic way. They consist of particular components which have various properties and interactions. The overall behaviour of the whole is generated purely by these components, their properties and their relations through the interactions of neighboring elements. Thus any explanation of the living must be a purely mechanistic one.

iii) All explanations or descriptions are made by observers (i.e., people) who are external to the system. One must not confuse that which pertains to the observer with that which pertains to the observed. Observers can perceive both an entity and its environment and see how the two relate to each other. Components within an entity, however, cannot do this but act purely in response to other components.

iv) The last two lead to the idea that any explanation of living systems should be non-teleological, i.e., it should not have recourse to ideas of function and purpose. The observable phenomena of living systems result purely from the interactions of neighboring internal components. The observation that certain parts appear to have a function with regard to the whole can be made only by an observer who can interact both with the component and with the whole and describe the relation of the two.

To explain the nature of living systems, Maturana and Varela focus on a single, basic example—the individual, living cell. Briefly, cells consist of a cell membrane or boundary enclosing various structures such as the nucleus, mitochondria and lysosomes, and many (often complex) molecules produced from within. These structures are in constant chemical interplay both with each other and, in the case of the membrane, with their external medium. It is a dynamic, integrated chemical network of incredible sophistication (see for example Alberts et al, 1989; Freifelder, 1983; Raven and Johnson, 1991).

What is it that characterises this as an autonomous, dynamic, living whole? What distinguishes it from a machine such as a chemical factory, which also consists of complex components and interacting processes of production forming an organized whole? It cannot be to do with any functions or purposes that any single cell might fulfill in a larger multicellular organism since there are single-celled organisms which survive by themselves. Nor can it be explained in a reductionist way in terms of particular structures or components of the cell, such as the nucleus or DNA/RNA. The difference must stem from the way the parts are organized as a whole. To understand Maturana and Varela's answer, we need to look at two related questions—what is it that the cell does, that is, what is it that the cell produces? And, what is it that produces the cell? I mean this in the sense of its ongoing existence rather than its reproduction.

What does a cell do? This will be looked at in detail in section 3.3 but, in essence, it produces many complex, and simple, chemicals and molecules which remain in the cell (because of the cell membrane) and participate in those very same production processes. Some molecules are excreted from the cell, through the membrane, as waste. What is it that produces the components of the cell? With the help of some basic chemicals imported from its medium, the cell produces its own constituents. So a cell produces its own components, which are therefore what produces it in a circular, ongoing process (Figure 3.1).

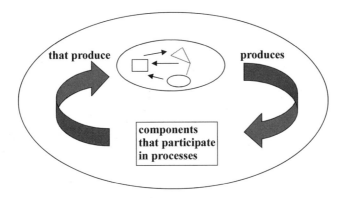

**Figure 3.1 Autopoiesis—Circular Processes Of Production**

It produces, and is produced by, nothing other than itself. This simple idea is all that is meant by *autopoiesis*. The word means "self-producing" and that is what the cell does, it continually produces itself. Living systems are autopoietic—they are organized in such a way that their processes produce the very components which are necessary for the continuance of these processes. Systems which do not produce themselves are called *allopoietic*, meaning "other-producing," for example, a river or a crystal. Maturana and Varela also refer to human-created systems as *heteropoietic*. An example of this is a chemical factory. Superficially, this is similar to a cell but it produces chemicals that are used elsewhere, and is itself produced or maintained by other systems. It is not self-producing.

At first sight this may seem an almost trivial idea and yet further contemplation reveals how significant it is. For example:

i)  Imagine trying to build an autopoietic machine. Save for energy and some basic chemicals, everything within it would have to be produced by the machine itself. So there would have to be machines to produce the various components. Of course, these machines themselves would have to be produced, maintained and repaired by yet more machines, and so on, all within the same single entity. The machine would soon encompass the whole economy.

ii) Suppose that you succeed. Then surely what you have created would be autonomous and independent. It would have the ability to construct and reconstruct itself, and would, in a very real sense, be no longer controlled by us its creators. Would it not seem appropriate to call it living?

iii) In terms of life originating on earth from a sea of chemicals, a cell in which a set of chemicals interacted such that it created and recreated its own constituents would generate a stable, self-defined entity with a vastly enhanced chance of further development. This indeed is the basis for current research in the origins of life (Fleischakes, 1990).

iv) What of death? If, for some reason either internal or external, any part of the self-production process breaks down then there is nothing else to produce the necessary components and the whole process will fall apart. Autopoiesis is all or nothing—all the processes must be working or the system disintegrates.

This, then, is the central idea of autopoiesis: a living system is one organized in such a way that all its components and processes jointly produce those self-same components and processes, thus establishing an autonomous, self-producing entity. This concept has nearly been grasped by other biologists, but Maturana and Varela were the first to coin a word for this life-generating mechanism, to set out its criteria (Varela 1974), and to explore its consequences in a rigorous way.

Considering the derivation of the word itself, Maturana explains (1980a, p. xvii) that he had the main ideas of a circular, self-referring organisation without the term autopoiesis. In fact, "Biology of Cognition" (Maturana 1970), the first major exposition of the ideas, does not use it. Maturana coined the term in relation to the distinction between *praxis* (the path of arms, or action) and *poiesis* (the path of letters, or creation). However, it is interesting to see how closely Maturana's usage of auto- and allo-poiesis is actually foreshadowed by the German phenomenological philosopher Martin Heidegger. Heidegger uses the term poiesis as a bringing-forth and draws the contrast between the self-production (heautoi) of nature and the other-production (alloi) that humans do. Many of the ideas of autopoiesis bear strong resemblances to the phenomenology of both Heidegger and Merleau-Ponty as will be discussed in Chapter 7.

## 3.2 Formal Specification of Autopoiesis

Having sketched the idea in general terms, this section will describe in more detail Maturana and Varela's specification and vocabulary[7].

---

[7] In terms of the source literature "Autopoiesis and Cognition" Maturana and Varela (1980) is the main original source and "Tree of Knowledge" is a popular introduction Maturana and Varela (1987). Maturana (1987a) is a more recent and comprehensive review. Other important papers are Maturana (1988), Maturana and Mpodozis (1995), and Varela et al (1974).

We begin from the observation that all descriptions and explanations are made by observers who distinguish an entity or phenomenon from the general background. Such descriptions will always depend in part on the choices and purposes of the observer and may or may not correspond to the actual domain of the observed entity (see Chapter 4 for further discussion of this). That which is distinguished by an observer Maturana calls a *unity*, that is, a whole distinguished from a background. In making the distinction, the properties which specify the unity as a whole are established by the observer. For example, in calling something a "car" certain basic attributes or defining features (it is mobile, carries people, is steerable) are specified. An observer may go further and analyze a unity into components and their relations. There will be different, equally valid, ways in which this can be done. The result will be a description of a composite unity in terms of components and the organisation which combines its components together into a whole.

Maturana and Varela draw an important distinction between the *organisation* of a unity and its *structure*.

"{Organisation} refers to the relations between components that define and specify a system as a composite unity of a particular class, and determine its properties as such a unity ... by specifying a domain in which it can interact as an unanalysable whole endowed with constitutive properties.

{Structure} refers to the actual components and the actual relations that these must satisfy in their participation in the constitution of a given composite unity ... {and} ... determines the space in which it exists as a composite unity that can be perturbed through the interactions of its components, but the structure does not determine its properties as a unity. (Maturana 1978a, p. 32).

The organisation consists of the relations between components and the necessary properties of the components which characterise or define the unity in general as belonging to a particular type or class. This determines its properties as a whole. At its most simple, we can illustrate this distinction with the concept of a square. A square is defined in terms of the (spatial) relations between components—four equal-sized lengths, connected together at right-angles. This is its organisation. Any actual square embodies these relations but has other characteristics such as size or colour as well. The total of these is its structure. Another example is a an aeroplane which may be defined by describing necessary components such as wings, power, steering, brakes, seating, and the relations between them such that it can fly. If a unity has such an organisation, then it may be identified as a plane since this particular organisation would produce the properties we expect in a plane as a whole. Structure, on the other hand, describes the actual components and actual relations of a particular real example of any such entity, such as the Boeing 747 I board at the airport.

This is a rather unusual usage of the term "structure" (Andrew 1979). Generally, in the description of a system, structure is contrasted with *process* to refer to those parts of the system which change only slowly; and the terms structure and organisation would be almost interchangeable. Here, however, structure refers to both the static and dynamic elements. The distinction between structure and organisation is between the reality of an actual example and the abstract generality lying behind all such examples. This is strongly reminiscent of the philosophy of classic structuralism in which an empirical surface "structure" of events is related to an unobservable deep structure ("organisation") of basic relationships which generate the surface.

An existing, composite unity, therefore, has both a structure and an organisation. There will be many different structures which can realize the same organisation, and the structure will have many properties and relations not specified by the organisation and essentially irrelevant to it—for example, the shape, colour, size, and material of a particular aeroplane. Moreover, the structure can change or be changed without necessarily altering the organisation. For example, as the plane ages, has new parts and gets repainted it still maintains its identity as a plane because its underlying organisation has not changed. Some changes, however, will not be compatible with the maintenance of the organisation—for example, a crash which converts the plane to a wreck.

The essential distinction between organisation and structure is between a whole and its parts. Only the plane as a whole can fly—this is its constitutive property as a unity, its organisation. Its parts, however, can interact in their own domains depending on all their properties but they do so only as individual components. A bird-strike can stop an engine; a short-circuit can damage the controls. These are perturbations of the structure—this may affect the whole and lead to a loss of organisation, or it may be compensatable, the plane still able to fly.

With this background, we can consider Maturana and Varela's definition of autopoiesis. A unity is characterised by describing the organisation which defines it as a member of a particular class, that is, which can be seen to generate the observed behaviour of unities of that type. Maturana and Varela see living systems as being essentially characterised as dynamic and autonomous and that it is their self-production which leads to this. Thus the organisation of living systems is one of self-production—autopoiesis. Such an organisation can, of course, be realized in infinitely many structures.

A more explicit definition of an autopoietic system is:

"A dynamic system that is defined as a composite unity as a network of productions of components that:

a)   through their interactions recursively regenerate the network of productions that produced them, and

b)   realize this network as a unity in the space in which they exist by constituting and specifying its boundaries as surfaces of cleavage from the background through their preferential interactions within the network, is an autopoietic system." (Maturana 1980b)

The first part of this quotation details the general idea of a system of self-production, whilst the second specifies that the system must be actually realized in an entity which produces its own boundaries. This latter point, about producing boundaries, is particularly important when it comes to attempting to apply autopoiesis to other domains, such as the social world, and will be a recurring point of debate. Notice also that the definition does not specify that the realization must be a physical one, although in the case of a cell it clearly will be. This leaves open the idea of some abstract autopoietic systems such as a set of concepts, a cellular automata, or a process of communications. What might the boundaries of such a system be? And would we really want to call such a system "living"? Again, this is the subject of much debate—see Chapters 4 and 8.

This somewhat bare concept is developed more by considering the nature of such an organisation. In particular, as an organisation it will involve particular relations between components. These relations, in the case of a physical system, must be of three types according to Maturana and Varela (Maturana and Varela 1975)— relations of *constitution*, *specification* and *order*. Relations of constitution concern the physical topology of the system (say, a cell)—it's 3-dimensional geometry. For example, that it has a cell membrane, that components are particular distances from each other, that they are the required sizes and shapes. Relations of specification determine that the components produced by the various production processes are in fact those specific ones that are necessary for the continuation of autopoiesis. Finally, relations of order concern the dynamics of the processes. For example, that the appropriate amounts of various molecules are produced at the correct rate and at the correct time. Specific examples of these relations will be given later, but it can be seen that these correspond roughly to specifying the "where," "what," and "when" of the complex production processes occurring in the cell.

It might appear that this description of relations "necessary" for autopoiesis has a functionalist, teleological tone. This is not really the case as Maturana and Varela strongly object to such explanations. It is simply that, if such components and relationships do occur it will give rise to electrochemical processes which will themselves produce further components and processes of the right types and at the right rates to generate an autopoietic system. But there is no necessity to this, it is simply a combination that does, or does not, occur, just as a plant may, or may not, grow depending on the right combination of water, light and nutrients.

### 3.2.1 Identifying Biological Autopoietic Systems

Having described the basic concepts of autopoiesis in an abstract sense the obvious question is how, or to what extent, can we identify these in actual systems? This task has been carried out reasonably successfully for physical systems—i.e., living organisms, but it is much less clear in the case of non-physical systems as we shall see later.

For biological systems, Maturana and Varela (Maturana and Varela 1975; Maturana and Varela 1980) showed in detail how the phenomenology of the cell embodied the autopoietic structure. They also developed a six-point key for identifying an autopoietic system (Varela 1974):

1. Determine, through interactions, if the unity has identifiable boundaries. If the boundaries can be determined, proceed to 2. If not, the entity is indescribable and we can say nothing.

2. Determine if there are constitutive elements of the unity, that is, components of the unity. If these components can be described, proceed to 3. If not, the unity is an unanalysable whole and therefore not an autopoietic system.

3. Determine if the unity is a mechanistic system, that is, the component properties are capable of satisfying certain relations that determine in the unity the interactions and transformations of these components. If this is the case proceed to 4. If not, the unity is not an autopoietic system.

4. Determine if the components that constitute the boundaries of the unity constitute these boundaries through preferential neighbourhood interactions and relations between themselves, as determined by their properties in the space of their interactions. If this is not the case, you do not have an autopoietic unity because you are determining its boundaries, not the unity itself. If 4 is the case however proceed to 5.

5. Determine if the components of the boundaries of the unity are produced by the interactions of the components of the unity, either by transformation of previously produced components, or by transformations and/or coupling of non-component elements that enter the unity through its boundaries. If not, you do not have an autopoietic unity; if yes proceed to 6.

6. If all the other components of the unity are also produced by the interactions of its components as in 5, and if those which are not produced by the interactions of other components participate as necessary permanent constitutive components in the production of other components, you have an autopoietic unity in the space in which its components exist. If this is not the case, and there are components in the unity not produced by components of the unity as in 5, or if there are components of the unity which do not participate in the production of other components, you do not have an autopoietic unity.

The first three criteria are general and structural, specifying that there is an identifiable entity with a clear boundary, that it can be analyzed into components, and that it operates mechanistically, i.e., its operation is determined by the properties and relations of its components. The core autopoietic ideas are specified in the last three points. These describe a dynamic network of interacting processes of production (6), contained within and producing a boundary (5), which is maintained by the preferential interactions of its components (4). The key notions, especially when considering the extension of autopoiesis to non-physical systems, are the idea of production of components, and the necessity for a boundary constituted by produced components. These criteria have been applied to the cell in Mingers (1995) and Zeleny and Hufford (1992) and Mingers has also exemplified the organisational relations of constitution, order and specification.

## 3.3 The Primary Concepts of Autopoiesis

The basic nature of living systems as autopoietic has now been described. They are characterised by a circular organisation of production processes that continually produce and replace the components necessary to that organisation. There are a number of important implications of this theory which will now be sketched out.

### 3.3.1 Structure-Determined Systems

One of the main principles underlying the concept of autopoiesis is that of *structural determinism* and, related to it, organisational closure. These concepts, particularly the second, have led to considerable misunderstanding and Maturana has tried to clarify this (Krull 1989; Maturana 1991b). I shall first briefly recap the difference between structure and organisation. By organisation Maturana refers to the relations between components that give a system its identity, that make it a member of a particular type. Thus, if the organisation of a system changes, so does its identity. By structure Maturana means the actual components and relations between them that constitute a particular example of a type of system. The organisation is realized through the structure, but it is the structure that can interact and change. So long as the structural changes maintain the organisation, the system's identity remains.

In considering change in a system, Maturana argues that all composite systems (i.e., those consisting of components) are structure-determined. He means by this that the actual changes that the system undergoes depend upon the structure itself at a particular instant. Any change in a composite system must be structural change—i.e., it must be a change in the components or their relations—and, as such, must be determined by the properties of the components. Changes will occur in response both to internal dynamics and to interactions with external systems, but even in external interactions the resulting change is determined internally; it is only triggered by the environment. This is a very important conclusion for it means that there can be no "instructive interactions." That is, it is never the case that an environmental action (be it physical or communicational) can *determine* its effect on a structure-determined system[8].

In general then, everything that happens in a composite unify is a structural change, and every structural change that occurs in a composite unity is determined at every instant by its structure at that instant. It follows from all this that composite unities are structure determined systems in the sense that everything is determined by their structure. (Maturana 1987a, p. 336)

---

[8] There are obviously limits to this—a nuclear bomb will impose its effects on most things.

The system is clearly affected by its environment, but the result depends on the structure of the system. We can say that perturbations in the environment trigger structural change or compensation. It is the structure that determines both what the compensation will be and even what, in the environment, can or cannot act as a trigger. In total, the structure at any point in time determines: i) all possible structural changes within the system that maintain the current organisation, and those which do not; and ii) all possible states of the environment that could trigger changes of state, and whether such changes would maintain or destroy the current organisation. Looking at some examples will show that this is reasonably straightforward, although we are accustomed to seeing things in a different way. The examples are biological, but the concept applies to all composite systems.

Living things are continually changing and developing, and these changes are determined by their own structure. Some changes, such as growth, leave the organisation the same; other changes result in a new organisation, for example, a caterpillar developing into a butterfly, or an egg into a chicken; whilst others, such as death, lead to the loss of both the organisation and the unity. Equally, what does, or does not, affect the organism, and the nature of that effect is determined by its structure. Humans have receptors for light and colour and so can be triggered by it, while bats can receive high-pitched sounds that humans cannot. Each organism has its own particular domain of interactions that can affect it and those which cannot. The effects are also structure determined. Berries that are poisonous to humans are food for other animals; carbon dioxide is necessary for plants but inimical to humans whilst oxygen is the opposite. In each case, the nature of the effect of a particular substance is determined not by the substance but by the organism. We humans will often label things as poisonous, and think that this is intrinsic to the substance when, in fact, it is only a reflection of ourselves.

### 3.3.2 Organisational Closure

All composite systems are constituted by an organisation and realized in a structure. But within this general class there are some systems that Maturana and Varela have termed organisationally closed, such as the nervous system, the immune system or a social system (Krull 1989). Autopoietic systems are also organisationally closed but they are a specific type in that they are also self-producing.

A system is organisationally closed if all its possible states of activity must always lead to or generate further activity within itself. In an autopoietic system, all activity must maintain autopoiesis or else the system will disintegrate. All processes are processes of self-production—the system's activity closes in on itself. Similarly, Maturana and Varela argue that the defining feature of the nervous system is that it is closed. All states of neuronal activity lead to further neuronal activity. All neurons both affect, and are affected by, others. Even the motor and sensor neurons are no exception to this—they do not "open" the nervous system to the environment. The motor neurons trigger sensor neurons through the activity they initiate, and sensor neurons are thereby also internally stimulated.

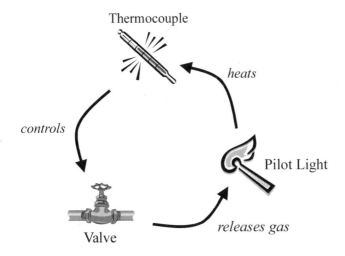

**Figure 3.2. Pilot Light in Gas Boiler.**

The particular nature of organisationally closed systems can be shown with a simple example. Consider a gas boiler and the pilot light which is used to start it. The gas heater itself is organisationally open, it takes in gas and puts out heat. However, the pilot light is closed (see Figure 3.2). When it is on, the pilot light heats a thermocouple which is connected to the gas supply which in turn fuels the pilot light.

Clearly this is a self-dependent, all-or-nothing, system. If the pilot light is not on, it does not heat the thermocouple, and there is no gas so the pilot cannot be on. This is why to light a gas boiler it is necessary to intervene from the outside, break in to the closed system and manually provide gas until the necessary temperature is reached. Once working, the system will carry on enabling itself until some other external force intervenes. This is organisationally closed but is certainly not autopoietic because it does not produce a boundary or any of its own components.

It can also be said that organisationally closed systems do not have inputs and outputs (Maturana and Varela 1980) (or, at least, are not characterised in such terms—see discussion below). Autopoietic systems are organisationally closed because the product of their organisation is that very organisation itself. They do not primarily transform an input into an output except in the sense of transforming themselves into themselves. All the possible states that they can enter must conform to or maintain the autopoietic organisation otherwise they will disintegrate. It may appear that the structure of an autopoietic system changes in relation to, or in response to, changes in its environment. But, for an observer to see such changes in the environment as an input and the structural change as an output is to mischaracterise the system as allopoietic, since the changes will, actually, have been devoted to maintaining autopoiesis. Such a description only pertains to the observer who can witness both the organism and its environment and relate the two together.

The notions that autopoietic systems are organisationally closed and have no inputs and outputs have often been misinterpreted. They have been taken to mean that such systems are completely isolated and have no interactions with their environment. This is not at all the case. Such systems are organisationally closed but interactively (or structurally) open. They interact with their environment through their structure. Maturana has said,

"I use the expression organisation closure to refer to systems whose organisation is closed but whose structure is open in order to highlight the fact that I am talking about their organisation and not their structure." (Krull 1989, p. 90)

Cells, for example, take in raw materials and energy and excrete waste products. Their structure is open to interactions, their organisation is closed.

### 3.3.3 Inputs/Outputs and Perturbations/Compensations

It is easy to become confused about inputs/outputs and perturbations/compensations in Maturana and Varela's writings. Autopoietic systems can only be perturbed by their environment, yet they appear to have structural inputs and outputs. The problem is partially clarified in Maturana (1991b) where it turns out that there are really two different questions involving input and output. The first concerns the organisation of the system—whether it is closed or open, and the second the level of description of the observer—whether we are interested in characterising the unity itself, as a composite entity, or whether we are interested in how the unity as a whole relates to some wider system of which it is a part.

First, all dynamic systems interact with their environment through their structure. In identifying a system as a composite entity we are interested in the organisation of the entity and its particular characteristics. Do we need to characterise the organisation (and thus the entity) in terms of inputs and outputs or not? If we are describing the autopoietic organisation (and other closed organisations) then we do not. But if we are describing an organisation which is not closed, then its inputs and outputs will be necessary for a proper characterisation. So, for example, organisationally, the cell is closed and has no inputs and outputs but the heart, as a blood pump, does.

The second question is whether we should refer to inputs and outputs or perturbations and compensations. This depends on whether we describe the entity in its own right, or as part of a wider system. In the former case, as all systems are structure determined all interactions should be described as perturbations which lead to particular compensations. However, if the entity is part of a wider system which produces repetitive perturbations then, *from that wider point of view*, the interactions may be seen as inputs and outputs. For example (from Maturana (1991b)), if a thermostat is seen as a composite entity changes in temperature will be perturbations, but if the thermostat is seen allopoietically as part of a heating system then temperature is an input and changes in heat is an output. Equally, a cell can be seen allopoietically as part of the liver, in which case it can be described in terms of inputs and outputs.

There is thus the organisational question of whether an entity is characterised by inputs/outputs or not; and the structural question of whether the level of description requires inputs/outputs or perturbations/compensations.

## 3.3.4 Structural Coupling

The concept of structure-determinism means that it is wrong to suggest that the environment determines or specifies what will be the changes of state of the system. This is difficult to accept initially because it appears as though organisms are so well adapted to their environments that the environment must have led to appropriate changes in the organism. The answer lies in the vital concept of *structural coupling* (Maturana 1978a, p. 35; Maturana 1980a, p. 70).

As we have seen, an autopoietic system is realized through a particular structure and the changes that it can undergo are determined by that structure so long as autopoiesis is maintained. These changes may preserve the structure as it is, or they may radically alter it (think of an acorn developing into an oak). Where change is possible the structure is said to be plastic. This plastic structure exists within an environment which perturbs it and can trigger changes. The environment does not determine the changes but it can be said to select states from among those made possible at any instant by the system's structure. In an environment characterised by recurring states (and an actual autopoietic system will require, for example, a continual availability of energy) continued autopoiesis will lead to selection in the organism of a structure which is suitable for that environment. The organism becomes structurally coupled to its environment and, indeed, to other organisms within that environment.

Structural coupling is a reformulation of the idea of adaptation, but with two important provisos. First, that the environment does not specify or determine the adaptive changes that will occur—they either will occur and thus maintain autopoiesis, or they will not and the system will disintegrate. Second, that the environment is not presumed to be fixed and unchanging. Rather, the environment consists of other structure determined systems that are themselves changing through their own processes of structural coupling.

"If a composite unity is structurally plastic, then adaption as a process of structural coupling to the medium that selects its path of structural change is a necessary outcome." (Maturana 1981, p.29)

At first sight this sounds rather abstract but examples will show how commonplace it is. The first example is a person interacting with a particular computer program. We can say that the computer and its software is itself an example of a structure-determined system that is interactively open but organisationally closed. The person can interact with the computer; they can type in information and get appropriate responses. However, the computer is structure determined since it is the structure of the program and the computer which determines what will or will not trigger it. Only pressing appropriate buttons will lead to appropriate responses and those particular triggering mechanisms are determined entirely by the nature of the system. Even simple operations of a similar nature vary from one software package to another.

When beginning a new package there is a feeling of insecurity, not knowing how to achieve what one wants, not knowing whether one has performed the right actions, pressed the right buttons. Gradually, through use, this feeling disappears until eventually one reaches a state in which it is almost unnecessary to think about the actual operations, one merely needs to think of what is to be achieved. This state of being able to interact without thinking consciously of what to do is called, by Heidegger (1962), a state of "being thrown"—the computer becomes *ready-at-hand* rather than *present-at-hand*. This process of becoming attuned is, in fact, the process of developing structural coupling.

The second example is the development of babies. In their first few months they are becoming structurally coupled to their physical environment. Their structures are developing in ways which reflect the interactions which they have with their environment. Then, up to 3 years, they also become structurally coupled in the linguistic domain. This is a very important domain of activity for human beings— indeed, it is probably their primarily distinguishing characteristic from other animals. Maturana describes language (see section 3.5.4) as a consensual domain, implying that the tokens we use in our language do not have meaning of themselves but depend upon a consensus amongst the people involved in using the language. This, of course, requires structural coupling. Once we have learnt a language we feel so comfortable and easy in using it that it appears as though the language and the words have inherent meaning in their own right. However, the above description reveals the true nature of the situation—namely, that communication is only possible to the extent that the systems involved are structurally coupled.

If structure-determined coupling is actually so obvious, why is it of importance? First, what it shows is that all interactions which we have as human beings, as autopoietic systems, are determined by our own structure. Things in our environment can only be triggers for our nervous system if our nervous system can react to them, and the reaction that they get will depend upon the state of our nervous system. We cannot, therefore, have interactions with anybody or anything which are in some sense pure—they all are generated by our own nervous system.

Organisms become structurally coupled not only to their medium, but also to other organisms. The behaviours of one become a trigger for the behaviours of the other through the selection of their individual structures. These interlocked triggering behaviours may have direct importance in themselves, such as a threatening gesture and a corresponding flight, or they may be purely symbolic and essentially arbitrary, such as a particular form of greeting in a particular language. In the latter case, it does not matter what the actual behaviour is; only that it has been implicitly agreed through structural coupling. This idea is of great importance in Maturana's cognitive theories, as it is the basis for his concept of a consensual domain, that is, a domain of behaviours (including, above all, language and description) which are both arbitrary and context dependent (see for example Maturana (1978a, p.47)).

Finally, Maturana calls the dynamic outcome of structural coupling, for a particular system, ontogenic structural drift (Maturana 1987a, p. 344). The analogy is with a boat, drifting uncontrolled in the sea, whose path is continuously determined by its structure and the effects of wind and waves. It is equally so for a particular, structure-determined, system. Such a system, in interaction with an environment, will conserve its organisation through structural coupling. Its particular structural changes will be triggered by occurrences in its environment and, just as the path of the boat is a determinate outcome of its history, so is the path of structural change of the system.

## 3.4 Implications of Autopoiesis

### 3.4.1 Implications for Biology

There is a worldview within biology, perhaps the dominant one, which places genetics and evolution at its core. Dawkins' (1978) classic work views the gene, and its survival and development through evolution, as the centrepiece of life. Individual organisms and groups of organisms are of secondary importance. This approach tends also to employ a functionalist mode of explanation (Lambert and Hughes 1988) which suggests that particular traits or components come about in order to fulfill a need posed by the environment. Maturana and Varela's work, which can be seen as an example of a structuralist approach to biology, presents quite antithetical views. Life is a property of the individual, autonomous entity such as the cell; reproduction and heredity are a secondary development of living organisms; and functionalist explanation is eschewed.

First, autopoietic systems are autonomous—they depend essentially only on themselves for their continued production and physically they define themselves through the production of their own boundaries (Varela 1977; Varela 1979; Varela 1981a; Tabary 1991). This occurs independently of an observer whose description may or may not correspond to these boundaries. The interactions which an autopoietic system can undergo are also determined by its autopoietic organisation. Interactions which do not allow the continuance of autopoiesis lead to its disintegration. An autopoietic system also has individual identity since, so long as it follows a continuous process of autopoiesis, it maintains its organisation despite significant change in its appearance (its structure).

Allopoietic systems, conversely, do not define their own organisation but depend on an observer to determine their identity. They rely on other systems for their continued production, and the result of their activity is something other than themselves. This is not to say that autopoietic systems cannot be treated as allopoietic either by an observer or by other entities with which they interact. For example, autopoietic cells do play an allopoietic role within multicellular organisms, but this in no way diminishes their primary autopoiesis.

Second, the actual processes which occur in a living organism depend only on the immediate neighbourhood interactions and reactions of the components involved and do not in any causal sense depend on a reference to, or representation of, or any supposed functions of, the system as a whole. Autopoiesis specifies certain necessary conditions and relations, and if these arise then an autopoietic unity will be established. This is entirely a contingent matter, however, and there is nothing in the theory of autopoiesis which suggests that autopoiesis brings about or causes particular structures to arise. There is no need for functionalist explanations or teleonomic ideas such as "purpose" in the explanation of living things, although they may be useful in the descriptive language of an observer who sees the components, the unity and its history of development:

"if living systems are physical autopoietic machines, teleonomy becomes only an artifice of their description which does not reveal any feature of their organisation, but which reveals the consistency in their operation within the domain of observation. Living systems, as physical autopoietic machines, are purposeless." (Maturana and Varela 1980, p. 86)

This may seem contrary to what we observe, namely the apparent fit or adaption of organisms to some independent environment. It is this which makes functionalist explanations attractive—the existence of tree-tops leads to the development of long necks in giraffes—but there never is such a causal relationship. Rather, Maturana developed the concept of structural coupling to explain the complementarity between organisms and their environments as explained in Section 3.3.4.

Third, reproduction has generally been seen as a defining feature of living systems but Maturana and Varela (1980; 1987) show that reproduction (i.e., the production of another entity) can come about only after the formation of a unity and is, therefore, derivative from it. Moreover, it is only with reproduction that the concepts of heredity and evolution, and indeed of species, can have meaning. Therefore, these too are not the primary features of living systems but secondary to the establishment of a single autonomous autopoietic entity.

The essence of reproduction is the production of another, distinguishable, entity of the same class as the first. This is, of course, quite distinct from autopoietic processes internal to the continual production of a single unity. Logically, therefore, reproduction requires the existence of an entity to be reproduced. However, this does not imply that reproductive capacity is a necessary characteristic of the living organisation. There can be living organisms which are biologically incapable of reproduction such as the mule (a cross between a donkey and a horse). Thus, the fact that the overwhelming majority of organisms can reproduce is not a defining feature of life. Rather, it reflects the simple logic that those which can reproduce will, over time, outnumber those which cannot.

## 3.4.2 Other Possible Autopoietic Systems

An interesting question leading on from the idea of the cell as an autopoietic system is whether or not there are other instances of autopoietic systems. Are multicellular organisms also autopoietic systems in their own right over and above the autopoiesis of the constituent cells? Are there chemical systems, e.g., auto-catalytic reactions, that that fulfil the autopoietic criteria but which we would not usually classify as living? Most controversially, are there non-physical autopoietic systems such as conceptual systems or even social systems?[9]

Chemical Autopoiesis

Three suggestions have been made of chemical processes that might embody the autopoietic organisation—auto-catalytic processes, osmotic growths, and self-replicating micelles.

A catalyst is a molecular substance whose presence is necessary for the occurrence of a particular chemical reaction, or which will speed it up, but which is not changed by the reaction. The complex productions of contemporary cells require many catalysts and this is one of the main functions of the enzymes. An auto catalytic process is one in which the specific catalysts required are themselves produced as a by-product of the reactions. The process thus self-catalyses. An example is RNA itself which, in certain circumstances, can form a complex surface that acts like an enzyme in reaction with other RNA molecules. Although this process can be described as a self-referring interaction, the system does not qualify as autopoietic because it does not produce its own boundary components and thus cannot establish an autonomous operational entity (Maturana and Varela 1980, p. 94).

Zeleny and Hufford (1992; 1992) have suggested that a particular form of osmotic growth can be seen as autopoietic. The growth is a precipitation of inorganic salt which expands and forms a permeable osmotic boundary. This is accomplished by putting calcium chloride into a saturated solution of sodium phosphate. Interaction of the calcium and phosphate ions leads to the precipation of calcium phosphate in a thin boundary layer. This layer then separates the phosphate from the calcium, water enters through the boundary by osmosis, and the increased internal pressure breaks the precipitated calcium phosphate. This break allows further contact between the internal calcium and the external phosphate, leading to further precipitation. Thus the precipitated layer grows.

Zeleny and Hufford argue that this system fulfils the six autopoietic criteria as set out above but Fleischaker (1992a; 1992b) argues that in fact it only meets the first three.

An approach with more potential developed by Bachmann and colleagues (Bachmann, Walde et al. 1990; Bachmann, Luisi et al. 1991; Bachmann, Walde et al.

---

[9] These will only be discussed briefly. For more detail see Mingers (1995).

1991) was first proposed by Luisi (1989). A micelle is a small droplet of an organic chemical such as alcohol stabilised in an aqueous solution by a boundary or "surfactant." A reverse micelle is a droplet of water similarly stabilised in an organic solvent. Chemical reactions occur within the micelle producing more of the boundary surfactant. Eventually, this leads to the splitting of the micelle and the generation of a new one, a process of self-replication. Experiments have been carried out with both ordinary and reverse micelles and with an enzymatically-driven system.

It is not clear that these systems could yet be called autopoietic. First, the raw materials (the water/lithium mixture or the enzyme catalyst) are not produced within the system. This limits the amount of replication which can occur—the system eventually stops. Even if these materials could be added on a regular basis, the system would still not be self-producing. Second, the single-layer surfactant does not allow transport of raw materials into the micelle. For this to happen, a double-layer boundary would be necessary, as exists in actual cell membranes. Moreover, the researchers themselves seem most interested in the fact that the micelles reproduce themselves, and seem to identify this as autopoietic. However, reproduction of the whole is quite secondary to the autopoietic process of self-production of components. Nevertheless, this does represent an interesting pathway towards generating real autopoietic systems.

Minimal Cells and the Origin of Life.

One of the key questions in evolutionary biology is that of the origin of life. At what point and in what way did primitive chemical systems become living? There are two main lines of approach to theories concerning the origin of life on Earth (Fleischaker 1988). In the first approach, based on study of the enzymes and genes, life is characterised as being molecular and a defining feature is the structure and function of the genes. In the second approach, life is characterised as cellular and its defining feature is metabolic functioning within the cell. Autopoiesis clearly lies within the second tradition and both Margulis (1993) and Fleischaker (1990; 1991) have utilised autopoiesis as part of their theoretical approach.

Higher Order Biological Systems

Having seen how cells embody the autopoietic organisation, it is natural to question whether more complex organisms such as animals are also autopoietic, at a higher level. At first sight, it would seem that these multicellular organisms are bounded and produce their own constituents, namely different types of cells, and thus are autopoietic. However, this is more complex than might at first appear and Maturana and Varela themselves do not give definitive or even consistent answers.

Clearly such a composite system consists of coupled autopoietic systems and provides a necessary medium for their continued autopoiesis. However, is it itself autopoietic as a unity? At first, whilst Maturana and Varela (1980) accepted that it was not necessarily the case they did claim that "This has actually happened on earth with the evolution of the multicellular pattern of organisation." (Maturana and Varela 1980, p. 110). However, in later publications they talk of "metacellulars" rather than multicellulars as collections of coupled cells and include within the definition organisms, colonies and societies. Such systems are second order autopoietic systems because they consist of first order autopoietic systems rather than because they are autopoietic in their own right. The question now becomes "are some metacellulars autopoietic unities? That is, are second order autopoietic systems also first order autopoietic systems?" (Maturana and Varela 1987, p. 87). Unfortunately, no answer is given. They are unable to say what molecular processes might constitute metacellulars as autopoietic systems. They are willing to say, however, (and this is one of Varela's main themes) that such systems are organisationally closed. That is, "a network of dynamic processes whose effects do not leave the network" (Maturana and Varela 1987, p. 89).

Maturana and Varela go on to describe third order structural couplings, that is, recurrent interactions leading to structural coupling between independent unities. Examples include social insects such as ants or bees, animals that form herds and packs, and humans forming societies. Phenomena arising through third order coupling are defined as social phenomena. If the organisms involved have nervous systems, the behavioural domain can become very complex, leading ultimately, as we shall see to language, self-consciousness, and the observer.

Non-physical Systems

The original definition of autopoiesis specified self-production but did not specify what was to be produced. This leaves open the possibility of autopoietic systems in the non-physical domain. For example, computer generated autopoietic models, human organisations and societies, abstract systems such as law or ideas, or social systems. There are two main questions here—can there be non-physical autopoietic systems? And, if so, are such systems living?

The first question is still open to debate. Certainly Maturana and Varela believe that their computer model does embody an autopoietic organisation, and so it should be counted as autopoietic. More contentiously, societies and law are claimed to be autopoietic by their proponents. An example of a non-physical system that is certainly very close to being autopoietic is the self-referential legal game called Nomic. This will be discussed in more detail in Chapter 8.

### 3.4.3 Epistemological Implications

Maturana and Varela are always aware of the epistemological implications of their ideas. This will be dealt with more thoroughly in Chapter 4, but a brief introduction to their ideas is in order here. As has been seen, they strongly maintain the distinction between the actual operational domain of an organism and the domain of descriptions of an observer.

"Everything said is said by an observer, to another observer, who can be himself" (Maturana 1975, p. 6)

Furthermore, Maturana and Varela's cognitive theories show that the domain of description is inevitably relative to the describer. The observer can generate descriptions of her interactions, but they will be embodied in states of relative neuronal activity, and so must be subordinate to the organisation and structure of the nervous system, and ultimately to the autopoiesis of the organism. This means that we, as observers, can never escape from the domain of descriptions and have access to an absolute, objective reality. Rather, independent events may trigger a response or description, but the neuronal representation they lead to will always be structure-determined and thus inevitably relative to the observer.

## 3.5 The Emergence of the Observer

The first section of the chapter introduced the concept of autopoiesis in the physical domain and its implications. Equally important, and developed at the same time, is Maturana and Varela's work on the nature of cognition in autopoietic systems, and their analysis of the organisation and workings of the nervous system. Most of the original papers are by Maturana and so I will generally refer only to him.

### 3.5.1 The Nervous System and Cognition

In general usage, the term "cognition" refers to the process of acquiring and using knowledge and, as such, it is assumed to be limited to organisms with a (fairly advanced) nervous system. The nervous system itself is viewed as a system which has developed to collect knowledge about the environment, enabling an organism to better survive.

Maturana's theories question both these beliefs (Maturana 1970; Maturana 1974; Maturana 1975; Maturana 1978a; Maturana 1978b; Varela 1984; Maturana 1988; Varela 1991; Maturana 1995; Maturana and Mpodozis 1995). He began his work in the area of animal neurophysiology, publishing a number of well-known papers (Maturana 1960; Maturana 1968). This tied in with his biological interest in terms of two seemingly unrelated questions. What is the nature of living organisms? And, what is the nature of perception and, more generally, cognition and knowledge? A central breakthrough was to see that the two questions are in fact linked. Perception and cognition occur through the operation of the nervous system which operates as part of the autopoiesis of the organism. As we have seen, autopoietic systems operate in a medium to which they are structurally coupled. Their survival is dependent on certain recurrent interactions continuing. For Maturana, this itself means that the organism has knowledge, even if only implicitly. The notion of cognition is extended to cover all the effective interactions that an organism has. The traditional dualism between knowing and acting is completely swept away—*acting is knowing, and knowing is acting*. This theme will be pursued in Chapter 7.

"A cognitive system is a system whose organisation defines a domain of interactions in which it can act with relevance to the maintenance of itself, and the process of cognition is the actual (inductive) acting or behaving in this domain. Living systems are cognitive systems, and living as a process is a process of cognition. This statement is valid for all organisms, with and without a nervous system." (Maturana and Varela 1980, p. 13)

The nervous system is an evolutionary biological development which increases the range of behaviour that can be displayed by an organism—its requisite variety. It does not, in essence, change the nature of operation of an autopoietic system. We can see how nerve cells (neurons) have developed as specializations of ordinary cells. If we consider a single-celled organism such as the amoeba it displays behaviour, for example, movement and ingestion. It has both a sensory and an effector surface—in fact they are both the same, its outer membrane. Chemical changes in areas of its immediate environment affect the elasticity of its membrane which in turn allows its protoplasm to flow in a particular direction thus leading either to movement or the surrounding of food. This eventually leads to the dying away of the environmental perturbation and the restoration of the status quo.

A neuron is like an ordinary cell that is specialized in two ways. First, it has developed very long extensions called dendrites which connect to many other, often distant cells. This leads to a separation of the sensory from the effector sites of the cell and allows for the possibility of the transmission of perturbations. Second, it has developed a generalized response—electrical impulses (although neurons are still affected by chemical changes)—as opposed to the specific physico-chemical sensitivity of different sensory surfaces. This has two vital consequences—the establishment of a universal medium (electrical activity) into which all the differing sensory/effector interactions can be translated; and the development of internal neurons which only connect to other neurons, responding to this electrical activity. These interneurons are particularly important as they sever the direct relationship between sensor and effector and vastly expand the realm of possible behaviours of an organism. In humans these have grown to outnumber sensory/motor neurons by a factor of 100,000.

The other main physiological feature of the nervous system is the neuron's method of connection—the synapse. The synapse is the point of near contact between dendrites and other cells—neurons or ordinary cells. Any particular neuron/cell will have thousands of these, each contributing a small amount to the cell's overall activity. A synapse is actually a very small gap across which chemicals called neurotransmitters can flow, triggering an electrical exchange. In effect therefore these are the sensory and motor surfaces of the neuron.

### 3.5.2 Characteristics of the Nervous System

There are a number of consequences which I will briefly outline. Some will be discussed more fully in later chapters.

Maintaining Internal Correlations

What is it that the nervous system actually does? Looking at the amoeba, a change in the sensory surface is triggered by the level of a chemical in the environment. This leads to motor changes and the movement of the organism through the environment. The process continues until the concentration is reduced and the balance between sensor and effector returns to the previous level. To the observer, the amoeba has moved or captured a prey. To the amoeba, state-determined structural changes have occurred restoring an internal balance or correlation between sensory and effector surfaces.

For Maturana, the nervous system functions in precisely the same way. It acts so as to maintain or restore internal correlations between sensory and effector surfaces. That it does so through an incredibly complex system of interacting neurons makes no difference to its fundamental operation. Touching a hot plate stimulates certain sensory neurons. These trigger motor neurons leading to the contraction of a muscle. This in turn results in withdrawal of the hand and removal of the sensory stimulation. Internal balance is restored.

Organisational Closure of the Nervous System

As mentioned above, the nervous system has a closed organisation. As observers, we see a hot plate and a hand moving quickly away. It appears that the nervous system is an open system, receiving an input from the environment and producing an appropriate response. Yet this account would be mistaken. The nervous system is in a process of continuous activity, the state of its components at one instant determining its state at the next. Thus states of relative neuronal activity are caused by and lead to further states of activity in an uninterrupted sequence. This seems clear for interneurons which only connect to other neurons, but do not the sensory and effector surfaces constitute some kind of open interface to the world? Maturana argues that they do in an interactional sense but not in an organisational sense.

The sensory surface is triggered by something in its environment and its activity contributes to the activity of the whole. This may lead to motor activity compensating for the disturbance. The result is a further change to the sensory surface, not directly, but through the environment. The hand moves, the temperature reduces. Relative activity leads to relative activity. This is equally true for sensory and effector surfaces which interact inside the organism. Excessive internal temperature leads to sweating and eventually to a restored temperature. In all cases nervous activity results from, and leads to, further nervous activity in a closed cycle.

Another way of saying this is that the nervous system is structure-dependent. Its possible and actual changes of state depend on its own structure at a point in time, not on some outside agency. At most, such an agency can only act as a trigger or source of perturbation. It cannot determine the reaction of the nervous system. This can easily be shown by recognizing that it is the structure itself that determines what can be a trigger for it. For instance, only systems with light sensitive neurons can be affected by changes in light.

These points, i.e., the maintenance of internal correlations and organisational closure, apply equally to organisms which have no nervous system. That the amoeba is affected by certain chemicals, and that they lead to particular changes, is determined exclusively by the structure of amoeba, not the nature of the chemical. The next two points, however, are particular consequences of the nervous system.

Plasticity of the Nervous System

A crucial feature of the nervous system is its plasticity—that is, its structure can change over time. This is because of the inter-neurons, which disconnect the sensory and motor surfaces, severing their one-to-one relations and vastly increasing the range of states open to an organism. It is this which allows changes in behaviour and that which we call learning. This plasticity does not mainly happen to the structure of connections between neurons and groups of neurons, but in the pattern of response of individual neurons and their synapses. Such changes occur both because of the specific activity of interacting neurons and through the general results of chemical changes in the blood supply.

Interactions with Relations

Apart from introducing plasticity and thus change and development of behaviour, the main feature of the nervous system is that it connects together cells that are physically separate within the organism. One vital result of this is that it allows the organism to interact in respect of the relations between events rather than the simple events themselves. An organism without a nervous system only interacts with isolated physico-chemical occurrences. However, in organisms with nervous systems that connect many different sensors, neurons develop that are triggered not by single events but by the relations that hold between events occurring simultaneously or, indeed, over time. Von Foerster (1984) gives an illustration of a network of neurons which is structured in such a way that it only responds to the presence of an edge— that is a sharp discontinuity between light and dark.

This may well be the most important consequence of the nervous system. It enables organisms to interact with the general as well as the particular and leads to the possibility of abstract thought, description and eventually language and the observer as will be shown in the next section.

## 3.5.3 The Emergence of Observing and the Observer

The nervous system allows the relations that occur at the sensory surface to be embodied in a particular pattern of nervous activity. With the growth of the interneurons this pattern no longer has a direct effect on the motor surface but constitutes a perturbation for the internal nervous system itself. The state of relative nervous activity becomes itself an object of interaction for the nervous system, leading to further activity. This is the basis for a further expansion of the cognitive domain—a domain of interaction with its own internal states as if they were independent entities. This is the beginning of what we term abstract thought.

The widened repertoire of behaviour and the potential for change and development constituted significant evolutionary advantage and stimulated an enormous expansion of the internal nervous system. Structurally, this development involved the nervous system projecting itself onto itself. The various sensory surfaces developed corresponding areas within the cortex, and these became functionally connected to each other and to various mediating structures. The human brain is vastly more responsive to its own internal structures than it is to its sensory/effector surfaces.

The next important emergence appears to be that of description and language. Maturana's ideas here are strikingly similar to those of George Mead (1934) although apparently developed independently. The evolutionary developments outlined above lead to organisms with well developed nervous systems capable of wide-ranging and adaptable behaviour. Such organisms are structurally coupled to their environment and to other organisms within it. Complex sequences of mutually triggered behaviours are possible. Always, however, such behaviour is ultimately structurally-determined within each organism (Rosseel and van der Linden 1990).

Within this context, Maturana distinguishes two types of interaction between organisms. The first is where the behaviour of one leads directly to the behaviour of the other, for example fight/flight or courtship. The second is less direct. The behaviour of the first organism "orients" a second organism, i.e., directs its attention to, some other interaction that the two have in common. The orienting behaviour stands for or represents something other than itself. What is important is that the behaviour symbolizes something other than itself, and its success depends on the common cognitive domains of the organisms. This leads Maturana to describe the domain of such behaviours as a consensual domain, and the interactions as communication.

Orienting behaviour is thus symbolic—its significance lies not in itself but in what it connotes or implies. This is the origin of the semiotic domain to be taken up in Chapter 5. In a very crude way it is an action that is a description of the environment of an organism. It is the basis for the emergence of a new domain of interactions—the domain of descriptions—which in turn forms the basis of language. Initially these symbolic gestures will be closely related, through metaphor and metonymy (Wilden 1977), to the activity that they connote. However, the nervous system can interact with the corresponding states of neuronal activity as if they were independent entities and thus generate descriptions of descriptions in an endless recursive manner. In this way the symbols become further removed from their origin and the domain of essentially arbitrary signifiers that we call language emerges.

As a result of this process, and a concomitant development of the neo-cortex, organisms have arisen that can make complex and recursive descriptions of their descriptions and thus they become observers. Moreover, within this linguistic domain a description of the self is possible, and thus descriptions of the self describing the self and so on. So is born the self-observer and self-consciousness.

To summarize Maturana's views so far, autopoietic systems exist structurally coupled to their medium. Their behaviours are implicitly based on presumptions about their environment and are thus cognitive. A nervous system does not alter this basic situation, but does permit the emergence of wider realms of interaction culminating in the self-consciousness of humans. Initially, the nervous system severs the direct connection between sensory and motor surfaces allowing a wider range of changeable behaviours, and interactions with relations rather than isolated events. Increasing encephalization (i.e., development of the brain) under evolutionary pressure widens the range of possible behaviours to include abstract thought, orienting behaviour and the domain of descriptions. Finally, descriptions of descriptions, and descriptions of self through language generate the observer and self-consciousness. At each stage emerges a domain of new and different interactions—interactions with relations, with internal nervous activity, with descriptions, with descriptions of descriptions, and finally with self-descriptions. All are made possible by the underlying biology, but none are reducible to it.

"The linguistic domain, the observer, and self-consciousness are each possible because they result as different domains of interactions of the nervous system with its own states in circumstances in which these states represent different modalities of interactions of the organism."        (Maturana and Varela 1980, p. 29)

### 3.5.4 Consequences of the Theory

Cognition as a Closed Domain

As explained in Section 3.3.2, an autopoietic system is organisationally closed and structurally determined—its changes of state depend on its own structure at a point in time and are not determined (although they may be selected) by events in the environment. The same is true of the nervous system even though it itself is not autopoietic. Every state of nervous activity leads to and is generated by other such states. This is true despite it appearing that the sensory/effector surfaces are open to the environment. The correctness of this counter-intuitive view will be illustrated by a number of examples. Further discussion occurs in Chapter 7 which examines Varela's later work on embodied cognition.

First were studies of colour vision in pigeons by Maturana, Uribe and Frenk (1968). It might be expected that there would be a direct causal relation between the wavelength of light and the pattern of activity in the retina, and that this in turn would create the experienced colour. In fact, it was not possible to directly correlate light wavelength and neuronal activity. The same nervous activity could be generated by different light situations while the same wavelength of light could lead to different experiences of colour (this is practically illustrated in Maturana and Varela (1987) p. 16–20. See also Thompson, Palacios and Varela, (1992)). However, it was the case that there was a direct correlation between retinal activity and the experience of the subject. In other words, a particular sensory activity with the nervous system (here the eye) always generates the same experience even though it may be triggered by different environmental situations.

Second, consider the sensory and effector surfaces of the nervous system between which lies an environment. Imagine a very simple nervous system with one sensor connected to one interneuron connected in turn to one effector. If the effector were itself connected directly to the sensor than the closed circular operation would be apparent. It is not, but neither are the other neurons in this simple system connected directly to each other. They are connected across a small gap—the synapse—which, therefore, forms the environment between each neuron. Moreover, each neuron can be seen as having its own effector and sensor surfaces. In principle therefore the relations between the sensory and effector surfaces of the nervous system are no different from those between any neurons. What is different is that we, as observers, stand in one environment and not the other and it is not apparent to us that functionally it is just as if we are standing within one of the synapses.

Third is the idea that the environment does not determine but only triggers neuronal activity. Another way of saying this is that the structure of the nervous system at a particular time determines both what can trigger it and what the outcome will be. At most the environment can select between alternatives that the structure allows. This is really an obvious situation of which we tend to lose sight. By analogy, consider the humming computer on my desk. Many interactions, e.g., tapping the monitor or drawing on the unit, have no effect. Even pressing keys depends on the program recognizing them, and pressing the same key will have quite different effects depending on the computer's current state. We say "I'll just save this file," and do so with the appropriate keys as though these actions in themselves bring it about. In reality the success (or lack of it) depends entirely on our hard-earned structural coupling with the machine and its software in a wider domain, as learning a new system reminds us only too well.

As adults we are so immersed and successfully coupled to our environments that we forget the enormous structural developments (ontogenetic structural drift in Maturana's words) that must have occurred in us, although observing the helplessness of young babies quickly brings this home. It is still easy, however, to imagine that the environment has caused us to become adapted to it, but this is as mistaken as to believe that the existence of tree tops caused the development of giraffes.

The Role of Information and Representation

The ideas of a closed, structure-determined system and a consensual domain of essentially arbitrary behaviours has major implications for current beliefs and theories about the role that information and representations play in living systems and their thought processes. They challenge a number of current notions. First, for example, it is currently held that DNA and the genes code or contain or transmit information about the structure of their parent organism (the genetic code):

"These experiments, and other related ones, have finally brought us to a clear understanding of the nature of the unit of heredity. Like the dots and dashes of Morse code, the sequence of nucleotides in DNA is a code. The sequence provides the information that specifies the identity and order of amino acids in a protein. The sequence of nucleotides that encodes this information is called a gene." (Raven and Johnson 1991, p. 305)

Second, it is currently held that the messages and communications between organisms are, in themselves, instructive. That is, that the messages contain sufficient information to determine an appropriate reaction in the receiver. Third, a major plank of cognitive science, particularly as embodied in artificial intelligence is that our minds work by creating and then manipulating objective representations of the environment and the tasks to be performed within it. Cognition is seen as a process of symbol manipulation and information processing.

All of these are so well established that they seem almost self-evidently true, yet autopoiesis suggests that they are all mistaken in the same fundamental way: they confuse the descriptions of an observer with the actual operations of an autopoietic system and ignore its structure-determined nature. As has been described above, autopoietic systems behave purely in terms of their particular structure and the neighbourhood interactions of their components at a point in time. Concepts such as "information" and "representation" pertain only to descriptions made by observers who can see both the internal interactions of a composite unity and the behaviour of the whole in a particular environment, and who can relate the two together.

"In fact, the notion of information is valid only in the descriptive domain as an expression of the cognitive uncertainty of the observer, and does not represent any component actually operatant in any mechanistic phenomenon of instructive interactions in the physical space" (Maturana 1975, p. 17).

A theory concerning the nature of information and meaning will be developed in Chapter 5.

Perception and Intelligence

Maturana's approach brings out characteristically novel insights into these domains (Maturana and Guiloff 1980; Maturana 1983). In both cases he asks not what is this phenomenon as an entity or characteristic? But, what is this as a process generating the observed phenomena (just as critical realism would expect)?

His analysis of perception has been introduced in section above. The process of perception does not consist in our grasping or representing an objective world external to us. Rather, it involves the operations of a closed neuronal network which has developed a particular structure of sensory/effector correlations through a history of structural coupling. For the observer, who sees the organism and its environment in apparent harmony, it seems that the organism must be responding to perceived changes in the environment. But the internal situation is rather like a robotic production line. Each robot is programmed to perform its own specific actions in orchestration with the others. Whilst these actions coordinate there appears to be purpose and communication but as soon as they become unsynchronised the resulting ludicrous spectacle reveals how fragile this illusion is.

Similarly, intelligence is normally seen as an objective property of a person or animal, like weight or strength, which can be measured in an objective way by, for example, solving problems or puzzles. Maturana argues that we must ask how behaviour which observers call intelligent is generated. His answer is that it must be the result of a history of structural coupling with the environment and/or other organisms, and that therefore any behaviour that is successful within a domain of structural coupling is intelligent behaviour. Intelligence is neither a property of the organism, or some part of the organism, nor is it directly observable. The word intelligence connotes the structure resulting from coupling in various domains and it is only manifest in particular instances of coupled or consensual behaviour.

There are a number of implications. First, all cultures, as consensual domains of biologically successful behaviour, imply equivalent although not identical intelligence in their members. Secondly, intelligence in general cannot be measured and certainly cannot be compared across cultures. IQ tests only reflect a subset of a particular culture and can only record the extent of an organism's coupling to that particular domain, and thus to the observer (test creator) who specifies it. They cannot therefore measure the organism's potential for structural coupling in other domains, or in general. Third, specific intelligence is not heritable for it is developed in the ontology of a particular organism's coupling. At most one can say that the general capacity for coupling in particular domains (e.g., the linguistic) is genetically dependent.

Language as a Consensual Domain

Just as it is mistaken to believe that the nervous system operates by manipulating the environment it is equally mistaken to view language as denotative, that is objectively indicating and pointing to an external world. Linguistic behaviour is *connotative*. The observed communication of meaning and the practical efficacy of language do not reside in the words and terms themselves but reflect similarities in the organisms' structures developed through their history of interactions.

Organisms which interact recurrently with each other become structurally coupled. They develop behaviours which reciprocally trigger complementary behaviours, and their actions become coordinated so as to contribute to their continued autopoiesis. Moreover, the particular behaviours or conducts are divorced from that which they connote—they are symbolic and thus essentially arbitrary and context-dependent. They only "work" to that extent that they reflect agreement in structure and this is what Maturana means by a domain of consensual action. They rely on a consensuality (rather than explicit consensus) between those involved (Harnden 1990).

When two or more organisms interact recursively as structurally plastic systems each becoming a medium for the realization of the autopoiesis of the other:

"the result is mutual ontogenetic structural coupling. ... the various conducts or behaviours involved are both arbitrary and contextual. ... I shall call the domain of interlocked conducts that results from ontogenetic structural coupling between structurally plastic organisms a consensual domain ... a consensual domain is closed with respect to the interlocking conducts that constitute it, but is open with respect to the organisms or systems that realize it." (Maturana 1978a, p. 47)

The consensual domain is thus a domain of arbitrary and contextual interlocked behaviours. Much animal behaviour involves coordinating actions of this type, e.g., courtship or nest-building. Some may be instinctive, e.g., the dance of bees, but most is learnt through the structural drift of the organism through its life. This learnt consensual behaviour Maturana terms linguistic, although it is not yet language. It is distinguished by its symbolic nature, i.e., that the action stands for something other than itself. For an observer, such coordinating conducts can be seen as a description of some feature of the organism's environment.

Linguistic acts by themselves do not constitute language. For Maturana, the process of using language or "languaging" can only occur when the linguistic behaviours themselves become an object of coordination. This, in turn, can only happen when the nervous system has developed in such a way that it can interact with its own symbolic descriptions. Thus linguistic behaviour is the consensual coordination of action. Languaging is a recursion of this, i.e., the consensual coordination of consensual coordinations of action.

Once this level of abstraction has been reached—i.e., the description of a description—the entire space of language is opened up, as is the observer and the self-conscious self-observer. In his early work Maturana talked of descriptions and descriptions of descriptions, but now he refers to consensual coordination of action. This emphasises his view that language is not essentially a descriptive domain but always an activity, embedded in the ongoing flow of actions.

Having uncovered the generation of human language, let us move to the level of its day-to-day use. Maturana (1988) has developed an elegant description of languaging around the concept of a conversation—that is an ongoing coordination of actions in language among a group of structurally-coupled observers. For the individual, such a conversation is actually a meshing or braiding of language and mood (or emotion). The linkage between these distinct domains occurs because they are both embodied in the body of the observer. Although often ignored in discussions of language and meaning, in real conversations our mood or "emotioning" is an ever-present background to our use of language. It conditions our stance or attitude—are we happy or sad, caring or self-concerned, deferential or confident, angry or upset—and thereby the course of our conversation. In turn, what we say and what is said may trigger in us changes of mood. For Maturana a conversation is an inextricable linking of language, emotion and body in which the nervous system is the medium in which all intersect.

As Winograd and Flores (1987) have recognized, this view is strikingly similar to the phenomenology of Heidegger (1962). He too argues that in relating to the world, in existing in the world, our basic attitude is always a practical one of doing, acting, having some aim in mind. Our consciousness (although we may not generally be conscious of this) is characterised by our state of mind or mood, and by our understanding of our situation which may be articulated in language. Generally, we are immersed in our daily tasks and do not notice most of the world as such. In using language within a conversation we bring out particular objects and highlight particular properties in the light of our concern at the time. It is also reflected in Luhmann's concept of the double contingency of interaction as will be discussed in Chapter 7.

It is important to note that the driving force behind these evolutionary developments is the advantage they afford through enabling cooperative and coordinated activity. Thus language itself is ultimately rooted in cooperative practical activity and its effects, rather than the abstract exchange of meaning and ideas. It also emphasises that language is itself an activity and of course is not restricted to verbal actions alone.

It is interesting to compare this with Habermas's (1979) analysis of language. For Habermas too language is a practical activity which arises out of the need for the social coordination of action. This has important consequences for the underlying nature of language, namely that for utterances to be practically successful they make, at least implicitly, certain claims as to their validity. Over and above being *comprehensible* they must be *true* in their description of the external world, *right* according to the norms of the social world, and *truthful* in their expression of the subjective world of the speaker. (See section 5.4.)

## 3.6 Conclusions

I think it is hard to overstate the importance of the major concepts that have been developed through the theory of autopoiesis. In particular:

- The basic circular and self-referring nature of both physical living systems and the nervous systems that have been such an important evolutionary development. Following from this the identification of the primary unit of biology – the fundamental "living system" – as the individual rather than the species.

- The organizational closure of the process of cognition and the implications of this for epistemology.

- The inextricable linking of mind and body, of cognition and action, leading to the support for an embodied view of cognition.

- A recognition of the importance of the development of languaging as the primary human characteristic, whilst stressing that languge is not essentially representative and denotational but consensual and connotative.

- An opening up of the possibility, at least, of considering whether non-physical systems, such as social systems, could also be autopoietic, and the considerable implications that would follow from this.

These will be seen to underlie much of the discussion and debate throughout the rest of this book.

# Chapter 4: Observing Systems:
# The Question of Boundaries

## 4.1 Introduction

It is an interesting paradox that a system boundary is one of the most fundamental concepts underlying systems thinking and yet it is one of the least discussed, especially in the seminal literature. Arguably, the concept of a "system" existing within an "environment" is the foundation for systems theory and yet what is it that separates a system from its environment, but the system boundary? In fact, defining a system in terms of its components and their relations is effectively to delineate its boundary. Or, put the other way, in order to define a system it is necessary to define its boundary. Thus the drawing of a boundary is in fact the most primitive systemic act that one can perform.

First I should substantiate my case concerning the omission. Table 4.1 covers a range of the primary systems literature since the 1960s. As can be seen, many books do not even index the term, and most others refer to it only in a cursory fashion.

If it were the case that this was a trivial act then one could understand the omission but with the advent of soft systems and second order cybernetics, which placed the observer's role in system definition firmly centre-stage, deciding on a system's boundary (and thus the constitution of the system), is highly debatable.

In this chapter I want to explore this question in an almost phenomenological way by considering what we can learn of the nature of boundaries in a whole range of different types of systems. Initially, I shall "bracket" the question of the observer and simply try to discover what properties boundaries have across a range of different systems. I shall begin with what seems the simplest—the boundaries of easily identified medium-scale physical systems. I shall move from physical boundaries to conceptual boundaries, beginning with mathematics where one might expect there to be the greatest concern with definition and precision and then going to more general conceptual boundaries, particularly linguistic. From there I shall consider the difficult question of boundaries for social systems. At this point I shall deal directly with the question as to whether boundaries are in fact purely observer constructs or whether we can in some circumstances take them as having independent ontological existence. As might be expected, given the critical realist stance, I shall come down on the side of existence. The chapter will finish with a consideration of systems which may bound themselves through organisational closure, and finally the setting of boundaries within organisational research and intervention.

### Table 4.1. Reference to Boundaries in Foundational Systems Books.

| Title | Reference | Coverage |
|---|---|---|
| *An Introduction to Cybernetics.* | (Ashby 1956) | Not in index |
| *A Methodology for Systems Engineering.* | (Hall 1962) | The system engineer's job is to define the boundary between system and environment (p. 102) |
| *Decision and Control* | (Beer 1966) | The detection of a system is a subjective matter. Two people will not necessarily agree on the boundaries of any system so detected (p. 243) |
| *The Systems Approach.* | (Churchman 1968) | Need to consider a richer way of defining the environment than a mere looking for boundaries. (p.35) |
| *An Approach to General Systems Theory.* | (Klir 1969) | Not in index |
| *Design of Inquiring Systems* | (Churchman 1971) | Boundaries should include all relevant parties – "the design of a Singerian enquiring system eventually becomes design of the whole social system" (p. 200) |
| *General Systems Theory* | (von Bertalanffy 1971) | Not in index |
| *Introduction to Systems philosophy* | (Laszlo 1972a). | Not in index |
| *The Systems View of the World* | (Laszlo 1972b) | Not in index |
| *An Introduction to General Systems Thinking* | (Weinberg 1975) | Sees boundary as essentially a physically based metaphor. Our experience usually leads us to make good choices. (p. 150) "A system is a way of looking at the world", (p. 52) |
| *The Systems Approach and its Enemies.* | (Churchman 1979) | Boundaries in social systems are chosen temporarily, through judgement, not fixed |
| *Systems Thinking, Systems Practice* | (Checkland 1981) | A definition in terms of the "formal system". "A distinction made by an observer which marks the difference between an entity he (sic) takes to be a system and its environment" |
| *Critical Heuristics of Social Planning* | (Ulrich 1994) | Significant discussion as boundary critique is the central message |
| *General System Theory* | (Rapoport 1986) | Not in index |
| *Soft Systems Methodology in Action* | (Checkland and Scholes 1990) | No real discussion but probably the same as Checkland above |
| *Facets of Systems Science* | (Klir 1991) | Little discussion of boundaries, but states that systems are constructs of the observer expressed in terms of distinctions. This constructivist view is "ontologically neutral" with regard to the existence of systems (p. 13) |

## 4.2 Physical Boundaries

To try to understand the nature of boundaries I shall begin with hard physical objects which would seem to be the most straightforward to deal with, moving on to conceptual, social and mixed ones.

### 4.2.1 Basic Forms of Boundary

<u>Type I—Edges and Surfaces</u>

The first and most primitive form of boundary is what we might call an edge or surface. That is, it is simply the limit of the extent of some entity or substance. Examples are: a pool of water, a table, a shadow or a sheet of paper. In each case the edge marks the transition from or difference between one substance and another (Bateson 1973). With an edge there are no specific boundary components, just a transition from one thing to another. To be more precise we need to distinguish an edge from a surface[10]. A surface is a two dimensional area of some extent. If it joins another surface then it forms an edge (and if two edges join they form a corner point). In two dimensions a surface is bounded by its edges although some surfaces do not have any edges, e.g., a sphere and are therefore unbounded (but finite!). In three dimensions a volume is bounded by its surfaces, e.g., a cube. A surface, such as a sheet of paper, can be seen to have two sides as well as its edges. These also form part of the boundary of the object as a whole since they are the interface between the object and another substance, e.g., air or a table.

It is the case that edges (and surfaces) are always fuzzy to some degree. Although an edge may appear to the observer as being very sharp if looked at it at a high enough resolution it will be seen to be imperfect. Some edges are, in any case, clearly imprecise either because of their rough (in a fractal sense—see Section 4.3.1) nature, e.g., rocks; or because of their dynamic behaviour, e.g., water lapping on the shore.

These latter observations show that what can be detected as an edge (or any other type of boundary) is always relative to time and the level of resolution. In general (and this is true of the systemic differentiation of structure and process), as we lengthen the period of consideration (at a given level of resolution) more will become dynamic and the more fuzzy the boundary will become. As we shorten the period, the more things will be unchanging and the more definite the boundary will be. Consider waves lapping on the sea shore. If we take a snapshot we will see a relatively fixed boundary between the water and the sand. As we lengthen the time period from seconds to minutes to hours the more variable the boundary will be, especially as the tides change. The same is true of resolution level. Seen from a

---

[10] Very precise definitions of such things can be found in geometry and topology—see section 4.3.

distance the edge of the paper is sharp, but as we magnify it more and more to an atomic level the original boundary virtually disappears.

## Type II—Enclosures

An edge simply demarcates or separates one thing from another. An enclosure or container is different in that it consists of specific boundary components that both mark a separation and keep in that which is included, or, equivalently, keep out that which is excluded. Examples are: a bottle, a bubble, a circle drawn on paper, an onion skin, a football, a suit of armour, insulation round a wire or pipe, or a fence. The important characteristics are:

1.  The enclosure consists of specific components different from, although related to, both inside and outside components. An enclosure has two surfaces, one facing in and one out.

2.  The enclosure is relatively impermeable, but never completely. It prevents the movement of certain substances but not others. A bottle contains liquids but not necessarily gases or radiation; a fence contains sheep but not insects or birds. The enclosure does not have to be complete to have an effect—an open bottle is still a bottle—although the effect may be different, e.g., the liquid may evaporate.

## Type IIa—Membranes

A membrane is a special example of an enclosure. It is an enclosure that is active rather than passive. In particular, it is a biological enclosure, which is one that is part of a living organism. Examples are: the cell wall, a person's skin, or an artery. A membrane is distinct from an enclosure in being part of the autopoietic structure in that its components are produced and maintained by the organism in an ongoing process. It is thus self-constructed by the autopoietic system rather than simply occurring as a result of physico-chemical processes such as a bubble or a gravy skin.

## Type III—Demarcations

We also need to consider the question of boundaries for physical systems that do not occupy contiguous areas of space. To what extent can they be said to have a boundary? Consider, for example, the solar system, a pendulum in a magnetic field, or a central heating system. The solar system is a system by virtue of the gravitational effect of the sun but it has no boundary components. Pluto may be the most extreme planet but there could potentially be others (indeed a new planet was claimed in 2004) as the gravitational force extends further out although decreasing in strength quadratically. So it does have a boundary surface or edge but constituted in terms of the limits of a force rather than a substance.

The pendulum I have in mind consists of a base with battery-driven magnet and a support holding a pendulum with a magnet over the base. The magnets repel each other and the pendulum undergoes chaotic (i.e., random) motion. Assuming that it is the dynamic behaviour that we are interested in then clearly the system needs to include both the physical components and the magnetic force connecting them. This means that there is not a contiguous edge or boundary physically surrounding the system. Instead the boundary becomes more of a notional device for separating conceptually what belongs to the system and what does not.

Considering next a central heating system there are potentially many different aspects (or systems) we could be interested in—the system that maintains a constant temperature in the house; the system of flows of water through the pipes; the system consisting of the boiler and its gas supply, and so on. Each will consist of a different set of elements, not all of which will be physical objects. For instance, the heat regulation system consists of the boiler, pipes, water, radiators, and thermostat but in order to work as a regulation system it needs to engage in information processing—comparing the information about actual temperature with desired temperature and then sending electronic signals to the boiler. Again, the various different boundaries pick out, for different purposes, the members of different systems.

In these three examples we can see that systemic thinking involves more than the simple recognition of particular objects. It begins with a particular phenomenon to be explained or purpose to be achieved. It then requires a degree of conceptualisation, rather than mere perception, to characterise an appropriate system in terms of components, relations and boundary. The boundary may in part have a material embodiment but generally it will simply represent a distinction or demarcation between that which has been selected as part of the system and that which is not. This does not mean that the boundary is purely arbitrary, or is wholly a construction of the observer. It rests on the components and relations that exist independently in the intransitive domain even though it is selected by the observer. This is demonstrated by the fact that the observer may *get it wrong*. Knowledge is always fallible and the real world will soon let us know if our choices of components, relations and boundaries do not in fact yield the appropriate behaviour.

## 4.2.2 Multiple Boundaries

So far we have assumed that an object has just one boundary but that is in general not the case. Systems may have many boundaries depending on the nature of the interactions they are undergoing. For instance, if we consider the body it is usually seen as bounded by the skin and this is so for many interactions, for example with light or with touch. But the skin is not a boundary for x-rays or for a very sharp knife for which the outside of the bones form a boundary. Equally, the skin does not form a boundary for particular chemicals, or for very small organisms that can enter in the pores.

To be accurate, therefore, in specifying a boundary we should also specify classes of interactions or agents for which the boundary is a boundary. In everyday language this is often assumed, or obvious from the context. It becomes more of an issue with complex social systems, such as "Kent University," which can have many boundaries in different dimensions.

An alternative to specifying it in terms of particular interactions, is to specify it in terms of the purposes of the observer. In general, an observer will have chosen some aspect of their experience which they wish to explain or perhaps change and this will shape the nature of the system or boundary that they focus on. This point will be discussed more extensively in Section 4.6.

### 4.2.3 Natural Wholes

The previous section raises a deep question. Are there some systems that form natural or integral wholes (Simons 1987) which observers may *discover* and then others, less tightly connected, where it is the observer who delineates the system?

For Maturana and Varela it is fundamental that we can treat a system either as a unity, that is an unanalysed whole, or we can study its parts and their interactions. These are distinct and irreducible domains. This certainly suggests that for them systems are natural wholes. Concepts such as structural coupling and structural determinism also presume that a system can be well-defined and separated from its environment. This seems very natural for biologists since organisms would obviously be prime examples of self-constructed wholes. However, as we have seen (Section 3.3.8) Maturana and Varela place the foundation for this with the observer and the distinctions they draw rather than with the external world. This will be discussed in Section 4.6.

I propose to take their basic argument but apply it to the intransitive domain. We can then argue that natural wholes exist in so far as the following are met:

1. The system possesses characteristic(s) or behaviour(s) that are only attributable to the system as a whole by virtue of it being a whole. They are not attributable to the parts. This implies that the system must be able to be clearly distinguished as a whole separable from its environment.

2. The system consists of parts and relations between the parts (its structure) that together are necessary in order to generate the characteristics of the system as a whole. In some cases this will include specific boundary components but this is not a necessity.

3. The relationship between parts and whole is recursive—the parts may themselves be whole systems.

Note that this does not imply that parts may only be a part of one system—they may be parts of several systems simultaneously. For instance, blood vessels are part of the blood circulation system and the immune system; my computer is part of my office system but also part of the university computer network. Equally, different systems may occur across the same set of parts depending on what particular characteristics are of interest.

Clearly there are many systems, both natural and designed, that meet these criteria and would generally be recognised as wholes even if they do not have specific boundaries. But as we move from the physical domain to the social and economic world there is a much more complex level of interaction between many different kinds of entities and wholes do not separate themselves out so clearly. Systems identification is much more dependent on the choices of an observer as will be discussed in Section 4.6).

We can summarise this section on physical boundaries by noting:

1.  Some characteristics of boundaries:

    a.  What we observe as a boundary is always relative to the space and time frame of the observations. As these change different boundaries come to be presenced. But, this is an epistemological point to do with our observations—the boundaries still exist ontologically.
    b.  Boundaries are inherently fuzzy if we take a high enough degree of resolution.
    c.  Equally, boundaries are never perfectly impermeable—they will always be open to some elements and closed to others.
    d.  Any particular physical object(s) will have several potential boundaries depending on the nature of the interactions or the purposes of the observer.
    e.  Moving away from single physical objects, the system will contain a variety of elements depending on the observer's purpose and the boundary will become more notional than actual.

2.  The effects of boundaries:

    a.  Separation or demarcation of different substances, elements or spaces.
    b.  Containment or inclusion/exclusion of substances, elements or spaces.
    c.  Self-production and functionality, e.g., permeability.

## 4.3. Mathematical Boundaries

If we move away from physical systems to conceptual ones then the most precise and well defined area of thought is probably mathematics. Here we can find many examples of boundaries, especially in terms of 2a and 2b above, i.e., separation and containment. Not being a mathematician I shall treat these informally.

### 4.3.1 Mathematics of Shape

Geometry

The most obvious area of mathematics relevant to boundaries is that of geometry which is the study of the properties of forms or shapes within Euclidian space[11], for example a circle on a plane surface. One of these properties is that the shape will usually divide the space into separable regions—inside and outside—and will thus form a boundary. Mathematically, these boundaries are *perfect* in the sense that they are infinitely thin and we can unambiguously determine whether a point lies inside or outside. Indeed, they can be defined algebraically rather than pictorially. The equation of the circle ($x^2 + y^2 = a^2$) is effectively a set of instructions to determine whether a particular point is inside, on, or outside the circle.

Geometry is obviously a good model for the sort of physical boundaries we have examined above although when it is applied in the real world, e.g., drawing circles or measuring distances, degrees of fuzziness come in. In fact traditional geometry is rather strict in many of its assumptions and it is interesting to consider two developments that relax some fundamental ones—topology and fractal geometry.

Topology

Topology is a kind of non-metric geometry (Flegg 1974) in that it also studies the properties of shapes but without considering distance or measurement. So in topology the circle, square, triangle or indeed any random shape that forms a closed curve are all considered the same. One property that remains central in topology is that of separating a plane into distinct regions, i.e., drawing a boundary, although surprising results can occur. For instance, if you draw a circle on the surface of a sphere it separates the surface into two regions and you cannot move from one to the other without crossing the line. The same is not always true on the surface of a torus, that, is a 3-D ring. If you draw the line around the torus, as if you were going to slice through it, then it does not create two regions since any point can be joined to any other without crossing the line. Thus some closed boundaries do not actually enclose anything.

Topology also investigates the properties of the surfaces the shapes are inscribed on. Usually a surface, such as a piece of paper, has two sides separated by an edge (a boundary curve) that must be crossed to move from one side to the other. But it is possible to construct interesting surfaces such as the Mobius strip which has an edge

---

[11] Euclidian space is an n-dimensional space of real numbers in which distances between points are measured using Pythagorus' Theorum.

but only one side and the Klein bottle which has only one side and no edges (an ordinary bottle has an inside and outside, and one edge—the rim).[12]

Bunge (1992), in one of the few recent contributions that aims to define the concept of system boundary, based his characterisation on topology, in particular, using the concepts of topological space and neighbourhoods. A topological space is a very abstract concept based on the relations between the members of a set of elements of any kind. Given a set (for example, of components of a system) the elements can be arranged in different groups or subsets. When taken together, open subsets do not include their boundary elements, while closed subsets do. For instance, the set of integers between 0 and 10 exclusive (i.e., 1–9) is open but the set of integers $\geq 1$ is closed since it includes its boundary element (1). A neighbourhood of a particular point, p, is a subset of elements that contains p and that is contained within an open set. Elements can have several neighbourhoods. From concepts like this we can generate the interior of a set (excluding its boundary), the closure of a set (the interior plus boundary), the exterior of a set (the interior of the complement of a set) and the boundary (that which is neither interior nor exterior).

From these ideas Bunge identifies the set of interest (relative to a given system) as consisting of all the components of the system and its environment. Relations between components are based on the idea of one component acting on another; and a neighbourhood of p is the set of components directly linked to (i.e., related to) p. The boundary components are then defined as those components which have neighbourhoods including both system and environment components. Elements whose neighbourhoods only contain other system components are part of the system, and elements whose neighbourhood only contains non-system components are in the environment.

How useful is this type of definition? First, several technical flaws have been identified by Marquis (1996) who provides a revised version based on the same general principles. However, from our point of view, that of identifying the boundaries of systems in the real world, this approach provides no help whatsoever. It begins with the assumption that there is a known set of system and environmental components and proceeds to deduce from these the boundary. But the whole point is to be able to identify the system in the first place by drawing its boundary. The identification of the system and the drawing of a boundary are two sides of the same act. If one has been done the other simply follows on. Indeed, even Marquis recognises this, concluding that:

"It is in fact tempting to say that the real problem has to do with the *criterion* for the boundary, that is, how we actually find in actual particular cases the boundary of a given system and that this question has no general solution. It is simply not the task of general systems theory to answer such a question." (Marquis 1996, p. 254)

---

[12] Note a sphere has two sides (inside and outside) but no edges. You cannot move from outside to inside without going through.

But that is indeed the question that we wish to address!

<u>Fractal Geometry</u>

The second development is fractal geometry which allows lines to be rough rather than smooth as is conventionally assumed (Mandelbrot 1982). Consider a coastline. When viewed on a map it is clearly not a smooth line but jagged and broken. You might think that if you looked at it at a different scale, say from the air, or down on the ground, it would become smoother. But this is not in fact the case. Remarkably, it has the same degree of roughness at whatever scale you observe it. Such lines are said to be self-similar at all scales. Real world shapes such as coastlines, mountains or rivers are statistically self-similar in that they are essentially random rather than ordered. Lines can display different degrees of roughness. A straight line between two points has a fractal dimension of 1. As the roughness increases the fractal number increases towards 2, the dimension of a surface or area. The Norwegian coastline has a fractal number of about 1.6. 3-D shapes such as mountains typically have dimensions of about 2.5 and a cube would be 3. Within fractal geometry, therefore, boundaries can be indefinitely fuzzy.

## 4.3.2 Sets and Operations

It has been argued since *Principia Mathematica* (Whitehead and Russell 1925) that sets may form the basis of mathematics and what is a set but a separation of a group of elements from everything else. A set is simply a list of elements, in no particular order, defined by a criterion of membership which is either *intensive* or *extensive*. An intensive criterion defines membership by a specific meaning or connotation as in "the vowels in English" whereas an extensive definition names or denotes individually all the members as in {a e i o u}.

The extensive definition is clearly the more precise, although even here it would be possible to make a mistake and wrongly include or exclude something. The intensive definition is the more general and useful but this ultimately rests on language and no matter how tightly definitions are drawn there will always be a degree of equivocation even in mathematics (e.g., Gödel's theorem) let alone in ordinary language.

What is different from the point of view of boundaries is that there is no actual boundary as such at all. No members of the set are marked out as boundary members, none can even be said to be closer to the edge in some sense, nor is there any visual representation as there is in geometry or topology. All we can say is that a distinction has been drawn (Spencer-Brown 1972) and it allows us to separate elements into members and non-members.

Having defined a set we can also consider operators or functions that can operate on members of the set. In a system's sense this is akin to moving from a static or structural view to a dynamic or processual view. The question is, when we apply the operator to one or more members of the set does the result also belong to the set or does it cross the notional boundary and become a non-member? In other words, is the set closed under that particular operation? To give an example, if we take the (infinite) set of positive integers then it is closed under addition but open under subtraction. Adding two positive integers always gives another positive but subtracting sometimes gives a negative which is not then a member of the original set.

Traditional set theory assumes that the boundary of the set is exact, i.e., that any element can be unambiguously assigned as a member or not. In practice this is often not the case and this has led to the development of fuzzy set theory (Zadeh). Suppose we are interested in the set of "tall" people. We could define tall arbitrarily as over two metres. This gives a hard boundary but does not really capture normal usage. Fuzzy set theory would instead define a point that was definitely not tall, a point that was definitely tall, and then have a membership function between the two points ranging from zero to 100%.

We can summarise this section on mathematics by noting the following:

- Geometry provides a formalism for considering boundaries, but it is too idealistic for dealing with real-world boundaries. Developments of geometry do go some way in this direction—topology only considers the relationships between shapes and not their distances or sizes, while fractals allow boundaries to be rough rather than smooth. Both still assume that the boundaries (lines) are perfectly impermeable (or "continent" to use a term from Spencer-Brown to be discussed in the next section).

- Set theory introduces the idea that elements can be separated without an actual boundary at all by a membership criterion. Moreover, operators can lead to entry or exit, i.e., input or output; a crossing or not crossing of the notional boundary. As in geometry set theory assumes a perfect distinguished boundary, but this is relaxed somewhat by fuzzy set theory.

## 4.4 Conceptual Boundaries and Language

Given that a boundary is primarily about separation and difference, then we can see that language, from individual concepts right up to whole languages, is essentially a play on boundaries. This is the insight of the semiotic linguists from Saussure (1960) to Derrida (1978), not to mention cyberneticians such as Bateson (1973). Perhaps the most interesting starting point, and one which provides a link between mathematics and language, is that of George Spencer-Brown's (1972) *Laws of Form*.

## 4.4.1 Spencer-Brown's *Laws of Form*

Spencer-Brown's primary aim was to uncover what lay underneath logic and, in particular, Boolean algebra[13]. The latter was created to provide a mathematical analysis of logic or, more precisely, the Aristotelian syllogistic logic. Logic can be defined as the science of abstract form (Lee 1961, p. 13) where form is taken to be organisation, pattern, structure, or relationship. Form, as such, cannot be shown separate from a particular content but it can be studied, in abstraction, through an appropriate symbolism. Thus logic can be seen as the study of relationship or order in general, abstracted from any particular content. Spencer-Brown's work was aimed at "the form in which our way of talking about our ordinary living experience can be seen to be cradled. It is the laws of this form, rather than those of logic, that I have attempted to record." (Spencer-Brown 1972, p. xxiv) [14].

His approach began with the realization that Boolean algebra, as the name implies, is purely an algebra and that no one has ever studied the arithmetic upon which this algebra is based[15]. He therefore set about trying to discover the primary, non-numerical, arithmetic for Boolean algebra. Logic and Boolean algebra concern the form of linguistic statements. To find an arithmetic therefore means going beneath the level of language to uncover that upon which language itself rests.

Spencer-Brown, like Maturana, sees language as essentially practical, not purely descriptive, and takes the most primitive activity as that of *indication* or *distinction*. To distinguish something is the most basic act we can perform. Before counting things we must be able to distinguish between them, and before distinguishing several different things we must be able to distinguish something. This is the basis of all language—to create from nothing ("the void") one thing, or state, or space which is distinct. The laws of form are concerned with the consequences of this, most primitive, act—the act of drawing a distinction. Spencer-Brown prefaces his book with a quotation from Lao Tzu: "The nameless is the beginning of heaven and earth."

What then is the nature of a distinction? "*Distinction is perfect continence*" (Spencer-Brown, 1972, p. 1) is the opening of Spencer-Brown's book. This sparse, but very precise definition is characteristic of the flavour of the rest of the book. "Continence" is derived from the Latin "continere," meaning to contain, and the definition is saying that a distinction, i.e., the drawing of a boundary, perfectly separates that which is on one side from that which is on the other.

---

[13] There are many websites about Laws of Form—see http://www.lawsofform.org/.

[14] Laws of form has close connections to C. S. Peirce's entitative graphs—see Roberts (1973).

[15] Briefly, the distinction between these is that an arithmetic uses constants whose values are known (e.g., 2, 5 etc.) whereas an algebra is concerned only with those properties of an arithmetic which hold irrespective of particular values (e.g., $a^2 - b^2 = (a-b)(a+b)$).

Out of the void we draw a distinction and we can then separate that which is to be distinguished from everything else. Moreover, once it can be distinguished it can be indicated or identified. A distinction will only be drawn if there is some reason (intention or motive) for doing so, and there must therefore be some difference in value (to the person making the distinction) between the contents of the two states. We can give a name to the contents which then indicates the value. Saying or calling the name identifies the value, and implies the distinction. Thus the act of indication, at this almost pre-linguistic level, combines naming, acting and valuing all in one. It is reminiscent of Wittgenstein's (1958, p. 3) proto-language where a builder shouts "slab" to his labourer and the labourer brings one. The shout distinguishes the slab from other things, values it, and generates an action.

As a direct consequence of this definition, Spencer-Brown claims that two axioms can be stated—the law of calling and the law of crossing.

*Axiom 1 The law of calling*: The value of a call made again is the value of the call.

*Axiom 2 The law of crossing:* The value of a crossing made again is not the value of the crossing.

For Spencer-Brown these capture the essence of a distinction—the difference between crossing and not crossing the boundary. The first axiom says that to draw a distinction and then to draw the *same* distinction again adds nothing new. To distinguish a circle and then distinguish a circle again leaves us with a circle. Thus, to re-call is to call. The second axiom involves us in crossing the boundary, and indicating the value by entering into the distinction. Now, if we draw another distinction, from within so to speak, we cross the boundary again and end up where we started with no indication. To distinguish a circle and then, from within, distinguish again must leave us with not-circle. Thus, to re-cross is to not cross.

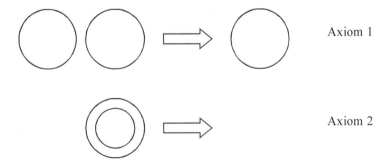

Axiom 1

Axiom 2

To explain it a slightly different way, if we make a distinction we have a single circle distinguished against the blank background. If we then make a second distinction, relative to the first, then it can either go outside or inside the first distinction (assuming, since a distinction is defined to be "perfect continence," that it cannot go across the boundary). If the mark goes in the same space as the first one—i.e., outside, then it is merely repeating the first one and so nothing is changed. If, however, it goes inside the first distinction then it is in a different space and, *from this space*, the second distinction can only take us back to the void.

One of the difficulties of grasping these is that they are at a pre-linguistic stage, yet we inhabit language so, as another example, consider a baby not yet able to talk. The baby cries (calls) for its mother's breast. This draws a distinction and values the contents. The distinction, the indication, and the value are one in the cry. The baby cries again and again, each cry drawing the same distinction and re-calling the same call. This is axiom 1. Then the mother arrives, the baby goes to the breast and the cries stop. The baby has entered into the distinction (mother's breast) and drawn another distinction (no longer need to cry for the breast) and peace returns. This is axiom 2.

These two rather unintuitive axioms form the basis of the whole calculus of indications as laws of form is sometimes called. But, what is the significance of this work?

First, all Boolean algebras rest on a group of assumptions, or a postulate set, which are stated without proof. All the theorems in Boolean algebra can then be rigorously deduced from this postulate set. There are numerous postulate sets for Boolean algebra (e.g., (Sheffer 1913) all of which are essentially equivalent and none of which have previously been proved. Spencer-Brown takes Sheffer's set and shows that each postulate can be proved as a theorem in his algebra. Thus the whole of Boolean algebra (and its tremendously important applications in set theory and logic) can be shown to follow from the two axioms above and these, in turn, are a direct consequence of the primitive act of drawing a distinction.

Second, and potentially the most significant claim, is that the laws of form provide an important foundation for understanding human knowledge. The argument, with variations, runs that indication and distinction are essential elements in our perceptions and conceptions of the world and that the laws of form are therefore the laws of our description of the world and therefore our knowledge. Spencer-Brown thinks that mathematics is a very special subject in that mathematical forms represent and are derived from internal ways of thinking and that these have as much if not more validity than knowledge of external reality. The discipline of mathematics is seen to be a way "of revealing our internal knowledge of the structure of the world" (Spencer-Brown 1972, p. xiii) and he later suggests that we have a direct awareness of the mathematical form as an archetypal structure (Spencer-Brown 1972, p. xvi).

That this is so, is important because Spencer-Brown is attempting to explore this internal world. He believes that this is complementary to a study of the outer structure of reality for what we approach, in either case, from one side or the other, is the common boundary between them, this boundary being the media through which we perceive the outside world. Thus the greatest significance of the laws of form lies in its explanation of this inner structure of knowledge in that it reveals the laws which must apply to our descriptions and understanding of the world, based, as they are, on distinction and indication. In this, Spencer-Brown is pursuing a similar task to the phenomenologists such as Husserl (1977) and his ideas have been drawn on by Luhmann who we will discuss shortly (Luhmann 1996).

### 4.4.2 Concepts as Difference and Distinction

It is interesting to bring in here the other authors mentioned above.

Ferdinand de Saussure (1960) revolutionised the subject of linguistics and provided the foundations for structuralism as later developed by people such as Levi-Strauss (1963) and Chomsky (1957). Prior to Saussaure, language was seen as primarily representational. That is, words were intrinsically associated with the objects they represented, be that actual objects or notional objects such as concepts and ideas. Moreover, there was a historical dimension in that if one traced back the roots of current languages and words one would expect to be able to see closer and closer links between the word and its object.

Against this, Saussure argued that in fact words bore very little relation to objects that they might stand for. Rather, a particular language is a complex system of differences and distinctions between terms—each language effectively cuts the world up in its own way. Particular terms or words then gain their meaning not directly from an object but only in terms of the system as a whole: only, in other words, through their similarities and differences to other terms in the language.

"… in language (langue) there are only differences. Even more important: a difference usually implies positive terms between which the difference is set up; but in language there are only differences without positive terms." (Saussure 1960 p. 120)

Saussure also brought in the important semiotic distinction between *signifier* and *signified* (already developed in a different way by Peirce—see Section 5.4.1). The word itself is a sign, a signifier, which goes with an associated idea, a signified, but does not relate strongly to a real-world object. Moreover, against the historical approach to language, a signifier has no intrinsic relation to its signified—it is arbitrary in that it could be anything—although clearly once the association has been instantiated there is a de facto relationship. These ideas were taken further by Jakobson and Halle (1956) in terms of two dimensions of meaning—the *syntagmatic* (metonymy) and the *paradigmatic* (metaphor) (see Wilden (1977, Ch. 2)). In the syntagmatic dimension, a term gains meaning through its combination with other terms in time or space. In the paradigmatic dimension, it gains meaning by its selection from other possibilities within a code or set of rules. For example, in the sentence "fetch me the hammer," the word "hammer" is combined with (syntagmatic) "fetch me the …" (it could have been "where is the hammer," or "hammer in the nail"), and selected from other possibilities (paradigmatic) such as "screwdriver" or "cup of tea."

Gregory Bateson is not primarily a linguist but a cybernetician although his work has been influential in many areas. In a seminal essay—"Form, Substance and

Difference" (Bateson 1973) he considers Korzybski's famous statement that "the map is not the territory"—in many ways the basic problem of epistemology.

"A map is *not* the territory it represents, but, if correct, it has a *similar structure* to the territory, which accounts for its usefulness. If we reflect upon our languages, we find that at best they must be considered *only as maps*. A word *is not* the object it represents; and languages exhibit also this peculiar self-reflexiveness, that we can analyze languages by linguistic means." (Korzybski 1933, p. 58).

For Bateson, the question is what gets on to the map? And the answer he gives is *differences*. The world, the territory, which of course we can never *directly* access, cannot be simply uniform for then nothing would get on the map. It must, at some level, consist of differences: in temperature, pressure, height, vegetation etc., and it is some selection of these that get transformed to become the map. The same is true in the process of perception and cognition. Differences in the environment are "picked up" subconsciously by the nervous system and transformed into that which we experience. The interesting questions are what get picked up out of the infinite differences that exist? And what do they become transformed into? Bateson called this the "difference that makes a difference" and identified it with the basic unit of information.

We have already considered this process at the neurophysiological level in Section 3.5 where we saw that the nervous systems was organisationally closed and structurally determined. This means that the differences that get "noticed," that "make a difference" are always determined by the structure and state of the nervous system itself from instant to instant, and that the effect that is generated will also be structurally determined. We must not forget of course that in evolutionary terms the structure of the nervous system itself develops in such a way as to enable the continuation of autopoiesis through its structural coupling with its environment.

Looking forward, we will also consider this process of difference transformation as a basis for the characterisation of the nature of information and meaning to be elucidated in Section 5.4.2. Foreshadowing that discussion we can say that information is carried by events in the world that exist in an analogue form of differences. Meaning is then generated from information by the nervous system through a process of digitalization that abstracts only some of the information available and presents it in discrete form. We might say that difference is converted into distinction.

### 4.4.3 The Boundaries of Language

In the previous section we considered the nature of individual concepts and the extent to which they were distinct and therefore bounded. But we can also look at the level of languages or forms of communication as a whole.

Consider first Luhmann, whose work we will consider in more detail in Section 7.3.1. For Luhmann, the basic social act is in fact *communication* (Luhmann 1986).

That is, an utterance or speech act which carries information and generates understanding (and thereby further action) in another person. Society is thus a network of communications continually generating further communications. Modern societies have become structurally complex embodying a range of functionally different subsystems such as the economy, law, science, politics or the mass media. Luhmann suggests that this demarcation occurs precisely through a differentiation of types of communications. The general, everyday, communications of the lifeworld differentiate themselves into specific subsets which have implicit closure, i.e., boundaries. Different subsystems, whether they are societal ones such as those mentioned above, or other social systems such as organisations, generate closure at two levels.

First, operations always generate other operations of the same type—thus communications generate communications (social systems), decisions generate decisions (organisations), and thoughts generate thoughts (psychical systems). There are connections between the different domains—what Luhmann calls interpenetration—where a particular element, e.g., a meaning, is part of both systems but it is not passed from one system to the other. The second form of closure is the type of communication. Thus a particular subsystem, say law, will only recognise or accept communications that are appropriate for law and those which are accepted will then generate further "legal" communications. The distinction (see laws of form above) as to what does or does not belong to the legal system is made by the system itself—it draws its own boundaries and is thus self-referential. These subsystems do interact with other subsystems but only in the autopoietic sense of triggering responses. Thus a legal communication about a fine may trigger an economic communication for payment.

We can also consider the boundedness of spoken languages such as English. A competent speaker of a language automatically generates sentences that are in that language. The sentence could be grammatically incorrect but it would still clearly be English rather than French. This is because there must be some underlying generative mechanism (Chomsky 1957) which automatically produces sentences in a language and at any particular time a person is actually speaking only one language. Bilinguals can of course switch from one language to another but they are always either within one or the other. Indeed, as mentioned in the note in Section 6.1.3, speaking a different language brings with it much more than just the language—it also involves gestures, emotionality and a whole way of being (Wittgenstein 1958).

Even here however the situation is not always that clear. For instance if you listen to a group of people from different countries talking they may use one language, say English, as a lingua franca but then bring in parts of other languages as they go producing a spontaneous and ill-defined polyglot[16].

---

[16] The term "lingua franca" is actually the name of just such a polyglot combination: a mixture of Italian with Provençal, French, Spanish, Arabic, Greek, and Turkish, formerly spoken on the eastern Mediterranean coast. Another example is "franglais"—French with added English.

### 4.4.4 Concepts, Language and Boundaries

What do these theories of difference, distinction and language tell us about the question of boundaries?

Taking first the *Laws of Form,* unsurprisingly perhaps given it relationship to mathematics, it makes the same fundamental assumption, that distinctions are "perfect," i.e., that the boundary created by a distinction is unambiguous and impermeable. But, as discussed in Section 4.3, whilst this may work in the conceptual world it does not when we try to apply it to the real world of objects, or indeed social categories. If we take the physical world it seems that there is a valid distinction between the table and not table although even here the distinction may not be so clear at the atomic or sub-atomic level. When we come to the social world and such concepts as good/bad, dominant/submissive, competitive/cooperative can we really say that each of these distinctions is crystal clear and that people can be assigned to the different categories without problem?

We can consider this in terms of Frege's distinction between sense and reference (Frege 1952). Words, or indeed concepts, have a sense or meaning, and they also have a reference—i.e., that to which they can apply or refer. So the "morning star" and the "evening star" have different senses or meanings even though they both refer to the same object—Venus. If we take a concept such as "terrorist" it is, in Spencer-Brown's sense, a distinction, which is the equivalent of its meaning or sense[17]. However, it is clearly a rather fuzzy term and it would be difficult to draw absolutely clear boundaries of what activities would constitute terrorism. And from Saussure's perspective any such meaning would come about not as a positive or even ostensive definition but through its differences to other, similar, terms such as guerilla, mercenary, soldier or freedom fighter.

In terms of its reference, i.e., whether or not it can be applied to a particular person, there is even more of a problem as Checkland (1983) points out since one person's terrorist is another person's freedom fighter. So, regardless of how precise or imprecise the term (i.e., the boundary) is, the application of the term always assumes a particular perspective or *Weltanschauung.*

Framing the discussion in terms of differences, rather than clear distinctions, does not seem to me to help for there is a mutually recursive relationship between the two. To speak of a difference implies that there must be a distinction such that there are two distinguished states between which there is a difference. So, the distinction comes before the difference. On the other hand, how do distinctions come to be made without there being differences—as Bateson says, differences that make a difference, i.e., create a distinction.

---

[17] An intensive definition in terms of set theory.

Where does this leave us? I think we have to accept both that concepts, and language generally, are intrinsically fuzzy and that the application of concepts to referents, especially in the social world, will always be based on perspective and values. However, in a way this is no different from what we discovered with physical boundaries. They too are not perfect but have degrees of fuzziness and impermeability about them but this does not stop them acting as boundaries so long as they have the requisite degree relative to the role they are playing. The same is true with language—concepts need only be clear and applicable enough for language to "work"; for us to be able to achieve mutual understanding (see Habermas in Section 5.4) and successful coordinations of action (see Maturana in section 3.5.4). That we do do this is manifestly the case. When language breaks down, or there is disagreement about meanings, then we should be able to follow Habermas's theory of discourse and initiate questioning and debate about implicit validity claims.

The fact that concepts are intrinsically relative and debatable does not make the whole matter purely arbitrary. In the same way that critical realism accepts the epistemic relativity of knowledge (Section 2.4.2) without thereby saying that all theories are equally valid, so we can make judgements about the more or less appropriate use of concepts. For example, Bhaskar (1994, p. 110) points out that genocide such as carried out by the Nazis could be described as "depopulation," "people dying," "people being killed," or "people being murdered." All of these are true, but the last one is the most precise and accurate—none of the others carry the full perlocutionary force and they are therefore less correct. Moreover, this is not a matter of personal perspective or value but of descriptive and explanatory adequacy. We should not confuse the map with the territory, but nevertheless the map is a guide to the territory and may be a better or worse one.

## 4.5 Social Systems Boundaries

The question of the boundaries of social systems, or even the existence of social systems, is extremely contentious because of major debates about the nature of the social world. We cannot deal with these debates here although they are overviewed in Chapter 8. We will confine ourselves to a few general comments from particular theoretical perspectives, mainly Giddens, Bhaskar and Luhmann.

### 4.5.1 Social Membership

Perhaps the most obvious form of social boundary is that of membership. People are members of many different groups, both formal and informal. Formal groups have specific and well defined criteria for membership, examples being religions, companies, political parties, or private clubs. In principle these criteria provide a clear demarcation between those who belong and those who do not. In practice there can be some degree of ambiguity—people who are in the process of joining or leaving, people who are connected with but not fully a member, and so on.

Informal groupings are much less precise. Examples are: the family (where do you draw the line on family members?), academic communities, friendship groups, or gangs (although some have very formal initiation rites). In boundary terms this is akin to mathematical sets. There are no boundary components as such—i.e., particular members who form a boundary with the outside—but it is possible to distinguish members from non-members and there are operations for joining or leaving a group.

### 4.5.2 Social Systems

One of the major debates within autopoiesis is the question as to whether social systems might be autopoietic—i.e., self-constructing. This will be thoroughly discussed in Chapter 8 but we can give a flavour of the problems now.

A major requirement of autopoiesis is that the system is organisationally closed and generates its own boundary[18]. This means that the network of processes involved must feed back upon themselves to form a circular concatenation and thereby implicitly demarcate itself from its surroundings. In the case of physical autopoiesis the boundary would be spatial and would involve specific components (e.g., the cell wall) but as Varela points out this is not necessary in the more general case of organisational closure where the nature of the boundary will depend on the type of components involved. Whether this condition can be satisfied is hard to answer in the case of social systems.

We can see many specific circular feedback loops involved within social processes. Giddens (1984) distinguishes three different types—homeostatic loops via unintended consequences of action, self-regulation through information filtering, and reflexive self-regulation involving conscious manipulation of social institutions, and uses the poverty cycle as an illustration of all three. We could obviously look empirically at any part of society and discover an enormously complex inter-meshing of causal loops involving both observable activity and events stretching over time and space and the underlying structure of positions and rules. The difficult question, though, is to what extent such circuits can be said to form a boundary, or at least demarcate themselves from the background. This is a strong but necessary feature of organisational closure as defined since it is what accounts for the systems' identity and its domain of possible interactions as a whole.

---

[18] To clarify the difference between organisational closure and autopoiesis per se, the latter is simply a special case of the former. Organisational closure occurs when processes within a system become circularly linked to each other thus generating an entity that has a degree of autonomy in defining its own boundary. These processes can be any, e.g., descriptions, computations, or productions (Mingers, 1997a). When the process is one of production, the systems is autopoietic (Varela, 1981a). The definition of organisational closure is identical to that given for autopoiesis in the Appendix but with "interaction" substituted for "production."

We can see how this applies to physical systems such as the nervous system or the immune system (Varela, Coutinho et al. 1988). In the case of a non-physical system if it is well defined such as a formal group we can say that at any point the system is able to distinguish inside from outside—valid members from invalid ones. But it is not obvious that we can actually identify such clear-cut examples within the mêlée of society as a whole. There are many different possibilities (Giddens 1990b, p. 303)—nations, states, or perhaps societies as such; Western capitalism as a whole; enduring institutions such as religions or political parties; particular collectivities such as organisations, clubs or social movements; small-scale groupings such as a family or a sports team; or, following Luhmann, functional subsystems such as the economy, law, and politics. The difficulties can be indicated by considering what might be the boundaries of a society and what could be its domain of actions as a unity.

Giddens (1981:45) has suggested three criteria for a social system to be considered a society: i) an association with a particular time-space location with a legitimate claim to make use of it; ii) a shared set of practices involving both system and structure; and iii) an awareness of a shared identity. In terms of time and space, societies will be localised to some extent and, especially in historical times, there may well have been particular examples such as nomadic peoples or forest tribes who were genuinely self-contained. We can look back and see different societies clashing with each other as in periods of colonisation. But in the modern world, with its tremendous global interpenetration through communications and transport, is it possible to draw any such lines any more? Societies certainly don't coincide with nation states being both wider, e.g., European society, and narrower, e.g., Scottish and English. Indeed it can be argued (Angel 1997) that nation states themselves will become of lesser importance than global companies. Luhmann (1982b) concluded that one had to go up to the level of the world society as a whole.

We can also to some extent pick out enduring social practices but at which ever level we look these are many and diverse. There may be greater differences within a notional society than between that society and another, especially with the tremendous intermixing of ethnic and cultural groups within modern societies. A sense of identity may be equally polysemous—one could feel Mancunian, English, British, European, or Western depending on whom one was interacting with. As Giddens concludes,

"It is important to re-emphasise that the term "social system" should not be understood to designate only clusters of social relations whose boundaries are clearly set off from others. … I take it to be one of the main features of structuration theory that the extension and "closure" of societies across space and time is regarded as problematic." (Giddens 1984: 165)

Thus, we can identify a circularity of relations both in the generic (re)production of structure and in specific causal chains, but, it is difficult in general to identify specific social systems that are clearly bounded and have identity. This may be possible in specific, well-defined instances but this would require empirical verification.

## *4.6 The Problem of the Observer*

So far we have largely ignored the problem of the observer simply discussing the characteristics of different types of boundaries as if they were observer-independent. However, we must now debate this issue.

In the early days of systems science, still under the thrall of empiricism, systems and their boundaries were assumed unproblematically to exist independently of the observer. Indeed this was the hallmark of positivist science—the elimination of any degree of subjectivity (Mingers 2000a). It is still the case today in some areas of GST and hard systems. However, from a relatively early time systems thinking did begin to recognise the involvement of the observer in determining systems and their boundaries. Beer, for example, in one of his early works states this very clearly:

"… the situation becomes still more confused when one stops thinking about physical objects and considers systems instead. The mouse and the plant may be physical objects but they can be understood only as systems. Moreover, the boundaries of these systems are not the same as the boundaries of the physical objects themselves. … At this point the scientist joins the philosopher in his assault on the classical notion of science: to measure aspects of a system—to observe it even—is to alter the system so measured and observed."    (Beer 1966, p. 96)

"A system is not something given in nature, but something defined by intelligence. … We select, from an infinite number of relations between things, a set which, because of coherence and pattern and purpose, permits an interpretation of what otherwise might be a meaningless cavalcade of arbitrary events. It follows that the detection of system in the world outside ourselves is a subjective matter. Two people will not necessarily agree on the existence, or nature, or boundaries of any systems so detected." (Beer 1966, p. 242–3)

Having made this strong assertion, it must be said that most of the book reads as though systems *do* exist unambiguously in the world and there is little discussion of the difficulties that this stance engenders. Organisations, for example, are taken to *be* complex systems even though there could be debate about their boundaries.

### 4.6.1 System Boundaries as Constructs

Two other systems thinkers took this stance more thoroughly and between them completely reoriented the disciplines of systems engineering (and operational research) (Checkland) and cybernetics (Maturana) to an interpretive or constructivist perspective. The move from first-order cybernetics (of the observed) to second-order cybernetics (of the observer) has been well documented by Hayles (1999).

Checkland's hugely important work (Mingers 2000b) began with the attempt to apply hard systems engineering methods, which worked well in designing complex physical systems such as chemical plants, to messy and unstructured organisational problems. The end result was the development of Soft Systems Methodology (SSM) the most well-known and successful systems methodology available (Munro and Mingers 2002). In making this change, Checkland has taken very seriously the idea that in the social world individuals construct their own interpretations and understandings of the processes and events around them. People endow their activities with meaning and purpose (Checkland 1983; Checkland 1989; Checkland and Scholes 1990; Checkland 1999).

This led to Checkland's argument that the concept "system" should be seen as epistemological, i.e., a mode of conceptualising, rather than ontological, i.e., existing in the world. The following is one of the clearest statements of this position:

"{we} need to remind ourselves that we have no access to what the world *is*, to ontology, only to descriptions of the world, ... that is to say, to epistemology. ... Thus systems thinking is only an epistemology, a particular way of describing the world. It does not tell us what the world *is*. Hence, strictly speaking, we should never say of something in the world: "It is a system," only: "It may be described as a system." ... The important feature of paradigm II {soft systems} as compared with paradigm I {hard systems} is that *it transfers systemicity from the world to the process of enquiry into the world.*' (Checkland 1983, p. 671)

Hence Checkland's brief discussion of boundaries featured in Table 4.1: that they are a distinction made by an observer marking something *taken to be* a system. We cannot assume that such systems and boundaries actually exist in the external world. For an extended explanation and critique see Mingers (1984).

The central tenet of Maturana's ideas—that the world we experience is a subject-dependent creation—was developed in Maturana (1988). An expanded discussion of the nature of science and scientific explanation is given in Maturana (1990). For an extended explanation and critique see (Mingers 1995, Ch. 7).

Maturana begins by adopting a very pragmatic view of explanation and its role in our lives—what he refers to as the praxis of living. As humans, we are linguistic animals; all our thoughts and experiences are mediated through language. And, much of our linguistic activity consists of explanations, to others or to ourselves, of our experiences.

Maturana then distinguishes between two fundamental ways of validating or accepting explanations (or as he calls them paths of explanation)—"objectivity-without-parenthesis" (transcendental objectivity) and "objectivity-in-parenthesis" (constituted objectivity). These two paths are primarily epistemological but they also have ontological implications—indeed, he uses the terms transcendental ontology and constitutive ontology. Each domain is characterised by criteria for validating explanations, assumptions about the nature of the entities involved, and actions (and therefore cognition) which are seen as legitimate.

The path of transcendental objectivity corresponds essentially to the (naïve as opposed to critical) realist view of reality. According to Maturana, the observer following this path accepts that much of reality takes place independently of the observer's activities; that things exist independently of the observer knowing them; and that knowledge can be gained through perception and reason. In this domain, explanations are held to gain their validity by their reference to an independent reality, which is the criterion of acceptability. The active participation of the observer in the constitution of reality is overlooked, and observers require and accept that there be a single domain of reality.

The path of constituted objectivity places objectivity or independent reality in parentheses. It recognizes that we are living systems and that our cognitive abilities have a biological base. As such we cannot assume that our perceptions correctly represent some independent environment. Neither, in neurophysiological terms, can we distinguish between reality and illusion. As we cannot access an independent reality, we should suspend our naive belief in it. Instead, we should acknowledge that existence for us is constituted by us through our linguistic distinctions. This is what is meant by "constitutive ontology"—we can only interact through linguistic entities and they come into being as they are constituted by us.

Such a stance can be seen to have extreme consequences, not just epistemologically, in limiting our access to reality, but ontologically in limiting that reality itself:

"… the physical domain of existence is one of many domains of reality that we bring forth as we explain our praxis of living … {O}utside language nothing (no thing) exists because existence is bound to our distinctions in language. … I am saying that all phenomena … are cognitive phenomena that arise in observing as the observer operates in language … Nothing precedes its distinction; existence in any domain, even the existence of the observer themselves, is constituted in the distinctions of the observer.… {I}f we ask for the characteristics of the transcendental substratum on which, for epistemological reasons we expect everything to take place, we find … that we cannot say anything about it, not even to refer to it as an it, because as soon as we do so we are in language (Maturana 1988 pp. 79–80)

Thus, although coming from different directions, sociology for Checkland, biology for Maturana, they both converge to a similar point at which the external world has become completely inaccessible and we are confined within the domain of the constructions of the observer. Not just boundaries, but systems and perhaps even objects are denied ontological existence.

With a single cut Checkland emasculates the force of systems thinking. Systems thinking began (in modern times) with the cyberneticians of the 1930s who found the concepts *necessary* to explain puzzling features of the world. The way in which organisms could display complex and apparently purposeful behaviour with no central control led to the concepts of negative feedback and information; the cyclical patterns of equilibriating and disequilibriating behaviour that occurred in so many different domains led to the notions of interacting positive and negative feedback loops; and the failure of reductionist thinking to explain the diversity and persistence of the biological world led to ideas of holism and emergence. These were more than mere epistemological devices to organise our thinking, they were genuine explanatory concepts in that the existence of such systemic processes in the world was *necessary* to explain the phenomena that were observed. To deny reality to systems concepts is to reduce them to an essentially arbitrary language game[19].

There is not space here to make these arguments fully (see Mingers 2000a) but I will summarise them briefly. Checkland is right to recognise that we do not have access to the world in a pure, unmediated way. Clearly, as human beings we can only ever experience anything through our perceptual and linguistic apparatus. It does not follow from that, however, either that our descriptions are unrelated to the world, or that we should deny existence to anything simply because our knowledge or perception are limited. This is to commit the *epistemic fallacy* (Bhaskar 1978), that is believing that statements about *being* can be analysed or limited by statements about our *knowledge*. Checkland is also right that we can never know definitively or prove conclusively the existence of systems. Again, however, this does not prove the converse, that they do *not* exist. We can move beyond the crude empiricist ontological criterion that *to be is to be perceived,* and instead adopt the critical realist view that causal efficacy is the proper criterion for existence. In other words, if some structure or system can be shown to have causal effects on the world then, whether we can perceive it or not, it can be said, putatively, to exist. Given this criterion, we can take particular phenomena that we wish to explain, hypothesise possible generative mechanisms which, *if they existed would generate the experienced phenomena*, and then attempt to confirm or refute them. This philosophical stance grants possible reality to both physical and conceptual systems whilst recognising the inevitable observer-dependence of our descriptions, and allowing that the social world is inherently different to the natural world.

### 4.6.2 System Boundaries as Process

I want now to consider a recent contribution by Midgley (2000). In general I am very much in agreement with much of the thrust of Midgley's work, not least the fact that he gives the idea of boundaries a central position. Midgley's primary interest is in methodology for systemic intervention, a topic that will be addressed in Chapters 9 and 10, but he sees that any intervention will require definitions or judgements to be made about the boundaries of the system to be considered.

He identifies the primary problem with boundaries as the implied separation between observer and observed and in particular with the traditional empiricist view that there

---

[19] In response, Checkland has said (private communication) "in my experience it is not a case of Hard ST or Soft ST as you imply but Softest/Hardest with Hard being the occasional special case of Soft. Usually I find myself working with various models with different W's; but occasionally it is fruitful and not harmful to choose to see a particular bit of the world as 'a system' and use HST. Operating with SST subsumes HST with the latter being a *conscious* choice." This does not seem to me to address the main argument as it implies choice rather than necessity.

could be objective, observer-independent observation. Midgley reviews four systems approaches each of which tries to resolve this problem—von Bertalanffy (1971), Bateson (1973), Maturana (1980), and Fuenmayor (1991). They are all found wanting "while each of these authors has managed to find an alternative to the radical separation of observer and observed a less naïve subject/object dualism is nevertheless still evident in their work." (Midgley 2000, p. 67)

To resolve these problems Midgley moves to what he calls (after Whitehead) a process philosophy. By this he means one that moves away from specifying particular content or boundaries to one that places primacy on the *process* of generating boundaries. I shall trace his arguments in some detail as I think it is an original, if ultimately flawed, approach.

Von Bertalanffy, Maturana and Bateson, in different ways, all specify particular types of systems in drawing boundaries, (or more generally for Midgley, creating knowledge)—open systems, autopoietic systems, systems of transmitted differences. Midgley wants to move away from privileging any one type of content to the *process* of specifying that content.

"… process philosophy involves identifying a process that is not dependent on further identification of a single type of system giving rise to that process. …If we regard the process of making boundary judgements as analytically prime, rather than a particular kind of knowledge generating system, then *subjects come to be defined in exactly the same way as objects—by a boundary judgement*" (Midgley 2000, p. 79 original emphasis)

Midgley suggests that we need to consider both outward-looking, first-order, boundary judgements about the world and backward-looking second-order judgements *about the system making the first-order distinctions*[20]. When we make this second step we can pick out many different possible observing systems and have many different theories about how these systems generate knowledge. All of these systems must, however involve what Midgley calls "sentient beings" (human or animal). This in fact means that there must be two second-order judgements—one concerning the boundaries, i.e., extent of the knowledge-generating system, and one concerning its nature. These judgements are not interest-free but depend on the purposes, values, and knowledge available at the time. As these change so the second order boundary judgements can change. Moreover, we can (and perhaps should?) examine the system *that is making the second-order judgements* and perform second-order boundary judgements on that, and so on ad infinitum. In other words we quickly end up with a plethora of potential systems: i) the first-order system boundaries that are distinguished "in the world"; ii) the different second-order

---

[20] Midgley acknowledges that this distinction is similar to that of first- and second-order cybernetics. His approach differs in not privileging either the first- or second-order view, but seeing both as an equal part of one process.

system boundaries that may be constructing those first-order systems; iii) the different "third-order"[21] systems that are distinguishing the second-order ones.

Midgley does not develop this in more detail on the grounds that to do so would be moving into specifying content. Thus he does not define what he means by "sentient beings"; nor does he elaborate on how boundaries are specified in general, although he does discuss certain particular instances, for example multiple stakeholders within organisations.

"Content philosophy presents a theory of exactly what counts as a knowledge generating system, while process philosophy allows for a variety of possible knowledge generating systems (with the proviso there are sentient beings identified as part of them). Also, content philosophy is mono-theoretical ... while process philosophy allows for theoretical pluralism. ... The reader may be left wondering why I have only talked in broad terms about the process of making boundary judgements ... The answer is that, as soon as we move away from discussing boundaries in general to a generative mechanism, we have moved away from process to content!" (Midgley 2000, p. 88–89)

Finally, and crucially, Midgley elucidates what his process view means we can, or cannot, say about "reality." He discusses this in relation to three major philosophical paradigms—realism, idealism and social constructivism[22]. His approach is to show that each paradigm makes particular, and different, judgements (often implicit) about the kinds of boundaries that can be drawn and the proper kinds of knowledge generating systems. He then goes on to argue that *each* of these paradigms is *compatible* with a process view in the sense that it can be explained in terms of first and second order boundary judgements. He does not see process philosophy as falsifying any of these paradigms, or as subsuming them, all it does is to allow us to avoid "slipping into a dogmatic insistence (sometimes found within these paradigms) that there is only one correct boundary to work with." (Midgley 2000, p. 98)

In evaluating Midgley's contribution I shall highlight several problems.

1. He is concerned to avoid the *ontological* dualism between subject and object and claims to replace it with an *analytical* dualism between first and second order judgements. He also claims to steadfastly avoid making assertions of content. I do not accept either of these claims. We have, in fact, just the traditional distinction between observed and observing systems (Von Foerster 1984), first- and second- order observers (Luhmann 1987) or systems as epistemology not ontology (Checkland 1989) cast in a different form. With all these earlier attempts to refrain from ontological commitment and place

---

[21] My suggestion

[22] There are many ways of classifying different paradigms and I do have some problems with Midgley's which I will discuss below.

priority on one side of the distinction only (the observer's) there are always ontological assumptions smuggled in. It is just impossible to theorise about anything without there being a "thing" to theorise about.

Midgley's approach is different in not privileging one side of the distinction, but still cannot avoid ontological commitments. If boundaries are being drawn by some system, first or second order, then clearly a system *exists* (or must be assumed to exist) that is drawing the boundaries, and the boundaries so drawn, in that they can have causal effect, must also have existence. Equally, Midgley's scheme only works if we assume the existence of a "real world" on which first order boundaries can be drawn, and some other, unnamed, system that is capable of drawing second-order distinctions.

Moreover, Midgley clearly does specify content when he says that second-order systems must include "sentient beings"—being evasive about what might count as such is merely avoiding the issue. And even more so when he says second-order judgments must include determining the nature as well as extent of such beings.

2.  Midgley's critique of existing philosophies is based on their exclusivity and commitment to a single theoretical paradigm. In the case of realism this is certainly not true of *critical* realism. As we have seen, CR is highly pluralistic both in its ontological acceptance of many different kinds of entities—physical, social, conceptual, or moral—and in its epistemological acceptance of a necessary range of different research methods from quantitative to qualitative. CR also takes as fundamental that there is an intimate connection between fact and value—something that Midgley espouses but presumes that realist philosophies do not.

3.  The whole "process" seems quite unhelpful in practice. If carried out properly it would lead immediately to a massive proliferation of systems and systems boundaries through an infinite regress of different orders of boundary judgements. Although Midgley does not actually propose such a comprehensive review, neither does he deny it. In the later practical chapters he is quite selective in doing this in particular contexts but little general guidance is offered (for this would presumably be content) as to how better or worse boundaries might be drawn (or are they all equally valid?) in any particular situation, or how the whole process could be effectively grounded in order to prevent the infinite regress.

4.  In overall terms Midgley seems to have gone to great lengths to avoid making commitments and has thereby thrown out the baby with the bathwater by remaining silent on the most fundamental issue—the relationship between the real world and the boundaries we draw about it. Midgley would no doubt see this as an unwelcome return to subject/object dualism but I make no apologies for that. The question that is never really answered is this: are all

boundaries *simply* constructs of the observer (the second-order knowledge generating system), i.e., independent of any world external to the observer?

If the answer is yes, then we remain in the subjectivist world of Checkland and Maturana. Surely this cannot fit in with Midgley's whole enterprise which aims at *intervention* into the world. Given this agenda then surely he must accept that there is such a world; that the boundaries we draw have effects on that world; and that we can therefore judge boundaries as being better or worse from some point of view.

If the answer is no, then there must be some relationship or interaction between the boundaries that are drawn and the world that they relate to. The implication is then that we must have a view about the nature of that relationship and particularly how boundaries drawn by observers relate to boundaries that may exist in the world.

### 4.6.3 Summary

We have explored in this section a significant challenge to the ontological reality of systems boundaries. Both Checkland and Maturana have arrived at similar points, albeit from different directions. For them, systems thinking is a question of epistemology rather than ontology; systems boundaries are distinctions brought into being by an observer and cannot be related directly to some external reality. Indeed, for Maturana such distinctions are themselves constitutive of reality. Midgley argues a slightly different point, that we must focus on the processes by which boundaries are constructed rather than the nature of the boundaries themselves. Ulrich (Ulrich 1994; Ulrich 2000) is also someone who has placed boundaries, or at least boundary critique, at the heart of his work. He fits in broadly with the writers in this section as he sees boundaries very much as the result of decisions or judgements made by systems inquirers or designers. However, as his work is primarily concerned with design and intervention is is better discussed in Chapter 10.

I have argued against both these views that system boundaries can, and sometimes do, exist in the world independent of human observers. The basic argument is the critical realist one that if we can show that boundaries are causally active then they must exist. Put another way, if we find it necessary to postulate the existence of a boundary in order to explain a particular phenomenon then we are entitled to accept its existence. This does not only hold for physical boundaries but potentially also for conceptual, psychological, or social ones. This argument does not mean that it is easy to identify actual boundaries in practice, or that we can ever be *certain* about them. In our work as systems theorists or practitioners we always remain in the transitive domain. Our systems models themselves are just that, humanly-constructed models, maps not to be confused with the territory. But as models, they can be said to be models *of something* intransitive, something different from themselves. And we can then discuss and investigate their relationship to that something.

## 4.7 Self-Bounding through Organisation Closure

In this section I wish to pick up the discussion in section 4.2.6 about natural wholes. There we were primarily concerned with physical systems, particular those occupying a particular area of space-time, and the extent to which they form boundaries independent of an observer. I want to extend that discussion to consider more complex systems which include non-physical components for which boundary identification is much more problematic. One approach is to consider the extent to which systems form their own bounds, or at least demarcate themselves from their environment, through some kind of organisational closure (in Maturana and Varela's terminology) or self-reference.

There is, however, a more general notion propounded by Maturana and Varela, that of organisational closure, of which autopoiesis is a special case (Varela 1977; Varela 1979; Maturana and Varela 1980). Mingers (1997a) argued that organisational closure simply requires some form of self-reference, whether material, linguistic, logical, or social, rather than the more specific process of self-production. However, as Teubner (1993, p. 16) has noted, there is considerable conceptual confusion around such terms in the general systems literature as well as within philosophy (Bartlett and Suber 1987) and even, on occasions, within Maturana and Varela's work. What is the difference between, for example, "self-reference," "self-production," "self-organisation," "self-regulation," "self-observation," "circular causality," "tautologies and contradictions," or "auto-catalysis"? Whilst not claiming a complete analysis of such systems, I offer the categorisation in Table 4.2 as a start.

In this typology, the numerical "Level" refers to Boulding's (1956) Hierarchy of Systems as modified by Mingers (1997a). The primary feature that distinguishes the different levels is the type of relation that emerges at each level. Systems at a particular level involve the relations of that level plus those from preceding levels. Level 1 systems are characterized by static relations of topology, level 2 by dynamic relations of order, level 3 by feedback relations, level 4 by relations of self-production, level 5 by relations of structural coupling between components, level 6 by symbolic relations, and level 7 by relations of self-awareness.

The first type of organisationally closed system is thus characterized only in terms of spatial or topographic closure since it is not dynamic or processual. I have called these self-referring systems. They are usually symbolic or representational in a general sense, and refer to themselves either by some form of pointing (e.g., a signpost pointing to itself); by containing an image of themselves within themselves; or by referring to themselves linguistically. They include all of the many paradoxes and tautologies (Hughes and Brecht 1978), for example, "This sentence is in French"; or "This assertion is not true." Pictorial examples are Escher's drawing (*Drawing Hands*) of two hands drawing each other, and Magritte's pictures, one (*The Treason of Images*) of a smoking pipe with the words (in French) "this is not a pipe," and another (*The Human Condition*) in which the picture contains a picture of part of the scene.

**Table 4.2. Typology of Organisationally Closed (Self-Referential) Systems.**

| Level in Boulding's Hierarchy | Type | Characteristic | Example |
|---|---|---|---|
| 1 | Self-referring systems | Structural references to self by position or symbolism (pictorial or linguistic) | "This is a sentence," Escher's *Drawing Hands,* Magritte's *The Treason of Images.* |
| 2 | Self-influencing systems | Dynamic systems that involve circular causality and causal loops. | Size and birth rate of population, inflation, the nuclear arms race. |
| 3 | Self-regulating systems | Maintenance of a particular variable at a particular level. | Thermostat, body temperature. |
| | Self-sustaining systems | All parts of the system are necessary and sufficient for operation of the whole, but do not produce each other. | Gas pilot light in heating boiler, autocatalysis. |
| 4 | Self-producing systems (autopoietic) | Autonomy, the system both produces and is produced by itself. | Cell, computer model of autopoiesis. |
| 5 | Self-recognizing systems | Systems that are able to recognize their own parts and reject others. | Immune system within an organism. |
| | Self-replicating systems | Systems that can build replicas of themselves. | Organisms that reproduce, computer viruses. |
| 6 | Self-cognizing systems | Systems that generate cognitive identity through recursive neuronal activity. | Animals with nervous systems interacting symbolically. |
| 7 | Self-conscious systems | Able to interact with descriptions of themselves. The observer observing the observer. | A person saying, "I acted selfishly today." |

It might be objected that as many of these are symbolic and linguistic examples they should be at a much higher level in the typology. This however is to confuse the output from a system with the system itself. While they may be the results of complex linguistic processes, in themselves they only embody Level 1 relations. By analogy, a table may be the result of a complex sociotechnical production process, but it, itself, is a simple Level 1 system.

At Level 2 are systems I identify as self-influencing systems. These are examples of what are often called causal loops or circular causality. That is, patterns of causation or influence which become circular: for instance, the larger a population, the greater the number of births, and thus the larger the population in the next time period. This is a positive loop leading to exponential increase or decrease and, more commonly, there are negative loops which lead to, at least temporary, stability—for example, the price/demand relations for a normal good. The economic and ecological domains are full of complex patterns of just such mutual causality.

At Level 3, I distinguish two types of systems: self-regulating and self-sustaining. Self-regulating systems are organized so as to keep some essential variable(s) within particular limits. They rely on negative feedback and specified limits. Obvious examples are a thermostat and the blood temperature control system. They are distinct from the self-influencing systems in that they maintain a prespecified level determined by the wider system of which they are a part. Self-influencing systems may stabilize through negative feedback but do so at essentially arbitrary levels.

The next type I call self-sustaining systems. In Maturana and Varela's terms these systems are organisationally closed but not self-producing. Their components and processes close in upon themselves so that their own elements are both necessary and sufficient for their own continuance. Such systems do not however produce their own components. A good example is the gas heater pilot light found on many central heating systems. In such a system, the gas pilot light heats a thermocouple which controls the flow of gas to the pilot light which allows the pilot light to function in the first place. Once it is in operation, it sustains itself. However, once it stops it cannot restart itself—it needs some form of outside intervention to begin the cycle again. Other examples are systems of auto-catalysis where a chemical reaction produces at least some of the chemicals that are necessary for the reaction to occur; and the nervous system where every state of nervous activity is triggered by a previous state and triggers, in turn, the next state.

At Level 4 we have autopoietic systems which are self-producing in both their components and their own boundary. They are more than self-sustaining in that they actually produce the components necessary for their own continuation. Such systems have properties such as autonomy, since they depend mainly on their own self-production, and identity, since they maintain their own individual autopoietic organisation despite changes in their structure. The main examples are living systems—molecular embodiments of autopoiesis—but it is also possible to conceive of abstract self-producing systems such as Nomic, a game that produces its own rules (Suber 1990; Mingers 1996a), and the computer model of autopoiesis produced by Varela (Varela 1974; McMullin and Varela 1997).

At Level 5 in the hierarchy (multicellular systems), I again distinguish two types: self-recognizing systems and self-replicating systems. The prime example of a self-recognizing system is the body's immune system (Varela and Coutinho 1991). This is a network of glands and chemicals throughout the body, one function of which is to fight off cells and organisms that do not belong to the body. In order to do this, it must be able to recognize its self—that is, its own cells as opposed to another organism's. Self-replicating systems are those that are capable of producing a copy or replica of themselves. This includes all living systems as well as, for example, a computer virus. Note that the ability to reproduce is not definitory of living systems: some individuals, or even species such as the mule, are sterile yet living, while most people would say a computer virus is not living.

At Level 6 are self-cognizing systems that are integrated by a brain and nervous system. The nervous system is an organisationally closed network of interacting neurons in which all states of relative activity lead to, and are preceded by, other states of activity thus leading to recursive closure. Certain parts of the nervous system (the effector and sensory surfaces) do interface to the bodily or external environment, and can thus be triggered by outside events, but the vast majority of the nervous system is composed of interneurons that only interact with each other. The coupling of the circular processes of the nervous system and the linear interactions of the organism as a whole over time, give rise to new domains of behaviour based on abstract and symbolic representations of the organism's interactions. This allows for the development of increasingly varied and ontogenetic modes of behaviour in the more developed species. It also necessitates, for the individual organism, the construction of their own cognitive self. The nervous system integrates the perceptions and actions of the organism as it operates as a whole within an environment. Through its circular, recursive operation it continually establishes and maintains the distinct, coherent self of the individual at the same time as projecting onto the environment a structure of signification that is relevant to its own self-continuance.

The symbolic interactions enabled by the nervous system lead to the emergence of many new domains of interactions—for instance, consensually coordinated behaviours, the distinctions of objects and the relations between them (observing), and finally self-consciousness. That is, systems that can, through language, create descriptions of themselves and then interact with these descriptions as if they were independent entities, thus recursively generating the conscious self. Human beings are the main example of such languaging systems at this point in time. Such interactions are mainly linguistic utterances, either latent or manifest, such as, "I am lying" or "I hereby promise to …," but can also be embodied in gestures or facial expressions.

One noticeable omission from this typology is a category of *self-organising* systems. This seems to me redundant within Maturana's terminology. All systems embody a particular *organisation*—it is what specifies their identity—and this organisation remains the same so long as they maintain their identity. What is generally meant by the term "self-organisation" is actually *structural* change rather than a change in the organisation, and here I would use my other categories depending on the particular type of change involved. A genuine change in organisation would involve a major change in category such as an autopoietic system dying and no longer being autopoietic. Also, the typology in Table 4.2 only goes up to the level of the individual. It is extended into the social domain in Chapter 7.

The general point of this section is that all these types of systems generate, through their own operations, a form of closure which is in essence a type of boundary. This is not necessarily a physical boundary, or one marked by particular boundary components, but it is nevertheless a self-generated, and therefore observer independent, demarcation of the system from its environment.

## *4.8 Boundary Setting*

So far we have been primarily concerned with recognising or determining the boundaries of systems that already exist in some way. But much of *applied* systems thinking is concerned with undertaking projects or interventions in the real world in order to bring about change that is in some sense desirable for particular actors. In these types of situation we are often in the role of setting rather than observing boundaries, or perhaps being the subject of boundaries that have been set by others. In a general sense we can classify these boundaries as relating to:

1. Boundaries that delimit the scope of the problem. They could be literally spatial, or at least geographical, as in which regions or areas are to be included. They define what problems or aspects of the problem situation are to be included (in the Strategic Choice Approach, Friend and Hickling (1987) discusses this under uncertainty about related problems). They also determine what range of stakeholders are to be included either as clients, problems owners or perhaps victims, and which are to be excluded (Midgley 2000) refers to these as the sacred and profane). The scope is strongly related to levels within an organisation—the greater the scope of the problem the more, and higher, levels that are likely to be involved (Beer's (1985) Viable System Model requires the specification of a "system in focus" and consideration of the levels directly above and below).

2. Boundaries that delimit the time horizon to be considered. The shorter the time period the more things that will be fixed or unchangeable and therefore have to be taken as given. Generally, therefore, the shorter the time scale the more narrowly will be drawn the scoping boundaries. Note that terms such as "short term" or "long term" are not absolute but relative to the nature of the situation. In the aircraft industry five years is short term, in bakeries a day.

3. Boundaries that place limits on what may be changed or what must be taken for granted. Any organisational setting will be sedimented with cultural norms, ways of working, and unquestioned assumptions about the nature of the situation. Mingers (2000d) refers to questioning rhetoric, tradition,

objectivity, and authority; and Ulrich's (2000) critical systems heuristics can be used to challenge expert judgements. These will often never be made explicit and yet they will powerfully shape the extent of potential changes. Indeed, one could see the process of bringing about change as essentially one of overcoming or transgressing boundaries (Mingers 1997b).

The importance of boundary setting for interventions in human organisations will be explored in Chapter 10.

## 4.9 Conclusions

This has been a long and complex chapter which has tried to re-consider the whole questions of the nature of boundaries within systems thinking—a long-neglected question. I am not sure that we have "solved" the problem of boundaries but we have hopefully addressed the important issues.

We began by considering, from an almost phenomenological view, what features of boundaries came to light when we looked at relatively simple physical systems. The main points I would wish to bring forward are:

- Boundaries do exist independently of an observer although it is always an observer who chooses to observe them. Boundaries are of different types— edges and surfaces, enclosures and membranes, and demarcations; and they have particular effects—separation, containment and constraint.

- Boundaries are never "perfect" but always to some degree fuzzy and permeable. This depends on the space-time frame with which we observe them. This does not mean, however, that they do not function as boundaries— they only need to be "good enough" relative to the role that they play.

- In picking out or "presencing" particular boundaries relative to some purpose, observers do not simply *perceive* systems but *conceive* them. That is, they are selective in the boundaries they draw dependent on that which they wish to understand or explain. Moreover, there may be multiple possible boundaries around a set of components, and a component may be a member of multiple systems.

From physical boundaries we moved to consider mathematical and conceptual boundaries:

- Geometry provides a formalism for considering boundaries, particularly spatial ones, but its assumptions are too idealised to apply directly to the real-world. Set theory introduces the idea that elements can be separated without an actual boundary at all by a membership criterion. Moreover, operators can lead to entry or exit, i.e., input or output; a crossing or not crossing of the notional boundary. As in geometry set theory assumes a perfect distinguished boundary.

- Concepts and language are similar to mathematics in the sense that underlying them is the idea of a perfect distinction, i.e., a completely clear demarcation of a concept from any others. Again, in practice this does not hold with distinctions and differences being both imprecise and inevitably judgemental in their application. But, as with physical boundaries, distinctions do not have to be perfect to work and allow us to communicate and interact.

After briefly considering social systems we moved to discuss a central cleavage within systems thinking—whether boundaries could be said to exist at all, ontologically, or whether they were in fact always simply constructs of the observer. Without replaying the debate, my conclusions basically followed critical realism. We have to firstly distinguish between the transitive (TD) and intransitive domains (ID). In the TD we are always dealing with our own human constructions and models and we, as humans, can never escape this domain. However, we can use the criterion of causal efficacy to argue that we can take boundaries to exist in the ID if we find it necessary to postulate them in order to explain our experiences. This is a powerful argument for the independent existence of both systems and their boundaries.

We concluded the chapter with two somewhat opposed domains—systems that were self-referential and were therefore in some sense self-bounding; and situations of practical intervention where it is clear that the boundaries or limits are set by the participants in the intervention—a topic to be covered more extensively in Chapter 10.

# Part II: Knowledge

# Chapter 5: Cognising Systems: Information and Meaning

## 5.1 Introduction

We have now developed the foundations for the rest of the book—critical realism as an underpinning philosophy in Chapter 2; autopoiesis as an explanation of living systems and in particular the biological abilities and limitations of the observer in Chapter 3; and a consideration of the problems of identifying systems and drawing boundaries in Chapter 4. We are now going to embark on the more substantive areas of development, exploring different levels of human activity, from the individual through to societies, as these form the context for engaged human action and intervention.

The first question to address is why should we begin by discussing 'information' and why relate that to 'meaning'? The concept of information is actually crucial as it is the nexus for two different domains of debate. On the one hand, it is now a truism to say that we live in the Information Age. The information technology revolution that is so strongly shaping our age clearly rests on the manipulation of information rather than energy or material and all the major human disciplines are trying to come to terms with this[23]. Yet, as we shall see, there is no fundamental agreement about the actual nature of information itself. Even information systems, the discipline that deals most directly with information and information technology, cannot agree about a definition of information (Mingers 1996b).

On the other hand, as we saw in Section 3.5, the autopoietic view of human cognition does have certain implications for information and communication:

1. The nervous system is organisationally closed and structure determined. Its activity cannot be determined but only triggered by external events.

2. The distinguishing feature of humans is that they are languaging animals. Consciousness of self develops through the self-referential nature of language.

3. Language is a consensual domain. It relies on implicitly agreed but essentially arbitrary signs and differences.

---

[23] See, for example, the following: in sociology Poster (1990), Poster (1995), Castells (1996), Lash (2002); philosophy Floridi (2002); information science Cornelius (2002); and economics Levine and Lippman (1995).

4.  Taken together these imply a particular view of human communication and the nature of information very different from that which generally prevails.

Taking these two arguments together shows the importance of having a clear and agreed conceptualisation of the nature of information both for information systems and human communication in general. That is the task of this chapter.

Information systems presumably could not exist without information, yet there is little agreement within the IS discipline over the nature of information itself. As Dretske (1981) and Lewis (1991) point out, few books concerning information systems actually define information clearly. There are, in fact, two competing views expressed within the IS literature, but there is little by way of rigorous discussion or debate about them. Lewis's (1991) survey of 39 introductory IS texts reveals the most common, traditional, view of information, when it was defined at all, was data that had been processed in some way to make it useful for decision makers. Philosophically, this view generally involves an implicit assumption that data is objective, that is, it has an existence and structure in itself, independent of an observer; and that information (processed data) can be objectively defined relative to a particular task or decision. An alternative view argues for the subjective nature of information—the idea that different observers will generate different information from the same data since they have differing values, beliefs, and expectations (Lewis 1993). Checkland formulates this view as "information equals data plus meaning." That is, by attributing meaning to data, we create information (Checkland and Scholes 1990, p. 303).

This chapter will argue that both views have significant weaknesses and that it is vital to develop an effective and consistent concept of information and the related but distinct terms "data" and "meaning." Put succinctly, it will be argued that meaning is created from the information carried by signs. The consequences are that information *is* objective, but ultimately inaccessible to humans, who exclusively inhabit a world of meaning. Meaning is essentially intersubjective—that is, it is based on a shared consensual understanding. The implication is that information is only a part of what we understand by an information system and that attention needs to be focused on the meaning systems within which information systems reside.

## *5.2 Foundations for a Theory of Semantic Information*

### 5.2.1 Stamper's Semiotic Framework

To study the nature of information, it is useful to use Stamper's (1997) framework based on semiotics (Morris 1938)—the study of signs—since information must ultimately be carried by or exist through signs. Stamper does not provide a formal definition of the word "sign" but illustrates it by examples. It is meant very broadly to be anything that signifies, or stands for, or can be seen to stand for, something else. A typology of different types of signs and symbols will be presented later. Stamper's framework distinguishes four levels of interest[24]:

1. *Empirics*. The study of sign transmission and the statistical properties of the repeated use of signs. This area is concerned with what might be termed communication engineering.

2. *Syntactics*. The study of structures or systems of signs and their properties without regard to their meaning or use. This area covers linguistics, the study of formal languages, logic, and so on.

3. *Semantics*. The study of the meaning of signs. This area covers the relationship between signifier and signified, between the sign and what it may represent.

4. *Pragmatics*. The study of the actual use of signs and systems of signs covering the relations between signs and behaviour.

For practical information systems development, empirics and syntactics are necessary, but it is the semantic and pragmatic aspects of information, where signs gain meaning and are used, that are crucial. For example, suppose that an information system displays the message that the costs of closing down a factory are £30m. What information is carried by or contained in this message (sign)? What meaning may this have for a particular person who comes across it? What information may they gain from it? What is the relationship between information and meaning? How, by whom, and under what circumstances was it generated? In what way might it be used? These are the type of semantic and pragmatic questions that must be addressed by an adequate conceptualisation of information.

In considering such questions, two particular theoretical perspectives will be employed. First, at the semantic level, Maturana and Varela's theories of cognition as outlined in Chapter 3 provide a consistent and coherent biological explanation for cognition and language. They show that perception and cognition are inevitably subject (i.e., person) dependent, but that language is intersubjective—based on common experience and implicit agreement. Second, at the pragmatic level, the work of Habermas (1979, pp. 1–68; 1984, pp. 273–338) on what he calls "universal pragmatics" aims to formalize the analysis of language in use—that is, active utterances seeking understanding and agreement rather than abstract sentences or propositions[25]. These theories will be placed within a critical realist perspective and

---

[24] Stamper (1991) has extended his framework to include the physical world and the social world as the bottom and top levels, respectively.

[25] Habermas's work on critical theory and a communicative theory of social action has already provided a number of ideas for conceptualizing information systems. For example, language as action, speech act, and intersubjectivity Goldkuhl and Lyytinen (1982); typology of social action, and knowledge-constitutive interests Lyytinen and Klein (1985); critical social theory,

then integrated with more specific theories about information and communication developed by Dretske and Luhmann.

## 5.2.2 An Evaluation of Existing Theories of Semantic Information

Both the objectivist and the subjectivist views of information have weaknesses. The main problem with the idea of objective or absolute information is that it assumes both that objective information has human-independent existence and that it produces a similar effect on all those who receive it. Against this latter assumption, Lewis (1993) shows how even conventional data analysis methods involve a large element of subjectivity. Moreover, Maturana's analysis of cognition and the nervous system shows that no sign, symbol or sentence determines its own effect on a receiver—it can never do more than trigger (or not trigger) particular changes in the structure of the body and nervous system.

"If the dynamics of states of the nervous system is (sic) determined by its structure, and this structure also determines what constitutes a perturbation for the nervous system, the description of the interactions of the nervous system in terms of information exchange, as if the environment were to specify the state that the nervous system adopts, is merely metaphorical. In fact, the notion of information is valid only in the descriptive domain as an expression of the cognitive uncertainty of the observer, and does not represent any component actually operant in any mechanistic phenomenon of instructive interactions in the physical space." (Maturana 1975, p. 17)

Thus, nothing is *intrinsically* informative for an individual, and no interaction is *inherently* instructive. They can only become so through the development of structural coupling between individual and environment.

Checkland (1990) claims that information is entirely subjective. A particular item of *data* must be interpreted by someone through their particular structure of *meaning* to yield *information* for that person. There are several problems with this formulation. First, the terms and their relationships are not defined precisely and clearly. Thus, what exactly are data, meaning and information? And how exactly do meaning and data interact to produce information? Second, information is conceptualised as a purely individual construction, thereby ignoring the intersubjective and socially structured dimensions of language. Third, it goes against everyday usages of the term "information." For example, books and train timetables could not be said to contain any information except for when they were being read, at which time the information provided would differ between individual readers. Nor could machines process information, or information systems contain information if this were the case.

---

knowledge-constitutive interests Ngwenyama (1991). Ngwenyama and Lee (1997); and typology of social action Lyytinen, Klein, et al. (1991).

These two approaches are not the only theories of information. Within the literature of philosophy, sociology, and particularly the cognate discipline of information science, there is a considerable range of theories, most stemming in some way from Shannon and Weaver's (1949) theory of information and communication[26]. For detailed reviews of the range of different theoretical positions see Mingers (1996b), Cornelius (2002), Newman (2001), Callaos and Callaos (2002) and Floridi (2002). These theories were evaluated for their relevance and usefulness within information systems in terms of four criteria: (1) the generality of the conception, that is, the extent to which they provide comprehensive and coherent accounts of both information and meaning; (2) the adequacy of their concepts for use as a fundamental base for information systems in both theory and practice; (3) their degree of fit with relevant theoretical and philosophical knowledge in other disciplines; and (4) the extent to which they correspond to common-sense usage of the terms "information" and "meaning." I will briefly summarise the results.

<u>Shannon and Weaver's Theory of Information Transmission</u>

Shannon and Weaver were engineers concerned with the correct transmission of messages. They developed a formula for measuring the amount of information that a particular channel or message might transmit, but their theory said nothing about the content or meaning of a message, as they made clear:

"The fundamental problem of communication is that of reproducing at one point either exactly or approximately a message selected at another. Frequently the messages have meaning … These semantic aspects of communication are irrelevent to the engineering problem. The significant aspect is that the actual message is one selected from a set of possible messages." (Shannon and Weaver 1949, p. 31)

Thus information theory is like measuring the volume of a container without knowing what it contains. Despite this, their work has formed the basis for the majority of attempts to generate a theory of *semantic* information. Their central idea is that the amount of information conveyed by a symbol or message is inversely proportional to the probability of occurrence of that particular message. The more unlikely it is, the more information it carries. The message "the prime minister is dead" is much less likely than "the prime minister is alive" and so carries more information. A two-digit code in binary can carry less information than one in decimal since any particular message would be 1 of only 4 possibilities, as opposed to 1 of 100. Thus the amount of information available from a particular source depends on the number of possible messages that it could generate and the relative probabilities of the different messages. Another perspective is that the receipt of a message could be said to remove uncertainty from the receiver, and the greater the

---

[26] Itself based on Hartley's (1928) earlier work.

uncertainty, the greater the amount of information conveyed. Mathematical formulae were produced to measure this quantity of information[27].

In some ways this is an intuitively appealing idea. If you were to learn in advance the result of a horse race then the more horses in the race and the more evenly matched they were (and thus the more evenly the odds were spread), the greater the amount or value of the information to you. If there were only one horse in the race the result would carry no information, as there would be no uncertainty. On the other hand, the concept suggests that a series of randomly chosen letters or words carries more information than messages in English since they are inherently more uncertain or unlikely than the patterned and structured linguistic messages. This information theory thus deals only with the observed statistical frequencies of occurrence of particular signs or messages. It does not address the semantic contents of messages at all.

I shall briefly review several approaches based on information theory.

1.   Bar-Hillel and Carnap (1952; 1964) claim that they can define and measure semantic information. They recognise at the outset that they do not deal with information in the communicational or pragmatic sense—i.e., how it is actually used by or between particular people (Bar-Hillel and Carnap 1964, p. 398–399). Nor do they consider anything but propositional statements—other types and forms of signs are excluded. In fact their theory is better described as concerning *logical* information. They consider a logical space of entities, predicates that can be applied to them, and combinations of propositions about these entities. Any particular statement will rule out some possibilities, but will be implied by others. The logical probability of a statement is related to the number of possibilities that it is compatible with and their probability. Finally, information is measured as the inverse of the probability.

     The limitations of this theory are: (i) in terms of generality it is limited to only restricted formal systems and linguistic propositions. It is hopelessly unrealistic and impractical for real-world languages and domains. (ii) While it provides a clear definition, it does not deal with the practical aspects of information use. The probabilities, and therefore the amount of information, are defined purely in terms of the number of possible state descriptions. iii) As admitted (Bar-Hillel and Carnap 1964, p. 298) the theory does not deal with meaning or interpretation for a particular person, given what they

---

[27] If a source can produce n possible, equally likely, messages then the probability of occurrence of any one is $1/n$. The amount of information it can carry is $-\log_2(1/n)$, and the amount of information of the source is $-\Sigma(1/n)\log_2(1/n)$. Thus a source generating randomly a single digit produces $(10/10)\log_2(1/10) = 3.32$ bits of information. A source generating randomly a character from the English alphabet produces $(26/26)\log_2(1/26) = 4.70$ bits. If the messages are not equally likely, the formula incorporates the actual (theoretical or empirical) probabilities: $\Sigma(1/p_i)\log_2(1/p_i)$

already know or what they intended, or communication of meaning between people.

2. Jumarie (1987) developed Shannon's theory to take into account the observer or receiver of information. This results in a two stage Shannon-like process. At the first stage a particular symbol (e.g., the word 'may') is generated. At the second stage an observer attaches a meaning to the particular symbol generated (e.g., 'is able to', 'is allowed to', 'fifth month of the year'). The meanings are related to the symbols by a system of conditional probabilities defined in advance by the subjectivity of the particular observer and dependent on the context. So the particular sentence in which 'may' occurs, and the prior expectations of the observer determine the conditional probabilities from instant to instant. Thus, there is a measure of the syntactic information of the source of messages, and a measure of the semantic information for each possible message dependent on the observer. The result is the overall measure of subjective information.

This approach does provide an extension to Shannon's formula to cope with the idea that a particular symbol may have a number of meanings, and it does provide a role for individual observers in assigning meaning to symbols. Thus it does provide a definition of information and distinguish it from meaning. However, it would seem to have very limited practical use. Like Bar-Hillel's scheme, it is completely impossible to operationalise in anything but a limited, artificial domain. And even if it were the result would only be a measure of the amount of information once again, in this case for a particular source/observer/time combination. Nothing is said about the content of particular messages.

3. Information as a reduction in uncertainty. Several authors have picked up on Shannon's basic idea that the amount of information is related to the degree of uncertainty and applied that to the receiver of information. Information is that which reduces uncertainty in the mind of the recipient.

Hintikka (1968, p. 312) defines information as: "the information of (a statement) s is the amount of uncertainty we are relieved of when we come to know that s is true."

Hintikka then considers various ways of measuring this reduction in uncertainty basing his ideas on Bar-Hillel and Carnap's concept of the number of states that a statement excludes. The amount of information is inversely proportional to the probability (of the truth of) the statement, or how surprising or unexpected the statement is. However, this reduction is assumed to be entirely independent of the particular receiver.

Nauta (1972) and Artandi (1973) do bring in the actual state of knowledge of a receiver. Nauta (1972, p.179) describes pragmatic information as "that which removes the doubt, restricts the uncertainty, reduces the ignorance, curtails the variance." This clearly makes information strictly relative to the receiver. The more prior knowledge that the receiver has, the less information that a message can provide. Indeed, a message that is repeated must convey zero information since it is already known by the recipient. Conversely, the message must be comprehensible to the receiver for it to reduce uncertainty, so messages in unknown languages or unfamiliar symbolic systems also convey no information for particular people.

This approach is certainly a significant step forward in moving information concepts towards the level of practical use. It begins to consider the actual content of messages by recognising that what they convey to someone will depend upon that person's prior knowledge and expectations, rather than being concerned only with the amount of information. It also represents one of the first attempts to consider the pragmatic dimensions of information by making the link between information and purposes and values. However, the approach is weak in terms of its actual definition of information. Is it the message or sign itself? This seems unlikely as the same information could be represented in quite different ways. It is the meaning of the message? This is a possibility but one of the weaknesses of the theory is that meaning is not discussed.

Aside from the detail of definition, is reduction in uncertainty actually a reasonable interpretation of information anyway? It seems to go against common usage of the term. For instance, it implies that books, newspapers, messages, and so on, do not carry information in themselves. Information comes into being only when someone reads them—so a library or information system does not contain any information when it is not being used. It also means that a message that is repeated carries information the first time but not the second. It seems more intuitive to say that the message still carries information but the second time it has no new information for the recipient. Moreover, it does not seem clear to me that information always reduces uncertainty—could not information increase it?

4.  MacKay (1969) explicitly tried to incorporate meaning into information theory by proposing the idea that information is some change in the cognition of the receiver. This approach has been further developed by Luhmann (1990b). I would argue that it is the approach which is nearest to providing a theoretical underpinning for Checkland's formulation of "information equals data plus meaning."[28]

MacKay's analysis is concerned primarily with intentional communication through language (although he does indicate that it could also apply to non-intentional signs and symbols). That is, a situation with a sender who has a

---

[28] Others whose work relates information to meaning are Pratt (1977), Otten (1978), and Mutch (1999).

meaning they wish to transmit, a message (statement, question, command) intended to transmit the meaning, and a receiver who is in a particular "state of readiness." This state of readiness can be interpreted as a set of conditional probabilities for different possible patterns of behaviour in different circumstances. MacKay refers to this as a conditional probability matrix (CPM). The intention of the sender is thus not to produce some actual behaviour but, through an understanding of the message, to alter the settings or state of the CPM.

There are three different "meanings" involved in such a communication: the intended meaning of the sender, the received or understood meaning of the receiver, and the conventional meaning of the message. There is clearly an enormous degree of complexity involved here. For example, the conventional meaning might be completely negated by a tone of voice or expression in an ironic or sarcastic comment. That aside, what is the exact nature of "meaning" implied here? MacKay argues that one cannot identify the received meaning with either the behaviour brought about, the change to the CPM, or the final state of the CPM. Rather meaning is a function or trigger, "the selective function of the message on an ensemble of possible states of the CPM" (Mackay 1956, p. 219). The three types of meaning now become the intended selective function, the actual selective function, and the selective function on a "conventional symbolic representational system."

Some illustrations of this concept are: two messages may be different but have the same selective function (meaning) for a particular receiver; the same message repeated still has the same meaning even though it brings about no change of state the second time and so produces no information; a message may be meaningless if it has no selective function for someone, for example if it is in an unknown language or is an inappropriate choice or combination of words. Note that this concept of meaning is relational-the selective function is always relative to a particular domain.

We can now connect meaning with information theory. What MacKay calls selective information content is the size or extent of the change brought about by a particular selective operation. This obviously depends on the prior state of the CPM. Thus, a repeated message will be meaningful but will have no information content since no change of state will take place, the CPM. will already be in the selected state. So meaning is a selection mechanism which may generate information for someone if it changes their state.

Luhmann (1990b) has developed MacKay's work further by tying it in with his sophisticated, phenomenologically-based, theory of meaning-constituting systems. Luhmann aims to move the discussion of meaning away from the perspective of the conscious intentions of individual subjects (as with MacKay) towards recognising that meaning is primary and should be defined without reference to the subject's intentions since the subject is already a meaning-constituted entity. Luhmann takes MacKay's idea that meaning is not primarily content, but a function for *selection*. Meaning functions at two levels the psychic (individual), where it frames or orders our experiences, and the social (society), where it makes possible intersubjective experience and communication. Meaning, in fact, connects these two levels and makes possible their differentiation.

Considering the individual level, we constantly experience a multiplicity of external and internal stimuli. This, in fact, constitutes a major problem for us—we are continually overburdened by possibilities and must in some way select or choose which of our immediate motor-sensory perceptions will become actual experiences for us. This is the function of meaning—to allow a selection from the many possibilities without at the same time losing that which is not selected. In selecting from our perceptions and presenting us with experience meaning always opens up further possibilities with its implicit references to the alternatives that have not been chosen.

Meaning is a relation between what is selected (presenced) and what is not. What is selected is only as it is by virtue of its difference from what it is not. Meaning connects present actuality to future possibility. It is the way the present is selected, and is the connection to the next instant's selection. It can be characterised by differences, or rather negations (what is not selected), in three domains—factuality—what is selected; sociality—who is selected; and temporality—when in terms of before/now/after. The particular selections made depend on our individual pre-existing set of readinesses or expectations, but the resulting experiences may, in turn, change our expectations. It is this change that Luhmann terms information—the surprisal value of a meaning complex for the structure of expectations. As before, information is always relative to the receiver while meaning is not. Thus the same message or event will produce different information for different people depending on the extent to which it accords with their prior expectations. And a repeated message retains its meaning but loses its information. More will be said about Luhmann's complex social theory of communication based on autopoiesis in Chapter 7.

MacKay's interpretation of meaning and information, as developed by Luhmann, is a clear advance over the Nauta/Artandi but does not overcome all weaknesses. In particular, it leaves us with information being entirely subjective and individual, unable to be carried or contained or processed in any way, as normal usage would have it. It is difficult to say what use could be made of such a definition other than to say we all experience the world differently.

5.   Dretske (1981) has developed a sophisticated theory that covers information, meaning and knowledge. As this forms the basis of my own analysis it will be covered in detail in the next section.

There are several theories of information that are not based on Shannon and Weaver's original approach. I will just mention them briefly here—most are reviewed in Mingers (1996b). Farradane (1976) identifies information with a particular *representation* of knowledge or thought; Belkin and Robertson (1976) suggest that information is that which is capable of changing the structure of a receiver; and Floridi (2002) defines information as being a collection of data that is well-formed, meaningful and as well as that *true*.

## 5.3 The Nature of Information

This section will develop a theory of information and its relationship to meaning. It will be based on Dretske's analysis as discussed briefly above, but will be augmented with concepts from Maturana and Varela, Habermas, and Luhmann. It will be compatible with critical realism both in terms of arguing that information does have a real, intransitive existence, and in terms CR's generative view of causation.

Following Bateson (1973), that which are most elementary are *differences*. If some area of the world were completely uniform, it could have no effects at all. It is differences that are transmitted endlessly around the physical medium. Differences in the surface of an object become differences in wavelength of light, leading to differences in the retinal neurones, which become different patterns of neural activity, which in turn become differences in body posture, and so on. For Bateson (1973), information is a "difference that makes a difference" which can be interpreted as one that generates an event, a sign, a symbol, or an utterance (the differences between these will be categorised later).

Dretske (1981) makes this more precise by suggesting that such events are not, in themselves, information but that they carry information about particular states of affairs in the world. A single event carries information, as Hartley (1928) and Shannon and Weaver (1949) saw, because it reveals a reduction in the possibilities of what might have happened. With the toss of a dice or the input of a particular data item into a computer, a number of possibilities are reduced to one. The amount of information carried or generated by the event reflects the reduction in possibilities thus brought about. The more likely the event, the fewer possibilities it eliminates, and the less information it carries. Note that the information that is available from the event is independent of any observer. Indeed, the event might not be observed—it may never move from the domain of the Actual to the domain of the Empirical (Chapter 2)—yet it still carries this information waiting to be tapped[29]. The average

---

[29] In fact, the situation is more complex than this. Although the actual information available from an event is independent nevertheless prior knowledge about the situation affects the amount of information that a particular observer can receive. This will be illustrated later.

amount of information carried by an event (e.g., a sign or utterance) can be measured, using formulae similar to Shannon's, both for individual events and for sets of possible events.

From a semantic, communicational point of view however, what is important is not the amount of information, but its content, and how it is transmitted from a source to a receiver. Considering first transmission, we must assume some causal link exists between the source and the receiver otherwise no information can be transmitted. The degree of correspondence between the two may vary from complete to zero. In general, the source will have a number of possible states, as will the receiver. These states will have differing probabilities of occurrence. The amount of information that can be carried is calculated for both source and receiver. The question is how much of the information at the receiver is caused by the source? If there is complete transmission, it means that every state of the source is linked with every state of the receiver and vice versa. In practice this situation is unlikely. The receiver will be affected by things other than the source (noise), and not all of the information from the source will affect the receiver (equivocation).

These situations can be seen in Figure 5.1. In 5.1a, S1 is a state of the source and R1–R3 are states of the receiver. S1 is associated with (can cause) R1, R2, and R3. Knowing that S1 occurs does not tell us which R will occur, although knowing R1, R2, or R3 does tell us that S1 has happened. This case represents *noise*—some factor other than the source must determine which of R1, R2, or R3 occurs. In probability terms, the conditional probability $Pr(R1|S1) < 1$. In the example, turning the key usually results in the starter motor turning and the engine starting immediately. Sometimes, perhaps if the spark plugs are old, the engine only starts after a while. And sometimes it may not start if there is some malfunction. Knowing S1 does not tell us with certainty which R will occur, but knowing R does tell us that S1 must have occurred. It carries the information that the key was turned.

On the other hand, in Figure 5.1b S1 and S2 can both cause R1. Knowledge of R1 does not carry the information that S1 happened, only that either S1 or S2 did. This

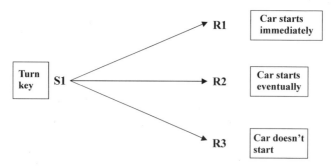

**Figure 5.1a. Noise in Signal Transmission.**

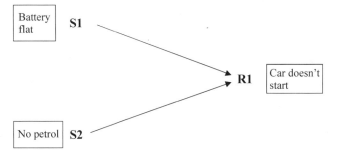

**Figure 5.1b. Equivocation in Signal Transmission.**

case represents *equivocation*—an output may result from a variety of causes. The conditional probability Pr(S1|R1) < 1. Knowing that the car didn't start only tells us that one (or more) of several malfunctions must have occurred.

Thus the amount of information that can be transmitted from a source to a receiver depends on the causal relations between them. Independent events can transmit no information, but a causally linked event carries information about its cause. Instruments (e.g., thermometers) are good examples. They are designed specifically to have some causal relationship to a particular state of affairs. Assuming that it is working properly, a particular thermometer reading carries information about the surrounding temperature.

It might appear that this formulation is quite against Maturana's view of autopoietic cognition in which he argues that information cannot of itself *cause* particular effects in a receiver. To resolve this we must distinguish between the signals and the information they carry on the one hand, and between information and meaning on the other. Anticipating what is to come, there must be a causal connection for the signal to be transmitted at all—something must impinge upon the nervous system in order for an interaction to occur at all. But once the signal has been received, the information that it carries triggers or generates *meaning* in the receiver in a subject-dependent fashion. A knock on the door generates differences in sound that are transmitted physically through the air, then through the ear, to trigger activity in the nervous system. The information carried by the signals results in the meaning "somebody is at the door" as a result of the structural coupling between the receiver and their environment.

Turning to *what* information is conveyed, Dretske argues that the content of the information carried by a sign is *that which is causally implied by the occurrence of the sign*. In other words, what must be the case given that the sign or event has occurred? Interestingly this is an almost identical transcendental approach to that of critical realism—given some phenomena, what causal mechanism must have generated it? This formulation provides a definition of information—*information is the propositional content of a sign*[30]. Thus, a sign carries information about the particular states of affairs that are implied by the occurrence of that sign. There are a number of consequences of this definition:

1. Information is an objective commodity. It exists whether or not there are people to observe or extract it, and it can be stored and transmitted by artefacts, e.g., books, newspapers, TV sets and computers. Information is distinct from the sign (which must ultimately be physically embodied) that it is carried by since the information has causal effects in its own right. The knock on the door causes someone to open it not because of its physical sound but because the physical sign carries the information that someone is there knocking.

2. However, the amount of information available to a particular person depends on their prior knowledge—in particular, their prior knowledge of the possible states of the source. For example, the message that the winner of a horse race was a grey carries more information for someone who knows there was only one grey than for someone who does not, since it enables the actual horse to be identified. Conversely, no information is available for someone who already knew the winner. Equally, a book written in a foreign language or a message in code carries information, but only for those knowing the language or code.

   This relativity of available information does not contradict the argument that information in general is objective and independent of the observer. It is equivalent to two observers looking at the same object from different angles—they see things differently because of their different positions but the object is nevertheless independent of them.

3. If a sign carries the information that a particular state of affairs obtains, it also carries all the information that is implied by that state of affairs (Dretske uses the term "nested in"). These consequences or necessary conditions could be *analytic* (that is, follow by definition), or *nomic* (that is, based on general scientific laws). A further possibility (in addition to Dretske's two) is consequences following from the logic of a social situation (for example, the rules and conventions surrounding the use of credit cards). Analytic consequences are those that follow from the definition of the event or entity. For instance, the information that something is square also carries the specific information that it has four equal sides and that its angles are right-angles, as well as the more general information that it is a square and not a triangle.

---

[30]More formally, Dretske (1981, p65) puts this as: *A signal r carries the information that s is F if and only if the conditional propability that s is F, given r (and k), is 1 (but given k alone, less than 1).* Where r is a signal; "s is F" means that some particular state of affairs, F, obtains; and k is any prior knowledge of the observer about the possible states of affairs—this may well be zero.

Nomic consequences are those that follow because of natural laws. For example, if water is boiling, its temperature must be 100°C at sea level. Consequences from the logic of the situation relate to social meanings and practices. For example, a sign saying "no credit cards" implies cash or a cheque will be required.

4.  Information can be transmitted along a chain provided that there are direct causal links. For example, people walking in a shopping mall cause changes in light waves which cause changes in the CCTV camera which cause changes to the wire which results in pictures on a screen and recorded on a tape. The pictures carry information about what went on in the mall and they do so whether or not anyone actually sees them.

We can illustrate the above with a simple example. Suppose that in a lecture I write the following number on the board "02476 522475" and ask the audience if this sign carries or conveys any information. Most people will probably say "no" as it will not mean anything to them. Some may say it looks like a phone number but of course it could be many other things or it could just be random. In fact, I claim that it does carry information because it is actually my work phone number. I knew that and I caused that particular number to be written on the board and so it carries that information. The fact that no one in the audience knows this just means that the information is not available for them. It could become available if I gave another message *about* the first one, saying that it was my phone number, or if someone in the audience already knew my number and recognised it. In these cases we can see that information has been transmitted because it can lead to action—someone could use the information to phone me up.

In fact, the sign carries its information even if no one actually sees it because the information that it conveys reflects its origin, its cause, rather than its receipt or interpretation as most information theories would have. Moreover it carries the information nested in or implied by it. That is, that I work, have a phone in my office, and so on.

Suppose that I had written up 0578 876573. Now I have just made up that number randomly and so it carries no information (except that it is a random number). Even if there is actually a corresponding phone number (or bank account, or passport, or safe combination …) this particular message does not carry that information since I did not know it; it is just a coincidence. So a message only carries the information that is causally connected to its occurrence, not that which is merely coincidental.

Suppose that I had written 03476 522475. Here I have made a mistake and put in a wrong digit. So this message does *not* carry the information about my phone even though I may think it does and I may tell other people that it does. *False* information is not information. We can tell this because it would not translate into action—dialling it would not get through.

## 5.4 From Information to Meaning

### 5.4.1 A Typology of Signs

Before discussing the relationship between information and meaning, it is important to clarify some terms. First, it is useful to have terms other than "information" and "meaning" themselves to use in a discussion about meaning. Second, there are various terms such as "sign," "signal," "symbol," and "data" whose meanings tend to overlap. The base discipline for the study of signs is called semiotics and the process of sign production and transmission is semiosis.

The most well known analysis of the sign is probably that of Saussure (1960) who saw a sign as consisting of two components, the signifier and the signified. The signifier is the word or image or sound pattern and the signified is the concept or meaning or idea that goes with it. This was a radical break for linguistics because traditionally words were assumed to link strongly to the objects that they represented[31]. In Saussure's theory objects do not really figure—language becomes disconnected from the world and the relation between signifier and signified is essentially arbitrary or, rather, conventional. Language itself (*la parole*) is conceptualised as a structure of distinctions or differences that are constantly changing and are primarily internal to the language rather than being based on a connection between language and its objects. This theory was very influential in the development of structuralism and ultimately post-modernism, but from a critical realist perspective the loss of the intransitive domain is a crucial problem.

A more interesting approach is that of an earlier (19th century) and currently less well recognised philosopher—C.S. Peirce—who actually coined the term semiotics. For Peirce (1965) there were three elements to a sign[32]—the *sign* itself (sometimes called a *representamen*); the *object* that the sign stands for; and the *interpretant*, the effect that it creates in someone (which may be another sign).

A sign, or representamen, is something which stands to somebody for something in some respect or capacity. It addresses somebody, that is creates in the mind of that person an equivalent sign, or perhaps a more developed sign. The sign which it creates I call the interpretant of the first sign. The sign stands for something, its "object." (Peirce 1965, 2.228)

This is an approach much more compatible with critical realism (Nellhaus 1998) since it brings in the object or referent of the sign. Bhaskar does actually discuss signs and proposes a triad of signifier, signified and referent which is quite similar (see Figure 5.2). These triads are known as the semiotic triangle.

---

[31] For example, Wittgenstein's *Tractatus* Wittgenstein (1974) has been described as a picture theory of language.

[32] Confusingly he uses the term "sign" both for the whole and for one of the parts.

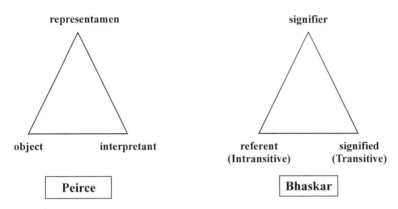

**Figure 5.2. The Semiotic Triangle.**

Peirce's scheme is actually a good deal more complex than this, Nellhaus (1998) provides a good overview from a CR perspective, but the only part I wish to mention is a classification of different types of sign in terms of their relation to their object. First there is an "index" which has a direct and real relation to its object, possibly part/whole or causal. For example, smoke and fire, a thermometer and temperature, or a sail and a boat. Second there is an "icon" which has a relationship of similarity with its object. This covers many categories such as pictures, descriptions, metaphors, models, mathematics. Finally there are "symbols" which have only a conventional, essentially arbitrary, relationship. Thus all of Saussure's signs are symbols in this sense.

Two further approaches are relevant. First Morris (1938) and then Nauta (1972) developed a five-term model of semiosis. This includes a sign (representamen), an interpreter, an effect (or interpretant), a denotation (or referent), and a context. It also stresses the importance of the internal cognitive state or representation of the interpreter (Newman 2001). Second, Bühler (1982), who was concerned more with purely linguistic utterances, suggested that a linguistic expression was at the centre of three relationships—one of *representation* to some particular state of affairs; one of *expression* to its sender; and one of *appeal* to its receiver. This was one of the sources of Habermas's theory of communicative action to be discussed later.

Drawing on these various ideas I have constructed the following typology of signs (Figure 5.3) that develop in increasing complexity from a simple event up to a full linguistic utterance. This allows us to be clear when discussing the relations between information and meaning in more detail.

At the first level, (a), we have an event, which I will call a 'trace', with its cause. It is not observed, or if it is it is not actually noticed as a sign of anything, but it still carries (and possibly transmits) information. For example, wet marks on the ground caused by rain; smoke caused by fire; or the electronic transmission of images from a CCTV camera. The arrow in the diagram indicates that the event carries information about its cause. In critical realist terms we can say that the event is in the domain of the Actual and has been caused or generated by mechanisms in the Real, but that this particular event has not been observed or experienced and so is not in the Empirical.

At the next level (b) we can see that the event has been observed or noticed and has become or been taken as a 'sign' of something by someone[33]. The event is seen, not for itself, but for what it is a trace of, what it points to. The sign therefore *signifies* something or, rather, it signifies that some other event has occurred—it has significance or more generally signification. The sign also 'means' something to the receiver; what I shall call its *import.* For example, a particular paw print in the ground might signify that a bear was there and might have the import for someone that that person ought to get away. The sign (signal) at this level has a direct, causal or part/whole, relationship to its cause. In Peirce's terms it is an index. Examples are: a knock on the door signifies that someone is there and could have the import that it's the postman; a reading on a thermometer signifies the temperature is 10°C and has the import of turning up the heating; a sail in the distance signifies that a boat is arriving and has the import of going to greet them.

We can now say with critical realism that the event, having been observed, has become part of the Empirical domain. This raises an important point within critical realism. As Nellhaus (1998) has noted, the exact nature or definition of the domain of the Empirical is left somewhat vague. Is it the purely subjective experiences of individuals? Is it only those experiences relevant to science? Is it only human experiences? Is it really social rather than individual? Nellhaus argues that we should in fact see the domain of the empirical very generally as constituted by semiosis— "The third ontological domain consists of meanings embodied in signs and semioses. I prefer to call it the *semiosic* domain." (p. 10).

At level (c) we move to 'symbols', that is, signs that do not have a direct relationship to what they signify. The paw print is physically caused or produced by a bear and could not have been otherwise, whereas symbols rely on an agreed, conventional set of rules governing their use—a system of *connotation.* For instance, blue on a map signifies water not because it was caused by water but because of the accepted rules of map-making. In this particular case the use of blue is not entirely arbitrary since often water does look blue, In Peirce's terms this category includes both symbols and icons. There are many types of symbolic system, e.g., icons, colours and shapes, gestures, numbers, and language. Symbols only work for the community of people who share the system of connotation.

Finally, in (d), we have an 'utterance', which is some combination of signs or symbols produced by someone at a particular time with some *intent.* This level therefore brings in the producer of a message. Typically an utterance will involve

---

[33] In fact, I would not restrict this to humans; clearly animals of all types have the ability, through their nervous systems, to respond to all kinds of sensory traces in their environments. One can go further and apply semiosis to situations such as the bee's dance, or antibodies 'recognition' of chemical markers Nellhaus (1998).

speech or writing but it could be a gesture, either symbolic, e.g., a referee blowing a whistle, or a non-symbolic sign such as holding up an empty glass to request more drink. Or it could be an input into an information system. Utterances may also have unintentional aspects (e.g., body language) that can act as signs for others.

A number of points can be clarified with this typology:

1.  Signs, symbols, and utterances will carry information about states of affairs in the world—what they signify. With signs the link is direct, but with symbols and utterances it is indirect, relying on an agreed background. The latter, therefore, only function for a particular community of observers to the extent that they share that background.

2.  The distinction between data and information can be made clear. Data is a collection of symbols brought together because they are considered relevant to some purposeful activity. Each symbol, or item of data, *carries some information*. It is not the same as the information, nor is information the result of some processing of the data. In the information systems context, data will usually be symbolic (numeric, linguistic, or graphic) utterances, produced in the system for a particular purpose.

3.  Foreshadowing the next section on information and meaning, we can distinguish two different usages of the term "meaning," and distinguish them both from "information." First, there is the idea of a system of meaning—the publicly available meanings within a language that enable sentences to be meaningful, i.e., that which actors draw upon, and reproduce (Giddens 1984; Luhmann 1990b), in their linguistic interactions. Within the typology this is the system of *connotation* that underlies a symbolic message. Second there is the specific meaning that a listener gains from a particular utterance, and that a speaker intends, which is possibly different. Within the typology, these are the *import* and the *intent* respectively.

4.  The "meaning" (import) of an utterance is clearly distinct from the information (signification) it carries. For example, the utterance "Yes, I killed her" spoken in a TV play carries very different information than if it is spoken in a trial for murder, and can lead to very different outcomes—the actress will not end up in jail—yet the meaning is the same. Conversely, in reply to the question "Did you go to the pub last night?" the answers "No, I stayed in" and "No, I went to the cinema," carry (some of) the same information but mean different things.

5.  The relationship of this typology to critical realism can be seen in Figure 5.4. As Nellhaus has argued it is possible to see the Empirical Domain as a domain of semiosis. Events occur in the Domain of the Actual and these can become signs, symbols and utterances. The information carried by a sign relates to the cause(s) of the event which is the sign and thus points back to the underlying generative mechanisms in the Domain of the Real.

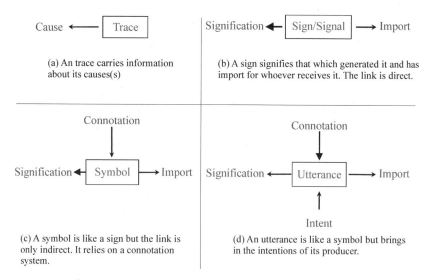

**Figure 5.3. A Typology of Signs.**

## 5.4.2 Information and Meaning

We have seen that events, and signs generated by these events, carry information that is objective—independent of observers and interpreters. The question now is, how is this information related to meaning (import)—the particular meanings that observers derive from the signs? The aim is to clarify that relationship by showing how objective information makes possible non-objective meaning.

This task will be accomplished using two related distinctions: analogue and digital, and difference and distinction. The physical world (in which all signs and signals are ultimately embodied) is essentially analogue (Wilden 1977) consisting of continuous rather than discrete effects such as heat, light and sound. It is a continuum of differences transforming and being transformed. All of these differences can be taken to carry a rich amount of information about the states of affairs that generated them. The digital, on the other hand, is discrete—it is yes/no, on/off, a distinction (Spencer-Brown 1972) rather than a difference. The analogue is full of information, yet it is ambiguous and imprecise. The digital is precise and well bounded, but it carries only limited amounts of information.

<u>Digitalizing the Analogue</u>

Dretske's argument is that the transformation of information into meaning involves a digitalization of the analogue. Consider the example of a photograph of an old man sitting in a chair. The photo contains a vast amount of information—about shape, light, colour, pattern, costume, furniture, decoration—in analogue form. The linguistic description given above carries only a very limited part of that information in digital form (Dretske 1981, p. 136). Most of the information available in the

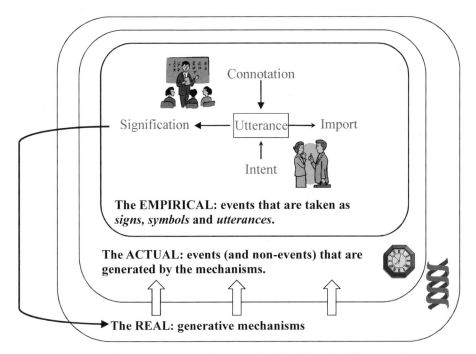

**Figure 5.4. The Typology from a Critical Realist Perspective.**

picture is not actually conveyed by the description[34]. That which is conveyed is what is stated in the description plus the information nested in that, i.e., that which follows analytically or nomically from the description. What is not conveyed is generally more specific information. In this example the man's appearance, his clothes, the type of chair, the room, the other furniture and so on.

Signs can carry both analogue and digital information. The information that is carried digitally by a signal is the most specific information that is available. In the verbal description, the most specific information about the chair was just that it was a chair. However, in the picture, we could see what type of chair, how big, what colour, and so on. Thus, the information that it is a chair is digital in the sentence, but analogue in the picture. Inevitably when analogue information is digitalized, a loss of information occurs. The digital signal carries less information than the analogue. The manifold differences are reduced to a single distinction, and information that is irrelevant to the distinction is pruned away. Effectively, a process of generalization occurs—a number of different states (different sorts of chairs) all produce the same final signal (that it is a chair not a table). All that matters for someone who wants to sit down is that it is a chair, not what type of chair. Note that digital information is not necessarily linguistic—for example, a simple thermostat digitalizes temperature.

---

[34] Remember a picture is worth a thousand words.

Dretske argues that our perception and experiences are analogue, while cognition and meaning are progressive digitalizations of this experience. For instance, light from a complex visual scene (analogue) triggers differences in the retina that remain largely analogue. These, in turn, through the very active process of perception involving all the senses, become seen as particular things—trees, houses, and people. Already some digitalization has occurred. Our attention picks out particular aspects of the scene. Eventually a linguistic signal, such as "the apples are ripe," is generated, by which time a full digitalization into meaning has occurred. The same thing happens with internal experiences. Toothache is a strong analogue experience but by the time we have digitalized it into a sentence almost none of the analogue information, the feeling, remains.

It can also be seen that this digitalization is a *selection* from a range of possibilities— it is a chair rather than a table or sofa or stool which fits with Luhmann's theory of communication to be discussed in Chapter 7.

This explanation reveals the relationship between information (signification) and meaning (import): objective information is converted into (inter)-subjective meaning through a process of digitalization. It fits well with Maturana's (1975) argument, outlined above, that information can only trigger subject-dependent structural changes, it cannot determine its effects on a receiver. At every stage the receiver's knowledge, intentions and context determine what counts as information and what particular aspects of the available analogue information are digitalized. Meaning and information are clearly distinct. A message may carry information but have no meaning for a particular person who does not understand the language since they are unable to digitalize it. Conversely, a message may have meaning but carry no information. The statement "I have toothache," is meaningful but carries no information if it is not true. Finally, while information must always be true, the meaning or belief we generate from information may be false—we may be mistaken.

To formalize the difference, a sign or utterance impinges on the sensory system. Its information is carried in analogue form. The nervous system strips away much of the detail to focus on a particular level. The result is the *semantic content* of the information structure carried by the sign—that information, *and only that information*, held in digital form (Dretske 1981, p. 177). The latter qualification is important, as we shall see shortly, for distinguishing between digitalization carried out in a meaningful, intentional way by humans from digitalization carried out by machines, such as cameras, thermostats, and computers. A further characteristic of the semantic content is that it must have some effect or action within the receiver, even if only internally. This semantic content is the meaning (import) generated from the available information.

Intentionality and Meaning

The information that is held digitally is the most specific information about something and carries with it the more general information nested in the description. But this nested information—analytic, nomic, or situational—must be held in analogue form, since it is less specific than that held digitally. This information is not part of the semantic content of the signal. Although it is carried by the signal, it is not what is meant by the signal. For example, saying that a glass contains water carries implications such as its boiling point and its chemical constituents and properties, but this is not generally what is *meant* by such a statement. These are not part of the semantic content unless they are relevant to the reason for the digitalization. If there was a question "can I drink this?" then the reply "it is water" does have the semantic content that it is drinkable.

It is this aspect of intentionality—of bringing forward only specific semantic content—that distinguishes humans from information processing machines. Some machines transmit all or most information they receive (e.g., a television). Some digitalize it to a greater or lesser extent (e.g., a sensor in the road converts pressure differences into a count of cars passing, which is then fed to a computer). In all cases they transmit the information that they carry and all its consequences—they are not able to impose a higher-order intentional structure on it and lose some of the information. They have not been able to discriminate between the relevance of different aspects of the information.

Summary

Information is different from meaning. Information is an objective, although abstract, feature of the world in the same way as are physical objects and their properties. Information does not depend on knowledge, beliefs, or understandings in itself, although the information available for a particular person does. Meaning, however, is generated from information by interpreters through a process of digitalization that abstracts only some of the information available. Large quantities of information, generally in analogue form, are carried by physical media. Yet humans can never experience or interact with it in an unmediated way, it is literally untouchable. Humans are always already in a world of interpreted, digitalized meaning. In this sense, computers have access to all the information they process, they just never know that they do. They are genuinely information processors. Humans, on the other hand, cannot consciously process information, only meaning.

## 5.4.3 Analysis of Some Examples

So far we have only considered the precise mechanism by which information triggers meaning: *how* meaning is generated, not *what* meaning is generated. We need now to bring in the semantic and pragmatic aspects of communication using the theories of Maturana and Habermas. This will be done initially by way of two examples that illustrate both the mechanisms outlined above and the link into semantics and pragmatics.

Example 1—a Non-Linguistic Sign

The first example is of a non-linguistic sign since language adds extra dimensions of complexity. Consider coming across a bear's footprint in the Canadian forests. What information does it carry and what meaning might someone gain from it? The information it carries clearly relates to its own existence. The most likely cause is a wild bear, and the sign carries the further information implied by that—a bear is an animal, carnivorous, often hostile and so on (analytic); as well as specific information such as size, weight, speed, and direction (nomic). Although a bear is most likely, it is not necessarily the case. One can imagine other, improbable, explanations—for example, a film being made, or a circus. In fact, the likelihood depends on the circumstances—wild bears are very unlikely in Hyde Park. This conforms to the critical realist interpretation described in Figure 5.4—an event is experienced in the Empirical domain and we then hypothesise possible causal mechanisms as explanations in the Real domain. This process has strong links to Bayesian probability theory (Mingers 2004).

Nevertheless, all this information is carried by the print even if it is never actually seen by anyone. If it is seen, however, it will trigger some meaning. Consider four different people. The first comes from the city, knows little about animals, and does not even recognize it as a bear print. They are able only to digitalize a very general meaning that it was made by some animal. The next person has come for a picnic with the family. They recognize it is a large bear and quite recent. They digitalize the meaning that the bear could be a danger to them and move away quickly. The third person is a hunter who can almost visualize the bear from the print and follows the tracks in eager anticipation. The final person is a technician from the film company who thinks the print is one of the fake ones they made but, unfortunately, is mistaken and is mauled by the bear.

What does this tell us? It shows the large amount and variety of information carried by the sign quite independently of its observation. It also shows how this information triggers specific meanings in people and how these differ substantially between people. Note that these meanings are not purely individual (subjective) but will be shared among different groups of people, living different forms of life (Wittgenstein 1958, p. 8–12), such as hunters or a film crew. Information is potential meaning. These meanings, in turn, lead to practical action in the world, generating new signs and signals of their own. The last case shows how the attribution of meaning can be mistaken. The sign was wrongly interpreted, and the resulting meaning was incorrect because of equivocation in the information.

Example 2—a Linguistic Utterance

This example follows the first, except that instead of seeing the bear print, the receiver is told about it, as in "I saw a bear track over there." What information does this linguistic sign carry? Once again, it carries information about its own existence—what has led this particular set of sounds to occur? Now, however, there are two different types of answer. One concerns the state of affairs that it describes—its propositional content. We could say that the fact there is a bear print (assuming the statement is true) has caused the statement. It therefore carries similar information to the previous example (although much less as it is digital). The actual cause of the statement, however, is the fact that it has been made by a particular person with particular intentions at a particular point in time. This points to the illocutionary or pragmatic content of the statement—what it is trying to achieve. Thus, in contrast to the non-linguistic sign the statement also carries information about its pragmatic dimensions. These can be analysed using Habermas's communicative validity claims (Habermas 1979; Habermas 1984; Habermas 1987).

This situation is quite different from before. In the first example, the relationship between source and sign was direct—the bear caused the print. In the second, it is indirect. We can gain information about the described state of affairs if we assume that Habermas's four validity claims, comprehensibility, truth, truthfulness, and rightness, can be justified for this speech act (see Table 5.1). If we do make these assumptions, we gain some of the information that would have been available by seeing the print, but not all. The print itself is an analogue sign that carries a large amount of information. The statement is a digital sign that carries relatively little—it loses much of the richness. A better secondary sign might be a photograph which maintains much of the analogue information.

Information is now also available, however, about the speaker's pragmatic intentions and the validity claims underlying the utterance. What possible motives could there be for the statement? What type of speech act was it: Answering a question? Making a statement? Ordering something? If the propositional content seems unlikely we may question the validity claims underlying the communication—is the speaker mistaken about factual matters (truth)? Have we understood the utterance correctly (comprehensibility)? Is the speaker sincere (truthfulness)? Is the speaker assuming different social norms and rules than we are (rightness)? Note that I do not restrict the term "speaker" to a single person. Rather, it can be seen as the ensemble of people, mechanisms, and procedures that lead to a particular sign being produced. In the case of data in an information system, it is not so much the person who types it in as the people and procedures that actually produce the data in the first place.

These examples illustrate how signs carry propositional information and, in the case of utterances, illocutionary information as well. They also illustrate how meaning can be extracted from the information and how meaning has both intersubjective (connotation) and subjective (import) dimensions. The process of meaning generation is examined in more detail in Section 7.4 after we have discussed Luhmann's communication theory.

## 5.4.4 Meaning and Semiosis

I should also like to point out at this stage that in dealing with linguistic signs we are not assuming some straightforward "picturing" of reality with a simple correspondence of a sign (word) to its referent or meaning. There are complex processes involved both in the way a word comes to have the meaning generated for it within a particular utterance; and how words change and develop their meanings over time and how they bring with them many different overtones and resonances that condition their meaning in a particular situation.

## Table 5.1. The Validity Claims of Communicative Action (after Habermas (1984).

| Validity Claim | Reference World | Purpose | Type of Speech Act | Form of Argument |
|---|---|---|---|---|
| **Truth** | Object world; that which obtains<br><br>External Nature | Presentation of knowledge | Constative<br>• propositions<br>• explanations<br>• predictions | Theoretical discourse |
| **Rightness (Legitimacy)** | Social world; normative relations and practices<br><br>Society | Establishment of social relations | Regulative<br>• promises<br>• orders<br>• requests | Practicate discourse |
| **Truthfulness (Sincerity)** | Subject world; private experiences<br><br>Inner Nature | Expression of self | Expressive<br>• beliefs<br>• intentions<br>• desires | Therapeutic discourse |
| **Comprehensibility** | Language | Understanding | | Explicative discourse |

One fruitful way of approaching this is with the fundamental distinction between metaphor and metonymy, which itself can be traced to Locke and Hume's principles of association (Hume 1967). Hume suggested that ideas could be connected by similarity or resemblance, contiguity in time or space, and cause and effect. Lacan (1970) developed Freud's ideas on dream processes working through *displacement* where one idea is displaced by a similar one, and *condensation* where several ideas are condensed into one. Jakobson and Halle (1956) (see section 4.4.2) used the terms metaphor and metonymy to describe how terms gain their meaning through their selection from other similar ones, and their combination within a message.

### 5.4.5 Summary of the Main Implications

First, and most significantly, this model provides a clear and consistent conceptualisation of the basic concepts of information, which is of particular importance to the disciplines of information systems and information science. In particular, distinctions have been specified between traces, signs, symbols, and utterances on the one hand, and between data (a collection of signs relevant to a particular purpose), information, and meaning on the other. The actual distinction drawn between information and meaning has a number of advantages over other characterizations:

1.  It corresponds to everyday usage of the terms—books, timetables, newspapers and computers contain or process information regardless of who does or does not observe them, and yet this information may mean different things to different people.

2.  It also corresponds to usage in other disciplines. For example, the use of the term "meaning" in the social sciences, and the idea of information processing in engineering and computer science.

3.  The particular approach adopted here covers both the semantic and pragmatic characteristics of information. It integrates significant theoretical work by Habermas and Maturana, but still relates back to Shannon's information theory at the empirical level. This spectrum could be completed by an analysis of information at the syntactic level based, perhaps, on the idea of logical information developed by Bar-Hillel and Carnap (1964).

4.  We should note that the view of communication (between people) implied by this model is not the traditional one of information in one person's head being transmitted or pipelined wholesale into someone else's. The sender's intentions (and perhaps unintentional information as well) do become embodied in a set of differences within a message. The message does carry this information to the receiver to the extent that it is transmitted correctly. But the effect that it has will be determined by the cognitive processes of the receiver. Different people will digitalize different meanings from the same message. To the extent that communication does occur effectively depends on the prior structural coupling of the two people.

Second, this formulation avoids the unproductive dichotomies between hard and soft or objective and subjective perspectives within information systems. It provides a place for each—objective information and (inter)-subjective meaning. More importantly, it proposes a mechanism that links the two, namely, the role of the body and nervous system in converting objective, analogue information into intersubjective and then subjective digital meaning, and then back into activity. This explanation focuses attention on the role of the physical body in cognition, a topic that has been neglected but is now receiving much more attention. The nature of "embodied cognition" will be discussed in Section 7.2.

Third, a clear framework is provided for analysing both the subjective and intersubjective dimensions of meaning. Producing and understanding symbols and utterances is only possible through a variety of shared, publicly available backgrounds of practices and meanings. In this sense meaning is intersubjective. Yet information also has its particular importance for an individual leading to subjective meaning and action.

Finally, one of the main conclusions of the analysis presented in this chapter is the distinction between information systems, traditionally conceived, and *meaning systems*. Computers process (transmit and transform) the signs (data) and the information which they carry. In itself, this information is quite meaningless until it connects to the wider meaning systems within which human beings operate. What we call information systems are really only a part of human meaning systems (see Fig. 5.5) in which signs and signals are continually produced and interpreted in an

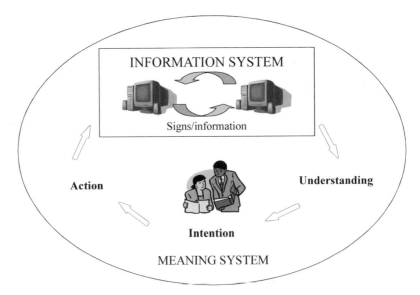

**Figure 5.5. Information Systems as Part of Meaning Systems.**

ongoing process of intersubjective communication. Information systems as a discipline needs to focus attention to the wider field of meaning systems if it is to make an effective contribution to human practice.

## 5.5 Conclusions

This has been a pivotal chapter in moving from the physical world of living systems to the human world of language, communication and meaning. We have considered the question of the nature of information—what is information in an ontological sense? And, how does information differ from *data* on the one side and from *meaning* on the other? The main conclusions of this enquiry are:

- Information exists objectively in the world, independent of human beings, as the propositional content of signs—that is, the state of affairs that must be the case for the sign (or, more generally, event) to have occurred. This means that it is not subjective, i.e., the effect of some sign or message on a receiver, as Checkland suggests.

- Information can be accessed or "picked up" by humans, and other organisms with a nervous system able to interact with relations, and used in a way that benefits the continuation of autopoiesis. This can only occur to the extent that the organism is structurally coupled to its environment. Signs, and the information they carry, are not *of themselves* instructive—they can only trigger or select particular changes of state in a structure determined manner.

- The information carried by signs is always inevitably converted into meaning by the receiver, and we humans live only in a world of meaning—information itself is untouchable for the instant we begin to process it we inevitably convert it into meaning. One implication of this is that whilst information systems can store, transmit and process information, people can only deal with the meaning generated from this information, and as we have seen, meaning is subjective, or perhaps intersubjective.

- This process of conversion can be seen as is a digitalisation of the analogue largely carried out unconsciously by the body. This leads to seeing that most cognition is actually embodied, a view that goes against the Cartesian split between mind and body.

- In moving from information carried by physical events and signs to human language and communication we bring in extra dimensions of truth, truthfulness and rightness which can be addressed through Habermas's theory of communicative action.

In future chapters we will look at: the relation between information, meaning and knowledge; the process of embodied cognition; networks of communication; and wider systems of social interaction.

# Chapter 6: Knowledge and Truth

## 6.1 Introduction

From the theory of information and meaning developed in the previous chapter we can move on to look at the relation with knowledge and thereby truth. Dretske certainly envisages this connection, titling his book "Knowledge and the Flow of Information" as we will discuss shortly.

Within information systems it is conventional (Boisot 1995; Davenport and Prusak 1998; Bell 1999; Freeman 2001) to draw up a ladder from *data* to *information* to *knowledge*, what Tuomi (1999) calls the knowledge hierarchy, and this is mirrored in the move from *information* management to *knowledge* management so pronounced in recent years. For Davenport and Prusak (1998) data are discrete facts about the world which in themselves are meaningless; information is data that has been processed or interpreted within a particular context to inform or reduce uncertainty; while knowledge is information that is even more valuable because of the addition of insight, experience, context or interpretation (Grover and Davenport 2001). Others who use the same basic model define knowledge in different ways. For example, knowledge is that which enables us to assign meaning to data (van der Spek and Spijkervet 1997); knowledge consists of truths, beliefs, concepts, judgements and expectations (Wiig 1993); or knowledge is tested, validated and codified information (Earl 1994).

Tuomi (1999) actually argues the opposite case for a reversed hierarchy, namely that knowledge precedes information which in turn precedes data. On this view, knowledge becomes articulated within a verbal and textual context to form an information structure. This may be embodied as a document, a diagram or a data structure or information system. Once this has become totally defined the "meaning" of the information is essentially fixed and this allows it to be populated or instantiated with items of data which would, by themselves, have no meaning at all. Put the other way round, data cannot exist without a pre-defined semantic and syntactic structure, which is information; and information is the articulation or explication of knowledge.

Other authors have developed more complex categorisations of knowledge itself. Miller et al (1997) concentrate on what the knowledge is about and specify know-what, know-why, know-how, know-who, and experiential knowledge which can involve any of the others. Blackler (1995), drawing on Collins (1993), focuses on where the knowledge is situated and distinguishes between knowledge that is embrained (cognitive), embodied (perceptual), encultured (social), embedded (systematised), and encoded (formal or symbolic). Other classifications have been suggested by, for example, Winter (1987), Fleck (1997) and Benson and Stauding (2001).

However, as has been pointed out by many commentators (Swan and Scarbrough 2001), the nature of knowledge itself is highly debatable and several authors are critical of the whole emphasis on knowledge as some objective, commodifiable entity. Alvesson and Karreman (2001, p. 995) argue that knowledge "is an ambiguous, unspecific and dynamic phenomenon, intrinsically related to meaning, understanding and process and therefore difficult to manage." Marshall and Sapsed (Marshall and Sapsed 2000, p. 12) emphasise the "importance of considering knowledge not simply as a stable and unproblematic object that can be effectively decontextualised and freely circulated, but as a complex, dynamic, and situated series of processes." They go on to argue that to know is essentially active—to be able to act effectively within a social situation. In practice, however, the overwhelming approach is to take a resolutely functionalist reading of knowledge as Schultze's and Leidner's (2002) research showed. They classified research articles on knowledge management between 1990 and 2000 into one of Deetz's four discourses of management—normative (functionalist), interpretive, dialogic (postmodern) or critical. Of the 75 papers, 71% were classified as normative with a further 25% being interpretive.

In this chapter I will argue that knowledge is certainly a multi-faceted phenomenon and that no simple move to knowledge management systems will be effective or indeed possible. And, I will present my own characterisation that tries to capture the rich complexity of the many different forms of knowledge. Going beyond that, I shall consider one very important aspect of knowledge that seems generally to be ignored by writers on knowledge management, whether they treat it positively or negatively, and that is the question of *truth*. One of the most fundamental questions in philosophy, at least since the Greeks, is how to distinguish knowledge from mere opinion. We may all believe certain states of affairs to be the case, or that we know how to do certain things, but ultimately in order to be *knowledge* these beliefs must be testable or able to be validated in some way, that is, there must be grounds for them to be considered to be *true*.

## 6.2 Forms of Knowledge

The first thing to be said is that, in everyday speech, the word "knowledge," or more actively "to know," are used in a multiplicity of ways: "I know it's raining"; "I know her well"; "I know how to ride a bike"; "I know right from wrong"; I know I left my key there"; "I know the feeling"; I know what black holes are"; "I know what the Marketing Department is like"; I know how the system works; "I know linear algebra." There is unlikely to be a single, uni-dimensional theory that could do justice to all these different semantics, but we can at least present a degree of classification.

Generally I will be talking about knowledge in the subjective sense, that is, in terms of an individual and what they know. Knowledge also exists in an objective sense as embodied in books, films, organisational practices and procedures, the internet etc. (World 3 in Popper's sense (Popper 1972)) but this ultimately depends on the knowledge of the individuals and groups who generate it and then access it. The biggest library in the world "knows" nothing even if it contains all knowledge. Polanyi (1958) argues that all knowledge has a personal dimension; that all knowing is personal knowing.

Bhaskar (1993, p. 232) recognises that knowledge needs to be seen as polyvalent rather than uni-dimensional. He highlights some distinctions that need to be made although he does not develop these in any detail. These are: ordinary vs. scientific; social science vs. natural science; know how, know that, know of; tacit vs. explicit; practical vs. discursive; and competence vs. performance.

There are some dimensions that all usages of "to know" have in common. First, any form of knowledge must be knowledge *of something*. There must always be an *object of knowledge* although by no means necessarily a material or physical object. In the above examples, such objects include states of affairs, people, skills, values, feelings and emotions, social practices, organisations and complex physical entities. Nevertheless there must be some object of knowledge and this connects immediately with critical realism. Knowledge itself, especially as it is an individual person's knowledge, is always in the transitive dimension but the objects of knowledge, even where they are concepts or ideas, are intransitive—objects available for investigation or debate (see Section 2.4.2).

Second, there must always be a source of knowledge—knowledge must come from somewhere, generally some aspect of a person's experience. Some possible sources of knowledge are: direct perception, a message or communication, learning as in a language, practice as in a skill, simple experience over time. It is here that the most direct connections with information and meaning come—information can be a source of knowledge, and existing knowledge shapes the information that is available from a source.

Related to this is the third dimension—the way the knowledge is stored or represented, particularly in terms of the degree of tacitness/explicitness. Some knowledge will be entirely conscious and explicit—we know we know it and can express it clearly. Some knowledge will have a degree of tacitness (Polanyi 1958)— we have the knowledge but are not necessarily fully conscious of it, or fully able to articulate it. For instance, we can speak a language without knowing the rules that govern it; or we can use a carpenter's plane and know when the blade needs changing. Finally, much of our knowledge, especially at a perceptual/motor level but also at higher levels as well (Mingers 2001b), is *embodied* at a pre-conscious level. It governs or shapes what we can be conscious of. This is discussed further with regard to the philosophy of Merleau-Ponty in Section 7.2.

Fourth, and most importantly, they differ in the *nature* or *form* of knowledge involved. It seems possible to identify at least four substantively different types of knowledge that cover the range of common uses of the term. I shall call these: propositional, experiential, performative and epistemological.

One very important facet of knowledge is its *truth*. This is supposedly what distinguishes knowledge from simply belief or opinion. However, the nature of truth is a very complex question and differs between different forms of knowledge so I shall leave this discussion until after I have considered the different types of knowledge.

## 6.2.1 Propositional Knowledge

This form of knowledge is our everyday, commonsense, relatively direct awareness of the world around us. To know in this sense is to know *that*—to be aware of or to be cognisant of states of affairs. It is to know that it is raining, that there is someone at the door, that there is a train at 12.15, that there are 35 widgets in stock, or that the petrol tank is half full. I call it propositional knowledge, in comparison with the other forms, because it is generally explicit and conscious, and can be represented in the form of propositional statements "I know that x is or will be the case."

We gain propositional knowledge from several sources. This first is our direct perception of the world, through any of the senses. In philosophy this kind of direct knowledge of things is called *de re* as opposed to that which we are told about—*de dicto*. In fact, Dretske, whose work we drew on earlier, actually restricts his theory of knowledge to only this kind of direct perceptual knowledge generated by the receipt of signs carrying information. Although this knowledge can be expressed propositionally, much of it is actually generated by the body and nervous system as embodied cognition. This discussion was already begun in Section 5.4.2 where we showed how the translation of information into meaning was a process of digitalizing the analogue carried out largely unconsciously by the body and will be developed in more detail in Section 7.2.

But I shall include more generally knowledge of states of affairs that we are told about through a linguistic (or indeed non-verbal) communication, and knowledge we get through books, papers, timetables and so on. Such knowledge is generally objective in the sense that the object of knowledge is independent of the particular person involved and could be verified by others.

## 6.2.2 Experiential Knowledge

We talk about knowing in this sense when we are referring to our own individual previous experience, particularly of people, places, events or feelings. To know in this sense is to be acquainted with or to be familiar with. Thus, I know Mary Scott, I know Birmingham, I know "that feeling," I don't know your school, or I know how bad toothache can be.

Knowing in this sense is a statement about the experience that someone has had, or not had, in the past. The depth of knowledge concerned is very variable—in saying "I know Mary Scott" I might just mean I know who she is, or I might mean that I know her very well. This form of knowledge is not primarily propositional. We can always make a propositional statement about it—"It is true that I know Mary Scott" but this is a second level statement the object of which is our first level experiential knowledge. We do not say "I know that Mary Scott."

Knowledge in this sense can be much richer and deeper than simple propositional knowledge. To know someone is not simply to know that they exist, it is to have a complex set of understandings, experiences, feeling and beliefs about that person. Much of this may be tacit and difficult to express explicitly. It is also deeply personal or subjective since my experience of a person or place may be very different from someone else's.

### 6.2.3 Performative Knowledge

Performative knowledge involves having some skill or competence in order to be able to do something—it is to know *how* rather than to know or to know that (Polanyi 1958; Ryle 1963). I include in this category much more than simple physical skills. So, we can talk of knowing how to ride a bike; knowing how to play the piano; knowing how to speak a language; knowing how to "play the game" as in office politics or a sport; knowing how to parent; or knowing how to cook.

What distinguishes this type of knowledge is that it goes beyond simple experience of something to involve particular skills and abilities that have to be learnt over a period of time. It generally involves explicit training in order to develop the necessary skills. I call it performative because it usually involves some kind of physical motor skills, some kind of performance—it goes beyond knowledge in a purely conceptual sense. For example, one could know plenty of the theory of music without being able to play the piano, and in its turn playing the piano does not mean that you can play the violin. Each skill has to be learnt over time and through practice—it is inscriptive rather than intellective (Hayles 1992).

This in turn means that performative knowledge is inherently embodied (Varela 1991)—that is it exists as dispositions or connective states of the body and nervous system itself and may well be pre-conscious (see Section 7.2). Even higher level skills such as language (Merleau-Ponty 1962; Merleau-Ponty 1969; Lakoff and Johnson 1987) or cognitive/mathematical activities such as navigation (Hutchins 1995) have significant bodily aspects. I once observed, at an airport, an English girl talking to her English friend. Their conversation was typically quiet and low-key. She then struck up a conversation with an Italian woman and it turned out she was herself half-Italian and could speak Italian. Her whole manner and disposition changed instantly becoming louder, more emotional, and much more animated as she unconsciously switched from *being* English to *being* Italian. This all ties in very strongly with Maturana's ideas of languaging as a braiding of language, body and emotion (Section 3.5.4); and of knowledge being effective action (Section 3.5.1).

Generally experiential knowledge will be evaluated in terms of practical success or failure rather than truth. Can one actually ride the bike; play the piano or converse in Italian? Although of course there will be degrees of ability in many of these activities. Dreyfus (1992) presents a useful analysis from a phenomenological viewpoint of the development of skills from novice to expert.

### 6.2.4 Epistemological Knowledge

By epistemological knowledge I am signalling a move away from the everyday *knowing that* things are the case towards deeper understandings of *why* things are as they are. It is to know *why*, to be knowledgeable about, to know the truth of, to be certain of, or to understand. It can be seen as related to or a development of propositional knowledge and I would include within this category what we call scientific knowledge—very much the subject of critical realism. I have called it epistemological knowledge to indicate that it is the most self-conscious about its validity and, more than the other forms of knowledge, is centrally characterised by its concern for truth.

This form of knowledge goes beneath the surface of what appears to be the case, the domain of the empirical, to be able to account for the empirical in terms of underlying reasons or causes. I would not want this to be seen in terms of some simple-minded, linear model of cause and effect. As we saw in Chapter 1, what actually occurs is often the unintended and perhaps unexpected result of the complex interactions of a variety of generative mechanisms. It is also useful to draw on Aristotle's Four Causes (*Physics* II, 3) or ways of explaining why things are as they are. The formal cause or underlying nature of something—what is it to be an x? The material cause or structure of something—what is x made of? The final cause or purpose of something—what is x for? And the efficient cause or causal grounds for something—what has generated x. Examples here are: to know how a diesel engine works, to know why inflation is falling, to know the difference between right and wrong, or to know "What Freud Really Said" to quote a well-known book.

This type of knowledge is in some ways the obverse of performative knowledge as it is almost entirely explicit and discursive and is judged in terms of its correctness rather than its success. It can be knowledge of an everyday kind—knowing how something works, but in the main it refers to scholarly knowledge that is generated according to well-defined procedures or methodologies. However, I do not only include knowledge of material things. Of equal importance (Habermas 1984; Habermas 1990b) is knowledge of the social world and the personal world, both valid interpretations of others and undistorted understanding of one's self (Sayer 2000).

## 6.3 Truth

Continually underlying this discussion of knowledge has been the implicit question of the relation between knowledge and truth. One of the most traditional debates in philosophy has been that of epistemology—that is the study of knowledge (*episteme*) as opposed to mere belief or opinion (*doxa*). When are we entitled to say I know something to be the case rather than merely I believe it to be so? Note that most truth theories concern the truth of propositions, and so only really apply to propositional and epistemological knowledge in our terms.

The most common view, in Western philosophy anyway, is that knowledge is *true, justified, belief (TJB)*. This stems from Plato's (2004) *Theaetetus* where Socrates argues that

"When, therefore, any one forms the true opinion of anything without rational explanation, you may say that his mind is truly exercised, but has no knowledge; for he who cannot give and receive a reason for a thing, has no knowledge of that thing; but when he adds rational explanation, then, he is perfected in knowledge"

Although going on to point out the self-referential difficulty of "knowing" what is a rational explanation. These three conditions have been taken to be both necessary and sufficient for a proposition to count as knowledge. In other words, to validly assert "I know that p ..." implies:

- You must sincerely believe that p is the case.

- You must have justifiable grounds or evidence for p.

- p must, indeed, be true.

Although this sounds clear, there are in fact many problems with each condition as well as their conjunction. For instance, there is much debate about what would constitute proper justification for such a belief—empirical evidence, rational argument, personal experience, perception or what? How in any case can we determine if something is actually true? There are a whole range of theories of truth—correspondence, confirmation, coherence or consensus, not to mention sceptics, e.g., (Rorty 1989), who would deny the possibility of truth in the first place. Indeed we might say that the question of truth is actually the same question as that of knowledge so defining knowledge in terms of truth makes little progress.

There is also the Gettier problem which provides cases where each of the conditions holds but we would still not wish to call it knowledge (Gettier 1963). For example, suppose you walk in to a room and think you see your friend John. You believe it to be John; you have grounds for believing it (he looks like John); but suppose you are mistaken and it is actually John's twin brother Mark. It would appear that the third condition is not met and you do not therefore "know" that John is in the room even though you believe it to be the case. Suppose however that John *is* actually in the room but hidden round the corner so you do not see him. Now the third condition becomes true, even though you are not aware of it, and so you are entitled to say you know, even though you are actually mistaken! One way out of this problem is provided by Dretske's theory as will be shown below.

## 6.3.1 General Theories of Truth

I shall briefly summarise the main philosophical theories of truth

- Correspondence theories (Russell 1912; Tarski 1944; Popper 1959; Wittgenstein 1974) are the main and most obvious view of truth. They hold that truth (and falsity) is applied to propositions depending on whether the proposition corresponds to the way the world is. It thus applies to the relationship between a proposition and the states of affairs it describes. Problems with this view are: i) in what sense can a linguistic statement be said to correspond to something quite different—an occurrence in the world? ii) We cannot directly access the external world so we are only ever comparing experiences and statements with other experiences and statements, so that we can never actually determine if a proposition is, in fact, true. Most other theories stem from the problems in maintaining a correspondence theory.

- Coherence theories (Bradley 1914; Putnam 1981; Quine 1992)] stress the extent to which a proposition is consistent with other beliefs, theories and evidence that we have. The more that it fits in with other well-attested ideas the more we should accept it as true. This approach avoids the need for a direct comparison with "reality." However, it is more concerned with the justification of beliefs rather than their absolute truth. From a Kuhnian perspective, fitting in with the current paradigm does not make the current paradigm correct. Quine held that coherent systems of beliefs were under-determined by empirical data and thus that no theory could ever be verified or falsified.

- Pragmatic theories (Peirce 1878; James 1976; Rorty 1982) hold that truth is best seen in terms of how useful or practical a theory is—that which best solves a problem is the best theory. A version of this is instrumentalism which holds that a theory is simply an instrument for making predictions and has no necessary connection to truth at all. This also leads into consensus theories. An obvious argument against this view is that a true theory is likely to be most useful and powerful[35] and therefore should be an important component of a useful theory.

- Consensus or discursive theories (Habermas 1978) accept that truth is that which results from a process of enquiry resulting in a consensus amongst those most fully informed—in the case of science, scientists. At one level we can see that this must be the case if we accept with critical realism the impossibility of proving correspondence truth. But, today's accepted truth is usually tomorrow's discarded theory and so this does not guarantee truth. See the discussion below about Habermas' more recent views.

- Redundancy and deflationary theories (Ramsey 1927; Frege 1952; Horwich 1991) argue that the whole concept of truth is actually redundant. If we say "it

---

[35] Although post-modernists argue that it is the theory that is deemed most powerful that is accepted as true.

is true that snow is white" we are saying no more than that "snow is white," the two propositions will always have the same truth values and are therefore equivalent. This seems to me largely a linguistic move as it does not touch upon the question of how we might know or believe that a proposition is actually the case.

- Performative theories (Strawson 1950) also deal with the linguistic use of the term. The suggestion here is that by saying "p is true" we are not so much commenting on the truth of the proposition as such but on our willingness or intention of accepting it as true and commending it to someone else. Again, this just seems to ignore large areas of the question of truth.

## 6.3.2 Critical Realism and Truth

Turning now to critical realism, what view of truth does it espouse? The first thing to say is that in general the whole approach is "fallibilist." That is, since it accepts epistemic relativity, the view that all knowledge is ultimately historically and locally situated, it has to accept that theories can never be proved or known certainly to be true. Thus, if provable truth were to be made a necessary criteria for knowledge there could be no knowledge within critical realism.

Bhaskar does briefly discuss the notion of truth and comes up with a multivalent view involving four components or dimensions (Bhaskar 1994, p. 62) that could apply to a judgement about the truth or falsity of something:

A. *Normative-fiduciary:* Truth as being believed by a trustworthy source—"trust me, I believe it, act on it." This sense would typically occur within a communication where the speaker states a proposition and the listener accepts their sincerity.

B. *Adequating:* Based on evidence and justification rather than just belief—"there's sound evidence for this." This goes beyond just the speaker's belief to warranted assertability but can still, of course, be false.

C. *Referential-expressive:* Corresponding to or at least being adequate to some intransitive object of knowledge. Whereas the first two dimensions are clearly in the transitive dimension and strongly tied to language, this aspect moves beyond to posit some sort of relation between language and a referent.

D. *Ontological and alethic:* This final level is the most controversial as it moves truth entirely into the intransitive domain. The truth of things in themselves and their generative causes. No longer tied to language although expressible in language.

Several comments need to be made here. First, the first three are relatively unproblematic and quite similar to the TJB formula although set within a communicative context. "This proposition is believable" (B); "don't just listen to me, there is some evidence for it" (J); and "it fits the facts" (T); none of these in themselves or, indeed, together *guarantees* that it is true.

Second, they are seen by Bhaskar as ordered or progressive. Thus the weakest form of truth is simply to have to believe someone with no further justification. Better, is to have some sort of warranted assertability, some evidence justifying the claim, although what the evidence is and how strong it is are debatable points. Better still, there should be some theory or description or model that can be related to real-world structures. This obviously moves in the direction of some sort of correspondence theory of truth. CR does tend towards this view whilst accepting inevitable limitations on it (Sayer 2000).

Third, the ontological/alethic aspect marks a major shift as it no longer concerns propositions at all. It is not predicated of a proposition but is said to be a characteristic the "real" nature and causes of things in themselves: "truth as *alethic*, i.e., the truth of or reason for things, people and phenomena generally (including in science most importantly causal structures and generative mechanisms), not propositions." (Bhaskar 1994, p. 64).

I find the full implications of this difficult to accept, as does Groff (2000). There does seem to be a need to go beyond the first three dimensions. For instance, the Greeks believed the sun orbited the earth (A); they had reasons to believe this as it obviously appears that way (B); and they even had a theory of rotating concentric spheres which seemed to correspond to the facts and gave a degree of predictive ability(C); however as we know the theory was false. In this sense for a theory to be ultimately true then it must include the actual causal and generative mechanisms that do in fact account for the phenomena in question. Unfortunately, as Bhaskar accepts, this is something we can never finally know; it will always remain putative or hypothetical. But even this is not quite what Bhaskar means by alethic truth since he does not apply it to our theories but to the intransitive world itself.

Groff argues that to do this is both unjustified and unnecessary. In proposing a radical view of truth as an ontological rather than epistemic or relational category, Bhaskar should provide justification and grounds that this move is both feasible and desirable. Yet he does neither, simply leaving it as a statement or definition. Against this view there are several arguments. i) If it does remain absolutely in the intransitive domain then surely it is just redundant. If y exists and x really is the generative cause of y what do we gain by calling this alethic truth? Why not just say x genuinely is the cause of y? ii) If it is to mean anything for us as human beings then surely there must be an implication not only that x causes y but also that we know of this and indeed are 100% certain of it. There are two problems with this—it seems to bring it back at least partly into the transitive domain and hard to distinguish from referential-expressive truth; and in any case it is against CR's fallibilism to believe we can be certain of anything. iii) It gives us no grounds or methods for validating such a belief. iv) Truth generally has an inherent connection to falsity, certainly insofar as it is predicated of propositions. But how could this be applied to alethic truth which by definition only describes causal connections that actually do occur?

### 6.3.3 Habermas's Theory of Truth

We can now move to consider Habermas's theories of knowledge and truth. His early work is known as the theory of knowledge-constitutive interests (KCI) (Habermas 1978). This suggested that humans, as a species, had needs for, or interests in, three particular forms of knowledge. The *technical* interest in moulding nature led to the empirical and physical sciences. For Habermas these were underpinned by a pragmatist philosophy of science (inspired by Peirce) and a consensus theory of truth. The *practical* interest in communication and mutual understanding led to the historical and interpretive sciences underpinned by a hermeneutic criterion of understanding. And the *emancipatory* interest in self-development and authenticity led to critical science which identified repressions and distortions in knowledge and in society. Its criterion of success was the development of insight and self-expression free from constraint.

This theory of transcendental interests was the subject of much criticism (see Mingers (1997b) for a review), and Habermas later transmuted it into the theory of communicative action (TCA) (Habermas 1984; Habermas 1987) as discussed in Section 5.4.3. Utterances and, I would argue, actions as well raise certain validity claims which must, if challenged, be justified. These claims are *comprehensibility*, *truth*, *rightness* and *truthfulness (sincerity)*. This is premised on the argument that utterances stand in relation to three different "worlds"—the objective or material world which consists of all actual or possible states of affairs; the social or normative world which consists of accepted and legitimate norms of behaviour; and the subjective or personal world that consists of individuals' experiences and feelings.

When such a claim is challenged the process of justification must always be discursive or dialogical. That is there should ideally be a process of open debate unfettered by issues of power, resources, access and so on until agreement is reached by the "unforced force of the better argument" (Habermas 1974, p. 240; Habermas 2003, p. 37), what Habermas calls the "ideal speech situation." Thus Habermas held a consensus or discursive view of truth both in the moral or normative domain of what ought we to do, as well as in the material domain of external reality. To say of a proposition "it is true" is the same as saying of an action "it is right," namely *ideal, warranted assertability."*

However, more recently Habermas (2003) has returned to the issue of truth and now rejects his discursive theory for propositions about the material world in favour of one with an irreducible ontological component. In essence, Habermas now maintains that there is a substantive difference between the moral domain of normative validity which can only ever be established through discussion and debate within an ideal speech situation, and the domain of propositional truth where properly arrived at and justified agreement may still be proven wrong by later events.

"I have given up an epistemic {based on reason and discussion—JM} conception of truth and have sought to distinguish more clearly between the truth of a proposition and its rational assertability (even under approximately ideal conditions)." (Habermas 2003, p. 8)

Habermas now accepts the basic realist view that there is a world independent of humans, that we all experience the same world, and that this places constraints upon us, whilst accepting that our access to this world is inevitable conditioned or filtered through our concepts and language. This, of course, leads to the age-old dilemma of trying to discover some external standpoint, outside of language and cognition, from which to judge the truth of one's propositions. The idea of ideal rational discourse is not wholly wrong, but is insufficient for the task (p. 252). Whilst it is necessary that we come to believe or accept the truth of propositions through a thorough process of rational discourse, that we do so is not sufficient to guarantee their truth. Even the most strongly held and well-justified views may turn out to be false.

"These objections have prompted me to revise the discursive conception of rational acceptability by *relating* it to a pragmatically conceived, nonepistemic concept of truth, but without thereby assimilating 'truth' to 'ideal assertability'" (Habermas 2003, p. 38) (original emphasis)

The basic outline of this nonepistemic concept of truth has a very Popperian ring to it. If we begin with our everyday purposeful activities within the lifeworld, we can see that our perceptual and conceptual apparatus unavoidably shapes our access to reality—we never meet it naked—but at the same time our interactions, and particularly our failures, lead us to revise our conceptual structure. In the lifeworld, whilst engaged in action, we presume and do not question the truths of the propositions we operate under. Only when these break down do we move from action to discourse and offer our beliefs up for debate and justification. Once we have become convinced of the truth of a proposition through the process of rational discourse we can then move back and adopt it within the sphere of engaged action. It is important in this process that the reasons we adduce for coming to believe a proposition are actually related to the experiences that have led us to question and debate. Within the true, justified belief definition of knowledge the justification must stem from the actual experiential learning that has occurred rather than being ad hoc or coincidental as in the Gettier example above.

Habermas's move away from an epistemic conception of truth is actually towards an ontological one. When we make what we take to be true assertions we are expressing beliefs that certain states of affairs do actually exist, and these in turn refer to entities or relations that do actually exist and establish a relation between truth and reference; between the truth of statements and aspects of an objective world. This is so even between different linguistic communities (spatial or temporal) where the same referents, the same objects of discourse, may well go under different descriptions. "The experience of 'coping' accounts for two determinations of 'objectivity': the fact that the way the world is is not up to us; and the fact that it is the *same* for all of us" (Habermas 2003, p. 254).

This does not of course guarantee that the "knowledge" is true—Habermas is fallibilist in the same way that Bhaskar is:

"Insofar as knowledge is justified based on a learning process that overcomes previous errors but does not protect from future ones, any current state of knowledge remains relative to the best possible epistemic situation at the time" (Habermas 2003, p. 41).

This is a view that seems not incompatible with Bhaskar's idea of epistemic relativity but not judgemental relativity.

Habermas's move is certainly welcome from a critical realist position. One criticism was always that his view of natural science was overly pragmatic or even instrumental. He tended to call it "empirical-analytic" and this, combined with the consensus theory of truth, lost touch with a realist view of ontology. It also meant that he was essentially anti-naturalist, seeing a radical disjunction between natural science and social science. This shift to some extent addresses both issues: accepting a causally constraining reality as discussed above; and also accepting a "weak naturalism" (Habermas 2003, p. 22) that there is an underlying evolutionary continuity between the objective world and the lifeworld, between nature and culture.

However, I would argue that he does not go far enough in this direction, and more specifically remains too strongly wedded to the idea that validity claims, including those of (nonepistemic) truth, can only be validated linguistically. In the model described above, problems and failures in the world of action lead to a switch to the world of discourse wherein questions of truth are decided through debate. Now whilst I accept that humans do always interact within language that is not to say that all activity is linguistic. Within the realm of epistemological knowledge (i.e., science) experimental activity is clearly the cornerstone of progress; with performative knowledge the measure is successful performance whether it is a motor skill such as riding or a social skill such as conducting a meeting; and with experiential knowledge claims to have had a particular experience can be investigated forensically, i.e., through some form of "detective" work. Thus it is the results of activity and action which will inform the linguistic debates.

## 6.4 Knowledge and Truth

In this section I want to put forward some tentative ideas about how the different forms of knowledge relate to truth.

There is not one form of knowledge but several distinct types with different characteristics. These differ in terms of their nature, their source, their form of representation, and their criteria for validity. Truth as usually understood does not apply equally to all of them. See Table 6.1 for a summary.

## Table 6.1 Forms of Knowledge and Truth

| Type of Knowledge | Object of Knowledge | Source of Knowledge | Form of Representation | Criteria for Validity |
|---|---|---|---|---|
| **Propositional** | States of affairs in the physical and social world.<br><br>*To know that x* | Direct perception, receipt of information, communications, the media | Generally explicit and propositional although some may be tacit | *(Ontological) truth*<br><br>Referential-expressive |
| **Experiential** | People, places, events we know through personal experience.<br><br>*To know x* | Personal experiences | Memories, some aspects of which may be tacit and embodied | *Sincerity*<br><br>Normative-fiduciary<br><br>Adequating |
| **Performative** | Skills, abilities and competences.<br><br>*To know how to do x* | Personal experience, learning, training | Embodied | *Competence, (Epistemic) rightness*<br><br>Alethic |
| **Epistemological** | Reasons for the (non-) occurrence of things and events.<br><br>*To know why x* | Formal methods of discovery, e.g., in science | Explicit, discursive, "objective," open to debate. | *Truth, rightness, sincerity*<br><br>Ontological, alethic |

*Habermas's validity claims*
Bhaskar's four dimensions

Actual human knowledge can never be certain or known to be correct (even an actually true theory could not be proved to be true). From a CR perspective this is because we can never have pure unmediated access to the intransitive domain; from a Habermasian perspective ultimate truth could only emerge from a never-ending, impossibly perfect discourse although now mediated by interactions with a constraining outer world. We therefore need to think of knowledge in terms of degrees of confidence and warrantability or justification rather than pure truth.

We can to some extent ally the different forms of knowledge with the different validity or truth claims. Thus:

a. Performative knowledge can best be judged by its actual success or failure. A claim to be able to do something, whether a physical skill or a social role, can only be vindicated by a performance. In some ways this is actually quite close to Bhaskar's concept of alethic truth which I critiqued above. To demonstrate that one is a pianist by actually performing validates itself without need of propositions or assertions. Even here there are of course

degrees of performance and competence. We can also bring in here
Habermas's validity claim of comprehensibility. Before a speech act or
indeed any other social action can be judged it must be understood, that is, it
must be performed in a competent manner. Habermas draws on Chomsky's
notion of a competent speaker of a language (Habermas 1979, p. 29) but this
can be enlarged to cover all the aspects of performative knowledge.

b.   Experiential knowledge must ultimately come down to a matter of
Habermas's truthfulness or sincerity (normative-fiduciary in Bhaskar's terms)
since it concerns a particular person's experiences or feelings. Of course one
does not just have to accept a person's discursive justification, one might try
to discover or provide some sort of evidence or justification as well which
could include documentary evidence—letters, photos, transcripts, and
certificates etc., or corroboration from other people (adequating).

c.   Propositional knowledge is explicit knowledge concerning the presence or
absence of particular states of affairs—truth for Habermas, referential-
expressive for Bhaskar. Here we can go beyond belief and even justification
towards confirming a relation between the proposition and the intransitive
world to which it refers. Indeed, if we follow Dretske we can see a direct
*causal* relation between information and the knowledge that it generates. The
information carried by the petrol gauge (which must be true to be
information) leads us to know that the tank is nearly empty and so our
knowledge in this case can actually be said to be true justified belief.

Indeed, this is a potential way out of the Gettier problem mentioned in
Section 6.3 and in relation to Habermas's theory. If we take the example of
the twins above, the problem was that whilst it was true that John was in the
room it was not this fact that actually caused it to be believed. Rather it was
the mistaken sighting of Mark. Following our theory of information we can
say that a belief is only justified if it is actually caused by information (which
by our definition must always be true—false information is not information
but misinformation). Thus we are not entitled to claim we *know* John is in the
room, even though he is, since our belief was generated by a
misinterpretation of information from the sight of Mark rather than actual
information from a sight of John.

Even so, we cannot finally prove our knowledge is true for we might be
mistaken either in our interpretation of the sign (the gauge might actually
read half full), or in believing it was (true) information when in fact it wasn't
(the gauge was faulty).

d.   Epistemological knowledge takes us to the realm of science where its primary
characteristic is the huge effort that is put in precisely in trying to ensure that
the knowledge generated is reliable even whilst accepting that we can never
be certain of it. This is ontological (incorporating a causal explanation) truth
for Bhaskar.

## 6.5 Conclusions

The main conclusions of this chapter are:

First, that the knowledge management (KM) literature implicitly assumes that knowledge is an integral, easily definable, commodity that can be extracted, stored and transmitted relatively easily. The literature that does not either presumes it to be some form of processed information; or categorises it on a single dimension such as tacit/explicit; or argues that it is too complex to manage at all. In contrast, this chapter has proposed a polyvalent view of knowledge that recognizes four distinctively different forms of knowledge—propositional, experiential, performative and epistemological—based on several different dimensions. It is argued that this typology does justice to the rich and varied ways in which people may be said "to know" something.

The second is to point out the intimate connection between knowledge and truth which is rarely discussed in the KM literature. Knowledge, to be knowledge rather than simply opinion, raises claims as to its truth or validity. Truth, too, turns out to be a complex concept and within the chapter it has been explored from a critical realist perspective. This grounds its concept of truth in terms of correspondence to an external, independent reality but recognizes that epistemologically knowledge is always provisional and relative. If truth can never be known with certainty then great emphasis must be paid to questions of justification and warrantability. What would lead us to accept a knowledge claim—accepting the trustworthiness of the source; witnessing an event; gathering evidence; or its consistency with our other beliefs?

This leads to the view that the different forms of knowledge imply different forms of truth or, rather, different way of justifying their claim to truth. Propositional knowledge of day-to-day states of affairs can be directly justified in terms of the (true) information that generates it. Performative knowledge can be justified by a successful performance. Experiential knowledge can be justified through the sincerity of the claimant or the discovery of adequate evidence, while epistemological knowledge brings in the full force of science, whether it be natural or social.

I would like to make it clear that although this chapter has concentrated on the subjective aspects of knowledge—the knowing subject, and has primarily developed somewhat static categorisations, I see this as only part of a much broader domain that is both processual and social. In terms of process, events in the world carry information and lead to experiences that generate meaning, ideas and knowledge for individuals. At the same time, as Tuomi (1999) indicated, our knowledge, and more generally our cognitive structure, conditions both how we experience events and what information is available to us from them. This dynamic interactive process involves the material world but even more significantly the social world. As individuals, we exist in multiple social networks or forms of life (Wittgenstein 1958) and much of our everyday knowledge is actually intersubjectively shared knowledge about acting effectively within these social systems.

# Chapter 7: Communication and Social Interaction

## 7.1 Introduction

In Chapter 4 I looked at the idea of organisational closure as a way of discovering the boundaries of systems and presented a typology of different levels of system and the nature of their closure (Table 4.1). This typology stops short of the higher levels of *social* organisation but that will be the subject of the Chapters 7 and 8.

I shall consider the nature of organisational closure in the social domain at four levels—the embodied individual, the social individual, the social group, and the organisation or societal sub-system. In Table 7.1 these are characterised in terms of their components, their structural[36] relations, their mode of organisational closure, and their emergent properties. Three of these are just standard systems concepts—the nature of the system's components, the nature of the relations between components, and the properties that emerge with each new level of system. The fourth mode of organisational closure is an attempt to describe the particular form of relational closure that occurs in each of the system types.

## 7.2 The Enactive Individual—Embodied Cognition

It might be useful at this point to give an overview of the position that I have been developing from critical realism through autopoiesis to information and meaning. This can be illustrated by Figure 7.1

At the philosophical level, critical realism provides a post-empiricist ontology and epistemology. It is accepted that we can have no objective, observer-independent, *access* to reality but against constructivism it is maintained that there is an independent external world constituted by structures or entities with causal powers (the domain of the Real). These are seen as generative mechanisms responsible for the events which actually occur, or which may not occur because of countervailing tendencies (the domain of the Actual). A subset of these events may impinge on and be noticed by humans—the domain of the Empirical. Epistemologically, science proceeds by hypothesising potential generative mechanisms that, if they did exist, would account for our observations and experiences. A distinction is drawn between the *transitive* and *intransitive* dimensions of science. The intransitive (ontological) dimension is the domain of the real objects of scientific knowledge; the transitive (epistemological) dimension is the domain of humanly-constructed cognitive objective of science such as theories, experiments and concepts.

---

[36] "Structure" is used here in its autopoietic sense as a contrast to "organisation."

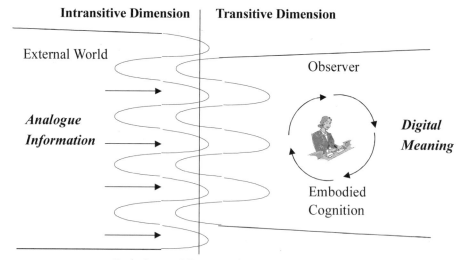

Relations of Structural Coupling

**Figure 7.1. Embodied Cognition.**

At the biological level, autopoiesis provides an explanation of our interactions with the world. As living systems, we have a closed (autopoietic) organisation, but are interactively open to our environment or medium. The nature and limitations of such interactions are determined primarily by our own physical structure (structure-determined) rather than by the environment. External stimuli provoke or trigger a response, but the nature of the response is determined by the structure of the organism at that instant, not by the stimuli. Moreover, it is the structure that determines what can or cannot be a stimulus for the organism—organisms without eyes or the equivalent cannot be triggered by light. Given this under-determination of the organism by its environment, how is it in fact that responses in particular situations are generally appropriate? This is answered through the concept of structural coupling. The maintenance of autopoiesis through recurrent interactions with the environment or other organisms will lead to the generation of mutually adapted structures that can be said to be structurally coupled.

Moving to the level of information and meaning, events or signs in the empirical world, especially symbolic and linguistic ones, carry information about their origins, the causal mechanisms giving rise to them. Such signs will be triggers or perturbations for the nervous systems of organisms or human observers but, as shown above, cannot determine or control the reaction or internal compensation that it provokes. We can see this process as one in which the *information*, carried in analogue form by the sign, it transformed into *meaning*, expressed in digital form for the observer. The information is objective in the sense of being independent of the observer, but the meaning that it generates is (inter-)subjective and observer-dependent. It is precisely this process of the digitalization of the analogue that is the main focus of this section as it is carried out, largely unconsciously, by the body and its nervous system. This *is* embodied cognition.

## Table 7.1. Modes of Social Organisational Closure.

| Level/Name | Type of components | Structural Relations | Mode of Organizational Closure | Emergent Property |
|---|---|---|---|---|
| The Embodied Individual | Body and nervous system; action | Relative neuronal and bodily relations | Enactive/ Embodied cognition | Distinction between information and meaning |
| The Social Individual | Direct interaction between people | Expectations of other's behaviour (structural coupling between individuals) in terms of meaning, emotion and behaviour | Double contingency | Distinction between action and communication |
| Social Networks | Recurrent interaction within groups | Structural coupling to a behavioural domain in terms of meaning, legitimation, power | Conversations as bodihood, language, emotion | Enduring social cultures / practices |
| Social Systems | Networks of social communications | Interaction generates society, society structures interaction. | Establishment of closed communicational domains | Closed networks of communications |

The section will argue for the importance of considering embodied cognition through the work of Merleau-Ponty and Varela. Merleau-Ponty[37] analyses the relationship between the perceiver and the world, which he sees as a reciprocal relationship—the world does not determine our perception, nor does our perception constitute the world.

"… The properties of the object and the intentions of the subject …. are not only intermingled; they constitute a new whole. When the eye and the ear follow an animal in flight, it is impossible to say 'which started first' in the exchange of stimuli and responses. Since all the movements of the organism are always conditioned by external influences, one can, if one wishes, readily treat behaviour as an effect of the milieu. But, in the same way, since all the stimulations that the organism receives have in turn been possible only by its preceding movements which have culminated in exposing the receptor organ to the external influences, one could also say that the behaviour is the first cause of all the stimulations. …. it is the organism itself ….

---

[37] The importance of embodiment and Merleau-Ponty's work from a critical realist perspective has been discussed by Archer (2000).

which chooses the stimuli in the physical world to which it will be sensitive. The environment (Umwelt) emerges from the world through the actualisation or being of the organism—{granted that} it can exist only if it succeeds in finding in the world an adequate environment." (Merleau-Ponty (1963, p.13); quoted in Varela et al (1991 p. 441))

Thus, the first task for Merleau-Ponty was to go below conscious thought to understand perceptual consciousness, to a consciousness that exists within a body living within a world and that presents perceptions that are inherently *meaningful* to us. This was first done in *The Phenomenology of Perception* (Merleau-Ponty 1962) which was a detailed examination of perceptual phenomena, especially of people with neural disorders, and psychological explanations of perception, both what he called empiricist (realist) and intellectualist (idealist). The empiricist simply takes the world as objectively given and sees cognition as a causal reflection of the world. But such explanations cannot account for the meaningful nature of perception; the differing perceptions that can be produced by the same stimulus (e.g., an ambiguous figure); and the impossibility of disentangling various sensory modalities such as movement, vision and touch (Hammond, Howarth et al. 1991; Crossley 1994). Intellectualism recognises that the subject is involved in constituting the experienced world, but it divorces the agent's thought and knowledge from their physical embodiment and is thus unable to account for the body's involvement in behaviour. For Merleau-Ponty, cognition is embedded in our body and our nervous system. It is the body that "knows how to act" and "knows how to perceive" on the basis of pre-formed readinesses and habits developed through its phylogenetic and ontogenetic interactions with the environment—what we would call structural coupling.

Empiricism and intellectualism both make similar mistakes: they create a split between subject and object and then privilege one over the other. Merleau-Ponty wants to portray the mutual interdependence of the two and, ultimately, their emergence from a more fundamental level that brings forth both the *seer* and the *seen*:

"... {w}e must rediscover, as anterior to the ideas of subject and object, the fact of my subjectivity and the nascent object, the primordial layer at which both things and ideas come into being." (Merleau-Ponty 1962, p. 219).

This is what Merleau-Ponty will later characterise as "the flesh" (Merleau-Ponty 1969). We can illustrate the basic model by considering the acquisition of habits and skills, of which perception is one of the most fundamental.

"The analysis of motor habit as an extension of existence leads on, then, to an analysis of perceptual habit as the coming into possession of a world. Conversely, every perceptual habit is still a motor habit and here equally the process of grasping a meaning is performed by the body." (Merleau-Ponty 1962, p. 153).

This shows two key elements of Merleau-Ponty's approach. First, that he always resists dualities such as perceptual/motor or object/subject and instead reveals their inherent mutuality and circularity (Madison 1981). Perception and action are indissolubly linked—perception always involves motor actions, but equally actions always generate new perceptions[38]. In picking up a drink we automatically register its spatial relation to us, its temperature, degree of fullness, smell and so on. Second, it points to our relationship to the world as one of mutual affordance rather than dominance of one over the other. As our bodies acquire skills and habits the world we can experience actually changes, affording us new distinctions and possibilities. As we develop from novices to experts in any activity (Dreyfus 1996) the repertoire of our actions, and corresponding possibilities in the world, grow together. Even the most taken-for-granted objects, such as a chair, only show up as "things for sitting on" in cultures that use them.

Two further aspects of our habituation are that developing a skill does not require explicit knowledge or conscious intention, and that it does not apply only to low-level physical perceptions, but also cultural and linguistic interactions. The extent to which the body "knows" and "acts" without conscious thought, representation, or intention is a major argument against the cognitivist view of cognition.

"A movement is learned when the body has understood it, that is, when it has incorporated it into its "world," and to move one's body is to aim at things through it; it is to allow oneself to respond to their call, which is made upon it independently of any representation … My body has its world, or understands its world, without having to make use of my 'symbolic' or 'objectifying function'." (Merleau-Ponty 1962, pp. 139–140).

"When we are engaged in acting in the world, we neither consciously control our bodies, nor do we 'think of' an intention and then issue an order to the body. Rather, the doing of the action is synonymous with the intention itself. Consciousness is in the first place not a matter of 'I think that' but of 'I can'." (Merleau-Ponty 1962, p. 137).

This clearly links back to the discussion of performative knowledge in Section 6.2.3. Whilst this seems reasonable for low-level perception and bodily functioning, can it be said to apply to higher level cognitive and cultural activities?

"The body is our general medium for having a world. Sometimes it is restricted to the actions necessary for the conservation of life, and accordingly it posits around us a biological world; at other times, elaborating upon these primary actions and moving from their literal to a figurative meaning, it manifests through them a core of new significance: this is true of motor habits such as dancing. Sometimes, finally, the meaning aimed at cannot be achieved by the body's natural means; it must then build

---

[38] Maturana and Varela (1980), Maturana (1983), Maturana (1987b) have an identical analysis at the neurophysiological level showing how each neuron is both an effector and a receiver, and how the nervous system as a whole is *organisationally closed*. There are many other deep isomorphisms between their work and Merleau-Ponty that cannot he explored in detail here.

itself an instrument and it projects thereby around itself a cultural world." (Merleau-Ponty 1962, p. 146).

So, certainly Merleau-Ponty includes cultural rather than purely biological activities insofar as they are primarily physical such as sports or music, but what about more essentially cognitive activities such as chess or speech itself. Surely here there is conscious thought *then* action. Dreyfus (1996) discusses chess and argues that whereas a beginner does learn the moves and basic strategy in a conscious, rule-governed way, an expert will often play moves in response to the general dynamics and pattern of the board rather than based on pure calculation. Similarly, Hutchins (1995) has described in detail how many of the skills of navigation are in fact tacit and embodied rather than representational.

Merleau-Ponty addresses the relationship to consciousness at the end of *Phenomenology of Perception* in terms of mathematical concepts which might be thought to be purely abstract. He argues that even these are only possible through and because of our underlying bodily engagement in the world. The concept of a triangle can be stated abstractly, but can only be grasped, visualised, or understood because we have contact with such things in a physical way:

"... far from its being the case that geometrical thinking transcends perceptual consciousness, it is from the world of perception that I borrow the notion of essence. ... The body ... is the condition of all possibility, not only of the geometrical synthesis, but of all expressive operations and all acquired views which constitute the cultural world" (Merleau-Ponty 1962, p. 388).

This resonates strongly with Lakoff and Johnson's (1987) argument that all language is based on bodily metaphors. This brings us to language itself and the processing of information into meaning and back again. Once again Merleau-Ponty's concern is to deny a split between some pure consciousness 'thinking thoughts' that then get turned into what is said in language. We can consider this in terms both of our use of language and our acquisition of language. When we use language it is the very process of speaking that is our thought. Consciousness only becomes articulate when we speak, whether it is to another or to ourselves.

"There is not *thought* and *language*: upon examination each of the two orders splits in two and puts out a branch into the other.... Expressive operations take place between thinking language and speaking thought; ... It is not because they are parallel that we speak; it is because we speak that they are parallel ... Speaking to others (or to myself), I do not speak *of* my thoughts; *I speak them* and what is between them." (Merleau-Ponty 1964, p. 18, original emphasis).

Equally, speech is essentially connected to the body: it is itself an act of the body; it is always accompanied or entwined with gestures, expressions, and emotional tones; and its fundamental categories spring from spatial and bodily activity. As Maturana says, a conversation is a braiding of language, body and emotion.

The way that we acquire language is also a skilled bodily habit rather than a rational, conscious learning of rules. Indeed, language is one of the best examples of the way we can routinely undertake complex and subtle activities without any explicit understanding of their structures or rules. Implicitly, such structures become embodied in the patterns of relative neuronal activity in the nervous system:

"The word has never been inspected, analysed, known, and constituted, but caught and taken up by a power of speech and, ... by a motor power given to me along with the first experience I have of my body and its perceptual and practical fields. As for the meaning of the word, I learn it as I learn to use a tool, by seeing it used in the context of a certain situation." (Merleau-Ponty 1962, p. 403).

This formulation of words gaining their meaning through use has a very Wittgensteinian flavour, although with more emphasis on the involvement of the body.

I shall draw this brief overview of Merleau-Ponty's thought to a close by considering his later work, especially that of his final, unfinished, book *The Visible and the Invisible* (Merleau-Ponty 1969). This does not mark some major change, but it does try to articulate a more radical vision of the earlier themes such as the circularity of the self and the world, and the relation between objective and subjective. Merleau-Ponty himself recognizes this when he says in a note: "{t}he problems posed in {*Phenomenology of Perception*} are insoluble because I start there from the 'consciousness'—'object' distinction." (Merleau-Ponty 1969, p. 200) thus marking an even more radical undermining of Husserlian consciousness and intentionality. He aims to go beyond (or rather below) the idea of an inevitable duality of consciousness and world to a primordial level *before* they can be differentiated, a pre-discursive and preconscious level out of which they spring[39]. This is a radical reworking of previous themes such as the "*tacit cogito*" that lies behind the spoken cogito: "the presence of oneself to oneself being no less than existence, (that) is anterior to any philosophy" (Merleau-Ponty 1962, p. 404)

Merleau-Ponty uses several terms to try and capture the quality of this almost nameless state such as "the flesh," or "wild Being" or the "abyss of self" or "brute being":

"{as} for the source of thought itself we now know that to find it we must seek beneath statements, .... fundamental thought is bottomless. It is, if you wish, an abyss.... Philosophy does not hold the world supine at its feet. It is not a 'higher point of view' from which one embraces all local perspectives. It seeks contact with brute being ..." (Merleau-Ponty 1964, p. 21–22)

---

[39] There is an interesting similarity here with the work of Spencer-Brown (1972), who also explained his *Laws of Form* as a journey to the primary distinction, the point before language.

Subject and object, consciousness and the world, are no longer to be seen as separate although inextricably related; rather they are both aspects or differentiations of the same underlying whole or Being—*the flesh.* The relationship is more like two sides of a coin or inside and outside of a glove. If we think of the body it is able to perceive, to sense the world. But, for it to be able to perceive, to be affected by events, it must itself be part of the world, it must be *sensible* (i.e., able to be sensed by others). At the same time it is not, for us, simply another object in the world for it is our (own) lived body and so is also sensible *for itself,* i.e., *sentient.* It thus has a dual nature of both seer and seen, toucher and touched. When we touch an object we are also touched by it and, even more reflexively, when we touch ourselves we are both toucher and touched in a dual sense. It is like a measuring instrument that measures its own internal states, or a closed neural network the inputs for which are its own outputs. We can see here the remarkable commonalities with Maturana and Varela's concepts of organisational closure, especially with regard to the closure of the nervous system (see Section 3.5.2). The nervous system is essentially closed, responsive to its own internal states. Yet, at the same time, sensorsy and motor neurons are affected by and affect, external events. They are literally both toucher and touched.

Merleau-Ponty recognizes the ambiguity of such an entity:

"… one can reply that, between the two 'sides' of our body, the body as sensible and the body as sentient …, rather than a spread, there is the abyss that separates the In Itself from the For Itself. It is a problem… to determine how the sensible sentient can also be thought" [Merleau-Ponty, 1969 #760, p. 136.

And, tries to use the concept of the flesh to provide an answer:

"… the seer and the visible reciprocate one another and we no longer know which sees and which is seen. It is this Visibility, this generality of the sensible in itself … that we have previously called flesh…. The flesh is not matter, is not mind, is not substance. To designate it, we should need the old term 'element,' in the sense it was used to speak of water, air, earth, and fire, that is, in the sense of a *general thing*, midway between the spatio-temporal individual and the idea." [Merleau-Ponty, 1969 #760, p. 139, original emphasis].

Merleau-Ponty's philosophy has been used by Varela *et al* (1991) in their theory of *enactive cognition*. The first point is that perception is neither objectivist nor purely constructivist—*pace* Maturana (Varela 1992) p. 254]. Rather, it is co-determined by the linking of the structure of the perceiver and the local situations in which it has to act to maintain itself. This is the basis of enactive cognition which has two aspects: i) that perception consists in perceptually guided actions; and ii) that cognitive structures emerge from the recurrent sensory-motor patterns that enable action to be perceptually guided (Varela 1991).

There can be no fixed point independent of the organism, nor can the organism construct its own closed world. The organism's activity conditions *what can be perceived* in an environment, and these perceptions in turn condition future actions. Varela (1991; 1992) assembles various neurophysiological evidence for this. For instance, in the area of perception, it is clear that colour and smell are by no means simple mappings of external characteristics. Rather, they are co-creations, dependent on the colour and smell 'spaces' constituted by a particular organism's nervous system, and only triggered by external stimulation. Equally, our perception depends for its effectiveness on movement, as can be shown by Held and Hein's (1958) kittens. Two groups of kittens shared the same, artificial, light conditions but one group were allowed to be active while the other group was passively moved around. When released, the active ones were normal while the passive ones acted as if they were blind even though their visual system was unimpaired. The organism must interact with its environment for its self-continuation and so the question becomes, how does it happen that the world it carves out is one which permits its continuance? The answer lies not in the world, but in the relations between the sensory and motor surfaces of the nervous system. How is it that these are such as to enable effective, perceptually-guided action in a perception-dependent world?

This brings us to the second of Varela's points—how action is selected and how the process generates higher cognitive structures. Our behaviour is seen as a constant switching from one task or activity to another according to our readinesses for action. How is it that one is chosen rather than another? This seems to occur as the result of what might be thought of as a competition between different sub-nets or 'agents' in the brain. Brain studies have shown that there are bursts of fast activity followed by more stable patterns as activities stop and new ones start. At each choice-point or breakdown there are many possibilities available, but eventually the historically conditioned structure leads to a selection and a new stability. It is next argued that this dynamic interplay liking sensor and motor activity gives rise to the higher cognitive structures. It does not determine them, but it does both enable and constrain the more conceptual and abstract modes of thought. The key here is the emergence of the symbol or sign, and thus language itself, as a new domain of neuronal activity.

## 7.3 The Social Individual: Action and Communication

We now move up a level in the hierarchy (Table 7.1) from the individual acting and interpreting in the world to consider communication—a reciprocal interaction between two individuals. We shall begin by looking at the work of Luhmann who has developed an extensive social theory based on autopoiesis.

## 7.3.1 Luhmann's Autopoietic Communication

Luhmann (1986; 1995) argues that communication (between at least two people[40]) is the most fundamental *social* category, more so than an individual social action whether communicative or not[41]. This is because first, actions need not be inherently social whereas communications are, although this does verge on the tautological since for Luhmann the social is defined as a system of communications. Second, social actions already presuppose communications in the sense that they rely on or raise the expectation of recognition, understanding, and acceptance by others. In other words, a social action is inevitably already a communication. Yet, third, a communication is more than simply an action. It involves and therefore includes the understanding of another party and so goes beyond the individual action to form the link necessary for social operations. A communicative act by an individual in itself leads to nothing; it is only when it generates some understanding in another that it can trigger a further communication.

It is important to be clear about Luhmann's conception of 'communication' since he uses the term in a very specific sense. He stresses that it is not what we might normally mean by a communicative act such as a statement or utterance made by a particular person. Indeed, it is at a different level to people and their thoughts and actions. For Luhmann, these are not part of the social system at all, but in its environment (he calls them psychic autopoietic systems). He characterises a communication as an event consisting of three indissoluble elements—*information, utterance* and *understanding*—which can enable further communicative operations to occur (Luhmann 1995:137)[42]. Each of these elements is a selection from a range of possibilities. It is the operation of the autopoietic system that defines and makes the selections. Broadly speaking, *information* is what the message is about—it's propositional content; *utterance* is the form in which it is produced together with the intentions of its sender; and *understanding* is the meaning that it generates (which can include misunderstanding) in the receiver. This means that there must be at least two parties involved in the communication and it is this that makes communication the most basic *social* element for Luhmann. All three elements are generated or co-produced together as a unity, and this event allows the possibility of further communications. It is important to stress that all three aspects are distinctions made by the communicative system—the system determines what, for it, is information; how it may be embodied; and how it may be interpreted. This is the closure of social systems.

---

[40] By 'person' Luhmann intends something wider that an actual, individual, human being. The addressors and addressees of communication may themselves be social systems—see Luhmann (1995).

[41] More detailed introductions to Luhmann's work can be found in Mingers (1995), Mingers (2003a).

[42] He sometimes uses the terms 'communication' or 'action' for 'utterance'; and 'comprehension' for 'understanding.'

Of the three, understanding stands in a particular relation to the other two. Understanding draws the distinction between information and utterance (Luhmann 1982a, p. 183) and recognises that they are selections in different dimensions. Even more importantly, it is the understanding of the receiver that ultimately determines the nature of the communication. Only when a further communication is generated (or perhaps not generated) 'in reply' does the nature of the initial communication become established. The question may have been interpreted as a command; the joke as a rebuffal. Information is the 'what' of the communication—it is produced by the system out of the perturbations the system undergoes, and the system determines whether it originates or refers outside the system to the environment. Information, following Bateson, is the "difference that makes a difference," it is that which actually triggers a selection, either in the sender or the receiver (Luhmann 1995, p. 67).

The utterance is the 'why now,' the 'how' and the 'who' of the communication and so is inevitably auto-referential. Again, these distinctions are made by the communication itself which is *attributed to* an agent rather than being the conscious production of an agent. It is this distinction between information and utterance, which allows for a degree of arbitrariness between the two, which provides the possibility of further autopoietic production for without it understanding would simply be perception rather than communication. This provides a model of the dynamism of communication both at the level of the individual interaction and moving up to the level of the social system.

Communication is not, however, the simple sending of a message. The event cannot be said to have occurred until the receiver has understood something, even if not what was intended. Indeed, the very nature of the communication remains undefined until it has been interpreted by the other. Nor can communication be understood as the *transmission* of some *thing* (information) from inside one person's head to inside another's. The utterance is a selection, a skilled performance chosen to provoke or trigger a reaction in the receiver. But it can never *determine* what the reaction will be for this too is a complex selection based on the receiver's own cognitive state.

The communicative event allows the possibility of further communications. This happens through a fourth selection, made by the receiver, the acceptance or rejection of the communication's meaning (Luhmann 1995: p. 147). This is distinct from understanding. Any communication generates meaning, whether intended or not. The fourth selection is the link to action—does the receiver respond in some way to the communication, perhaps to question or disagree, or does the receiver fail to respond and thereby terminate the communicative sequence?

We can see the relationship of communication to meaning, (Luhmann 1985; Luhmann 1990a) which is a fundamental category in Luhmann's sociology (Luhmann 1990b). The production of communication is precisely a set of selections from the multiple possibilities—distinguishing what is by what it is not. It is these related events and possibilities that constitute the system of meaning. Meaning is the openness of all possibilities: all the distinctions, relations and denials that could be generated provide an ongoing underpinning that connects a particular communication both to those that come before and after, and to those others that are or could be occurring. It is that which provides newness and difference between communications. On the other hand, a particular communication closes this off—it fixes one possibility in order that something might actually happen. Autopoietic communication can thus be seen as meaning-processing (Luhmann 1989a: 17), generating distinctions to convert the open field of meaning into the particular information/utterances, which thereby constitute a society.

The closure of this systemic interaction can be seen in terms of what Luhmann (1995, Ch. 4) calls the problem of 'double contingency.' In initiating a communicative interaction, A needs to consider what B's expectations are, but equally B needs to consider what A's expectations are. "I will do what (I think) you expect of me if you do what (you think) I expect of you." Given that each individual is opaque to the other the interaction is under-determined—how is it that communication occurs at all? For Luhmann, it is the resolution of this problem in practice that generates social structure itself. Presupposing at least a minimal interest in the relevance of the other's communication for the self the two self-referential systems will interact based only on what they can observe of the other, and the influence that their actions have.

"In this way an emergent order can arise that is conditioned by the complexity of the systems that make it possible but that does not depend on this complicity's being calculated or controlled. We call this emergent order a social system" (Luhmann 1995, p. 110).

The inherent uncertainty (contingency) in this system becomes stabilised through the generation of shared expectations that in turn constrain or limit future interactions. For Luhmann, social structure is precisely the structure of expectations that develop in response to the double contingency of interaction.

How does this view of information and communication compare with that developed in Chapter 5? Luhmann's formulation is in some ways similar, although with the terms reversed. *Meaning* is something external to the observer that serves a function at two levels. For the individual it frames or orders experience, while for society it makes possible intersubjective interaction and communication. In terms of the typology in Chapter 5 this is similar to what was called the system of *connotation*. Meaning allows the individual to select from the multiplicity of possibilities that which will be noticed or experienced without losing that which was not (see Figure 7.2). The utterance thus gains its meaning through the interaction of the psychic and social systems of meaning (intent and connotation).

What then of information? First it is a selection in the sender, it is that which is to be communicated and which partly selects the form of communication—the utterance. Thus it is the signification of the utterance in Figure 7.2. But it also exists for the receiver. The actual selections made by the receiver depend on their own prior

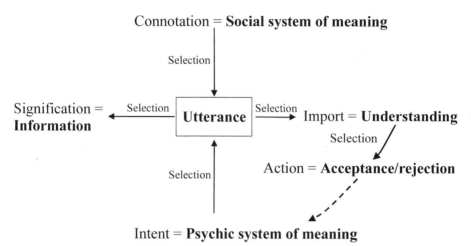

**Figure 7.2. Luhmann's model mapped onto the typology of signs
(Luhmann's concepts in bold).**

experiences, but they are selected from a pre-existing structure of meanings. Once selected (unconsciously, of course), the resulting experience may well change the individual's structure of expectations or readinesses. If it does then this is information for the receiver in Luhmann's theory. Of course, it is not necessarily the same as the information generated by the sender. This is what was termed *import* or meaning in the typology and is therefore subjective—dependent on the receiver. For Luhmann, an utterance received again still has meaning but will no longer have information as the change to the receiver's expectations will have already have happened. For my theory, the utterance will still carry the same information although its meaning for the receiver (import) will be different the second time.

So, in crude terms, for me information is objective, meaning subjective, while for Luhmann it is the other way round. Arguments for preferring the former are given in Mingers (1996b).

## 7.4 The Process of Meaning Generation

We can now pick up the discussion from Chapter 5 concerning the process by which information is converted into meaning. We will use Luhmann's basic model but with the terms information and meaning transposed. That is, for us information is objectively available independent of the receiver and this is then converted into meaning through a process of embodied cognition, the first stage of which is "understanding" as in Luhmann.

We have seen how meaning can be generated from information and leads on to action. The examples (in Section 5.4.3) have shown that the initial perception of a sign, and comprehension of its meaning (connotation) if it is linguistic, quickly brings in context, knowledge, and intention to create the complex, individual meaning (import) for a particular person. There is, here, a continuum of meaning that ranges from initial, public, intersubjective meaning of the utterance to the private, individual, subjective implications for action for the receiver. We can distinguish, analytically, three different levels of meaning within this complex continuum. They apply to both linguistic and non-linguistic signs, although they are more revealing in the linguistic case. They are referred to as 1, 2 and 3. Initially, they shall be explained from the viewpoint of a receiver gaining meaning from signs. It is equally important, however, to look at the *producers* of signs and utterances, and the relations between their meanings and the signs produced (see Figure 7.3). Much of the processing of information into meaning is actually done un- or sub-consciously by the body and the nervous system—a process of embodied cognition as discussed in Section 7.2. The process can also be seen in Luhmann's terms as one of continual (unconscious) selection from a range of choices.

Meaning 1—Understanding

The first level of meaning is that in which the receiver comes to understand the primary meaning of a sign or linguistic message. The observer recognizes the bear print as such (taking the example from Section 5.4.3), or understands the sentence as saying that there is a bear print. This is the level of understanding that can be expected from all competent speakers of a language—all those who share a particular language or symbol system. It corresponds to the semantic content outlined in Chapter 5—that is, the digitalized information without its analogue nesting. The main Habermasian validity claim (see Table 5.1) it involves is that of comprehensibility, although others may be involved.

It is not always easy or simple, however, to gain this understanding. Much work in ethnomethodology (Hassard 1990) and hermeneutics (Bleicher 1980) show how difficult it can be to understand a particular utterance. Often a negotiation or interchange is necessary to establish it, especially when speakers are not straightforward or sincere, and employ irony or sarcasm to negate the surface meaning. If comprehensibility is a problem, it may reflect a lack of adequate structural coupling (Maturana 1978a) between speaker and receiver—the signs do not have common connotations—or it may call into question other validity claims, particularly sincerity.

Meaning 2—Connotation

This level brings in the complex of other meanings, beliefs, and implications that are associated with the primary meaning, for example, the knowledge and experience that the receiver has about bears. This level of meaning will not be primarily individual but will be differentiated between groups of people—for example, bear hunters, zoologists, and picnickers. Such people share forms of life with meanings that are unavailable to outsiders. This level of meaning extends the initial digitalization to include nested consequences known and available to the receiver.

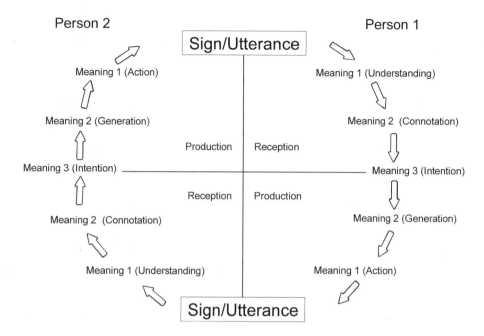

## Figure 7.3. Levels of Meaning.

This level is mainly concerned with the validity claims of truth and rightness. Is the propositional content of the sign actually correct? Does the state of affairs actually exist? Are its assumptions about social rules and roles acceptable? This demonstrates the two-way relationship between information and knowledge as mentioned in Section 6.5.

<u>Meaning 3—Intention</u>

Meaning 3 is, finally, the individual meaning for a particular person and the implications of that meaning for action—what intentions will it lead them to have. Their own personal experiences, feelings and motivations at a particular time will be brought in and result in a particular activity, which may be simply remembering it for future use. This level of meaning is subjective rather than intersubjective.

At this level, sincerity will be a primary validity claim. Is the source truthful? Did the speaker mean what they said? Are they reliable? Questioning these implicit claims may lead to the conclusion that the speaker was acting strategically rather than communicatively and thereby to appropriate action.

We can now move to the production of signs from meaning. Here we are concerned with the obverse of meaning generation—that is, sign production. This is of much greater importance in the indirect symbolic systems such as human language where questions of truth and truthfulness arise. We can trace three similar stages from the intention of the speaker through the actual enactment of the sign or utterance. In terms of the analogue/digital distinction, production is the obverse of digitalization—a case of generating an analogue sign (i.e., an utterance or a gesture) from a digital meaning.

### Meaning 1—Intention

The first stage concerns the intention of the sender or producer of the sign. An intention to communicate might come about de novo or it might be in response to a previous utterance. Questions at this level concern the nature of the intention (for example communicative or strategic action), and its sincerity.

### Meaning 2—Generation

This level is concerned with converting an intention into a specific form that can then be expressed through particular signs or utterances. There are a wide range of possibilities. At one extreme—say the cry of "help" in response to danger—the transition from intention to action is almost instinctive and involves little work. On the other hand, to pick up an earlier example, estimating the cost of closing a mine will involve much research, a number of people, and theories, assumptions, calculations, and procedures. It will be a highly political process.

The generation stage always occurs within the context of particular forms of life and draws on social structures and constraints such as language, practices, skills, resources and power. The main validity claims are rightness, truth, and, in the case of strategic action, effectiveness.

### Meaning 3—Action

Finally, a comprehensible utterance or sign must be generated. This clearly implies competence in the semantic and syntactic rules of the language or sign system if the sign is to be understood. The process produces an analogue sign from a digital meaning, the obverse of digitalization. This is clear in the case of a gesture or picture but is equally so in linguistic interactions through, for example, tone of voice and body posture. Maturana (1988) describes a conversation as a meshing of language, emotion, and body. It is interesting to note that signs produced in a computer lack most of these analogue dimensions and communities of e-mail users often recreate their own stylized forms.

## 7.5 Conclusions

This chapter has marked a significant move from information and knowledge as concepts related to the individual person and their interaction in the world, to the beginnings of the social level. The level at which that which is distinctively human occurs—communication and language. The main conclusions are:

First is the embodied nature of cognition. Against the prevailing Cartesian separation of mind and body, this chapter has argued that most of what we call thought and cognition is inextricably bound to our *embodied* selves. This is a reversal that has also occurred in phenomenology, as we have seen, beginning with the difference between Husserl's (1970) analysis of pure consciousness and Heidegger's (1962) focus on concernful, day-to-day, activity. Our natural attitude, our being-in-the-world, cannot be expressed in, nor does it consist of, conscious beliefs, ideas, rules and intentions; rather, it is a sub- or pre-conscious attitude that has been socialized into us. Being, our (human) way of interpreting and dealing with the world, is inherent in the practices of our culture and society, and is continually enacted by us in an unmindful way.

This trend has been continued by Merleau-Ponty who took phenomenology down to the level of action and perception, the level at which it is the body that knows how to think and how to act. This argument has important consequences for disciplines such as information systems and artificial intelligence for they must move beyond the dualism of mind and body to recognize that human cognition and social action are inherently embodied. The extent to which various kinds of knowledge depend on embodiment has been shown in Chapter 6. The body is a nexus for the interaction of both the individual and society, and action and cognition, and is, therefore, of central importance both for developing more effective information-based systems, and for observing the effects of such systems on people and society.

The second theme has moved from individual cognition to what is arguably the basis of human society, that is communication. The term "communication" here is used in a specific sense. It does not refer to a communicative act by one party alone, but specifically to the reciprocality between parties. One person makes a gesture or speech act but communication can only be said to have occurred when this generates or provokes a response in the other. It is this linkage that makes it a fundamentally social act and which thereby forms the basis of our sociality.

We must also be aware that communication is not to be seen as the transmission of something from inside one person's head to another. Chapter 3 showed us that the nervous system was organisationally closed and that external interactions could only trigger, not determine, internal changes of state. Chapter 5 showed us that information was received and transformed into meaning through a process of embodied cognition dependent very much on the body and nervous system of the receiver. Given this, then we can see that communications could never *determine* their effects on the receiver. Rather they trigger changes or make selections from the various possible states that the receiver is able to enter. That communications *does* occur, in the sense that people *do* come to understand one another and act coherently, reflects their degree of structural coupling within a linguistic domain rather than the transmission of information.

# Chapter 8: Social Systems

## 8.1 Introduction

This chapter will examine different conceptions of how we might theorise the nature of society and social systems (level four in Table 7.1), and the relationship of structure to agency. In fact, both of our foundations—critical realism and autopoiesis—have had much to say about social systems. In terms of critical realism, Bhaskar (1979; 1989) argued first for a modified naturalism in the philosophy of science, i.e., that the basic critical realist approach applied, although in a modified form, to social science as well as to natural science. He went beyond this however to produce his own social theory—the transformational models of social activity (TMSA) (Bhaskar 1994)—which has been developed significantly by sociologists such as Archer (1995; 2000), Sayer (2000) and Danermark *et al* (2002).

From an autopoietic perspective, the original authors (Maturana and Varela) were rather circumspect about its applicability to the social domain, but several others have been keen to claim that social systems were in fact autopoietic (Robb 1991; Robb 1992; Zeleny and Hufford 1992) and, as we saw in Chapter 7, a major sociologist—Luhmann (1995)—adopted autopoiesis as the basis for his social theory. Giddens' structuration theory will also be shown to have significant links to both autopoiesis and the TMSA.

Before looking at social systems and societies as a whole, we will consider the third level of social forms from Table 7.1, that is social networks.

## 8.2 Social Networks

At the third level we can consider patterns of repeated social communication within groups or networks of individuals such that particular cultures or practices emerge that transcend the individuals. Individual members of such groups may join or leave but the social *organisation* (Maturana 1980b) carries on. Examples are families, clubs, email discussion groups, informal subcultures within organisations, communities of practice, and other informal but enduring networks.

For Maturana, such systems are not themselves autopoietic, but constitute the medium in which other autopoietic systems exist and interact in such a way that the interactions become bound up with the continued autopoiesis of the components. In other words, a group of living systems (not necessarily human) take part in an ongoing series of interactions with each other. These coordinations of action will contribute to the continued survival of the individual autopoietic systems. This will generate networks of particular interactions and relations through the structural coupling of the organisms and these networks will become involved in the continued autopoiesis of the organisms. The resulting system, consisting of the living components, their interactions, and the recurrent relations thus generated, is characterised by a particular organisation—the *social organisation*.

The relationship between people and their social networks is a circular one. The participants, as structure-determined entities, will have properties and behaviour determined by their structure. These properties and behaviours realise the particular social systems to which they belong. But this, in turn, selects particular structural states within the participants as in all structural coupling. In other words, a social system inevitably selects or reinforces behaviours which confirm it and de-selects those which deny it. People are members of many different social networks. They may enact them successively, or at the same time. These domains all ultimately intersect in the body and nervous system of the individual and may well involve different and possibly contradictory modes of behaviour. Membership is very important in human social systems. To become a member means taking on the behaviours appropriate to the domain (consensual co-ordinations of action), becoming structurally coupled, and then being accepted as such by other members. Decisions about acceptance and rejection are emotional rather than rational and form an implicit boundary for the system.

The mutually reinforcing nature of social networks means that they are inevitably conservative in the sense that they operate so as to maintain their present organisational relations. Change can only come about through a change in the behaviour of the participants—it cannot be imposed in some sense by the system. Such change can happen, despite the homeostasis of the social system. An individual may enter a social network and not become structurally coupled to it, instead altering the behaviours of the other members by becoming structurally coupled to them in the course of co-ordinations of action that do not confirm the social system. Or, already existing members can reflect upon their experiences in other domains and choose to modify their own behaviours thus realising an altered social network. For humans, interaction is essentially communicational and social systems can therefore be seen as networks of recurring conversations (series of interlocked communications). Conversations are a braiding of language, emotion and bodyhood and social interactions involve all three. This is in fact the mechanism whereby the structural coupling of the social system takes place since linguistic interactions are inevitably physical involving the body and the nervous system.

The rest of this chapter will be to begin with an examination of why autopoiesis might be attractive as a theory of social systems and criticisms of this view. We will then look at specific social theories, those of Luhmann, Bhaskar and Giddens, and try to evaluate the success or otherwise of social autopoiesis.

## 8.3 The Attractions of Social Autopoiesis

The very concept of a self-producing or self-constructing system has interesting and radical implications. Traditionally, systems theory has dealt with open systems that process or transform inputs into outputs. Such a view can be applied to, say, an organisation quite easily—resources are taken in, undergo production processes, and result in products and services. Within sociology, systems theory was initially associated with Parsons (1951) and its main concern was seen as explaining pattern and order within society, rather than more dynamic processes of change and development. As such it was generally condemned for being overly functionalist although there has been a revival in interest in Parsons' work, see for example Habermas (1987: Ch. VII)[43]. Buckley (1967; 1968) tried to address the problem of change with a much more dynamic view of systems. Societies were seen as complex adaptive systems that used internal feedback processes to change their structures to better survive in a turbulent and changing environment.

There are, however, severe problems with this open-systems view. First, it gives primacy to the environment—it is the system that has to adapt itself to the environment. This seems to imply that it is the environment that somehow specifies or determines the structure of a social system. Yet, what exactly is the environment within which a social system, more especially a society, might exist? Is it the physical world, or other societies, or what? More generally, how would one draw a boundary to demarcate off some well-defined social system that then interacts with an equally well-specified environment? Second, what could possibly be the inputs and outputs of such a system? Does it really make sense to conceptualise a society, or part of it such as a family, as a processor of inputs into outputs?

An autopoietic system however is quite different—it does not transform inputs into outputs, instead it transforms itself into itself. The outputs of the system, that which it produces, are its own internal components, and the inputs it uses are again its own components. It is thus in a continual dynamic state of self-production. We reviewed the implications of this in Chapter 3 and we can see several reasons why the theory might be attractive for sociologists:

i)     The distinction between organisation and structure allows for radical change
       and development in a system without loss of its identity. This is very
       common in the social world where we see many groupings—families,
       companies, religions, cultures and societies—that exhibit long-term stability
       and persistence despite enormous changes in their environment, and their
       own internal membership and structure.

ii)    The organisational closure of the system means that we do not have to
       specify external inputs and outputs, nor do we have to see the system as
       functionally dependent on other systems. Its "purpose" is simply its own
       continual self-production.

iii)   The idea of structural determinism places the origin of change and
       development firmly within the system rather than from the environment,

---

[43] Luhmann was actually a student of Parsons and his work can be seen as trying to synthesise the insights of phenomenology and functionalism.

whilst the concept of structural coupling shows how, nevertheless, systems and their environments can mutually shape each other.

iv)    The focus on self-production fits well with the ideas of Giddens (1984) and Bhaskar (1979; 1997) who both emphasise the way in which social structures are continually (re)produced and transformed through the social activities that they govern. It also resonated with Luhmann's (1982a) conception of a society functionally differentiated into subsystems, each essentially closed with respect to the others.

v)    The acceptance of self-reference and the ideas concerning language and observation also fit in well with the linguistic and communicative turn (Habermas 1979; Habermas 1984; Habermas 1987; Luhmann 1989a) in sociology and the greater recognition of the importance of the body (Turner 1984; Featherstone, Turner et al. 1991; Shilling 1993; Synnott 1993; Grosz 1994).

vi)    It resonates well with social constructivist (Gergen 1999) viewpoints— Maturana (1988) emphasises the extent to which we "bring forth" the world we experience through our own linguistic distinctions.

vii)    Within law especially, autopoiesis has the potential to reconcile major problems. For instance, the split between the "pure theory" view of law as autonomous and the sociology of law view that it is societally dependent (Ewald 1987); and the paradoxes generated by the fundamentally self-referential nature of law (Teubner 1990)—"only laws make laws."

We can see that autopoiesis represents a major advance over previous systems theories in its sophistication and its potential for addressing many of the concerns of current social theory. However, there are major difficulties in simply applying the biological theory of autopoiesis to social systems and these will now be outlined.

## 8.3 The Problems of Social Autopoiesis

Whilst the idea of autopoietic organisations and social systems is very attractive there are fundamental difficulties involved in such an application. If the concept is only to be used metaphorically, as Morgan (1986) suggests, to generate interesting insight then no great problems emerge—it is simply a matter of whether or not it is fruitful. To go beyond metaphor, however, and suggest that an organisation or a social system *is* autopoietic raises significant ontological claims that are very difficult to substantiate (Brown 1988; Stokes 1990; Veld, Schaap et al. 1991; Meynen 1992; Kickert 1993). This is already explicitly addressed in autopoiesis at the physical level where a clear distinction is drawn between the observer's descriptions and the operational autopoietic system. The problem is more acute with social systems. We, as observers, are trying to observe systems of which we are only a part, the constitution of which is still the subject of much debate. Without discussing these difficult philosophical problems in general, a number of aspects particular to autopoiesis need to be mentioned.

If it is to be claimed that social systems are autopoietic, then we must examine very carefully the specific definition or criteria for autopoiesis and evaluate the extent to which they can be met by whatever we take to be social systems. There are three essential elements in the definition of autopoiesis:

i)     Fundamentally, autopoiesis is concerned with processes of production—the production of those components which themselves constitute the system. It is therefore essential to identify clearly what are the components of an autopoietic social system, and what are its processes of production.

ii)    The autopoietic organisation is constituted in terms of temporal and spatial relations, and the components involved must create a boundary defining the entity as a unity—that is, a whole interacting with its environment. In the case of social systems, is it possible to identify clear demarcations or boundaries that are constructed and maintained by the system?

iii.)  The concept of the autopoietic organisation specifies nothing beyond processes of self-production. It does not specify particular structural properties or components. It is thus so abstract or general that in principle it should be applicable to systems of any kind. It should not, therefore, need to be modified to deal with social systems. If it is, can we still use the term "autopoietic"?

In applying these ideas strictly there are obvious problems. Is it right to characterise social systems as essentially processes of production and, if it is, what exactly is it that they are producing? If human beings are taken as the components of social systems then it is clear that they are not produced by such systems but by other physical and biological processes. If we do not take humans as components, then what are the components of social systems? The emphasis on physical space and a self-defined boundary consisting of components produced by the system is also problematic. Whilst space is a dimension of social interaction, it does not seem possible to sustain the central idea of a boundary between those components which are both produced by and participate in production, and those which are not. Again, taking people as components, they can choose to belong or not belong to particular groups or networks, and will be members of many at any time. What is it then that could constitute the boundaries of such a systems? What might be its environment? And, how can it be said that such a social system can act as a unity or whole—surely it is only individual people who act?

If it seems difficult to sustain the idea that social systems are autopoietic, at least in strict accordance with the formal definition, is it possible that a more generalised version, such as Varela's (1979) idea of organisational closure that does not specify processes of production, could be fruitfully applied. A more radical approach is to apply autopoiesis not to physical systems (such as groups of people) but to concepts or ideas or rules. Maturana defines a unity as "… an entity, concrete *or conceptual*, defined by an operation of distinction" (Maturana 1975, my emphasis), and thus opens the possibility of a non-physical autopoietic system. Such a system might consist of concepts, or descriptions, or social practices, or rules, or communications which interact and self-produce.

## 8.3.1 An "Ideal-Type": Nomic, a Self-Producing Game

To sharpen the issues about social autopoiesis, this section will introduce an abstract model or ideal-type that, I would argue, encapsulates the requirements for a social embodiment of autopoiesis. This is a very unusual game called 'Nomic' invented by Peter Suber (1990) and based on legal self-reference.

Nomic was created to demonstrate the reflexivity of law—that is, the idea that only laws can create laws. All legal systems have a set of rules (i.e., laws) that govern how the system itself is to be changed, how particular laws can be created, repealed or amended. These can be seen as "meta-laws." However, there must also be provision for these meta-laws to be changed (meta-meta-laws), although generally changing these is harder and more complex than changing ordinary laws. Potentially this leads to an infinite regress but in practice all legal systems actually stop at a certain point, although this may be multi-layered and there may, at the limits, be ambiguities or irresolvable situations. Nomic is based on this context but has only two levels—what are called "mutable" and "immutable" rules, although the immutable rules can, in time, be changed. The point of Nomic, and that which makes it self-producing, is that the object of the game is *nothing other* than making changes to the rules.

The players take turns and, as the rules are initially set up, a turn consists in proposing, discussing, and then voting on a change to the rules. A change could be: (1) the deletion, creating, or amendment of a mutable rule; (2) the deletion, creation, or amendment of an amendment; (3) the transmutation of an immutable rule into a mutable one or vice versa. If the vote is in favour of the change it is adopted henceforth. Thus, by playing the game the rules by which the game is played will change. Initially, the immutable rules govern the main features of the game, for example that a play of the game is a proposed change to the rules, while the mutable ones govern the minor features such as the voting majority. However, since the immutables can themselves be changed, albeit in two stages by first making them mutable, it is possible to change even these rules and hence the entire nature of the game. It would be possible, for example, to begin playing Nomic and end up playing chess!

This fascinating game has many interesting aspects, but I will just bring out the relations with autopoiesis and social systems. First, it appears to qualify as a genuine example of non-physical autopoiesis. Its components are the rules, which are essentially conceptual although they may be embodied in writing, speech, or cognitive activity. These constitute the structure of the system in Maturana's terms. During any particular play of the game this structure may well change drastically even though the identity of the game continues throughout the process. What constitutes the identity of the game, as a game of Nomic, is precisely its organisation as one of self-production—the modification and generation of its own components, i.e., the rules.

Note that under this interpretation the players are *not* a constitutive part of the autopoietic system since they are not produced by the system. It is necessary to bracket the players and focus exclusively on the interaction and evolution of the rules alone. This is in fact quite plausible since the players need not even be humans, they could conceivably be suitably programmed computers. One divergence from the formal definition of autopoiesis is the lack of specific boundary components—there are no rules that can be said to be boundary rules. However, it may be that with self-producing conceptual systems it is only necessary for the system itself to be able to clearly demarcate inside from outside. In this case to be able to distinguish "genuine" rules that apply at a particular time from "false" ones that have not been incorporated correctly, or indeed from everything else, e.g., the players.

Second, it is easy to make parallels with social theorists such as Giddens and Bhaskar who emphasise the duality of social structure. The players participating in a game are an example of Giddens' social *system*, while the rules of the game are equivalent to his social *structure*. The rules both enable and constrain the actions of the players, while the playing of the game directly reproduces and transforms the structure (rules). A question arising here is: could the same be said of any game, or only of a reflexive game like Nomic? Consider chess: while the rules govern the possible moves and actions there is no feedback from moves to rules. Nothing in the play of the game can alter the rules. However, if we consider not the formal rules of chess but the informal knowledge of tactics and strategy then the same situation does seem to apply. For a knowledgeable player moves are governed by informal (as much as formal) rules while the history of past chess games generates the informal knowledge. Thus ordinary games have a degree of self-production within externally fixed constraints but Nomic is radically autonomous by incorporating its constitutive rules within its own domain of possible changes.

## 8.4 Society as a System of Autopoietic Communication

We move now to consider the work of Niklas Luhmann who has, in fact, embraced autopoietic theory whole-heartedly and put it at the centre of his systemic social theory. Luhmann's work up to autopoiesis is well covered in *The Differentiation of Society* (1982a), while his major development of autopoiesis is *Soziale Systeme* (1984; 1995 (translation)). Much of his theoretical writing is extremely abstract, but two translated books apply it to ecological problems (Luhmann 1989a) and the mass media (Luhmann 2000b).

Luhmann's starting point is the idea that modern society has become a functionally differentiated one. Societies are faced by an environment (all that is not society, not just the physical environment) that is inevitably more complex than they are. Over time, societies have responded by becoming increasingly complex themselves, that is increasingly internally differentiated. This has occurred in many different forms (Luhmann 1982a: 232ff), for example segmentation—the generation of many, essentially identical, subsystems such as villages in the middle-ages; or stratification where society split into unequal subsystems forming a hierarchy such as capital and labour. Modern society can be seen as a development from stratified to functional differentiation. Subsystems become established in terms of the particular tasks that they carry out—for example, the economy, politics, law, science, the mass media, education and religion. These subsystems become highly autonomous, distinguishing themselves from their environments self-referentially. Society no longer has a centre or controlling subsystem, but becomes the indeterminate outcome of the interactions between these independent but interdependent domains.

Luhmann brings in autopoiesis by arguing that all these subsystems, and society itself, are autopoietic unities and are thus organisationally closed and self-referring. In doing this, he recognises the problems in defining social autopoiesis, in particular the exact nature of the components and the processes of their production (Luhmann 1986, p. 172). He accepts that social systems do not consist of, or produce, the (physical) people who participate in them. So, in what sense can they be autopoietic? His answer is similar to Varela's in suggesting that there can be closed, self-referential systems that do not have physical production as their mode of operation. These include both social systems and psychic systems (human consciousness). He differs from Varela in that he calls all such systems autopoietic whereas Varela restricts that term to living physical systems.

### 8.4.1 Society as the Production of Communication

So what are the basic elements of social systems that continually produce themselves? Not conscious thoughts, nor behaviour or actions, nor even language, but *communications* or, rather, communicative events.

"Social systems use communications as their particular mode of autopoietic reproduction. Their elements are communications which are recursively produced and reproduced by a network of communications and which cannot exist outside such a network." (Luhmann 1986: 174)

Each subsystem defines itself what is and is not a communication for it, and then consists of networks of particular communications which always refer to previous communications, and lead on to other ones. Society as a whole encompasses all of the communications of its subsystems as well as the more general communications of the lifeworld. Section 7.3.1 has already explained Luhmann's particular view of a communication and how this relates to the theory of information and meaning developed in Chapter 5.

"A social system comes into being whenever an autopoietic connection of communications occurs and distinguishes itself against an environment by restricting the appropriate communications. Accordingly, social systems are not comprised of persons and actions but of communications." (Luhmann 1989b: 145)

Society differentiates itself into subsystems each of which is an autopoietic network of recursive communications. Society itself is also autopoietic consisting of all these communications plus all others not specifically involved in subsystems—the communications of the lifeworld (Luhmann 1989b). As such, it distinguishes itself from its environment—that which is not communication. Thus, not only the physical environment but also people and their consciousnesses are in the social system's environment. Only thoughts can generate thoughts and equally only communications can generate communications. Society is a closed system in that it cannot communicate directly with its environment since the environment, by definition, does not communicate. Events happen in the physical world (e.g., pollution) but this does not affect society until it becomes the subject of a communication—society cannot communicate with but only about its environment according to its capacities for information processing. This does not mean that society is totally isolated—it is like physical autopoiesis, organisationally closed but interactively open. The environment (especially people) can trigger or irritate society and society may then generate a communication but its nature and form will be determined by society or a particular subsystem, not by the environmental disturbance.

In a similar way, the subsystems also distinguish themselves within society and specify their own boundaries. They too form closed networks of communications— each one only being able to process or deal with communications of its own type. Luhmann analyses their workings in terms of codes and programs. He argues (Luhmann 1989b: 36ff) that each subsystem utilises a particular binary code representing the good/bad, positive/negative for that subsystem. For example, the code for the law is legal/illegal, for the economy to pay/not pay, for science truth/falsity, for politics the holding/not holding of office, for the mass media information/non-information. The code provides the basic guidance for a subsystem for without it the self-referential operations would be entirely undetermined. The code itself is just the particular categories, and it therefore requires some means or criteria for assigning events to a category. This is the program—the rules for coding. This separation is one way in which variety can be increased since it allows the program to be changeable even though the code is not. For example, the historical development from natural to positive law involves a shift from defining legality in terms of religious or natural criteria that were unchangeable to criteria that are defined by society and are thus open to change.

For subsystems, the other functional subsystems exist as part of their environment and there are much greater interactions and dependencies between subsystems than between society and its environment. The subsystems have become autonomous and independent, but at the same time more interdependent since they rely on the existence of the other subsystems to carry out particular functions. Interactions between subsystems are reasonably well defined—legal communication can give rise to economic ones which in turn trigger political ones. When a subsystem is triggered by its environment and generates a communication about a particular matter, this is called resonance.

There are several types of (structural) couplings. First, the coupling of communication (i.e., society) to sense-systems, that is, individual consciousnesses, but not, he argues, to the general physical world. Then there is the coupling of subsystems to society itself. Indeed, this coupling is most close, since the subsystems are not something other than society but part of its very constitution. Nevertheless, they do distinguish themselves through their operation. Finally, there is structural coupling between subsystems, and here he details a few specific combinations. The economic and legal subsystems are mainly linked through the law of property and contract, and politics and the legal system by constitutional law. Events in these particular fields generate communications in both the connected subsystems which then become part of the subsystems' autopoietic operation.

We are thus left with a view of society very different from the traditional one. Society is essentially centreless—there is no core or fundamental division driving it, and there is no privileged position from which a rational overall view can be developed. Instead we have self-defined autonomous subsystems in a constant process of renewal and redefinition, locked together in a fragile balancing act, resonating amongst themselves but relatively unresponsive to society's external environment.

## 8.4.2 Luhmann's Autopoiesis—Evaluation

The question now is, to what extent can we accept Luhmann's social theory as genuinely and correctly embodying the underlying theory of autopoiesis as set out above? The conditions to be met were articulated above—to be able to clearly specify the components and concomitant processes of production of those components, and, to be able to identify a clearly demarcated boundary so that the system can be said to act as an organisationally closed unity and to produce itself as a whole.

Certainly Luhmann's work represents a bold attempt to theorise an autopoietic unity in the non-physical domain. It defines the basic components of such a system—in this case communications—and holds consistently to this without confusing domains by, for example, including people within the system. The nature of production is shifted to a production of events rather than of material components. Finally, the circular and self-defining nature of the production network is brought out well, as is the combination of organisational closure and interactive openness. Examining it in more detail, however, shows up several problems.

First, let us consider the notion of components and their production. That the components are events does not seem a particular difficulty—ultimately it is just a matter of time scale. Given long enough, all production processes become events since the produced component will exist and then disintegrate. Equally, with a short enough time horizon all events themselves become processes as we observe their unfolding.

However, I would argue that there is a problem with the notion of production, specifically with the claim that it is communications (rather than people) that produce further communications. Put another way, there is little attempt to show how societal communication, as an independent phenomenal domain, emerges from the interactions of the human beings who ultimately underpin it. Without human activity there would be no communication. Maturana is always careful to show how new domains arise out of the interactions of observers, but with Luhmann the observer is lost completely in favour of the observation. This is an important lacuna with a number of concomitant problems, some of which are also identified by Habermas (1985). How do communications actually occur? It is one thing to say analytically that communications generate communications, but operationally they require people to undertake specific actions and make specific choices. Is not the claim that "communication produces communication" stretching the notion of production too far? One communication may stimulate another but surely it does not produce or generate it. How does this interaction occur? What factors affect the selections that are actually made? In general, what is the relationship between the psychic systems of individual consciousness and the social system of communication?

Luhmann does consider this analytically with his concept of interpenetration. This describes the way in which something can be an element in two systems at the same time. Thus an action (e.g., an utterance) is part of the psychic system of human activity. At the same time it can be used, as an element, within a social system of communication, but it will not be the "same" element in the two systems—it will have different functions. "{I}nterpenetrating systems converge in individual elements—that is, they use the same ones—but they give each of them a different selectivity and connectivity, different pasts and futures" (Luhmann 1995: 215, original emphasis). Whilst this would seem to be true descriptively, it does not seem to provide sufficient explanation of the complex interaction between the two levels.

Luhmann's theory would seem to rely on his concept of meaning as the link between the two. A communication opens up possibilities through its meaning to people whose selections then generate new communications. However, this appears to be a very individualistic analysis. Little attention is paid to the constituting of these subjects as subjects and the major role of language in this. In Maturana's terms, Luhmann ignores the importance of languaging and consensuality which provides an already existing, a priori, structure generating an intersubjective domain of interactions. Such an approach would provide a general bedrock in the lifeworld out of which the particular specialised communicative subsystems can be seen to arise.

Secondly, how does Luhmann's theory deal with the question of boundaries? At first sight it looks promising. In defining components as communications it draws a clear distinction from that which is not communication, e.g., the physical or psychological domains. It then specifies functional subsystems within society as a whole that demarcate themselves by distinguishing their own communications. Whilst this does not actually involve boundary components, it does (to the extent that it is successful) generate a clear cleavage in the communicational space.

The question is whether, empirically, subsystems can be properly described in such a pure fashion. In the economic sphere, for example, it may be that the ultimate operations underlying it are monetary payments, but if we seek to explain particular happenings we immediately find that social, political and legal factors are at work. This is because it is people who make economic decisions—to buy, or sell, or invest, or lend—and people form a nexus between all the different subsystems. Their decisions are affected by their expectations which are conditioned by communications from other domains. Moreover, communications can often be said to belong to more than one domain. For example, signing a loan agreement both generates a transfer of money and establishes legal obligations. Gaining a research grant is both a communication about academic status and a payment. As another example, Luhmann characterises organisations as recursive networks of communications about decisions and only decisions (Luhmann 2000a). Yet, this seems an incredibly reductionist view of the rich complex of social interactions within an organisation (Mingers 2003a).

To summarise, this section has developed the following conclusions concerning the application of autopoiesis to social systems by Luhmann. In terms of components and processes of production, we can take the components of such a system to be communicative events, where communication consists of information, utterance, and understanding. However, there are problems in accepting that communications are produced by other communications alone rather than by people within social interaction. This is part of the problem of the totalising nature of the definition of society as communications and only communication, leaving the mutual interaction between people and society under-theorised.

In terms of organisational closure, the idea that society, and its subsystems, define their own boundaries through communications that do/do not belong to them has some potential but it is difficult to accept empirically that subsystems can be adequately characterised in such a pure and separable manner.

## 8.5 Structuration Theory, Critical Realism and Autopoiesis

Giddens' concept of structuration is one of the main developments in recent social theory and it does have definite resonances with autopoiesis:

Giddens' concern with the continual, recursive, (re)production of social structure through time is clearly linked to the idea of self-producing systems (Mingers 1996a; Mendoza 1997). In places, the idea of circular self-production is very clear[44]:

---

[44] Giddens himself mentions autopoiesis: "The most relevant sources of connection between biological and social theory ... concern recursive or self-reproducing systems. There are two

"By its recursive nature I mean that the structured properties of social activity—via the duality of structure—are constantly recreated out of the very resources which constitute them" (Giddens 1984, p. xxiii)

"Human social activities, like some self-reproducing items in nature, are recursive. That is to say, ... in and through their activities agents reproduce the conditions that make these activities possible." (Giddens 1984, p. 2)

"all social life has a recursive quality to it, derived from the fact that actors reproduce the conditions of their social existence by means of the very activities that—in contexts of time-space—constitute that existence." (Giddens 1987, p. 221)

Both theories (autopoiesis and structuration) emphasise that explanations should be non-functionalist and non-teleological. Both distinguish between that which is observable, having space-time existence, and that which is not but is still implicated in the constitution of a system (*structure/organisation* for Maturana, *system/structure* for Giddens). And both take an essentially relational view of social systems and identify the same three sets of relations: constitution/space, order /time and specification/paradigmatic[45].

At the same time, a related conception of social systems (the transformational model of social activity—TMSA), developed within critical realism, is becoming influential. This was first articulated by Bhaskar (1979) as part of a comprehensive post-positivist, but realist, philosophy of natural and social science, and further developed in later works (Bhaskar 1993; Bhaskar 1994; Archer, Bhaskar et al. 1998; Harvey 2002). At first sight this appears compatible with structuration theory with talk of the duality of structure, of the continual reproduction and transformation of society, and that social structure only exists in and through the activities it governs. However, there has been considerable debate about the degree of similarity as will be discussed below. Even more pertinent, however, is that Bhaskar specifically uses the term "autopoiesis" to describe fundamental aspects of the TMSA although nowhere does he actually reference Maturana and Varela's writing. To give some examples:

In discussing the nature of scientific knowledge, he says:

"These resources comprise the transitive objects of knowledge; their transformation is the transitive process of knowledge-production; and its product, knowledge (of an

---

related types of theory involved here ... {the theory of automata} ... is not of as much interest to the conceptualisation of social reproduction as recent conceptions of cellular self-reproduction (autopoiesis)"... Giddens (1979).

[45] Giddens (1981). To unpack this slightly, these three relations/differences are the *where*, the *when*, and the *what.* Space and time are straightforward and can be seen as syntagmatic dimensions. The third dimension of difference is paradigmatic—that is a specification or selection from a domain of differences. For Giddens, the first two relate to system and the third to structure.

intransitive object or topic) in turn supplies resources for further rounds of enquiry. This imparts to the cognitive process a quasi-autopoietic character, with the production of knowledge accomplished by means of (anterior) knowledges." (Bhaskar 1986, p. 54)

"The quasi-autopoietic conception of scientific activity ... implies that science is a continuous process of production, dependent on the imaginative and disciplined research (productive) and educational (reproductive) transformative activity of (wo)men." (Bhaskar 1986, p. 83)

Here we can clearly see the primary concept of circular processes of self-production. Even more fundamentally, the basic mechanism of societal production is described as autopoietic:

"The activity-dependence of social structures entails its auto-poietic {sic} character, viz. that it is itself a social product, that is to say, that in our substantive motivated productions, we not only produce, but we also reproduce or transform the very conditions of our production. ... Thus we can situate the *auto-poetic, conceptualised* and *geo-historically dependent* character of social structures alongside their *social relation dependence* as four ontological limits on naturalism." (Bhaskar 1993, p. 156, original emphasis)

And finally he characterises emergence itself as being autopoietic:

"In emergence, generally, new beings (entities, structures, totalities, concepts) are generated out of pre-existing material from which they could have been neither induced nor deduced. ... This is matter as creative, as autopoietic." (Bhaskar 1993, p. 49)

Thus there is clear *prima facie* evidence that the theory of autopoiesis has been influential for both Giddens and Bhaskar.

In the next section I will first briefly cover the Giddens/Bhaskar debate and argue that the two are in fact potentially compatible, and then consider the extent to which autopoiesis may be involved in this conceptualisation. Before that it is necessary to mention a fundamental objection to the whole notion of social autopoiesis—that social systems or social structures do not exist in a causally efficacious sense at all.

The basic contours of this debate are as old as sociology itself. They used to be defined in terms of individualism versus collectivism and now tend to be discussed through the agency/structure distinction. Critical realism (strongly) and structuration (less strongly) maintain that social structure(s) exist, and have causal effects, over and above the actions of individual people. Upward conflationists, to use Archer's term (Archer 1995) (downward reductionists as I would call them), deny causal reality to social structure, which they see as simply an effect or epiphenomenon of individual social interaction. This case has been argued strongly in terms of the primacy of hermeneutics by King (1999a; 1999b; 2000) against both Giddens and

Bhaskar, and has been rebutted by Archer (2000). There has been a related debate couched in terms of whether or not social structure can be causally efficacious between Varela and Harré (Varela and Harre 1996; Varela 1999; Varela 2002) and Lewis (2000) and Bhaskar (2002).

I do not wish to enter these debates directly for that would subvert the main purpose of this chapter[46] but it is clear that any attribution of autopoiesis to the social world must presume the existence and efficacy of social structure. To accept the opposite would immediately foreclose the possibility of social autopoiesis. So, for the purposes of this chapter I will simply take as given that the social world is not exhausted by the individual's meanings and actions whilst recognising that this is actually an ongoing debate[47].

## 8.5.1 Giddens and Bhaskar: Similarities

It is inevitable within social science that particular authors will use certain basic terms such as "society," "social structure," or "social system" in different ways. There is then much debate about these terminological differences that may obscure the similarities of the underlying conception or model. Certainly there are differences of substance and emphasis between Bhaskar and Giddens, not least because they approach their common object from different directions—philosophy and sociology respectively, but within the wide realm of social theory as a whole they seem to me to occupy essentially the same niche[48].

Bhaskar's central realist propositions have been explained in Chapter 2. For Bhaskar, society exists as an object in its own right, emergent from but separate to people and their activities, and with its own properties[49]. Society always pre-exists individuals who do not therefore create it but only transform or (re)produce it. Nevertheless, society is *necessary* for social activity and it only *exists* in virtue of that activity.

---

[46] Section 4.6.1 has a related discussion about the ontological reality of systems boundaries.

[47] Very briefly, my argument against the hermeneutic critique is the obvious one that understanding is never transparent to itself either in terms of its grounds or its consequences. With regard to causality, we can accept that people are the only source of intentional, efficient causation but, as with any system (including physical ones such as amoeba) the parts act in a way that generate the emergent properties of the whole but, at the same time, the configuration of the whole shapes the behaviour of the parts. With a more Aristotelian view of causation we can accept that only people act (efficient cause), but that society shapes that action (material and formal cause).

[48] In this, I largely agree with New (1994), but disagree with Wright (1999), who takes criticisms of Giddens largely on trust.

[49] Bhaskar contrasts this with a "dialectical" view of the relationship (as advocated by Berger and Luckmann (1967). *The Social Construction of Reality*), which, he claims, sees people and society as two moments or sides of the same process, rather than as two distinct, but interacting, objects. This is a criticism that has been applied to structuration theory. Archer (1996).

Society therefore conditions social activity and is either maintained or changed as an outcome of that activity (*the duality of structure*). Equally, human action (praxis) is both a conscious production, i.e., intentional bringing about of purposes, and an unconscious (*re*)production of society (*the duality of praxis*).

"At the heart of this idea is the conception of human agency or *praxis* as transformative negation of the given ...; and at the same time as both enabled and constrained by and reproductive or transformative of the very conditions of this praxis, so that these conditions are *activity-dependent* or auto-poietic ..." (Bhaskar 1994: 93, original emphasis)

Society is said to be an "ensemble" of structures, practices and conventions, where structures are relatively enduring generative mechanisms that govern social activities. Being more specific, Bhaskar suggests that there must be a linking mechanism between human action and social structure and that this mediating system consists of *position-practices*, that is combinations of roles that can be filled and practices that are then engaged in. It is important to note that position-practices are relational—they develop to form a system in relation to each other and this is separate from any network of relations between those who happen to occupy them. Whilst emphasising the ontological reality of social structures, Bhaskar recognises that they have significantly different properties from physical objects. In particular:

- Social structures do not *exist* independently of the activities they govern;

- Social structures cannot be *empirically identified* except through activities;

- Social structure is not independent of actors' *conceptions* of their activity;

- Social structures are *relative* to particular times and cultures.

Despite these differences they are still suitable subjects for scientific theorising even if they lead to particular epistemological difficulties (Bhaskar 1979).

Structuration theory also has a core distinction at its heart—that between social *structure* and social *system*. Taking first social structure, this does not describe empirically observable patterns or regularities as in functionalism but underlying sets of rules that generate the observed regularities more akin to structuralism.

"Structure, as recursively organised sets of rules and resources, is out of time and space save in its instantiations and coordination as memory traces, and is marked by an 'absence of the subject.' The social systems in which structure is recursively implicated, on the contrary, comprise the situated activities of human agents, reproduced across time and space." (Giddens 1984, p. 25)

Structure is thus seen as similar to a code or set of rules that governs possible selections of social action. It is constituted as an "absent set of differences" that is not empirically observable as such, but is only exhibited in particular social interactions. Its existence is said to be "virtual." In fact, structure should really be seen as the structuring properties of social systems and these properties can be understood as rules and resources, recursively implicated in the reproduction of social systems. Social systems, by contrast to structure, do exist in time-space, and consist of observable activities and practices. The regularities that we can observe in social systems occur both spatially and over time and this observable patterning and inter-dependence is brought about and sustained through the virtual (unobservable) structure governing their activity.

The relationship between system and structure is provided by the concept of *structuration*, a two-fold process which Giddens sometimes refers to as the duality of structure. First, structure organizes the practices that constitute a social system—actors draw on the structural rules and resources in the production of interaction. But, secondly, it is precisely and only these interactions that reconstitute (and possibly transform) the structure. "The structural properties of social systems are both the medium and the outcome of the practices that constitute those systems" (Giddens 1979, p. 69). This is the central kernel where both the TMSA and structuration appear to be an embodiment of autopoiesis.

## 8.5.2 Giddens and Bhaskar: Differences

In the beginning there appeared to be clear resonances between structuration theory and Bhaskar's early social theory as even Archer (1995, p. 147) accepts[50]. The following could easily be describing structuration theory:

"On this model, unintended consequences and unacknowledged conditions may limit the actors understanding of their social world, while unacknowledged (unconscious) motivation and tacit skills may limit his or her understanding of himself or herself" (Bhaskar 1986: 125)[51]

However, on deeper inspection it became clear that there were in fact substantive differences. Bhaskar wrote:

"This {analytically discrete moments of social interaction} is a feature which, as Margaret Archer has convincingly demonstrated, distinguishes it {TMSA} from structuration, or more generally any 'central conflation' theory" (Bhaskar 1993, p. 160, my insertions).

These differences revolve around the ontological status of social structure in the two theories. For Bhaskar, there is a *dualism* of two distinct entities—people and their social activity on the one hand, and the social structure(s) that emerge from and also

---

[50] Bhaskar relates his work to Giddens, Bhaskar (1979), and Giddens also uses Bhaskar's arguments Giddens (1984).

[51] This is repeated in one of Bhaskar's later discussions of the social Bhaskar (1994).

enable and constrain such activity on the other. Both are equally real. For Giddens, there is a *duality* between observable social systems and their unobservable, virtual structural properties.

Several writers from the critical realist camp have been deeply critical of structuration theory, for instance, Archer (1990; 1995), Layder (1985; 1987; 1989), Craib (1992), Thompson (1989) and Porpora (1989). The fundamental claim, made by each author in different ways, is that Giddens does not give sufficient ontological independence to social *structure* (or system). That he essentially treats agency and structure as though they are inseparable, two sides of the same coin, with centrality being afforded to the encompassing notion of social practices. This means that Giddens remains too much on the subjectivist side of the fence, refusing to accept the leap into an objective, constraining social structure. I accept that there is force to this argument. Giddens adopts a perspective that puts much greater emphasis on the knowledgeable activities of agents and does not recognise a separately existing social structure in the way that Bhaskar does. However, I will argue that the anti-Giddens camp goes too far and erects something of a straw man in their characterisation of Giddens, who would not hold some of the extreme positions that they impose on him. This then allows us to consider a possible synthesis of the two models.

Let's begin with Archer (1995) whose position can be summarised as follows:

"A realist ontology which regards structural and cultural systems as emergent entities is at variance with the Elisionists' {Giddens *et al*} view which holds, (a) that such properties possess a 'virtual existence' only until, (b) they are 'instantiated' by actors, which (c) means these properties are neither fully real nor examinable except in conjunction with the agents who instantiate them" (Archer 1996: 692, my insertion).

This, according to Archer, has several consequences:

- Both elements, agency and structure, are denied autonomy and their own separate properties since both are subsumed under social practices. This has the effect of flattening ontological strata losing both that of social system and that of psychological individual.

- This means that we cannot investigate each as a separate entity, except in the limited sense given by Giddens' methodological bracketing; nor can we consider the ways in which agency and structure, as independent entities, might causally interact with each other.

- The time dimension is lost. Since structure and agency are simply different reflections of the *same process*, they must be simultaneous. We cannot conceptualise how structure at time t conditions activity at t+1 which then transforms or reproduces structure at t+2. Archer suggests that Giddens moves from the obvious "no people: no society" to the questionable "this society; because of these people here present." (Archer 1995, p. 141)

- This also makes it difficult to understand under what conditions social activity will change rather than simply reproduce the pre-existing conditions. This can be put another way in terms of the difference between *social* and *system* integration. For Giddens the distinction is primarily one of scale—face-to-face relations as opposed to relations between collectivities at a distance. Archer argues that there cannot therefore be a disjunction between the two. Whereas a separation of the two would allow different degrees of integration/conflict in the two domains so that, for example, social conflict may or may not result in systems change.

Porpora (1998b) examines four different concepts of social structure—stable patterns of aggregate behaviour (e.g., Homans or Collins); lawlike regularities among social facts (e.g., Durkheim or Blau); systems of relations among social positions (Bhaskar); and virtual rules and resources (Giddens). He argues that Giddens is a realist in accepting that structural rules and resources do causally affect social activity, but is not sufficient of a realist to also grant causal efficacy to the "objective" social relations to be found in Giddens' social system. Rules and resources are important, but are ultimately subjective (or intersubjective) in necessitating some degree of at least tacit understanding and knowledge on behalf of actors. In contrast, Porpora suggests that of more fundamental importance are the material, objective social relationships such as the distribution of income, the division of labour, and job opportunities that act as external constraints on individuals. The heart of the disagreement is that "Giddens gives analytical priority to rules and in fact denies that the relationships of a social system have any causal properties independent of the rule-following activities of human actors." (Porpora 1998b, 350, my emphasis). Whereas Porpora maintains that social relations do constrain in a way that is independent of the actor's knowledge of them.

Layder's (1985; 1987; 1989) critique seems to rest on a rather partial reading of Giddens' work. For instance, one of his main arguments is that the idea that social system and social structure must always be instantiated through social activity loses an essential distinction between such activity and pre- and post-existing system/structure. He quotes (Layder 1987, p. 34) Giddens' "social systems only exist in so far as they are continually created and recreated in every encounter as the active accomplishment of subjects" in support of his view. But Giddens is saying something rather different: not that social systems only exist at all in the moments of their instantiation but that they will no longer exist if they are not continually re-enacted. He is simply making the point that particular practices will only remain in existence if they are, in fact, practiced. Indeed, the use of the term "recreated" in the quote clearly acknowledges the fact that there is something already existing, which is recreated or reconstructed through social activity.

A similar misinterpretation occurs in Layder's discussion of the extent to which social structure can constrain action. He construes Giddens as saying that constraints can only be identified with that which is internal to a particular episode of social interaction and indeed ultimately with the psychological motivations of the actors involved. What Giddens actually says, as quoted by Layder (1987, p. 39), is

"Structural constraints do not operate independently of the motives and reasons that agents have for what they do. ... The only moving objects in human social relations are individual agents who employ resources to make things happen, intentionally or otherwise." Layder then makes the illicit equivalence that "The word 'operate' doubles for the word 'exist'" (Layder 1987, p. 40).

Again, I would argue that Giddens is saying something significantly different and that *operate* does not in fact equal *exist*. Giddens' point, and it is a very fundamental one that I believe is accepted by Bhaskar and Archer, is that only people can actually undertake social activities. Systems, structures, practices or whatever do not, *of themselves*, act—only people can do that. So structural constraints can only have effects (operate) by affecting people, and in particular by shaping their motives and reasons for action. This does not mean that such constraints do not *exist* independently of and prior to the activities of particular individuals. It simply means that the powers of the constraint are not actualised (to use a Bhaskarian term) except through people. Nor does it mean that the actors involved have full transparency over the process. Giddens accepts that there are both unacknowledged conditions of action and unknown consequences of action. So it is quite possible for constraints to determine aspects of the contexts within which people find themselves and thereby shape the choices made without those involved being fully aware of it.

With regard to the fundamental question of ontology, it seems to me that there is a substantive difference between Bhaskar and Archer's dualist model and Giddens' dualism at least in so far as social *structure* is conceptualised, although both see social structure as only *existing* and *observable* through social activity, and inevitably dependent (to some extent) on actors' knowledge of what they are doing. But I do not accept Archer's (and Bryant's (1995, p. 97)) view that Giddens cannot therefore be seen as a realist because of the *virtual* nature of his concept of structure. I would argue that this is a mistaken interpretation of the term "virtual." Giddens uses this in contrast to those things that have space-time presence—that is that happen at particular times and places. Virtual rules and resources do exist; they are *real*; they are as Giddens says "generative"—they do have causal effects; but they endure and underlie the events that they enable. Indeed, the distinction is very close to that which Bhaskar makes between the domain of the *real* (enduring mechanisms) and the domain of the *actual* (particular events). Thus it is not virtual as opposed to real, but virtual as opposed to actual.

I do, however, think there is a substantive difference in the way Giddens and Bhaskar conceptualise the term "structure" and this is the basis of much of the problem. Bhaskar takes a traditional view that out of the social activities of people a new entity emerges—*society*. This is said to consist of various *structures*—that is relational systems of position-practices that govern, and are reproduced/transformed by, social activity. This is essentially the same as Giddens' social system[52],

---

[52] Although Giddens might disagree on the extent to which "society" can be clearly identified—see later.

consisting of practices which, when long-standing and widely spread, are termed institutions, a term also used by Bhaskar. What Giddens then does is to highlight a particular aspect of the mechanism whereby social systems govern activity and the activity reproduces the system—that is rules and resources. Practices and institutions, which can be observed, must have rules[53] underlying them for the activities to occur although these will not be observable save through the activities. In calling these rules and resources "structure" Giddens recognised that he was moving away from the common usage of the term although he was not uncomfortable with its continued traditional use as in "class structure" (Giddens 1984: p. 19). It could be said that Bhaskar's usage of structures as "generating mechanisms" is itself a new development.

I would suggest that the two views can be reconciled by using "structure" in Bhaskar's sense and saying it consists of positions, practices, and the rules and resources that underlie them[54] but then using much of Giddens' substantive theorising about how such a complex and stratified structure interacts with praxis[55]. Although it might be objected that this would return from duality to a dualism, there are elements of structuration theory that seem to fit and to answer some of the more detailed points raised by Archer above.

First, Giddens recognises that structures may be transformed, not simply reproduced. In fact he identifies four different mechanisms of social change (Giddens 1990): *system reproduction*—the gradual and unintended drift of social practices; *system contradiction*—conflicts of interest within and between social systems; *reflexive appropriation*—conscious shaping of social systems, especially organisations; and *resource access*—changes generated by changing availabilities of resources. This implies that there is a degree of distanciation between structure and system—rules are not causally determinative but may be enacted in different ways, and the consequences of action, intended or not, may bring about structural change rather than reinforcement[56].

Second, Giddens does recognise the temporal element in the structure/action relation, the idea that actors do not create *de novo* but always transform or reproduce something that pre-exists them.

---

[53] Interpreted in Giddens' general sense of procedures for enacting practices: Giddens (1984).

[54] Cohen (1989), one of the main interpreters of Giddens' work, also suggests that Bhaskar's notion of position-practices could usefully be incorporated in Giddens' structure.

[55] An interesting anomaly in Giddens' concept of structure has been pointed out by Sewell (1992). It is said to consist of rules and resources, and resources can be authoritative (power over people) or allocative (power over objects). Allocative resources are themselves material, e.g., raw materials, technology, goods (Giddens 1984), and so how can they be part of structure which is virtual?

[56] For an analysis of the effects of change and reflexivity in late modernity see Giddens (1990a), Giddens (1992).

"Human societies, or social systems, would plainly not exist without human agency. But it is not the case that actors create social systems: they reproduce or transform them, remaking what is already made in the continuity of praxis" (Giddens 1984: p. 171)[57].

Further, in discussing the structuring of institutions he says that this "raise{s} once more the problem of history, since the absent others include past generations whose time may be very different from that of those who are in some way influenced by residues of their activities" (Giddens 1984, p. 37). He even accepts that all social life, from the micro to the macro, is inevitable "episodic" (Giddens 1984, p. 244), that is it can be regarded in terms of sets of events having specifiable beginnings and ends during which significant changes to the social structure may occur. This all goes against Archer's assertion that structuration theory limits itself to the activities of presently existing people and is unable to recognise the effects of an already existing structure.

Third, when considering specific mechanisms by which social institutions are reproduced, we can see causal relations between system and structure. The concept of structure itself is stratified into different levels of abstraction (Giddens 1984: 185). The most abstract and enduring are "structural principles" which underlie the organisation of whole types of society—e.g., capitalist. At the next level are "structures" which are particular sets of transformation relationships between elements within a society, e.g., the relations between commodities, money and capital[58]. Finally, there are "structural properties" or "elements of structuration" which are the most concrete, linking specific systemic occurrences with wider societal institutions. An example is the division of labour—a general structural property that is enacted within particular organisations. These are linked to dynamic processes of reproduction or change—what Giddens calls homeostasis and reflexive regulation[59] or circuits of reproduction (Giddens 1984: 190). An example is the poverty cycle of deprivation—poor schooling—poor jobs – deprivation – poor schooling. Clearly such causal loops can be seen as structural generating mechanisms the exercise of which results in particular, observable phenomena.

With regard to Porpora's criticism, I suggest that he is imposing a rather crude dichotomy onto what is actually a complex mix of known and unknown conditions of action. Giddens (1989) himself speaks of three ways in which action may be constrained—first, the material constraints of the body and the physical world (which can of course be changed through technology); second, constraints stemming from the direct application of some form of power or sanction (which can vary in

---

[57] In a note at this point Giddens refers approvingly to Bhaskar.

[58] And sound very much like Bhaskar's generative mechanisms.

[59] Giddens (1979). These are taken unchanged from systems theory where they would be called multiple cause feedback loops.

intensity); and, third *structural* constraints imposed by the context of action of an individual.

In this latter case, Giddens recognises constraints deriving from the pre-existing social situation and from the social relations in which actors find themselves:

"All structural properties of social systems have a similar 'objectivity' *vis-à-vis* the individual agent. How far these are constraining qualities varies according to the context and nature of any given sequence of action" (Giddens 1984: 177).

He goes on to accept the legitimacy of a sociological explanation in terms of social forces (such as technology) "without reference to agents' reasons or intentions." However, structural constraints are not causally determinative in the way that physical forces sometimes are, and they also differ in always being enabling of action as well as constraining it. He insists that ultimately all such constraints must work through individual (or groups of) actors by restricting the range of choices available in particular situations—the greater the degree of constraint, the less options available. Thus, there is in principle always some degree of choice even when actors feel they have but one course of action. This does not imply that actors are always (or ever) fully aware of many of the conditions or consequences of their activity. There are limits here in terms of both unconscious motivations and unknown conditions of action.

"It is equally important to avoid tumbling into the opposing error of hermeneutic approaches and of various versions of phenomenology which tend to regard society as the plastic creation of human subjects." (Giddens 1984, p. 26)

To summarise this section, I have tried to show that Giddens' and Bhaskar's conceptions of society and social structure, while different, can usefully be synthesised. Social structures, consisting of position-practices, rules, and resources, are generating mechanisms that, through their complex interactions, enable and constrain observable social activity which in turn reproduces and transforms these structures. Society is then a particular combination of both praxis and structure that is historically and temporally located.

### 8.5.3 Autopoiesis and Social Structure

There are two questions to be answered in this section—whether it is possible to apply autopoiesis to the social theory outlined above? And, if it were, what benefits this would bring?

We can see elements of circularity, self-reference, and production in the above description. First and foremost, as illustrated by the quotations at the beginning of this section, is the mutual dependence of praxis and structure. Social activity could not occur without a pre-existing structure, but the structure itself is only produced and reproduced through the activity. In a very general sense this must be seen as self-production—to take Bhaskar's two dualities, structure continually produces itself through its enactment in praxis, while praxis continually produces its own pre-conditions through its crystallisation in structure. Going below this generality, we can see that Giddens especially has identified many specific causal loops or circuits of reproduction that can be seen as akin to the sorts of chains of chemical reactions which occur within cells. However, is this enough to accept social autopoiesis? The conditions to be met were articulated above—what are the components and what are the processes of production of those components? And can we identify a clearly demarcated boundary so that the system can be said to act as an organisationally closed unity and to produce itself as a whole?

With regard to the components it seems clear that they cannot be the actors themselves for they are the result of systems of biological production. I also do not think that it could be their actions or activities as such, for whilst these may be conditioned by social structure they are surely not, in general, produced by it, in the same way that the structure of language enables and constrains what *can* be said, but not what *is* said. Peoples' actual actions surely result from their own stratified and historically situated self, albeit reacting to a particular social context or situation, and expressing itself through legitimised forms of behaviour. This only leaves the elements of social structure—rules, positions, practices etc.—as potential components for social autopoiesis, but this fits in quite well with the paradigmatic example of non-physical autopoiesis, Nomic, discussed in in Section 8.3.1. Here, it was specifically the rules of the game that were the self-producing system rather than the players or their actual moves.

If these are the components, what then are the processes of production that generate them? First, we need to consider what sense can be given to the term "produce" here as this is one of the problems Varela himself highlights—instantiating the concept of production within the realm of social systems.

"In order to say that a system is autopoietic, the production of components in some space has to be exhibited; further, the term production has to make sense in some domain of discourse. Frankly, I do not see how the definition of autopoiesis can be *directly* transposed to a variety of other situations, social systems for example." (Varela 1981b: p. 38)

When applied to biological systems it refers to processes of molecular interaction that generate new molecules which then participate in further interactions. It is clear from the discussion of structuration that actors do not produce structure anew but rather reproduce or transform that which already exists. However I do not see that this is incompatible with a notion of production since one could say that molecular production does not create something from nothing, but simply reorganises or recombines components (atoms and molecules) that already exist. One significant difference from the Nomic example is that in the game the moves are intended to change the rules—that is their primary purpose—and the players will be conscious of this, whereas most if not all social activity is *not* intended to reproduce structure, this is merely an unintended and probably unrecognised consequence. Again, I do not see that this invalidates the notion of production—all that is necessary, and indeed both

Giddens and Maturana stress this non-functionalist view—is that (re)production of structure actually occurs. If it does, whether intended or not, autopoiesis continues; if it doesn't, the particular social practices will die out[60]. A tentative conclusion thus far is that we can, contra Varela, identify components and processes of production.

The second major requirement of autopoiesis is that the system is organisationally closed and generates its own boundary. This means that the network of processes involved must feed back upon themselves to form a circular concatenation and thereby implicitly demarcate itself from its surroundings. In the case of physical autopoiesis the boundary would be spatial and would involve specific components (e.g., the cell wall) but as Varela points out this is not necessary in the more general case of organisational closure where the nature of the boundary will depend on the type of components involved.

Whether this condition is satisfied is harder to answer in the case of social systems. Taking firstly the question of closure under some type of circular relationship, there is clearly a form of closure between the social structure in general and the social activity through which it is (re)produced. However this is rather different to the circularity of physical autopoiesis where molecules interact with other molecules to produce yet more molecules. In the social case the relation is between two different strata—social structure and social action rather than within the one strata[61]. To be strictly analogous to the physical example we would have to look for circularity among the elements of structure—position-practices and rules producing more of the same. There no doubt there are many relationships between these components, indeed Bhaskar (1979: p. 41) defines them relationally, but since social structure only exists through social activity, positions and rules cannot simply produce themselves. This situation is clear in Nomic—the rules are only transformed through the activities of the players. This of itself does not preclude organisational closure, but we would have to accept that social systems are different from material systems in the ways Bhaskar suggested above.

Apart from the general notion that action (re)produces structure, we can also see many specific circular feedback loops involved in this process. Giddens distinguished three different types—homeostatic loops via unintended consequences of action, self-regulation through information filtering, and reflexive self-regulation involving conscious manipulation of social institutions, and uses the poverty cycle as an illustration of all three. We could obviously look empirically at any part of society and discover an enormously complex inter-meshing of causal loops involving both

---

[60] This aspect of social reproduction, although not stressed by Giddens, is easily observable. As technology develops old practices die out, simply because they no longer occur and are therefore not reproduced.

[61] Mathematically, closure can be clearly defined. A particular domain of objects is closed with respect to a particular operation if the result of the operation always remains in the same domain. Thus the domain of positive numbers is closed with respect to addition but not with respect to subtraction.

observable activity and events stretching over time and space and the underlying structure of positions and rules. The difficult question, though, is to what extent such circuits can be said to form a boundary, or at least demarcate themselves from the background. This is a strong but necessary feature of organisational closure as defined since it is what accounts for the systems' identity and its domain of possible interactions as a whole.

"Thus a unity's boundaries, in whichever space the processes exist, is indissolubly linked to the operation of the system. If the organisational closure is disrupted, the unity disappears. This is characteristic of autonomous systems. ... It is also apparent that once a unity is established through closure it will specify a domain with which it can interact without loss of identity." (Varela 1981a: p. 15)

We can see how this applies to physical systems such as the nervous system or the immune system (Varela, Coutinho et al. 1988). In the case of a non-physical system, if it is well defined, such as Nomic we can say that at any point the system is able to distinguish inside from outside—valid rules from invalid ones. But it is not obvious that we can actually identify such clear-cut examples as Nomic within the mêlée of society as a whole. There are many different possibilities (Giddens 1990b, p. 303)— nations, states, or perhaps societies as such; Western capitalism as a whole; enduring institutions such as religions or political parties; particular collectivities such as firms, clubs or social movements; small-scale groupings such as a family or a sports team; or, following Luhmann, functional subsystems such as the economy, law, and politics. Considering what might be the boundaries of a society and what could be its domain of actions as a unity can indicate the difficulties.

Giddens (1981: p. 45) has suggested three criteria for a social system to be considered a society: i) an association with a particular time-space location with a legitimate claim to make use of it; ii) a shared set of practices involving both system and structure; and iii) an awareness of a shared identity. In terms of time and space, societies will be localised to some extent and, especially in historical times, there may well have been particular examples such as nomadic peoples or forest tribes who were genuinely self-contained. We can look back and see different societies clashing with each other as in periods of colonisation. But in the modern world, with its tremendous global interpenetration through communications and transport, is it possible to draw any such lines any more? Societies certainly don't coincide with nation states being both wider, e.g., European society, and narrower, e.g., Scottish and English. Indeed it can be argued (Angel 1997) that nation states themselves will become of lesser importance than global companies. Luhmann (1982b) concluded that one had to go up to the level of the world society as a whole.

We can also to some extent pick out enduring social practices but at which ever level we look these are many and diverse. There may be greater differences within a notional society than between that society and another, especially with the tremendous intermixing of ethnic and cultural groups within modern societies. A sense of identity may be equally polysemous—one could feel Mancunian, English,

British, European, or Western depending on who one was interacting with. As Giddens concludes,

"It is important to re-emphasise that the term 'social system' should not be understood to designate only clusters of social relations whose boundaries are clearly set off from others. ... I take it to be one of the main features of structuration theory that the extension and 'closure' of societies across space and time is regarded as problematic." (Giddens 1984: p. 165)

### 8.5.4 Summary

This section has developed the following conclusions concerning the application of autopoiesis to social systems as seen from a broadly structurationist perspective.

In terms of components and processes of production:

- We can take the components of such a system to be those of social structure developed above—rules, resources, positions and practices;

- We can identify processes of production (in terms of reproduction and transformation) of these components provided we accept that with social systems production involves the transformation of an existing structure, and a duality between social structure and human activity.

In terms of organisational closure:

- We can identify a circularity of relations both in the generic (re)production of structure and in specific causal chains;

- But, it is difficult in general to identify specific social systems that are clearly bounded and have identity. This may be possible in specific, well-defined instances (for example, Nomic) but this would require empirical verification.

Thus we cannot conclude in general that social systems, conceptualised as a synthesis of structuration and critical realism, *are* autopoietic. Nor can we follow Varela and say they are not autopoietic but organisationally closed. However, most of the key elements of self-producing systems can be seen in social systems, and it may be that particular examples could embody them all.

## 8.6 Conclusions

The purpose of this chapter was to evaluate in detail the extent to which social systems could be conceptualised as self-producing, autopoietic, in an ontological rather than simply metaphorical sense. The first step was to specify clearly what we took to be the essential core of the theory of autopoiesis—a specification of particular components that participate in processes of production of similar components within a well-bounded whole. The next step was to consider the extent to which autopoiesis was compatible with, or contributed to, existing social theories. For this purpose Luhmann's communication theory, Giddens' structuration theory, and Bhaskar's transformational model of social activity have been examined.

In the case of Luhmann, the conclusions were that his social theory did consistently embody a version of autopoiesis although not being wholly compatible with Maturana's original formulation. The components were clear (communications) and a mechanism was specified for generating closure, but the production processes and the supposed isolation of various systems was considered problematic. However, this theoretical purity was only obtained at the expense of a very abstract and impoverished view of social processes and interactions.

In the case of structuration theory, we had first to construct a synthesis from two different versions developed by Giddens and Bhaskar respectively. The conclusion then was that components and processes of production could be identified (rules, resources, positions and practices), but that it was extremely difficult to identify empirically the bounded closure of a particular social system.

Thus, the overall conclusion is one of agnosticism. Autopoiesis as a social theory has many attractions, and there may be very specific social situations, exemplified by Nomic, where it could be identified. But, in general, I do not believe that social autopoiesis has yet been demonstrated. Nevertheless, further research in this area is certainly to be encouraged:

- Attempting to demonstrate empirically a self-constructing social system along the lines described in the paper. Paterson and Teubner (1998) have tried this but the attempt seems to me to be rather superficial.

- Developing further Maturana's other theoretical ideas concerning the biological basis of observation, languaging, and embodied cognition. This leads to a particular view of interacting human agents at the individual level which could possibly be combined with modern complexity theory (Byrne 1998) at the system level to produce an interesting new synthesis.

- Synthesising Giddens' and Luhmann's theoretical systems which seem to me to be potentially complementary. They could be developed as an orthogonal pair of distinctions—that between observable system and underlying structure on the one hand (Giddens), and, within the system, that between individual interaction and societal communication (Luhmann).

Part III: Action and Intervention

# Chapter 9: Management Science and Multimethodology

## 9.1 Introduction

We have now reached a significant change of direction in the book. In Part I we considered some fundamental underpinnings for systems and management science—critical realism as a basic philosophy of science; autopoiesis as a theory of biology and cognition; and the nature of boundaries as a key element of systems theory. In Part II we developed from this some substantive theorising at a hierarchy of levels—the nature of information, meaning and knowledge; communication and interaction between people; and the autopoietic character of social systems. We now move away from knowledge to action which is, after all, the point of management science. By "action" in this context I do not mean general human behaviour but purposeful activity directed towards particular objectives within human activity systems (Checkland 1981), and in particular direct interventions of the sort that management scientists[62] carry out. I include within this management *research* which I view as a particular type of intervention.

What are the main themes that emerge from the first two Parts that have implications for action and intervention[63] such as this?

- The first is that knowledge and action are much less separable than is commonly presumed. The traditional Cartesian view that underlies much of Western philosophy is that cognition and action are almost separate domains (witness the great mind vs. matter debate). More recently, people such as Checkland (1998) have emphasised their interlinking—for example, action research should always be based on prior theories or knowledge, the application of which then feeds back to change and develop them. But from the work of both Maturana and Merleau-Ponty (Sections 7.2) knowledge and action are not merely linked, but are indissoluble—two sides of the same coin. Action is the enactment of knowledge and knowledge is the sedimentation of action.

- Following from this, and linked to the discussion of multiple forms of knowledge in Chapter 6, is recognition of the importance of the person or agent(s) who is actually carrying out the intervention. Traditionally, discussion

---

[62] Including within this term operational research, information systems applied systems thinking, and other management disciplines aimed at improving the process of management rather than simply studying it.

[63] I shall use the term "intervention" generally to mean purposeful action within a particular organisational context of concern. This could be one person or a group and they could be internal or external to the organisation(s).

within management science about different methods and methodologies has been just that, disembodied and totally disconnected from the users of such methodologies. But the intertwined nature of knowledge and action, and the experiential and performative aspects of knowledge itself mean that we have to bring agents into the picture in debating practical methodologies.

- The next important theme is that which underpins multimethodology itself and that is the multi-dimensional nature of the real world of organisations. Both critical realism and Habermas's theory of communicative action demonstrate that we cannot rely on methods or methodologies from just one paradigm. The world has material aspects that can be measured and counted, but it also has social aspects that must be shared and understood, and indeed personal and individual aspects that must be experienced and expressed. This calls for the judicious and knowledgeable combination of a variety of research and intervention methods.

- Finally, the discussion of boundaries in Chapter 4 pointed to the fundamental importance of the judgements that we make about boundaries and constraints, both in the problem situations and in ourselves as engaged and involved agents.

We shall in these last two chapters assume on behalf of the reader, a basic familiarity management science and its various methods and methodologies. For those who come from other disciplines I will just contextualise briefly. Management science (also sometimes known as operational research—OR) developed during the second world war when scientists (physicists, mathematicians, biologists, psychologists) began to use their scientific approach to tackle operational military problems (Trefethen 1995). This often involved data collection and mathematical modelling. The success of OR led, after the war, to its transfer into business and organisations and many original methods and techniques were developed such as linear programming, simulation, network analysis, inventory control and forecasting. These were largely quantitative.

In time, however, it was realised that many aspects of organisational problems were not measurable and could not be modelled mathematically. This led to the development of new methods, known as "soft" OR as opposed to "hard" OR, such as soft systems methodology (SSM) (Checkland and Scholes 1990), cognitive mapping (Eden and Ackermann 2001), and strategic choice approach (SCA) (Friend 2001). At first there was considerable conflict within the discipline (Ackoff 1979; Checkland 1983; Mingers 1992) between hard and soft but in time both came to be viewed as important although individuals often worked within only one area. The question then became how to decide which method to use in a particular situation—methodology choice (Jackson 1989b), or how to combine together different methods within the same intervention—multimethodology (Mingers and Brocklesby 1997).

## 9.2 Introduction to Multimethodology

At its simplest, *multimethodology* just means employing more than one method or methodology[64] in tackling some real-world problem. For instance, one could be using SSM but feel that some cognitive mapping might be useful in understanding how certain managers are thinking. Or one could use SSM as a whole to gain agreement on desirable changes, and then build a simulation model to help implement them. Or you could do some cognitive mapping and then develop this into a causal-loop diagram and ultimately a system dynamics model. It is often sensible, especially for beginners, to use one main or overall methodology, such as SSM, and then augment it by bringing in techniques from others.

In fact, we can distinguish several ways in which such combinations can occur, each having different problems and possibilities:

- *Methodology combination*: using two or more whole methodologies within an intervention.

- *Methodology enhancement*: using one main methodology but enhancing it by importing methods from elsewhere.

- *Single-paradigm multimethodology:* Combining parts of several methodologies all from the same paradigm.

- *Multi-paradigm multimethodology:* as above, but using methods from different paradigms.

There are three main arguments in favour of multi-paradigm multimethodology. The first is that, as Bhaskar has argued (Chapter 2), the world is ontologically stratified and differentiated and therefore real-world problem situations are inevitably multidimensional. There will be physical or material aspects, social and political aspects, and personal ones. Different approaches tend to focus attention on different aspects of the situation and so multimethodology is necessary to deal effectively with the full richness of the real world. The second is that an intervention is not usually a single, discrete event but is a process that typically proceeds through a number of phases, and these phases pose different tasks and problems for the practitioner. However, methodologies tend to be more useful in relation to some phases than others, so the prospect of combining them has immediate appeal, combining a range of approaches may well yield a better result. Third, combining different methods, even where they actually perform similar functions (such as cognitive mapping and rich pictures) can often provide a "triangulation" on the situation, generating new

---

[64] I will generally talk of "methods" but some approaches, e.g., soft systems methodology (SSM), are referred to as "methodologies." The glossary at the end of the Chapter clarifies some of these terms.

insights and providing more confidence in the results by validating each other. The next section will look at each of these points in more detail.

There are several other approaches to pluralism within management science that I will discuss in section 9.4.

### 9.2.1 The Multi-Dimensional World

Adopting a single approach is like viewing the world through a particular instrument such as a telescope, an x-ray machine, or an electron microscope. Each one reveals certain aspects of the world but is completely blind to others. Although they may be pointing at the same place, each instrument produces a different, and sometimes seemingly incompatible, representation. These very general ways of looking at the world are sometimes called paradigms. In adopting only one paradigm you are inevitably gaining only a limited view of a particular real-world situation—for example, attending only to that which may be measured or quantified; or only to individuals' subjective meanings and thus ignoring the wider social context. This argument is a strong one in support of multi-paradigm interventions suggesting that, ideally, it is always wise to utilise a variety of approaches.

To explain more clearly the main dimensions of a problem situation, a framework developed from Habermas (1984; 1987) is shown in Figure 9.1. It suggests that it is useful to distinguish our relations to, and interactions with, three worlds—the material world, the social world, and the personal world.

Each world has different modes of existence, and different means of accessibility. The material or physical world is independent of human beings. It existed before us and would exist whether or not we did. We can shape it through our actions, but ultimately we are always subject to its laws. Our relationship to this world is one of *observation* rather than *participation* or *experience*. But we must always be aware of the limitations of the observations we make. They will depend on the particular theories and beliefs we hold, and the measuring instruments and processes of data collection that we employ. We can characterise this world as objective in the sense that it is independent of the observer, but clearly our observations and descriptions of it are not.

From this material world, through the process of evolution, human beings have developed the capability for language and thus the possibility of communication and self-reflection. This has led to the social and personal worlds. The personal world is the world of our own individual thoughts, emotions, experiences, values and beliefs. We do not observe it as outsiders, but each *experience* it. This world is subjective in that it is generated by, and only accessible to, the individual subject. We can aim to express our subjectivity to others and, in turn, appreciate theirs.

Finally there is the social world that we (as members of particular social systems) share and *participate in*. Our relation to it is one of intersubjectivity since it is, on the

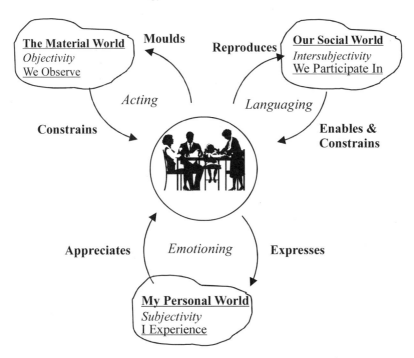

**Figure 9.1. Habermas' Three Worlds.**

one hand, a human construction, and yet, on the other, it goes beyond and pre-exists any particular individual. It consists of a complex layering of language, meaning, social practices, rules and resources that both enables and constrains our actions and is reproduced through them.

Thus, any real-world situation into which we are intervening will be a complex interaction of substantively different elements. There will be aspects that are relatively hard and observer-independent, particularly material and physical processes, which we can observe and model. There will be aspects that are socially constituted, dependent on particular cultures, social practices, languages, and power structures, which we must come to share and participate in. Finally, there will be aspects that are individual such as beliefs, values, fears, and emotions that we must try to express and understand.

## 9.2.2 Intervention as a Process

The second argument is that intervention is not a discrete event but a process that has phases or different types of activities predominating at different times. Particular methods and techniques are more useful for some functions than others and so a combination of approaches may be advantageous to provide a successful outcome. To help design an intervention in practice it is useful to have some categorisation of the phases of a project, against which the strengths of various methodologies can be mapped. The following four phases have been identified (Mingers and Brocklesby 1997): ·

**Appreciation** of the situation as experienced by the practitioners involved and expressed by any actors in the situation. This will involve an initial identification of the concerns to be addressed (especially the consideration of constraints and boundaries), conceptualisation and design of the study, and the production of basic data using methods such as observation, interviews, experiments, surveys, or qualitative approaches. Note that this cannot be an "observer-independent" view of the situation "as it really is." The practitioners' previous experience and their access to the situation will condition it. In terms of critical realism's retroductive methodology (Section 2.3.2) this corresponds to the first two stages of Resolution and Redescription:

**Analysis** of the information produced so as to be able to understand and explain why the situation is as it is. This will involve analytic methods appropriate to the goal(s) of the intervention and the information produced in the first stage. Explanation will be in terms of possible hypothetical mechanisms or structures that, if they existed, would produce the phenomena that have been observed, measured, or experienced. This phase mirrors CR's move from the Empirical to the Real (Retroduction)

**Assessment** of the postulated explanation(s) in terms of other predicted effects, alternative possible explanations, and consideration of ways in which the situation could be other than it is. It includes interpretation of the results and inference to other situations. This corresponds to CR's Elimination stage where different possible mechanisms and changes are explored and Identification of the appropriate one.

**Action** to bring about changes, if necessary or desired. In CR terms this fits the Diagnosis, Explanation and Action model for practical problem resolution or the Description, Explanation and Transformation model for normative change.

Put colloquially, these phases cover: What is happening? Why is it happening? How could the situation or explanation be different? And, what shall we do? At the beginning of an intervention, especially for a practitioner from outside the situation, the primary concern is to gain as rich an appreciation of the situation as possible. The next activity is to begin to analyse why the situation is as it appears, to understand the history that has generated it, and the particular structure of relations and constraints that maintain it. Next, in cases where change to the situation is sought, consideration must be given to ways in which the situation could be changed. This means focussing attention away from how things are, and considering the extent to which the structures and constraints can be changed within the general limitations of the intervention. Finally, action must be undertaken that will effectively bring about agreed changes. We should emphasise immediately that these activities are not to be seen as discrete stages that are enacted one by one. Rather, they are aspects of the intervention that need to be considered throughout, although their relative importance will differ as the project progresses. Equally, different projects will place their emphasis at some stages rather than others.

It is clear that the wide variety of methods and techniques available do not all perform equally well at all these phases. To give some brief examples: collecting data, carrying out questionnaires and surveys, developing rich pictures and cognitive maps, and employing the twelve Critical Systems Heuristics (CSH) (Ulrich 1991) questions, all contribute to finding out about the different aspects of a particular situation. Whereas building simulation or mathematical models, constructing root definitions and conceptual models, using role-playing and gaming, or undertaking participant observation helps to understand *why* the situation is as it is, and to evaluate other possibilities.

### 9.2.3 Triangulation of Results

There are other advantages to combining methods (Tashakkori and Teddlie 1998)— i) triangulation—seeking to validate data and results by combining a range of data sources, methods, or analysts; ii) creativity—discovering fresh or paradoxical factors that stimulate ideas and solutions; and iii) expansion—widening the scope of the study to take in other aspects of the situation that may be of importance. One approach is to use a variety of methods to carry out a similar function—for example using rich pictures, cognitive maps, and CSH questions to appreciate a situation; doing a simulation and then using queuing theory as a rough check; or using drama theory and strategic choice to consider different ranges of options. The other is to use some quite different method to get a new insight on the problem. For example, having developed a particular model or even proposed solution challenge it with the CSH questions, or perhaps SSM using an antagonistic Weltanschauung. Another idea is to take a particular method and then use it in an unusual way. For example, instead of assuming an LP is an objective model of some aspects of reality, treat it like a cognitive map and develop several, incorporating different assumptions and values (Mingers 2000c).

## 9.3 Barriers to Multimethodology

Having put forward arguments for the desirability of multimethodology we must also recognise the inherent problems and assess its overall feasibility. We should remember that we are concerned particularly with linking research and intervention methods that would normally be seen as belonging to different paradigms.

Four levels of problems can be identified: i) *philosophical*—particularly the issue of paradigm incommensurability; ii) *cultural*—the extent to which organisational and academic cultures militate against multi-method work; iii) *psychological*—the problems of individual researchers who are often only comfortable with a particular type of method; and iv) *practical*. Each of these is a major research area in its own right and in this chapter all we hope to do is to outline the main debates and provide at least *prima facie* evidence that the problems are not insurmountable. More detailed arguments will be found in Mingers and Brocklesby (1997).

## 9.3.1 Philosophical Feasibility—Paradigm Incommensurability

The paradigm incommensurability thesis asserts that because paradigms differ in terms of the fundamental assumptions that they bring to organisational inquiry, researchers must choose the rules under which they do research from among the alternatives on offer. They must then commit themselves to a single paradigm, although sequential movement over time is permissible. Multimethodology is proscribed for a number of reasons, the most notable of which is the supposedly irreconcilable objectivist/subjectivist ontological and epistemological dichotomies that exist between the empirical-analytic and interpretive paradigms respectively. There are other related dichotomies such as structure versus agency, determinism versus voluntarism, causation versus meaning, and object versus subject—some of these have been discussed in Chapter 8. The opposing positions in each dichotomy represent alternative competing "truths" about the world and, as such, it is said that they resist reconciliation or synthesis (see Tashakkori and Teddlie 1998).

However, several arguments have been put forward within philosophy, social theory, and organisation studies against a strong view of paradigm incommensurability. First, it is argued that the characterization of paradigms as separate and mutually exclusive domains may have been overstated (Gioia and Pitre 1990). Although the central prototypical characteristics are incommensurable, paradigms are permeable at the edges, in their so called "transition zones." It is possible, these authors argue, to "construct bridges" across paradigm boundaries that are ostensibly impenetrable. Moreover, the distinctions that are generally drawn between different paradigms are themselves fuzzy and highly questionable, and there is no one agreed set of paradigms (Smaling 1994). Second, it is not necessary to accept that research methods are wholly internal to a single paradigm (Smaling 1994; Mingers and Brocklesby 1997). Rather, it is quite possible to disconnect a particular method from its normal paradigm and use it, *consciously and critically*, within another setting. For example, the use of quantitative data need not imply the acceptance of a positivist, objectivist epistemology. Rather, such data can (and should) be interpreted in the light of relevant social meanings, and their production as a social construction.

Third, it is claimed that the whole idea of paradigm incommensurability based upon the objective-subjective duality is fundamentally flawed (Orlikowski and Robey 1991; Weaver and Gioia 1994). Giddens' structuration theory has been used to demonstrate that it is not possible to separate out objective and subjective dimensions. Reality, according to structuration theory, emerges out of the dialectic interplay of forces of structure and meaning—structural regularities are created out of subjective meanings, and through socialization processes, structures then "act back" upon individuals' meanings. Finally, generalizing the previous argument, different paradigms provide us with different perspectives or insights into a reality that is forever more complex than our theories can capture (Booth 1979; Guba 1990; Smaling 1994). It is therefore quite wrong to wholly accept the postulates of any one paradigm.

We have seen in Chapter 2 that critical realism provides a firm underpinning philosophy that rejects both empiricism and interpretivism alone whilst encompassing multiparadigm combinations such as intensive/extensive (Sayer 1992; Layder 1993) or distant/engaged (Nandhakumar and Jones 1997). It also has strong arguments against incommensurability (Bhaskar 1986, p. 70). If we have two theories or paradigms the first question is are they actually in conflict or are they about totally different things? If they are not about the same thing there is little point in comparing them. If there is point in comparing them then they must both refer to some aspects of the world in common and it must then be possibly to consider grounds for choosing between them. As CR argues, accepting epistemic relativity does not entail judgemental relativity. One such criterion would be the extent to which theory A explains everything that theory B does as well as explaining other phenomena that B does not (Einsteinian and Newtonian theories are a good example of this). This is not to say that comparing and choosing between paradigms is easy or always successful but simply to say that it is not impossible.

Critical realism emphasises an acceptance of plurality at many levels— philosophical, social, and methodological—but also grounds this from a perspective that adopts a critical stance towards the necessity and validity of current social arrangements. This is clearly seen as a new paradigm—it is not meta-paradigmatic. Nor does it take the extant paradigms' assumptions at face value—for example, that quantitative data could be pure, unmediated reflections of an external reality.

## 9.3.2 Cultural Feasibility—Paradigm Subcultures

The question here is whether the existing cultural constitution of a research community such as information systems or management science—the extent to which it is split into paradigm subcultures—will facilitate or act as a barrier against the widespread adoption of multimethodology as a research strategy. Obviously this depends upon the size of the "cultural gap" between where we are now, and where— in relation to multimethodology—we would like to be. This issue has been discussed in some detail with regard to the domain of management science (Brocklesby 1994; Brocklesby 1995; Brocklesby and Cummings 1995) and information systems (Mingers 2001a). Certainly Applegate and King's (1999) description of the problems faced by a junior researcher trying to undertake non-standard research is an excellent illustration of paradigm sub-culture at work.

Some empirical evidence in the UK is both interesting and surprising. Galliers *et al* (1997) report on a survey of UK IS academics (the sample frame was the 535 members of the UKAIS of whom 20% replied) part of which dealt with academic background and use of research methods. Surprisingly (in comparison with the above research), nearly 70% came from a *social* science background (36% economics), and a further 21% came from operational research. Almost none had a specifically technical or scientific training. Given this, it is not surprising that the most common research area was in the organisational and human impact if IT (16%) and that the most commonly used research methods were intensive ones such as case study, interviews, and qualitative analysis (41%). The most common epistemological positions were interpretivism (40%) and "common sense/ad hoc" (12%), with positivism (10%) and pragmatism (10%) coming next. Finally, the survey specifically asked if research methods were used in combination and 70% replied "always" or "often," although no further details are available. The predominance of a social science background is unexpected in the light of common presuppositions that many IS people come from a technical background. There may of course be some bias in the sample—either the UKAIS in general, or the subset who chose to respond—but it would be interesting to replicate this research in the US, and with IS practitioners rather than academics. The high proportion who regularly combine methods is encouraging, although these may well be methods within a single paradigm.

This does not mean that the institutionally entrenched single-paradigm, even single-method subcultures that pervade IS are inviolable. Cultures do change, albeit often slowly and in response to specific conditions and events. Perhaps the most basic condition that might trigger the sort of transformation we are talking about would be an unexpected failure in traditional ways of working combined with a consciousness of the limitations of one's preferred paradigm and knowledge of what other options might be available. This, indeed, does seem to be happening following the numerous, well-publicised commercial information systems failures such as the London Ambulance system (Beynon-Davies 1995) and the London Stock Exchange system, *Taurus* (Drummond 1996). Then, of course, there is the question of capability. Changes would have to be made in the curriculum to develop a better awareness of the range of ontological and epistemological options that are available, and to broaden knowledge and research skills. Changes would need to be made in the criteria required to recruit staff. These changes present a number of challenges, but they do not represent insurmountable obstacles.

### 9.3.3 Psychological Feasibility—Cognitive Barriers

The next potential difficulty in multimethodology research concerns the cognitive feasibility of moving from one paradigm to another. Spanning a wide range of disciplines, there is now an extensive literature that has explored the extant links between personality traits, cognition and research preferences, and the production of knowledge. A major issue raised in this literature is the question of whether entrenched cognitive predilections may be altered to facilitate multi-method work. Research based on a Jungian personality schema (Slocum 1978; Nutt 1979; Blaycock and Rees 1984; Nutt 1986; Stumph and Dunbar 1991) suggests that the preferences of the "analytical scientist" type seem to reflect many of the exigencies of doing hard, quantitative research. Empirical studies of these "types," for example, show that they value precision, accuracy and reliability, and they perform best when they can impose models on a decision situation to specify the relevant data needed and provide formats for logical analysis. The two "feeling" types—the "particular humanist" and the "conceptual humanist"—in contrast, provide a closer approximation to the interpretive/soft systems style of research. Particular humanists, for example, prefer to conduct research via personal involvement with other people; they prefer qualitative data; and report through personalized descriptive accounts.

Employing a variety of different methods requires a range of competencies on the part of the practitioner. This is particularly so when combining hard and soft approaches—the skills of a quantitative analyst are very different from those of a facilitator, a point made by Dando and Sharp (1978), Eilon (1975), and Fildes and Ranyard (1997). A survey by Munro and Mingers (2002) into the use by OR/systems practitioners of multimethodology asked respondents about their original academic disciplines and the extent to which they had moved discipline or become multi-disciplinary. 72% came from a technical background (with 15% from social science) and 20% reported that they had moved from their original discipline to another one while 63% felt that they had now become multidisciplinary. None of those from a science discipline claimed to still be within that discipline.

### 9.3.4 Practical Barriers

Finally, we must recognize that there are practical, but none the less real, constraints on multi-method research. The current situation seems well captured by Deetz (1996) in a paper on the nature of paradigms within organisational studies. He argues against the traditional, epistemological, version of paradigms developed especially by Burrell and Morgan (1979), that has dominated organisational and management studies. This, he claims, is too rigid and representational; is founded in a strong objective/subjective distinction; and is too easily taken as being "true" (or perhaps "false") rather than simply more or less stimulating or interesting. In its place he proposes to identify different discourses[65] (rather than paradigms) that characterize different research communities within organisational research. And, he argues, movement across or between these discourses, whilst desirable is very difficult in practice.

"Different orientations have developed specific ways of answering the types of questions they pose and do not work terribly well in answering the questions of others. The choice of orientation, to the extent that it can be freed from training histories and department/discipline politics, can probably be reduced to alternative conceptions of social good … I, like many others, sometimes wish we were all multilingual, that we could move across orientations with grace and ease, but this type of Teflon-coated multiperspectival cosmopolitanism … is often both illusionary and weak." (Deetz 1996, p. 204)

At the same time, academics are increasingly under publication pressure and it is certainly much easier to sell clear-cut, well-defined, mono-method work both to funding agencies and to journals. This is particularly crucial to less senior faculty still needing to establish their reputation and tenure—Applegate and King's (1999) vignette of the pressures and conflicts faced by a junior researcher rings very true. In the United Kingdom we have suffered from the Research Assessment Exercise

---

[65] Four discourses are identified—normative, interpretive, critical, and dialogic—based on two underlying dimensions: whether theoretical concepts are local/emergent or elite/*a priori,* and whether the research is generally focussed on consensus/order or dissensus/conflict.

(RAE). This major undertaking aims to assess research quality across all subjects in all universities and its results are a significant determinant of research funding. However, its crude methodology, largely couched in terms of *numbers* of publications rather than quality, has effectively penalized longer-term, more complex research projects in favour of short-term, often trivial, journal articles. It is also true, of course, that any project must have self-defined or externally-given boundaries, and particular questions that it sets out to answer. It cannot aim to discover everything about everything.

However, despite the practical problems raised in this section I believe that the approach set out in this chapter does not ask for the impossible. It simply suggests that in any piece of research or intervention, even one where a tightly drawn research question overwhelmingly implies a particular method, thought be given to the influence of a range of factors in the situation (including the predilections and experience of the researcher), and the extent to which other methods may add to the richness and validity of the results. It is certainly true that multiparadigm intervention and research *is* occurring increasingly across a range of disciplines—see surveys by Lewis and Grimes (1999), Munro and Mingers (2002) and Tashakkori and Teddlie (1998)—and there is no reason to suppose that the barriers outlined above apply any less to these other disciplines. Also, to some extent these problems can be alleviated when research is organized into a research program. Individual projects may be largely mono-method, but their results and conclusions can be linked to others that adopt a different approach and may be carried out by other researchers, resulting in the overall program being rich and multi-method.

## *9.4 Other Pluralist Approaches*

Although in this book I am concentrating on my particular approach to multimethodology, based on critical realism, that I term "critical pluralism" (Mingers 1997b) several others, mainly from the systems world, have proposed their own versions—coherent pluralism (Jackson 1999; Jackson 2000), discordant pluralism (Gregory 1996), pragmatic pluralism (White and Taket 1997) and theoretical pluralism (Midgley 2000). All accept the general arguments for the combination of different methods from different paradigms but they differ in the underlying rationale and the particular approach taken. Jackson (2000, Chapter 11) provides a reasonably fair overview despite being a proponent of one particular approach.

Jackson's view of pluralism, which has changed considerably since his espousal of the system of systems methodologies (SOSM) (Jackson 1990) and total systems intervention (TSI) (Flood and Jackson 1991) can be characterised by three principles:

1.   That there should be the flexibility to use the widest range of methods, methodologies, and parts of methodologies (decomposition) in the planning and during the execution of an intervention. However, to be theoretically informed and to avoid the trap of pragmatism methodologies must be used within an appropriate paradigm (functionalist, interpretive, emancipatory or

postmodern). Jackson has developed what he calls "generic" methodologies for each of the paradigms.

2. That a range of paradigms *should be* employed in all interventions, and at all stages of them. This is because of the inherent complexity of the world and in order to maintain a radical edge and not lapse into unthinking imperialism or support for the status quo.

3. That we have to accept a degree of incompatibility between paradigms. There can be no overarching or underpinning paradigm that subsumes them all to provide coherence or consistency. Instead, debate and critique should be conducted between the paradigms.

My version of pluralism, critical pluralism, accepts some but not all of the above. It accepts the idea that one should be able to use the widest possible range of methods, and that this should include the "decomposition" of methodologies into their parts. Indeed, this was first suggested by Mingers and Brocklesby (1997). However, it does not accept that each one must be employed from within a currently existing paradigm or generic methodology. It also accepts that a range of methodologies should be employed within a single intervention. This was one of the main critiques of SOSM and TSI put forward by Mingers (1993a; 1993b; 1997b), that it legitimated the use of only one methodology, and usually a functionalist one, within a particular intervention even though others may have been considered.

The main point of disagreement, however, concerns point 3 that we have to accept the validity and in some sense equality of currently existing paradigms rather than try to go beyond them. I see no justification for accepting the validity of the paradigms as currently formulated since each has been legitimately critiqued by the others. Indeed, Jackson's book (2000) does a reasonable job of pointing out the limitations of each of his four paradigms.

Critical realism has developed in debate with a large range of philosophies, beginning with positivism and proceeding through to postmodernism. For instance, positivism in its various forms is covered in Bhaskar (1978), hermeneutics and methodological individualism in Bhaskar (1979), neo-Kantianism, Popper, Kuhn, Feyerabend, and the sociology of knowledge are discussed in Bhaskar (1986), Bachelard, Rorty and materialism in Bhaskar (1989), Marxism and dialectics in Bhaskar (1993), and postmodernism more generally in Bhaskar (1993) and Norris (1997). Its general style of argumentation is "immanent critique." This means that it takes some aspect of a competing position and then tries to show how this cannot in fact be explained according to the position's own premises, but can be accommodated within critical realism (Archer, Bhaskar et al., 1998, p. 4). CR does not however just dismiss competing philosophies but tries to incorporate within itself that which is valuable.

So, the question arises that if it has been shown that these paradigms all have serious flaws or limitations why should we consider as valid research or intervention that is carried out wholly within one such paradigm? Surely it is much better to try to develop new paradigms, and research methods, that draw on the strengths but avoid the weaknesses? Critical realism is one such paradigm, and one that I obviously favour. This does not mean that it can be *proved* to be correct, or that it has no limitations of its own (see Section 2.4) and in keeping with its own fallibilist stance it may well be superseded itself in time.

Thus the *critical* pluralist approach is to welcome a wide variety of different methods and methodologies, and to use them together in an intervention. But, to be critically aware of both their theoretical and paradigmatic origins, and the limitations and critiques of these origins, and thus to use them in a sophisticated rather than naïve way. I will illustrate this with two commonly used methodologies from different paradigms—statistical modelling and soft systems methodology (SSM). These originate in empiricism and interpretivism respectively but, contra Jackson, I argue that they should not be employed from within these paradigms but rather from within a critical realist perspective.

### 9.4.1 Statistical Modelling—Critique of an Empiricist Methodology

Statistical modelling (including regression, other multivariate techniques, time-series decomposition and ARIMA) is an approach that, in varying degrees, goes against critical realism in being essentially empiricist. In this section I shall show the weaknesses of the conventional interpretation of statistics, but also how it can be better employed within a critical framework. Consider first multiple regression, a technique used in a range of social sciences as well as OR/MS. It claims to be a causally-oriented technique (in comparison with, say, time-series analysis) that aims to explain the variation in a dependent variable in terms of a set of supposedly causally-related independent variables. A linear functional form is assumed and parameters are estimated from a sample of data. Inferences are drawn towards a wider population. In practice, where it has been used extensively, for example in econometrics, its predictive ability has been extremely poor (Lawson, 1997). From a CR viewpoint this is hardly surprising since there are severe limitations in this approach.

i)   The notion of causality is impoverished being essentially the Humean one of a constant conjunction of events as underlying empiricism (Ron 1999). A set of empirical observations is made, and a mathematical procedure produces an equation that best links them on the basis of an assumed model (typically multivariate normality). The equation is then often used for predictive purposes. The justification for this procedure is either that the variables "really are" linked by some such universal law that the regression is capturing, or the instrumentalist version that the model is useful predictively even though it is not representing "real" relationships. The main problem with this is that it remains in the superficial world of the empirical, with no attempt to get at underlying mechanisms that may be responsible for the observed regularities. This is manifest in the truism that the correlation coefficient only identifies association not causality. This remains just as true in complex and sophisticated regression models as it does at the level of a simple bivariate correlation. There is no way from the model to decide if a correlation is genuine or spurious.

ii) The procedure rests on an implicit assumption of closure (Sayer 1992; Olsen 1999) which, as we have already seen in Chapter 2, cannot be expected to occur in social systems. By this I mean that the stability of the coefficients, and their statistical significance, rests on assuming that the factors that have not been included, usually because they are unknown or impossible to measure, have only a small and essentially random effect. In practice, the effect may well be large and there is no way of knowing what the influence will be outside of the sample data.

iii) The main assumptions of regression—multivariate normal distributions, independence of variables, one-way causality, linearity, etc.—are highly implausible to say the least. As we have seen, the real world is characterised by complex, often circular, chains of interaction that occur at many different levels. This undermines the traditional idea of significance tests, the logic of which is: if we assume that the model is true in reality (null hypothesis) then alpha is the probability of obtaining the observed values (and then wrongly rejecting the null hypothesis). Since, almost by definition, the model will not be "true," it makes no real sense to accept that it is.

iv) All of this makes it very difficult to choose between competing models for the same data. Elaborate methods have been devised—e.g., stepwise, best-subsets, fragility analysis—but in practice many different models are developed and choices made on essentially subjective grounds such as experience, usefulness, or perhaps just intuition (King 1991). Even more problematic is the very nature of the data itself which tends to be taken for granted, but which CR would recognise as being highly dependent on the processes of its production (Mingers 1989).

Given these problems, it might seem that CR would abandon statistical analysis all together, especially since empirical verification is not a necessary feature of a realist scientific explanation (since causal tendencies may be possessed but not actualised). This is not the case, but it does require a re-thinking of the purpose of such analysis, and also a differentiation between different techniques. Critical realism proceeds by trying to discover underlying structures that generate particular patterns of events (or non-events). Statistical analysis can help in several areas: i) It can be very useful in the exploratory stage in detecting particular patterns within the data. Any non-randomness must imply some structure or set of constraints that is generating it, although, of course, this may be just as much a result of the mechanism of data production as any underlying generative mechanism. Nevertheless, detecting such patterns within large sets of multivariate data is very difficult and methods such principal components, factor analysis, cluster analysis, and regression are very valuable. The results, though, will merely be the starting point for more substantive investigations. ii) Some techniques do lend themselves more towards identifying underlying structures, especially something like factor analysis, which aims to identify common factors generating observed variables, or path analysis (Olsen 1999) that involves a series of inter-related equations. Even here, however, the results are merely suggestive, not conclusive. iii) Perhaps the main use might be in validating possible explanations by corroborating, or falsifying them. This could be done either by testing the implications of a theory through collecting and analysing data (Porpora 1998a). Or, more sophisticatedly, by regarding the analysis as a quasi-experiment, inducing artificial closure on a system by controlling for the influence of normally uncontrolled factors (Ron 1999). Techniques such as multivariate analysis of variance and covariance are useful here.

These points can be illustrated with a practical experience of my own using time series decomposition, a technique that at face value is even more empiricist than regression in ignoring outside causal factors completely. The project concerned a major UK bank that wanted to better control the amount of cash kept in cash machines. This required good forecasting of daily cash demand at individual machines. There was a large dataset of actual withdrawals from machines over two years and also ideas about particular underlying factors influencing demand (generative mechanisms). The project proceeded in two ways—the data itself was interrogated to identify particular seasonal patterns and, at the same time, theoretical suggestions were investigated by seeing if the data supported them. Examples of such factors are: a weekly effect where withdrawals were greatest on Fridays and Saturdays; a monthly effect where withdrawals fell towards the end of the month, then picked up as people were paid; the effects of particular events such as Christmas; the influence of the location of the machine, for example those in universities had different patterns from those on high streets, and those near race-courses were affected by the occurrence of a race meeting. The overall approach, which I believe is typical of OR/MS, was one of developing hypotheses about causal mechanisms and using the data both for discovery and justification without becoming trapped in the purely empirical domain of the data in itself.

### 9.4.2 Soft Systems—Critique of an Interpretive Methodology

Soft OR is too diverse to cover overall, so I will confine discussion to cognitive mapping and SSM as two of the most well known approaches. Cognitive mapping is a diagrammatic technique for depicting the way an individual thinks about a particular issue or problem. In appearance it is similar to an influence diagram but it clearly aims to map *a person's beliefs about* an issue, rather than "objective" aspects of the situation. It is primarily used within strategic decision making as part of a wider process that was known as SODA (Eden 1989) and is now called *Journeymaking* (Eden and Ackerman 1998). Cognitive mapping is based on Kelly's psychological theory of constructs and is subjectivist in limiting itself to exploring people's beliefs about the world. It can, therefore, clearly be seen as interpretive or hermeneutic in character and as such in opposition to the intransitive world of real structures and objects. However, I would argue that this is not wholly the case. It is part of a wider process within which the actor-independent world is considered. Different peoples' individual maps can be compared and, through discussion, group maps can be developed. This process becomes less and less subjective, and can result in substantive, real-world research.

"It is usual for a SODA workshop to identify opportunities for further analysis, such as financial model building, simulation modelling, market research, and statistical analysis." (Eden 1989 p. 39).

In one documented case (Bennett, Ackerman et al., 1997), cognitive mapping was combined with a system dynamics model that was explicitly aiming to be demonstrably valid in depicting actual occurrences. Overall, it is better seen as a qualitative component within a pluralist research framework.

Moving to SSM, this could also be seen at first sight as being antithetical to CR. Checkland denies the ontological reality of "systems," instead reserving this concept for *thinking about* the world. He also distinguishes strongly between natural and social science, or rather positivist and interpretivist approaches within social science, and allies SSM clearly with the phenomenological tradition. I shall have to restrict myself to making a few observations on SSM from a CR perspective. The main problem is that Checkland takes positivism as the only alternative to interpretivism as a philosophy of (social) science. This inevitably means that he has to adopt a full-blown phenomenological position that then generates all kinds of contradictions and problems in dealing with a "real-world" external to the observer; that is, after all, what SSM aims to improve (Jackson 1982; Mingers 1984). The major advantage of a critical realist approach is that it maintains reality whilst still recognising the inherent meaningfulness of social interaction.

It might be said that SSM only concerns ideas or concepts (root definitions or conceptual models) and that these are somehow less real than objects. Or, that it is strongly relativist in accepting all viewpoints as being equally valid. Against this, critical realism demonstrates that ideas, concepts, meanings and categories are equally as real as physical objects (Bhaskar 1997). They are emergent from, but irreducible to, the physical world, and have causal effect both on the physical world (e.g., in the generation of technology) and the social and ideational world. They are also inevitably social products and participate in transformations of the social world, just the sort of transformations that SSM aims to bring about. With regard to relativism, CR makes a distinction between epistemic relativism and judgmental relativism—people may well hold different beliefs about processes in the world but this does not mean that we are unable to rationally judge between them and prefer one to another given some particular purpose. Equally, ideas once expressed are no longer wholly subjective—they become intransitive and available for investigation, debate and judgement by others. This is an example of a more general idea—referential detachment (Bhaskar 1994, p. 52)—that any communication must refer to something, that which it is about (even if it is self-referential), and this immediately establishes an intransitive dimension. Bhaskar goes further in arguing against the positivist distinction between facts and values (which would fit in well with both soft and critical OR/MS), and eventually to a moral realism—i.e., the idea that there could be moral truths (Bhaskar 1994, p. 108).

A final point is the weakness of SSM with regard to the origin of the Weltanschauungen that it explores, and an understanding of the difficulties of individual and organisational change. These both stem from the individualistic social theory that it embodies. With a critical realist interpretation both of these are avoided. On the one hand we can generate explanations of why particular actors may hold the beliefs they do in terms of their social and organisational position; their history of experiences particularly as these relate to underlying social characteristics such as gender, race, and age; and, of course, their individual personalities (Whittington 1992). We are also in a position to understand the psychological and social structures that may impede or facilitate learning and change.

## 9.5 Conclusions

This chapter has considered the theory underlying a multimethodology approach before looking at its use in practice in Chapter 10. The primary argument is against the views either that there is only one appropriate paradigm for research and intervention—usually positivism/empiricism, or that there can be several valid paradigms only one of which need be applied in a particular situation. Drawing on earlier parts of the book concerning critical realism, information and meaning, embodied cognition and the nature of the social world it is instead claimed that the multi-dimensional nature of the world and of particular interventions in it forces us to routinely employ multi-paradigm multi-methodology.

## Glossary

This section will clarify a set of terms (e.g., methodology, method, technique) that is used throughout the chapter. Words such as "paradigm," "methodology," "method," and "technique" are open to many interpretations so while I shall endeavour to use the following definitions consistently it must be recognised that these are not claimed to be the "correct" ones, and that inevitably some latitude will be required in applying them across a variety of areas.

### Methodology, method, technique

Interventions and research are conducted by undertaking particular activities such as building a simulation model, doing cognitive mapping, developing root definitions and conceptual models, or administering and analysing a survey. These basic activities will be termed *methods* or *techniques,* using these words synonymously. They are generally well defined sequences of operations that, if carried out proficiently, yield predictable results. However, there is often a confusion between the terms "method" and "methodology."

For this chapter it is useful to distinguish three usages of the term *methodology.*

The most general meaning is "method-*ology*" meaning the study of methods. One might use this meaning to refer to a course in OR Methodology that covered a whole range of different methods.

The most specific meaning is when talking about "the methodology" of a particular project. In this sense the term refers to the actual method(s) or technique(s) used and thus every project has its own, individual, methodology.

The third usage is a generalisation of the second. Particular combinations of methods occur many times in practice, or are deliberately designed *a priori*, and come to be called "a methodology." Examples are Soft Systems Methodology, SODA, and Strategic Choice.

Using the term in this third way, "a methodology" is more general and less prescriptive than a method. It is a structured set of guidelines or activities to assist in undertaking interventions or research. It will often consist of various methods or techniques, not all of which need be used every time. This chapter is generally concerned with combining research *methods* or *techniques*, but it is also possible to combine these more generic *methodologies.*

## Paradigm

Methodologies, and therefore methods, make implicit or explicit assumptions about the nature of the world and of knowledge. It has been conventional to call particular combinations of assumptions *paradigms*. A paradigm is thus a construct that specifies a general set of philosophical assumptions covering, for example, *ontology* (what is assumed to exist), *epistemology* (the nature of valid knowledge), *ethics* (what is valued or considered right), and *methodology*. In simple terms, we can say that a methodology specifies *what* to do, a paradigm defines *why* this should be done, and a method or technique provides a particular *how* to do it There can only be a relatively small number of paradigms existing within a discipline at one time although there may be different ways of classifying them. This chapter uses the idea of different paradigms to emphasise the desirability of combining together methodologies that have distinctively different assumptions, but does not thereby wish to remain wedded to the particular paradigm boundaries that exist at the moment. To fit in with current literature, I will generally refer to three—hard or positivist, soft or interpretive, and critical.

# Chapter 10: The Process of Multimethodology

## 10.1 Introduction

In Chapter 9 we argued that there can be many benefits in combining different intervention and research methods together, both to deal with different dimensions of a situation and because of the different phases of an intervention. But, given that there are many, many different methods and methodologies, how should an analyst choose which to use in a particular intervention? In this section several frameworks will be presented that can help the practitioner to design a multimethodology suitable for a particular situation. They will be incorporated into a general description of a design process in the next section.

## 10.2 The Context of Practical Interventions

The general context for the use of multimethodology is the purposeful engagement of an agent(s) with some aspect of their social or organisational world. Checkland interprets such situations in terms of two notional systems, a *problem-solving system (PSS)* and a *problem-content system (PCS)*. The use of multimethodology clearly lays extra emphasis on the various methodologies and techniques available, and so a framework with three systems, and the relations between them, is more useful as shown in Figure 10.1.

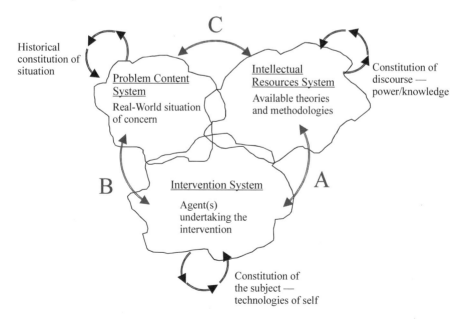

**Figure 10.1. Context of an intervention.**

The Intervention System (IS) consists of the particular people engaged with the Problem Content System (PCS), and possibly being ordinarily part of it. And the Intellectual Resources System (IRS) consists of those theories, methodologies, and techniques that could potentially be relevant to the problem situation, although not necessarily within the practitioners' or researchers' current repertoire.

More important from the point of view of multimethodology are the relationships *between* these notional systems (labelled A, B and C in Figure 10.1)—those between agents and methodologies/techniques (A), those between the agents and the situation (B), and those between methodologies/techniques and the situation (C). It is these relationships that are unique to a particular intervention and it is consideration of these that will guide the agents in their methodology choices. Some of the important dimensions of these relations can be highlighted in a series of questions. These are shown in Table 10.1. Of course, these relationships are not independent of each other. For example, in considering relation A, what methodologies the agent might use, it is also necessary to consider (B) the agent's relationship to the situation (e.g., am I expected to be a facilitator or an expert?), and (C) the relation between methodologies and the situation (e.g., does the organisation have any experience of this particular methodology?).

These three systems, and the relations between them, constitute the context for an intervention. Consideration of these sorts of issues will determine both the initial actions taken and the planning or design of the intervention as a whole. During an intervention they both condition, and change in response to, what happens. Thus they serve as continual reference points for the process of critical reflection that is necessary to structure the methodological choices made during the process.

## *10.3 A Framework for Mapping Methods*

Given that the main argument of this chapter is the potential advantages of combining together different methods, it is necessary to provide some way of characterising them so that a practitioner can use them in an informed way. The framework described next allows methods to be mapped in terms of the different aspects of a situation that they can deal with. In the earlier section on the desirability of multimethodology two important features of interventions were described—their multidimensionality and the different types of activity that need to be undertaken. Combining these two factors produces a grid (see Table 10.2) that can be used to map the characteristics of different methodologies to help in linking them together.

The logic of this framework is that a fully comprehensive intervention needs to be concerned with the three different worlds—*material*, *personal*, and *social*—and the four different phases of an intervention—*appreciation, analysis, assessment,* and *action*. Thus each box generates questions about particular aspects of the situation/intervention that need to be addressed. Such questions cannot be answered purely objectively, that is independently of the agents involved. Rather they should provoke ongoing debate, construction and reflection amongst the actors participating in the intervention from which decisions about the methods to be used should emerge.

## Table 10.1 Questions of Context

A) **Relations between practitioner(s) and intellectual resources**

- What is my level of critical awareness/understanding of potential methods?

- What is my experience and skill in using them?

- What is my personality/cognitive style comfortable with?

- To what extent can I work in varied paradigms?

- Nature of relation B)—intervention system to problem content system—e.g., what might I be able to use in this situation?

- Nature of relation C)—problem content system to intellectual resources system—e.g., what methods might be relevant to this situation?

B) **Relations between practitioner(s) and problem situations**

- What has initiated this engagement?

- What, if any, is my history of interactions in regard to this situation?

- What are my commitments to various actors in the situations?

- Who do I see as clients/victims/problem owners, etc.?

- What resources and powers do I have?

- Nature of relation A)—intervention system to intellectual resources system—e.g., what methods am I experienced in that may be useful? What might I have to learn?

- Nature of relation C)—problem content system to intellectual resources system—e.g., what methodologies may or may not be seen as legitimate here? What methods have they experienced?

C) **Relations between problem situation and intellectual resources**

- What is the culture of the organisation/situation with regard to methods?

- What is the history of past methods use?

- What methods are likely to be useful in this situation, given the particular tasks or concerns initiating the intervention? For example, is the task technical or strategic, well-defined or messy, uncontentious or political?

- To what extent are the values embedded in the methods appropriate to the situation?

- Nature of relation A)—intervention system to intellectual resources system—e.g., will the agent's experience allow the use of a particular method here?

- Nature of relation B)—intervention system to problem content system—e.g., does the practitioner's history with this organisation suggest particular methods?

## Table 10.2 Framework for Mapping Methods

|  | Appreciation of: | Analysis of: | Assessment of: | Action to: |
|---|---|---|---|---|
| **Social World** | Roles, norms, social practices, culture and power relations | Norms, practices, culture and underlying social structures | Ways of changing existing practices and culture | Generate enlightenment of social situation and empowerment |
| **Personal World** | Individual beliefs, meanings, values, and emotions | Differing Weltanschauungen and personal rationalities | Alternative conceptualisations and constructions | Generate understanding, personal learning and accommodation of views |
| **Material World** | Material and physical processes and arrangements | Underlying causal structures | Alternative physical and structural arrangements | Select and implement best alternatives |

The framework can be used to map various methods and methodologies on to it so that it is possible to easily see their strengths and weaknesses: which aspects of the situation and which phases of the intervention a particular methodology can be helpful with. In order to do this in a systematic way and in order to have a clear view of the actual purposes or outputs of a particular methodology, there needs to be a general, comparative, classification of the whole gamut of management science methods and methodologies that detailed both the primary purpose and the underlying assumptions of the method(ology). This would assist multimethodology users in understanding both the implicit or explicit assumptions underlying methods, and their principal aims and purposes, in order to be able to make more informed and critically-aware choices when designing particular combinations in practice. To some extent such a classification follows on from the system of systems methodologies (SOSM) (Jackson and Keys 1984; Jackson 1990), and other meta-frameworks (Bunge 1977; Bahm 1981; Muller-Mehrbach 1994), but is a significant development in giving a much richer picture. The classification involves seven dimensions rather than two, and does not try to pigeonhole methods into specific, narrow, categories.

We must also recognise that some methods may be used in ways that are quite different from that envisaged when they were developed and that, indeed, they may be employed from within an alternative paradigm. For instance, mathematical modelling, usually seen as a quantitative and relatively objective method, can be used in a soft way to facilitate a debate between different groups (Bryant 1988). This will be illustrated in Section 10.4.2

## 10.3.1 A Characterisation of Management Science Methods

In order to classify *all* management science method(ologies) we must identify the most general characteristics that they all share. I believe, and it is obviously open to debate, that they can be adequately captured by the following:

A management science methodology is essentially about taking action. It provides its users with particular *activities* that they can undertake in response to questions that they have about how they might transform some aspects of a situation (including simply their own understanding). The users may include both external analysts and internal clients. The overall approach is one that aims at synthesising the objectivity of the analyst with the commitment of the client (Eden 1989).

All management science methodologies (and this is a distinguishing characteristic) share the idea of developing *models* (representations) of aspects of the situation but they differ in terms of what they form models *of*. The models are usually expected to be amenable to some form of formal, logical or systemic analysis. There are, however, many different types of models—mathematical, computer-based, logical, diagrammatic, or linguistic.

Different methodologies, incorporating different approaches to modelling, all make implicit or explicit philosophical assumptions about:

- *Ontology*—that is, what types of entities are taken to have existence for the model. This is exemplified by what kinds of entities the method will build models of.

- *Epistemology*—that is, the forms of knowledge and knowledge creation the method uses. This is realised in terms of where the model comes from (e.g., "the world," someone's beliefs, or an abstract viewpoint), and the form in which it is represented.

- *Axiology*—that is, what is valued or considered good within the modelling approach. This is manifest in what the purposes or uses of the model are, and who (e.g., analyst, facilitator, participant) develops and uses the model.

It is also true to say that different methods will, to a greater or lesser extent, draw on particular bodies of theory. This could be seen as a differentiating characteristic, and it would certainly be valuable, when learning a new method, to understand something of its theoretical background. However, I do not think it would be useful to include it in this particular classification which is oriented towards the practical purposes of a method and any underlying presuppositions.

From the above three assumptions a root definition for a generalised management science method(ology) has been produced. This was developed in the "do P by Q in order to achieve R" form advocated by Checkland (1990, Ch. 2).

> A system to **do** *the process specified*, **by** developing models of *that assumed to exist*, in the *specified form of representation*, based on *necessary information*, gained from *particular sources*, **in order to** assist *users* achieve *specified purposes*.

This root definition makes explicit the three types of modelling assumptions as described above. They are identified by the different forms of underlining:

*Ontology*:    *that assumed to exist*—e.g., real measurable objects, or conceptual systems, or causal relationships.

*Epistemology*:    *form of representation*—e.g., equations, diagrams, software; *necessary information*—e.g., quantities, measurements, meanings, beliefs; *source of information*—e.g., real-world objects, participants, groups.

*Axiology*:    *users*—e.g., analyst, facilitator, participant, stakeholder; *purpose* e.g., optimising, learning, experimenting, challenging.

This root definition (RD) was then used to produce Table 10.3 covering a range of methods and methodologies. Clearly there are many others that could or perhaps should have been included (see for example the list in Munro and Mingers (2002)) but these were felt to cover the main, and most commonly used, types.

Table 10.3 was constructed on the basis of a thorough review of the literature, both theoretical and practical, for the various methods. It has also been seen by the originators of the methods where that was possible and their comments have been taken into account, although responsibility for the precise wording in the Table rests with the author[66].

To describe the Table in more detail, the first column records, as specifically as possibly, what the methodology *does* rather than *why* it does it (i.e., its purpose) or *how* it does it, which are covered in later columns. This is the "Do P" part of the root definition. On the basis of this, it is possible to infer what ontological assumptions are implicitly being made (column 2). Each method will focus on or bring out certain aspects of the world and not others. This does not necessarily deny the existence of

---

[66] I would like to thank Russ Ackoff, Peter Bennett, Colin Eden, John Friend, Werner Ulrich.

other characteristics or dimensions; the method simply makes no reference to them. That which is assumed to exist is those entities and relations, physical or conceptual, that are captured by the model. For example, mathematical programming assumes that there are entities and processes with measurable characteristics that can be described by linear or non-linear inequalities, together with an agreed and measurable objective(s). Interactive planning assumes groups of stakeholders with differing but reconcilable views about desirable futures.

The next three columns deal with the epistemological assumptions of the method. The first describes the form that the model takes, its type of representation. This is the "By Q" part of the root definition. Thus, mathematical programming uses a set of simultaneous inequalities together with an objective function and an optimisation method; whilst SSM uses a combination of rich pictures, root definitions, etc. From the form of representation, it is possible to derive what information it is necessary to have or produce, and from where it is assumed the information will come—the next two columns. The latter point is at the heart of the epistemological differences between methods. In particular, does a method assume that the information is derived from objective measurements on the external world, independent of any observer or agent; or is it assumed that it is individual subjective views gleaned by interviews and discussion; or perhaps group views or social practices explicated through discussions, workshops, or even participation in the situation?

The final two columns describe the use of the method—the "In Order To R" part of the RD. In particular, who will use the approach, and what is its primary purpose. The three main categories of user are: *analysts* who are external (to the particular situation of concern) experts in the method and use it, by themselves, on behalf of others (e.g., clients or problem-owners); *facilitators* who use a method with actors in a situation to help the actors resolve the problem; and *participants* who are themselves actors in the situation who also enact the method, possibly assisted by a facilitator. A flexible methodology such as SSM can in fact be used in all three ways: it could be used privately by an analyst to help that person in performing an intervention; it could be used by a facilitator without actually revealing it to the participants; or it could be used in a fully transparent way with the participants producing their own root definitions and conceptual models.

The final column is in some ways the most important of the table, as it attempts to give a brief description of the specific results that the method aims to bring about. This may well provide the main practical benefit for users of methods, as it can help them select a method on the basis of what they need to achieve at a particular point within an intervention, whether it be the initial design of an intervention strategy, or some way through the process. When dealing with a generic methodology such as SSM it would probably be helpful to take this one stage further and break it down into its component methods, specifying the purpose of each, rather than remaining at the level of the methodology as a whole. For an example see the decomposition of SSM presented in Section 10.4.1.

**Table 10.3— A Framework for Characterising the Philosophical Assumptions Underlying OR/MS Methodologies and Techniques.**

| Methodology/ technique | What it does A system to.... | Ontology What it assumes to exist | Epistemology Representation by modelling.... | Necessary information | Source of information | Axiology Users | Purpose in order to.... |
|---|---|---|---|---|---|---|---|
| Mathematical programming | Model the relationships between many variables using linear or non- linear equations and optimises the value of an objective function. | Relations between the measurable attributes of entities and processes, together with explicit objective(s) | Variables, linear and non-linear constraints, optimisation software. | Relevant variables and necessary data to model the relationships between them | Observation and measurement of real world processes | Analyst | Evaluate many different options and decisions thereby optimizing an objective(s). |
| Visual discrete-event simulation | Simulate the behaviour of particular entities and the activities they undergo in a visual interactive form | Entities and activities with stable patterns of statistical behaviour that form inter-linked processes. | Activity-cycle diagrams, entity life cycles, visual, interactive software | Entities, their interactions, and the behavioural patterns. | Observation and measurement of real world entities and procedures | Analyst | Explore the operation of complex real-world interactions between discrete entities to aid understanding and control |
| Systems dynamics | Simulate the dynamic behaviours of physical and social flows and processes, and their causal relations | Material and immaterial stocks and flows, and their causal feedback relations, information and decisions that link them | Influence diagrams, systems dynamics diagrams, icon-based interactive software | Structure of causal relations between flows, ideally with quantified data and mathematical relations | Observation and measurement of real world together with judgement and opinion | Analyst | Explore the operation of a complex real-world systems to aid understanding and control. |

| Methodology/ technique | What it does — A system to... | Ontology — What it assumes to exist | Epistemology — Representation by modelling.... | Necessary information | Source of information | Axiology — Users | Purpose — in order to.... |
|---|---|---|---|---|---|---|---|
| SODA (including cognitive mapping) | Represent explicitly an individual's views about a particular issue or event in their own language. | Individual beliefs about particular issues expressible in terms of inter-related constructs | Psychological constructs and their mutual influences in the form of a map, software for representing, analysing and merging maps. | Personal constructs and their inter-relations. | Interviews/ workshops with (groups of) participants. | Facilitator, researcher, participants | Surface and understand individual beliefs, and generate consensus about possible strategic actions |
| Soft Systems Methodology | Explore different worldviews relevant to a real-world situation and contrast them in a process of debate | Real-world problem situation; conceptual human activity systems (holons); worldviews Ws. | Systems concepts; rich pictures, analyses 1,2,3; RD/CMs; logical relationships | Hard and soft information concerning structure, process, climate, and relevant worldviews | Concepts, language, logic and participation by concerned actors. | Analyst, researcher, facilitator, participant | Learn about and improve a problematic situation by gaining agreement on feasible and desirable changes |
| Strategic Choice Approach | Assist groups of users in making incremental progress toward implementable decisions by recognising and managing uncertainties | A network of inter-related problems, decisions and uncertainties as viewed by participants | Models of the decision space, inter-connected decision areas, decision schemes and commitment packages. Walls, flip charts, software | Participants' views concerning decisions, options, uncertainties, and feasibilities as well as real world data. | Workshops with (groups of) participants | Facilitator, participant | Structure decision choices under conditions of uncertainty and reach agreements and commitments for action. |
| Interactive Planning | Prepare a vision of how an organisation should be now and plan how to realise the design. | Stakeholders with differing values that can be reconciled in designs for the future that are preferable for all. | Constrained or unconstrained idealised designs that are technologically feasible operationally viable, and improveable. | Stakeholders' views about desirable designs for their own spheres of influence, and their interrelations. | Involvement by all the stakeholders in the design/planning process. | Analyst, facilitator, stakeholders | Plan and design futures that are desirable for different' stakeholder groups, and then jointly realise them. |

| Methodology/ technique | What it does A system to... | Ontology What it assumes to exist | Epistemology Representation by modelling.... | Necessary information | Source of information | Axiology Users | Purpose in order to.... |
|---|---|---|---|---|---|---|---|
| Critical Systems Heuristics | Use specified boundary questions so that the involved and affected can challenge the "expert" decisions of planners and designers, and their normative consequences. | Premises and boundary judgements made by designers that have normative implications for affected by the design | Twelve critical questions concerning the motivation, control, expertise and legitimation of a design that can be used "polemically." | Information concerning the plans including subjective viewpoints | Discussions with those involved and affected by plans and designs | Citizens, planners | Provide support for planners and citizens to raise, explore and critique the normative implications of plans and designs |
| Viable Systems Model | Use cybernetic principles of viable existence in the diagnosis and design of an organisation. | Principles of cybernetic viability that are applicable to organisations | Organisations in terms of VSM structure of five inter-related subsystems and their communication links | Purposes, structure environment and communications of an organisation. | Cybernetic principles and research into an organisation. | Analyst | Diagnose and improve organisational structure and functioning. |
| Strategic Assumption Surfacing and Testing (SAST) | Surface a variety of contrasting strategic options and achieve consensus through a debate. | Groups with competing views, and the assumptions underlying these from different stakeholder viewpoints | Diametrically opposed viewpoints, underlying assumptions, and relevant stakeholders. | Options, individual characteristics and viewpoints, stakeholders and their interests, | Formation of maximally different groups to present and debate different viewpoints | Facilitator, participants, stakeholders | Synthesise competing viewpoints about complex interactive messes |
| Drama Theory/ Hypergames | Represent a competitive situation involving different players and interacting decisions using a variety of game-theory based modelling tools | Complexes of interacting decisions consisting of competing players, strategies, viewpoints, and preferences under conditions of uncertainty | Game matrices, trees, decision arena models | Competing players, their interests, options and strategies, and the decisions and uncertainties involved. | Various real-world players and parties involved in the decisions. | Analysts, players | Clarify the competitive structure of a situation in terms of interactive and conflicting decisions and possibilities for cooperation. |

## 10.3.2 Mapping Methods

The first aim of the characterisation was to assist with the mapping of methods and methodologies onto the framework shown in Table 10.2. Some results are shown in Figures 10.2a-c.

Each grid shows a mapping for a particular method(ology). The shading shows which area of the grid the method can support and the depth of the shading represents a judgement about the strength of the support. By the idea of support is meant specifically that there are activities within the method that can help the user in that particular area. So where a particular cell is left blank, the implication is not that that aspect of the situation doesn't need to be dealt with, only that the particular method does not have a specific activity for it. Note that methods can be used in non-standard ways—this will be dealt with in the next section.

In mapping methods on to the grid I have had to be quite strict—it is relatively easy to suggest ways in which almost any method *could be used* to support a particular cell but this would not help in discrimination between the methods. So I have only mapped onto a particular cell when it can be shown that the method explicitly deals with it, either by having a specific activity concerned with it, or by explicitly addressing it in its underlying assumptions, or occasionally where the method has commonly come to be used for that purpose in practice. I recognise that these are judgmental decisions about which there could be debate. Mabin et al (2005) have used this framework to map the Theory of Constraints (TOC).

Let us consider some examples. Mathematical programming assumes measurable variables and known (usually linear) relationships between them. This would seem to confine it to the material dimension. It has strengths in analysing an existing situation (via its model) and assessing many alternatives. There are no specific activities for appreciating the situation initially. Although there are no specific activities assisting with implementation, the information available from various solutions can clearly be used to justify and support particular courses of action. Considering next system dynamics, this too generally assumes quantifiable variables and relationships and so is strong in the material dimension. The use of causal loop diagrams before developing the actual model does provide support for the appreciation phase. However, most system dynamicists (Lane 1999; Lane 2000) are happy for models to incorporate social practices even though these are only estimated or judgmental and therefore it can contribute (weakly) in the social dimension as well. The same is true of discrete event simulation (Robinson 2001) although this is less common.

Cognitive mapping may seem to be similar to the causal loop diagrams used as a precursor to system dynamics but it is epistemologically distinct in explicitly being subjectivist. That is, a cognitive map is clearly viewed as a representation of an *individual's beliefs* about a situation, rather than a map of the situation itself. This

## Discrete Event Simulation

| | Appreciation of | Analysis of | Assessment of | Action to |
|---|---|---|---|---|
| **Social** | social practices, power relations | distortions, conflicts, interests | ways of altering existing structures | generate empowerment and enlightenment |
| **Personal** | individual beliefs, meanings, emotions | differing perceptions, personal rationality | alternative conceptualizations and constructions | generate accommodation and consensus |
| **Material** | physical circumstances | underlying causal structure | alternative physical and structural arrangements | select and implement best alternatives |

## Cognitive Mapping

| | Appreciation of | Analysis of | Assessment of | Action to |
|---|---|---|---|---|
| **Social** | social practices, power relations | distortions, conflicts, interests | ways of challenging power structure | generate empowerment and enlightenment |
| **Personal** | individual beliefs, meanings, emotions | differing perceptions and Weltanschauung | alternative conceptualisation's and constructions | generate accommodation and consensus |
| **Material** | physical circumstances | underlying causal structure | alternative physical and structural arrangements | select and implement best alternatives |

## Mathematical Programming

| | Appreciation of | Analysis of | Assessment of | Action to |
|---|---|---|---|---|
| **Social** | social practices, power relations | distortions, conflicts, interests | ways of altering existing structures | generate empowerment and enlightenment |
| **Personal** | individual beliefs, meanings, emotions | differing perceptions, personal rationality | alternative conceptualizations and constructions | generate accommodation and consensus |
| **Material** | physical circumstances | underlying causal structure | alternative physical and structural arrangements | select and implement best alternatives |

## System Dynamics

| | Appreciation of | Analysis of | Assessment of | Action to |
|---|---|---|---|---|
| **Social** | social practices, power relations | distortions, conflicts, interests | ways of altering existing structures | generate empowerment and enlightenment |
| **Personal** | individual beliefs, meanings, emotions | differing perceptions, personal rationality | alternative conceptualizations and constructions | generate accommodation and consensus |
| **Material** | physical circumstances | underlying causal structure | alternative physical and structural arrangements | select and implement best alternatives |

**Figure 10.2a. Mappings of Particular Methodologies.**

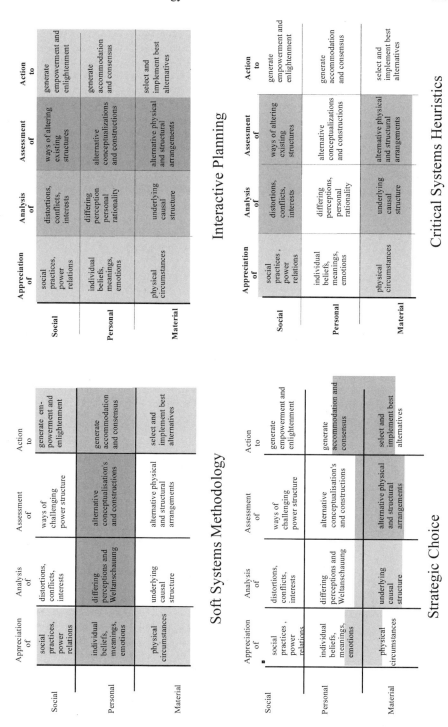

**Figure 10.2b. Mappings of Particular Methodologies.**

**SAST**

| | Appreciation of | Analysis of | Assessment of | Action to |
|---|---|---|---|---|
| Social | social practices, power relations | distortions, conflicts, interests | ways of altering existing structures | generate empowerment and enlightenment |
| Personal | individual beliefs, meanings, emotions | differing perceptions, personal rationality | alternative conceptualizations and constructions | generate accommodation and consensus |
| Material | physical circumstances | underlying causal structure | alternative physical and structural arrangements | select and implement best alternatives |

**Hypergames**

| | Appreciation of | Analysis of | Assessment of | Action to |
|---|---|---|---|---|
| Social | social practices, power relations | distortions, conflicts, interests | ways of altering existing structures | generate empowerment and enlightenment |
| Personal | individual beliefs, meanings, emotions | differing perceptions, personal rationality | alternative conceptualizations and constructions | generate accommodation and consensus |
| Material | physical circumstances | underlying causal structure | alternative physical and structural arrangements | select and implement best alternatives |

**Viable Systems Method**

| | Appreciation of | Analysis of | Assessment of | Action to |
|---|---|---|---|---|
| Social | social practices, power relations | distortions, conflicts, interests | ways of challenging power structure | generate empowerment and enlightenment |
| Personal | individual beliefs, meanings, emotions | differing perceptions and Weltanschauung | alternative conceptualisation's and constructions | generate accommodation and consensus |
| Material | physical circumstances | underlying causal structure | alternative physical and structural arrangements | select and implement best alternatives |

**Figure 10.2c. Mappings of Particular Methodologies.**

means that its main contribution must lie within the Personal dimension as a way of articulating and exploring individual peoples' viewpoints. But cognitive mapping, and SODA more generally, does have an underlying theory of organisations as negotiated social reality (Eden and Ackermann 2001) and the later stages of SODA can help in the social dimension.

Moving to SSM, it is clear that the major philosophical thrust of SSM is in surfacing and exploring individual participants' beliefs and values. It therefore contributes mainly in the personal dimension. Here, it is particularly strong in generating and assessing alternative possibilities. It is less strong in terms of activities to bring about consensus and change. The use of rich pictures is a good way of exploring the situation in the material dimension, and Analyses 1, 2, 3 focus attention on the social and political dimensions of the problem situation. SSM has been criticised for its lack of a social theory (Jackson 1982; Mingers 1984) and does not have specific activities that address the later stages in this dimension but has in practice been used to bring about social change and so contributes weakly in these areas.

Strategic Choice Approach has specific methods for covering all phases of a project, and its commitment package has been commonly used in a multimethodology context as a good way of securing agreement for action. I have placed it across the personal/material divide because whilst it recognises there may be different stakeholders and viewpoints, it does not explicitly model these, but concentrates on the production of a shared model of "reality."

Ackoff's interactive planning is the only methodology, I would argue, that covers all the possibilities to some extent. It recognises a plurality of stakeholders and the need for discussion and consensus (as Ackoff (1977) argues, objectivity is a combination of subjectivities); it both analyses the existing situation and considers alternative "desirable" futures; and in its means planning it recognises both material and organisational aspects. Finally, the whole approach is aimed at securing agreement and action about realising a vision. This may explain why, for example, Ormerod (1995; 1996b) has often used it as an overall framework.

The second use of the framework (an example is shown in Table 10.4) is in the design of a particular intervention. Here the focus is on the individual boxes. The practitioner can ask which of the boxes are of most importance for the particular intervention. In theory, of course, all are relevant but in practice limitations of time, resources, and competence, and the actual problem of concern may well make it necessary to focus most of the attention on only certain aspects of the problem space. Then, for each of the boxes focus methods can be chosen that are particularly strong in those areas. The user can also look at the final column of Table 10.3 which tries to encapsulate the primary purpose of each methodology.

Some caveats are in order in using the framework. First, it is not intended that methodologies be slotted into particular boxes in the manner of Jackson and Keys' (1984) system of systems methodologies. Rather they are mapped across all the different areas to which they can contribute. Second, clearly the precise placing of a particular method or methodology is debatable (see Ormerod (2005) and Mingers (2005)). I would be happy for further debate to result in the scope of methodologies being widened on the framework subject to them not becoming so wide that the framework is no longer of use in discriminating between them.

## 10.4 The Process of Multimethodology Design

The design of multimethodology interventions occurs in two stages: at the initiation of a project a broad plan will be specified detailing what combination of methods and techniques may be used in the light of the questions outlined in Table 10.1. Then, as the project proceeds, there will be a continual monitoring process of reflection and design to adjust the activities in the light of actual occurrences both internal and external to the project. The balance between these two may differ— some projects may be well-specified in advance, while others may be deliberately left to evolve as the project develops—but it is important to maintain a clear mental distinction between the ongoing design of the project and its actual operation, as Figure 10.3 shows.

The two lower cylinders show the ongoing process of the intervention in which the practitioner(s) take action in the problem content system. The fact that the two

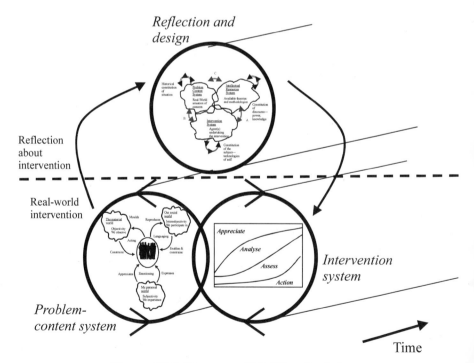

**Figure 10.3. Process of Multimethodology.**

circles are not contiguous represents the fact that both systems have lives of their own outside, but conditioning, the intervention. The upper cylinder shows the metalevel activities of *reflection* and *design* that appreciate and respond to the intended and unintended consequences of previous actions by specifying the next steps to be taken and methods to be used. There are four key subactivities:

- Reflection:

    - *Review* the current situation.

    - *Determine* which areas of the problem situation currently need addressing.

- Design:

    - *Understand* what methods or techniques could possibly be useful.

    - *Choose* the most appropriate to use in relation to the project context as a whole.

These subactivities are posed here at a rather general level, but the frameworks described above have been developed to assist in undertaking them.

At the start of the intervention especially, attention must be paid to the general context—PCS, IS, and IRS (Figure 10.1) and the list of critical questions (Table 10.1) should be used to help produce a set of feasible methodological choices. These will reflect the nature of the task to the extent that it can be defined, the organisational context, and the knowledge and experience of the practitioners. This initial consideration may suggest only one or two possible methods, or it could leave open a wide range. To help narrow this choice down, it is useful to consider the different dimensions of the problematic situation—material, social, and personal (Figure 9.1), and the different stages of a project—the 4 As (Sections 9.2.2) and the methods or techniques that may be particularly useful at each phase. These last two aspects can be considered together using the framework for mapping methodologies (Table 10.2). One could then end up with a selection of methodologies, or their parts, mapped onto the framework, showing how they will fit together within the project as a whole. An example of such a multimethodology design is shown in Table 10.4.

This should not be seen as a generic multimethodology design, but simply one that could be suitable for a particular intervention. In this example, several methods are used in the first, Appreciation, phase—SSM rich pictures and analysis 1, 2, 3, CSH "is" questions, and some data production and analysis. In the Analysis phase, cognitive mapping and SSM conceptual modelling are used to make sense of the information produced in the first phase. Consideration then turns to Assessing various possible alternative solutions using conceptual modelling again, the viable systems model for organisational design, and the CSH "ought" questions. Finally, as the project moves to the Action phase, a strategic choice type commitment package is agreed.

**Table 10.4. An illustrative multimethodology design.**

|  | Appreciation of | Analysis of | Assessment of | Action to |
|---|---|---|---|---|
| **Social World** | Critical Systems Heuristics—"Is" SSM—Analysis 1,2 3 |  | Critical Systems Heuristics—"Ought" Viable Systems Model |  |
| **Personal World** | SSM – Rich Pictures | SSM – RDs and CMs Cognitive mapping | SSM—RDs and CMs | Strategic Choice—commitment package |
| **Material World** | SSM—Rich Pictures Data production and statistical analysis |  | Viable Systems Model |  |

With an understanding of the issues that need to be addressed at a particular point in time and an appreciation of the contribution that various methods and techniques can make, the methodology choices can be made and put into action. However, the final decision about which methods and techniques to use brings us back to the individual practitioner (or team) for it is ultimately their choice (in negotiation with the client), and it will necessarily and appropriately reflect their personal skills, experience, values, and personality. Some might argue objectivity requires that the nature of the task, rather than the analyst, should determine the choice of approach. But from the multimethodology perspective this is impossible both philosophically and practically. Philosophically because, as Ackoff (1977) has said, objectivity can only be the result of many subjectivities: it is value-full not value-free; practically, because individuals' skills and experience actually matter in their choices of method. Everyone is not equally competent across a wide range of quantitative and qualitative approaches, and we all tend to have our own favourites with which we feel most comfortable. This follows very much for the discussion of embodied cognition in Chapter 7 which denies the easy separation of mind from body. It is often more effective to use a somewhat inappropriate method well than an appropriate method badly. In the longer term it is important that practitioners review their range of knowledge and skills and develop their methodological competence (Ormerod 1997).

## 10.4.1 Partitioning/Decomposing Methodologies

One approach to multimethodology is that of linking together *parts* of methodologies (rather than combine whole ones), possibly from different paradigms. This requires detailed study of the different methodologies to see where fruitful links can be created, but is in any case dependent on the idea that techniques or methods can be detached from one methodology and used in another. Generally, such a transfer will conserve the original function, for example, using cognitive mapping within SSM to explore actors' viewpoints. However, it is possible to transfer a methodology or technique into a setting that makes different paradigm assumptions. For example, system dynamics models are usually seen as hard or positivist, being possible models of *external reality*. However, they could be used in an interpretive way, as models of *concepts*, i.e., as models of how things might be from a particular viewpoint in a similar way to cognitive maps.

This linking process requires that methodologies be decomposed or partitioned in some systematic way to identify detachable elements and their functions or purposes. It is proposed this can be done in terms of distinctions between underlying principles (*why*), methodological stages (*what*), and techniques (or methods) (*how*). The primary focus of a methodology is its stages—a conceptual account of what needs to be done. These are justified by the underlying philosophical principles and actualised by a set of activities or techniques within a methodology. The techniques may be complementary to each other in that several must occur, or they may be substitutes, any one being potentially satisfactory.

It seems potentially possible to detach pieces of a methodology either at the level of techniques or at the higher level of methodological stages. The former is more straightforward and is particularly useful when enhancing a whole methodology (e.g., SSM) with techniques from another (e.g., cognitive mapping). Whilst a technique does have a particular purpose or output, this needs to be interpreted within the context of the particular methodological stage that it realises. Thus in moving a technique from one methodology (and possibly paradigm) to another, its context and interpretation may be changed. To take one of the examples above, if a system dynamics model is built as part of a hard methodology its context will lead to the results being interpreted as a model of reality. If it is detached and used within a soft setting it will be interpreted as a model of a notional system or concept. The model-building process will be essentially the same, although the previous stage of generating inputs to the model will be different.

Figure 10.4 shows a decomposition of SSM and concentrates on the stages concerned with expressing the real-world situation and with modelling relevant conceptual systems. Each of these stages has particular techniques that help accomplish them, for example, rich pictures and analyses 1, 2 and 3 for expressing the situation. Some techniques may have lower-level tools such as CATWOE or a computerised system for drawing rich pictures (CASE tool). It is these techniques (and their lower level tools) that can be disconnected from the methodology, as shown by the thick lines, and used in other contexts within other methodologies. The figure also shows how techniques can be imported into the methodology, for example, cognitive maps (and the associated computer tool COPE) instead of, or as well as, rich pictures; Ulrich's (1991) critical systems heuristics (CSH) as a complement to Analysis 3; or a viable systems model (VSM) (Beer 1985) to aid development of a conceptual model.

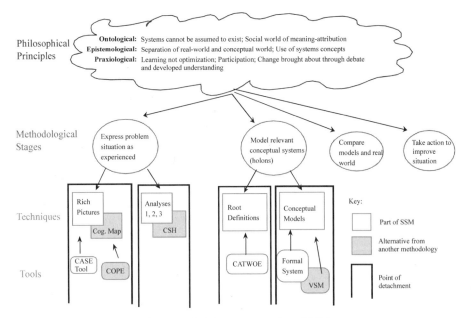

**Figure 10.4. Decomposing SSM.**

The main emphasis in Figure 10.4 is on the disconnection of techniques from their "home" methodology. The second possibility mentioned above, of detaching at the higher level of stages, is possible and occurs in both methodological enhancement (adding a stage to another methodology that is deficient) and multimethodology (combining various stages to construct a new, ad hoc, methodology). It is, however, more problematic, particularly in the multi-paradigm case since the stages are more strongly related to their philosophical paradigm. For example, "Modelling relevant conceptual systems" clearly expresses the soft rather than the hard view of model building.

## 10.4.2 Using Methods in Non-Standard Ways

The framework in Table 10.2 assumes that all the methods and techniques are being used in the way that they were originally intended—in the standard manner. However, it is possible to use them in non-standard ways within a different framework of assumptions or paradigm (Mingers 1997b; Mingers and Gill 1997), a possibility that has also been recognised by Bryant (1988), and Flood and Romm (1995) who call it the "oblique use of methods." Thus, for example, mathematical programming models are generally held to be models of an objective (i.e., observer-independent) reality, and hence the ontological assumptions listed in Table 10.3. But one could build a model that was consciously taken to be a model of a person or group's subjective beliefs rather than external reality. Such a model could be used as the basis for discussion and debate between the participants or stakeholders, leading to some sort of agreed action, rather than being seen as providing definite, objective solutions. Many of the techniques that are usually viewed as "hard" could be used in this non-standard way.

**Table 10.5. Examples of Methodologies Being Used out of Context.**

| Method(ology) | Description of non-standard use | References |
|---|---|---|
| Mathematical programming | Use mathematical programming models as subjective descriptions to formalise a debate between different actors.<br><br>Of particular interest is multi-objective or goal programming This allows for several competing objectives. Models could be built with broadly similar sets of constraints but with goals representing the views of different interest groups.<br><br>Data envelopment analysis (DEA) is concerned with the relative efficiency of similar organisational units in terms of the balance between inputs and outputs. Different models could be built representing competing views as to the purpose and thus the relevant inputs/outputs of the units. | (Bryant 1988) |
| Systems Dynamics | Systems dynamics was originated as a tool to build quantitative models of the real-world. Recent developments have stressed its qualitative use to model different peoples' perceptions and beliefs about particular events and occurrences. The models can be used as part of a learning and group decision making process alongside other soft approaches such as cognitive mapping and SSM. | (Wolstenholme and Coyle 1983; Wolstenholme 1993; Vennix 1996; Lane 1998) |
| VSM | The VSM is usually interpreted as a model of the human nervous system that can be applied to organisations. However it is also possible to see it instead as simply a model of a concept that can be useful as a heuristic in a debate or conversation between participants in a problem situation. Flood and Romm have also suggested the use of VSM in an "oblique" way in order to subvert the powerful within a coercive or organisational context. | (Harnden 1989; Jackson 1989; Flood and Romm 1995) |
| Cognitive Mapping | Cognitive mapping is usually seen as providing descriptions of subjective viewpoints. However, it is possible to "firm-up" a qualitative map and gradually develop it into an influence diagram and finally a fully quantified systems dynamics model. | (Eden 1994; Ackerman, Eden et al. 1997; Bennett, Ackerman et al. 1997) |
| SSM | There has been much interest in using SSM in the design of information systems. One approach is to link the conceptual models within SSM into a traditional hard IS design methodology (ISDM). There are a variety of approaches, some simply front-ending SSM to the ISDM, others involving more integration and the eventual embodying of the conceptual model in an actual IS artefact.<br><br>Flood and Romm have also suggested the use of SSM in an "oblique" way in order to subvert the powerful within a coercive organisational context. | (Flood and Romm 1995; Mingers 1995; Savage and Mingers 1996) |

It is also possible to move in the opposite direction by taking a "soft" technique and using it in a hard, objectivist way, or at least linking it to other hard techniques. For instance, an SSM conceptual model could be taken to be real-world rather than conceptual and actually instantiated or put into practice. Or, a cognitive map could be processed into becoming a system dynamics model taken to be a model of reality. Some examples of these alternative approaches are given in Table 10.5, together with references where known. Where methods are used out of context, then clearly the assumptions from Table 10.3, and the subsequent mappings, do not apply.

## *10.5 Multimethodology in Practice*

So far we have looked at combining methods rather in the abstract but in this section we will flesh out these ideas by briefly considering the two multimethodology interventions described by Richard Ormerod (2001), and then discussing more generally the use of multimethodology in the practitioner world based on an empirical survey and a literature review.

### 10.5.1 Sainsbury's and PowerGen Examples

These two interventions were carried out independently of the frameworks outlined in this chapter, but nevertheless exemplify many of the points very well. In both examples we can see the two stage process of design—a preliminary, and here quite well-defined, decision about which methods were to be used, and then a continual reflective adjustment of the design as events unfolded. These decisions were made in the light of the requirements of the organisational and project contexts as well as the practitioner's expertise and experience. As can be seen, particularly in PowerGen, the process needed to be quite creative, not just a slavish following of methodological stages. The decision to base the project around senior management participation required agreement from the company, and also determined to a large extent the possible methods to be used. It is interesting that commitment to participation at PowerGen was not at first forthcoming and had to be generated later in the project. The importance of context, and the interaction between problem content system, intervention system and intellectual resources system (Figure 10.1) is clearly shown.

In both cases the intervention was guided by an overall methodology, Ackoff's interactive planning, and then various other methods were brought in at particular stages. In terms of different types of multimethodology this is an example of methodology enhancement at two levels—interactive planning is enhanced by other methodologies (cognitive mapping, SSM, strategic choice) which are themselves further enhanced (e.g., Porter's five forces and VSM). Ormerod's description of the phases of the Sainsbury's project is very similar to the phases outlined in this chapter, and the sequence of methodologies—cognitive mapping for appreciation, SSM for analysis and strategic choice for assessment—fits well with the mapping presented in Table 10.4. The majority of the methods used were soft, fitting mainly into the personal and social dimensions of the situation, but harder, quantitative, techniques were also employed, particularly in the evaluation of various proposals.

## 10.5.2 Survey and Review

Munro and Mingers (2000) have recently carried out a survey of OR and systems practitioners to discover the extent of multimethodology use, and the particular combinations of methods that work well together. 64 respondents gave details of 163 different interventions each employing a combination of methods. Table 10.6 lists the most popular combinations occurring in threes (sometimes combined with other methods as well).

Actual examples of multimethodology use do show particular combinations that work well together. Some of the main points of interest are:

- SSM is used extensively as a methodology that can be combined with many others. SSM itself is very flexible and can be used to structure the whole

### Table 10.6. Most popular triads of methods.

| Method 1 | Method 2 | Method 3 | Frequency |
| --- | --- | --- | --- |
| Strategic Choice | SSM | Interactive Planning | 4 |
| Maths. Modelling | Simulation | Statistics | 3 |
| Maths. Modelling | Simulation | Heuristics | 2 |
| Statistics | Influence Diagrams | Cognitive Mapping | 2 |
| Statistics | SWOT | SSM | 2 |
| Statistics | SSM | Cognitive Mapping | 2 |
| Statistics | Project Networks | Forecasting | 2 |
| Statistics | Forecasting | Inventory | 2 |
| SSM | VSM | Strategic Choice | 2 |
| SSM | VSM | TSI | 2 |
| SSM | VSM | CSH | 2 |
| SSM | Interactive Planning | CSH | 2 |
| SSM | Scenarios | CSH | 2 |
| Cognitive Mapping | Delphi | Scenarios | 2 |
| Hypergames | Delphi | Scenarios | 2 |
| Cognitive Mapping | Delphi | Systems Dynamics | 2 |
| Cognitive Mapping | Decision Analysis | Strategic Choice | 2 |
| Cognitive Mapping | Influence Diagrams | Systems Dynamics | 2 |

intervention. It is often used as the dominant method augmented by other techniques. It has been used extensively in information systems development (Stowell 1995) both as a "front-end" to harder, structured systems analysis techniques, and as the controlling method throughout the systems development.

- Cognitive mapping is a general approach to capturing peoples' thinking about particular complex issues and as such is compatible with many other methods. It is particularly synergistic with system dynamics, as a map can be converted into an SD model; and it is also often used in the early stages of SSM to enhance the appreciation of the problem situation. It has also been used with strategic choice, decision analysis, and Delphi.

- Strategic choice can also be combined with SSM, particularly in the later stages of an intervention when decisions about, and commitments to, action are being negotiated.

- The viable systems model (VSM) is useful where organisational change is concerned, as it focuses attention on the necessary structural and communicational features of an effective organisation.

- Hard methods are combined together, e.g., mathematical modelling, simulation and statistics, but it is rare to mix hard and soft. This may well reflect the practitioners' skills and predilections rather than a lack of potential success.

## *10.6 The Nature of Critical Engagement*

So far in Part III we have discussed management science practice in a rather general way through the different forms of methods and methodologies that can be used in trying to bring about change. In this last section I want to move to a more engaged view of the realities of intervention and discuss how the approach of critical pluralism outlined so far embodies a form of *critical engagement.* This is motivated by three of the central themes of this book (see Section 9.1) that are themselves intertwined: the duality of knowledge and action (and the embodied nature of cognition); the importance of the individual agent in designing and then enacting multimethodology; and the significance of boundaries and constraints in interventions

We can structure the discussion using the three notional systems outlined in Figure 10.1—the intellectual resources system; the intervention system, i.e., the actual agents involved; and the problem content system. I wish to show that at the heart of almost any intervention are questions concerning the *mutability* of boundaries and constraints believed to exist within the situation. This view draws on several, quite disparate, theories—Midgley's theory of boundary critique, Bhaskar's view of explanatory critique, Foucault's and Habermas's (distinct) views of the nature of emancipation and critique, and, from a more direct management science perspective, the Theory of

Constraints (TOC)—as well as my own practical experiences of OR interventions. I also want to approach it from two different directions, or rather two intermeshing systems—that of structures and events within the situation of concern, and that of structures and events within the world of the agent(s) undertaking action (Figure 10.3).

In Section 10.6.1 we shall discuss what we might mean by the term "being critical" in general, drawing particularly on the work of Habermas and Foucault. In 10.6.2 these ideas will be applied to the OR practitioner—the agent actually engaged in struggling to improve a real-world situation. 10.6.3 then moves to consider the nature of this process in practice and argues that it can be conceptualised as a continual testing and stretching of constraints and boundaries.

## 10.6.1 Intellectual Resource: What is it to be Critical?

This section will discuss, at a general level, what it is to be *critical*—the nature of critique and emancipation and the relevance of this for intervention and indeed management as a widespread practice. To begin with, I will draw some distinctions between the related themes of *critique (and critical theory), enlightenment, emancipation, morality and ethics.* The term "emancipation" derives from the Latin "to release" and connotes the freeing of a person or people from some form of **constraint** (I highlight the word because of its importance later on). It has been used in connection with the ending of slavery, the attainment of women's suffrage, and by Habermas (1978) in terms of a human species interest in autonomy and freedom from distorted knowledge. This latter usage is clearly related to Kant's view of *enlightenment*, a process by which people would use their reason and knowledge to free themselves from dogma. Thus enlightenment can be seen as a particular means towards certain forms of emancipation. This process can also be seen as one of "critique," that is a deliberate questioning of prevailing forms of knowledge or of particular, oppressive, social and institutional arrangements. Critical theory (or critical systems) is a specialised type of knowledge used within the process of critique. Finally, "morality" concerns general principles of valued human behaviour (i.e., that which is accepted as good /bad or right/wrong) and "ethics" refers either to processes of determining moral principles, or to particular sets of principles held by individuals or groups.

In terms of traditions, the pre-eminent one has been the modernist-rational tradition beginning with Kant, extending through Hegel and various forms of Marxism, to Habermasian critical theory. It is certainly this tradition upon which critical management science has drawn. The central themes have been the possibility of attaining some oppression-free, ideal social situation; the employment of reason, rationality and knowledge in achieving such a state; the constraining and distorting effects of power; and the role of the autonomous human subject in this process. Some of the strands of diversity have been an idealistic concentration on a critique of ideas as opposed to a materialistic emphasis on action to change society. And, particularly with Habermas (1984; Habermas 1987), a switch to communication and language, and to discourse and dialogue rather than individual cognition (Young 1990; Benhabib 1992). Habermas' later work aimed at developing what he terms "discourse ethics" (Habermas 1990a; Habermas 1992; Habermas 1993; Habermas 1993). This will be discussed later.

A second strand, particularly within the domain of ethics, is communitarianism, (MacIntyre 1985; Spaul 1995; Munro 1996) reviving traditional Aristotelian ideas concerning the "good life." The main argument is against the Kantian notion that a universal, rational morality can be created. General morality is seen to be firmly anchored in individual personal values and these in turn can only be generated through historical interactions amongst a group of people within a community. Morals cannot be prescribed from the outside as appropriate for all because, in total, there is such divergence of experiences, situations, and viewpoints. There can be no universal moral viewpoint to be aimed at. Instead we should encourage the development of localised communities within which agreements about worth and value may develop.

Recently, however, many of the assumptions of the traditional approach have been challenged from a post-modern perspective, particularly through the work of Foucault (Foucault 1980; Foucault 1980; Foucault 1982; Taket and White 1993; Brocklesby and Cummings 1996). This draws on another tradition stemming from Nietzsche and Heidegger and sharply undermines the very roots of modernism. It questions the idea that rationality and reason can be neutral tools suggesting instead that they themselves are inevitably entwined with the exercise of power; it questions the idea that power is simply a constraining imposition that can be removed, seeing it as inextricably constitutive of our everyday practices; and it emphasises the extent to which the subject can never be autonomous but is always constructed through the disciplining practices of society.

In broad terms, the situation of engaged action is envisaged as follows. An agent or agents[67] will commit themselves to taking action within a situation regarded as problematic. They may have no previous relationship to the situation or they may have some history of interactions such as previous projects, on-going consultation, or actual employment. Whatever the case, we can distinguish two types of continual activity—actual actions within the problem situation some of which may draw on particular methodologies and techniques; and critical reflection *about* the intervention determining the particular combinations of actions and methodologies that are employed as explained in Section 10.4.

We have already noted that the problem content system (PCS) can be seen to have three fundamental dimensions—the material, the social, and the personal. This

---

[67] This chapter is written largely from the perspective of a single agent or practitioner. In practice, interventions will often involve teams of people with a variety of relationships to each other and the problem situation. The extra complexity generated by this differentiation is not addressed here, but one approach would be to apply multimethodology at a meta level to the working of the team. That is, to make this a problem situation in itself. The practicalities of this will be pursued in further work.

analysis was based on Habermas's theory of communicative action and in particular the validity claims that any speech or action implicitly raises, that is comprehensibility, truth, rightness and sincerity. These were initially described in Table 5.1, Section 5.4.3, and then later in Section 9.2.1. They are reproduced and expanded in Table 10.7

Apart from the dimensions of mode of interaction and form of science discussed above, there are two other dimensions of particular importance for critical intervention—of *power/knowledge* or technology of reason (Foucault 1988b), and *axiology*, i.e., that which is valued or considered right.

Power/Knowledge—Technologies of the Self

It has generally been considered that the works of Foucault and Habermas are mutually contradictory, particularly concerning the limits of rationality and the nature of power. However, a number of commentators (McCarthy 1991; Bernstein 1992; Ingram 1994; Kelly 1994; Probert 1996; Ashenden and Owen 1999) have argued that in fact the differences are not that great and that the two are better seen as complementary. Foucault himself said (about the Frankfurt School in general rather than Habermas in particular):

"Now, obviously, if I had been familiar with the Frankfurt School, if I had been aware of it at the time, I would not have said a number of stupid things that I did say and I would have avoided many of the detours that I made while trying to pursue my own humble path—when meanwhile, avenues had been opened up by the Frankfurt School. It is a strange case of non-penetration between two very similar types of thinking which is explained, perhaps, by that very similarity. Nothing hides the fact of a problem in common better than two similar ways of approaching it." (Foucault 1988a, p. 26)

### Table 10.7. Habermas' Validity Claims with Foucault's Technologies of Power.

|  | Mode of Interaction | Validity Claims | Form of Science | Power/ Knowledge Technologies | Axiology |
|---|---|---|---|---|---|
| **Linguistic** | We communicate through | Comprehensibility | Semiological | Signification/ Meaning | Expressiveness |
| **Material** | We observe and mould | Truth, possibility | Empirical/ Analytical | Production/ Manipulation | Effectiveness, concern |
| **Social** | We participate in and reproduce | Rightness | Sociological/ Cultural | Power/Conduct | Morality |
| **Personal** | We experience and express | Truthfulness | Hermeneutic/ Phenomenological | The Self/ Transformation | Ethicality |

This is certainly the position that I adopt, and I will provide two examples of resonances between Habermas and Foucault.

Foucault's complex work can be seen as moving through three stages as mentioned above (Foucault 1988c). From an initial concern with the formation of science and knowledge; to recognition of the importance of power and domination in both knowledge and our relations with others; to a study of the ways in which power and knowledge condition the formation of the self as a subject. In thus examining the nature of human experience, Foucault (1988b) categorised four techniques or technologies that apply to our understanding and action: technologies of production that allow us to manipulate objects, technologies of signs that allow us to communicate, technologies of power that control our conduct with respect to others, and technologies of the self that we use for self-transformation. These four technologies relate, in essence, to Habermas' three worlds and to language. Moreover, one of the technologies of self is the concept of "self-examination"—a scrutiny of our thoughts and conscience. Foucault (1988b, p. 46) categorises three types of self-examination—the relation between our thoughts and reality, the relation between our thoughts and rules of conduct, and the relation with our own hidden thoughts. These three correspond almost exactly with Habermas' three validity claims—truth, rightness, and truthfulness.

From the viewpoint of critical intervention, Foucault offers many useful insights into the subjugation and suppression of knowledge, the practical mechanisms of power and resistance, and the nature of the individual's constant struggle with the constraints of their own subjectivity. His work shows the necessarily bounded and local nature of critique and emancipation, and that critique should no longer be seen as the discovery of universal and necessary limits, but an exploration of the contingency and plasticity of constraints and boundaries:

"The point, in brief, is to transform the critique conducted in the form of necessary limitation into a practical critique that takes the form of a possible transgression ... critique will be genealogical in the sense that it will not deduce from the form of what we are what is impossible for us to do and to know; but it will separate out, from the contingency that has made us what we are, the possibility of no longer being, doing, or thinking what we are, do, or think...." (Foucault 1988d, p. 46)

Axiology—what is good or valued

The next dimension of importance to all three worlds is that of axiology, i.e., what we value or judge to be right or good. This ultimately provides the criteria by which we evaluate possible actions and make choices. Here, Habermas' (1990a; 1992; 1993; 1993) work on "discourse ethics" provides a useful framework. Habermas considers that the question "how should I act?" differs according to different contexts—the *pragmatic*, the *ethical*, and the *moral*. Pragmatic contexts are those of purposive rational action—situations where we are concerned with the most effective choice of means (given ends) or of ends (given preferences)[68]. Ethical questions are deeper, concerning the self-understanding of the individual. They address the Aristotelian, communitarian issues of the nature of the "good life"—that which is important or good for the individual (or the community). Finally, moral questions concern our relations with other people (and possibly nature, e.g., animals), our duties and responsibilities, justice, and acceptable norms and practices. Habermas appears to see these three as mutually exclusive alternatives, i.e., situations are of one or other type, but from a multimethodology perspective it is more helpful to see these as dimensions, all of which are relevant to any particular situation.

What is Habermas' approach to these issues? First, he accepts that in our fragmented and pluralistic age it is not possible to determine universal and abstract answers to these questions. We cannot specify what everyone must accept. Instead, we can specify procedures to enable people to determine and apply such standards in a rational way. The main principles of the procedure are: first that it consists of a process of *actual* dialogue and debate by real people. So individuals cannot determine principles in a lone monological way, nor can there be purely imagined or conceptual debates—it must be engaged actors involved in a communal situation. Second, for standards to become generally accepted they must be such that everyone affected by them would agree that they should be obeyed by all. Third, that in participating in such debates we should make a genuine effort to put ourselves in the place of the other(s).

Clearly these are highly idealistic in the sense that they are unlikely to be realised in full in practice. However, they can stand as an ideal towards which we can aim and against which we can judge actual arrangements.

## 10.6.2 The Intervention System: The Agent

Any consideration of critical action must begin (and ultimately end) with the actual, embodied and embedded, agent(s) whose choice and action it is. This is because first, in the light of post-modernism, it is no longer tenable to maintain, with traditional critical theory, the idea of a universal, historical, rational (male) subject— the critical analogue to "economic man." The Cartesian cleavage of mind from body, relentlessly pursued by Kant and Husserl, has broken down in the light of, for example, the recognition of the embodied nature of cognition (Chapter 7); the cultural and temporal relativity of knowledge and reason itself as highlighted particularly by Foucault; the post-modern insistence on the importance of difference and heterogeneity (Taket and White 1993; Taket and White 1994); and feminist theory, has revealed the implicit masculine bias in critical conceptions of rationality (Young 1990). Habermas himself has to some extent accepted these points (Habermas 1994), recognising that processes of enlightenment only ever refer to particular individual subjects (rather than an "emancipated society" he refers to "undisabled subjects"); that one cannot specify the future nature of a utopia, only

---

[68] Very much the domain of traditional, hard OR/systems.

conditions under which it might be generated; and that reason must not wipe out separateness and difference.

Second, with multimethodology a particular combination of methodologies is woven together anew each time by a particular agent to meet a unique set of circumstances. This, of necessity, is dependent on the characteristics of the agent—their knowledge, history, relationship to the situation, personality, values and commitments, and perhaps gender (Kotidiatis 2005)—and so, inevitably brings them centre-stage. Third, I would argue that no critical theory or methodology can, *of itself*, compel its users to employ it critically. No matter what principles or commitments a methodology or framework has, its mechanisms and procedures can be used in antithetical ways. It is, indeed, one of the dilemmas of critical management studies in general that its own methods and knowledge could be used to further oppression rather than emancipation (Alvesson and Willmott 1992). Thus, any methodology or framework of ideas is ultimately subservient to its users.

Given this starting point, we must now consider the cognitive and social context of the agent, beginning with a brief historical/evolutionary perspective. As we have traced in earlier chapters, the physical medium gave rise to the self-producing, autonomous entities that we distinguish as "living." It afforded both possibilities and constraints for the material domain of interaction. Through evolution, there developed organisms with nervous systems that could interact with abstract relations, and finally human beings with the capacity for self-consciousness and language. The advent of language brought into existence two new, intimately related, domains of interaction—the personal and the social. Language (interpreted broadly and any form of communicational interaction) provides the medium for the social and personal in the same way that physical forces do for our material world. It is significantly different however in that it is, ultimately, dependent on humans and their cultures in a way that physical forces are not.

Thus, the embodied agent exists in a pre-structured world of language, practices, norms and values, oppressions and distortions. A social world that is, of its nature, moralised and value-laden. From what position can we both be constituted from this and yet stand outside it? And what would be the motivation for this? The motivation can only ever arise from the desire of the individual (Young 1990; Maturana 1991a) that things be different from how they are. From the recognition that all action (or inaction) either reinforces or struggles against the status quo, and thence reflection on one's own response to that inevitability, there can arise the desire that currently unrealised possibilities be brought about. That either unnecessary and unwanted **constraints** be removed, or that absences be filled (Bhaskar 1989; Bhaskar 1994). These two possibilities correspond to the dual nature of power, power as constraining and restricting, and power as enabling and productive (Foucault 1982; Mingers 1992).

This perspective brings in another factor that is seldom considered—the *emotions* of the agent. Most of the theory of methodology is concerned with the *rationality* of approaches to intervention, but real embodied people always act in a way that is conditioned by their emotions (Heidegger 1962; Maturana 1988). Indeed, it is precisely their emotional relation to a situation that motivates action in the first place, whether it is anger, sympathy, interest, or desire for gain, and sustains it through the intervention. However, traditionally emotion and rationality would have been seen as in opposition with rationality displacing emotion as a basis for choice and action. I would argue that emotion cannot be eliminated from human action but needs to be seen in terms of a positive synthesis with rationality. This critical moment occurs in the agonistic (Foucault 1982, p.208) question faced by agents, *what should I/we do?* which continually confronts us in our praxis. We always have to make choices, to act or not to act, to move in this way or that, circumscribed by the apparent **constraints** and absences of the social and material worlds on the one hand, and our own personal world on the other.

### 10.6.3 The Problem Situation: Constraints and Boundaries

I want to begin this section with some simple examples from practice to show that what I have just argued above, which sounds quite abstract and obscure, is in fact extremely practical and day-to-day.

The first example concerns a project I undertook for a toothpaste manufacturer. The project was for the Purchasing Department which had to buy over 1.5m tubes of varying types each year. There were only two suppliers who could produce in the required volumes. There were complex contracts with each supplier specifying various discount and rebate levels depending on the amount bought over the year as a whole. The buyer's problem was having to, each month, allocate the requirements for 24 different types of tube between the suppliers in such a way as to balance short-term costs against longer-term discounts whilst ensuring security of supply.

Technically, this was relatively easy to formulate as a mixed integer programming problem with the integer variables dealing with the discounts, and after a fairly short time I was able to show the buyer a solution for the next two months' requirements which was considerably cheaper than his manual allocation. He looked at it and said that he could see it was logically correct but it was not practicable. Because one supplier was cheaper across the board the model had allocated almost everything to that supplier. The buyer said that two suppliers must be maintained in case of problems and that meant giving a reasonable amount to each, even though one was more expensive. I added a constraint to allocate at least 40% to each supplier and produced another solution. This time the buyer realised that not only did there have to be a split across the whole order but there also had to be a split in each particular type of tube otherwise one supplier would not be able to utilise its production facility properly. Again these extra constraints were added in and the model solved again. Now the buyer said that you had to give the suppliers an estimate one month in advance of the next month's order and then keep roughly to that. Again, another set of constraints and another, more expensive solution. After several more iterations with new constraints emerging, the buyer was finally satisfied that the solution was realistic, although by now the costs had risen until they almost matched his manual solution.

Two other brief examples: the first was a harbour where we were asked to help with work scheduling. After some investigation it became clear that little could be done to improve things given the current pattern of shifts and breaks. However, we were told that we had to take those as fixed since they were the result of hard negotiations with the unions after a damaging strike the previous year, and so the boundaries on our investigation were effectively fixed. The second concerned scheduling a steel mill that had to take on a new and larger order book after the closure of another plant. It was apparent that there were many constraints within the mill. Some of these were clearly fixed, e.g., the rate at which the slab could be cast and the cooling down and heating up times of the equipment, while others had more to do with traditional practices and could potentially be changed. However, the main constraints turned out to be concerned with the railway that shipped the finished slabs away to a nearby port for transport to Sweden and this was actually owned by another company. It was very difficult to determine the extent to which these limitations were fixed or could be varied with sufficient discussion and debate.

The common theme in these examples and, I wish to claim, in *all* real-world interventions is twofold: first, the extent to which the situation is full of constraints and potential constraints on the ways in which things can occur; and, second, that the difficult question is the extent to which the constraints are real and justified and do have to be taken as definite boundaries, rather than being potentially mutable. My contention is that, in fact, OR interventions consist largely of testing and exploring constraints both within the problem content system and within the intervention system. We will now look at several approaches that take the testing of boundaries and constraints as central.

Theory of Constraints

One approach from within traditional management science that has constraint at its core is what has become known as the Theory of Constraints (TOC). This began quite narrowly as a concern with improving the productivity of factories and production facilities. Goldratt (1984; 1997) saw that if you looked at a particular set of machines and resources you would always be able to find that there was one major limiting factor—one machine or resource (including people skills) that was restricting the throughput of the whole system. This was the one core constraint. The only way to improve overall throughput was to identify this constraint and then either develop it or, if that was not possible, reorder the rest of the system to utilise that constraint to the fullest extent. If the constraint was developed then of course some other factor may in turn become the core constraint.

Where the constraints are reasonably easy to identify, a five-step focussing approach was developed:

1.  Identify the constraint—the operation or resource that is the limiting or binding constraint of the system.

2.  Exploit the constraint—ensure that it is being used as efficiently as possible.

3.   Subordinate everything else to the constraint. This could involve re-ordering workflow; ensuring that there are always high levels of buffer stock; or investing in appropriately skilled operators.

4.   Elevate the constraint—invest in the constraint to improve its throughput.

5.   Check that, as throughput increases, some other constraint becomes binding and repeat the process on that.

TOC was initially developed within the specific domain of production/operations, but it was soon generalised to potentially cover all of the activities of a company or organisation (Mabin and Balderstone 2003). Constraints could then be seen as one of three types: *physical*, such as machines, raw materials, labour time, skills; *policy*, such as rules and procedures—"how we do it"; and *behavioural*, such as habits, customs and cultures.

Constraints such as these are usually much messier and difficult to identify than purely physical ones (and indeed the first stages of a multimethodology intervention—appreciation and analysis—are very much concerned with this) so TOC developed a different approach known as the "thinking process" which has a selection of tools to aid identification and development (Mabin, Forgeson et al. 2001). These tools, such as "current reality tree" and "future reality tree" are mainly diagrammatic and are quite similar to many other systems based techniques.

Boundary Critique

Within the systems literature, the importance of boundaries[69] in interventions has been highlighted by Churchman, Ulrich and Midgley. Churchman (1970) was one of the first to recognise that boundary setting was very much a decision made by the agents involved in an intervention rather than something given by the nature of the situation. In setting a boundary you are limiting both the range of stakeholders whose views are considered, and the range of possible changes. A solution considered good within a narrowly defined boundary may not appear so if the views of wider groups are brought into play. Churchman was therefore of the view that boundaries should be pushed out as widely as possible to try to ensure that changes were suitable for the "whole system." Churchman also recognised that there would inevitably be different, conflicting viewpoints about proposed changes so that decisions about boundaries were not technical or neutral questions, but very much value-based or ethical ones. He therefore argued that we should always subject our proposals to deep critique. They should be opposed by their "deadliest enemies" in a Hegelian dialectic that should lead to more robust and widely acceptable improvements (Churchman 1971).

---

[69] A boundary distinguishes what is included from what is excluded. A constraint is a boundary that also carries the connotation that it cannot be crossed, that it is imposing a limit on that which is within.

This was the underpinning for Strategic Assumption Surfacing and Testing (SAST) (Mason and Mitroff 1981) and Soft Systems Methodology (SSM) (Checkland 1981).

It was also one of the foundations of the work of Ulrich (1994; 2000) who was not so much concerned with organisations, but with planning processes in which ordinary people were often subject to the dictates of experts and planners without being able adequately to question such decisions. He recognised the importance of pushing boundaries but also saw that ultimately boundary decisions would have to be made and that a procedure for questioning and justifying boundary judgements was necessary. Importantly, this would often need to support the viewpoints of those affected by the decisions (who were often not part of the decision making process) against the technological rationality of the experts. Drawing on the work of Kant and Habermas, he developed a list of twelve questions that can be used to challenge the boundary judgements of a design in terms of what the system *is* and what it *ought* to be (Critical Systems Heuristics). This covers issues such as the client, the decision-taker(s), the designers, witnesses representing the affected, the sources of knowledge and expertise, and the underlying worldview.

Midgley (2000) has drawn on Churchman's and Ulrich's work in elaborating a theory of boundary critique. This begins with the recognition that boundary judgements reflect the values of stakeholders and that therefore there may potentially be conflict between them. What happens when one group want to draw a narrow boundary but another group wishes to draw a much wider one, bringing in other issues and groups? If we assume that the narrower boundary is fully contained within the wider one, then there will be a set of elements within the wider one but not in the narrower one. Midgley refers to these as "marginalised" elements, reflecting their ambivalent status. These will be the focus of debate between the two viewpoints or stakeholder groups (of course in practice there may be an interaction between more than just two). The marginalised elements will be judged positively ("sacred") or negatively ("profane") from the perspective of the two different boundary judgements. The situation will become stabilised when one viewpoint or the other gains the upper hand and the marginalised elements are designated as sacred or profane.

This model can be used in practice in a variety of ways. Clearly, one use is simply to bring these mechanisms to peoples' attention and thus open up for debate issues or assumptions that may not generally obvious explicit. Another may occur when there actually appears to be consensus over boundaries. This may just reflect the fact that only a limited number of stakeholders have been involved. In this case raising the question of who or what is marginalised by the particular agreement can be valuable, as can deliberately bringing in other stakeholders, or at least their viewpoints, to disrupt the taken-for-granted consensus. The model can also be used in the situation where the two boundary judgements are only partially overlapping. This could occur where two organisations, or departments, both have a particular issue or concern in common. They may view the other positively and sacred, or they may be antagonistic and view them as profane, or indeed some mixture of the two.

Critiquing Validity Claims

I have developed a third approach which stresses that critique, or being critical, can take the form of a deep questioning of the validity of the assumptions, often unthinkingly made, about forms of and constraints on, proposals for action and change (Mingers 2000d). Four different dimensions of questioning or scepticism were identified. The rationale for these was based, by analogy, on Habermas' theory of communicative action and discourse ethics and, in particular, his theory of the validity claims of speech acts as discussed in Section 10.6.1. Habermas argues that any communicative utterance aimed at generating understanding and agreement implicitly raises four validity claims—that it is *comprehensible,* that it is factually correct or in principle possible *(truth),* that it is acceptable normatively *(rightness),* and that it is meant sincerely *(truthfulness).*

In a situation of intervention within an organisation we are concerned with more than simply speech acts—for example, plans, proposals, actions, and designs; and they may well not be communicative (i.e., oriented towards understanding) but may well be strategic (oriented towards getting one's way). Nevertheless, by analogy we can say that proposals for action (or reasons why certain actions cannot be taken) involve implicit assumptions or validity claims that should be questioned. First, the logical soundness of the argument and its manner of expression *(critique of rhetoric);* second, the taken-for-granted assumptions about factual matters and acceptable social practices and values *(critique of tradition);* third, assumptions made about legitimacy and whose views should be privileged *(critique of authority);* and fourth assumptions concerning the validity of knowledge and information *(critique of objectivity).*

i)      Critical thinking—the critique of rhetoric

The first sense that is considered is that known as *critical thinking.* At the simplest level this concerns being able to evaluate whether peoples' arguments and propositions are sound in a logical sense (Hughes 1996). Do the conclusions follow from the premises? Are the premises themselves justifiable? Is language being used in a fair way, or is it deliberately emotive or misleading? This might appear to be a simple technical skill concerned with the logical analysis of language, but in real situations it can become extremely difficult to fully understand what is meant or claimed by some assertion, or to discover whether particular claims are or are not valid.

Critical thinking can be defined more widely (McPeck 1981) to involve a scepticism or suspension of belief towards particular statements, information, or norms. To think critically is not purely abstract but is always *about* some particular problem or domain. It therefore requires knowledge and skills specific to the problem or disciplinary domain although Paul (1990) argues that critical thinking is a general skill rather than being domain specific. It should also be *reflective* scepticism—being aware of its purpose *(*why am I adopting this particular attitude?*)* and being capable of offering alternatives. This aspect of being critical could be called the critique of rhetoric as it is particularly concerned with the use of language[70].

ii)    Being sceptical of conventional wisdom—the critique of tradition

The other senses of the term critical that we will consider are really developments of this sceptical attitude, taking less for granted and questioning deeper and more fundamental assumptions that we usually make. One of the most common assumptions we meet in organisations (and society more generally) is that of tradition or custom—the taken-for-granted "way we do things around here." Or, indeed, the reasons why things are not done in a particular way—the constraints that are taken for granted. Organisations and parts of organisations develop particular cultures and particular practices. These may have originated for good reasons, or simply by chance, but they tend to become accepted and, indeed, unseen. However, they may well not be the most appropriate way of doing things either because the situation has changed, or because in fact they never were, or because they deny or contradict moral values such as sexism, racism or environmentalism.

It is often not so much the long-standing practices or traditions of an organisation, but assumptions that relate to a particular project or plan. These can be seen as boundary judgements as discussed above, often set by technical experts or powerful groups, which limit (perhaps implicitly) what may be debated or challenged. Questioning such practices or judgements can often provoke strong reaction and the weight of tradition and authority may well be used to support them. Trying to change them can be extremely difficult as it will inevitably change the status quo and upset established patterns of power and authority. This can be called the critique of tradition.

iii)    Being sceptical of the dominant view—the critique of authority

Another, sometimes deeper, assumption is that there should be just *one* right or dominant view as opposed to a plurality of different but valid perspectives. For many people this will be particularly difficult to accept since much of their education and experience will have been aimed at learning the "correct" answer or the proper way of doing things, on the assumption that there is one. They will not have been encouraged to question the validity of their superiors or teachers. The situation in the organisational world, which does not split itself into well-defined disciplines and problems, can be highly complex with many different stakeholders involved. These interest groups will all have different experiences of the situation, different relationships to it, and stand to benefit or lose in different ways. Recognising that there is a multiplicity of perspectives, questioning the dominant view or privileged

---

[70] The term "critique" is taken to mean a particular critical appraisal or evaluation of some problem or situation; "rhetoric" is used is its general sense of the effective use of language.

position, and trying to "see the world through another's eyes" (Churchman 1968; Checkland and Scholes 1990) could be called the critique of authority.

iv)      Being sceptical of information and knowledge—the critique of objectivity

The final level to be considered is questioning the validity of the knowledge and information that is available, and recognising that it is *never* value-free and objective. At the simplest level we have to see that even seemingly objective "facts" such as numerical data do not simply occur but are the result of particular processes involving a whole variety of people, operations, and decisions/choices. Which factors are recorded and which are not? How are they recorded or measured—there are usually several possibilities? Can important factors be measured at all or do we have to use some surrogate? Do the non-quantifiable judgmental factors get given their due weight (Mingers 1989)? Even when some data has been produced, it only becomes useable as *information* when someone interprets it from their point of view and for their particular purposes. A simple table of data embodies many assumptions and has as many interpretations as there are readers.

At a broader level it can be argued that information and knowledge always reflect or are shaped by the structures of power and interest within a situation (Foucault 1980; Foucault 1988c). Which problems are raised and which are not? Which decisions get taken and which are always put off? To what extent are particular interest groups able to promote or suppress certain information, or shape the agenda's of discussion and meetings? This aspect of critical thinking can be called the critique of objectivity as it calls into question the whole idea of there being objective, value-free knowledge.

## Summary of Section 10.6.3

In this section we have explored the view that much of what happens within organisational interventions is concerned with the boundaries and constraints that we face. We push against these constraints, always testing their immutability by a continual reappraisal of our *appreciation* (understanding how the situation is), our *analysis* (explanation of why the situation is as it is), our *assessment* (exploring the potential for change), and finally our *actions*. The process is renewed through the consequences, both intended and unintended, of our actions both for ourselves and for others. In this ongoing process, we are continually concerned with all three of Habermas' worlds and the types of methods that may help us deal with them, regulating our choices with regard to effectiveness (what works), morality (what is just) and ethicality (what is desirable, individually), in which power is an ever-present, unavoidable force that is both enabling and constraining.

## 10.7 Conclusions: Implications for the Critical Practice of Multimethodology

In this section I will highlight briefly some of the main implications of the position expressed above for the practice of critical methodology. This should not be seen as a fully worked-out, practical methodology, but some guidelines that should inform such a methodology.

The starting point for a critical employment of multimethodology must be the real, situated, embodied, activities and desires of actual agents, not abstract theories, frameworks or methodologies themselves. As agents, we find ourselves in a context of an always/already constituted and moralised situation, where all our actions (or inactions) will have effects both on ourselves and on others. We can never be neutral or disinterested. The motivation for action is emotional—desire that the situation be other than it is. That unnecessary and unwanted constraints be broken, or that absences and needs be fulfilled.

Change and emancipation will be local, context-dependent and often very limited: a challenging or transgressing of boundaries, both social and individual. This can take place through four stages of critical reflection—*appreciation* of the situation as it is, *analysis* of *why* it is as it is, *appraisal* of how the situation might be different, and *action* towards generating movement. The drawing of boundaries is central to this process for in drawing a boundary we are separating that which we consider (at a particular moment) unchangeable from that which may be. The more that we accept as fixed the narrower will become the domain of possible change and development.

Our actions (linguistic and otherwise) stand in relation to three analytically separate domains—the material world, our social world, and my (the individual's) subjective world. These three worlds provide a second dimension to the concept of critical reflection. Each of the four stages mentioned above should concern itself with to each of the worlds. Our actions involve both validity claims—*truth, rightness,* and *truthfulness,* and axiological claims—*effectiveness, morality* and *ethicality*—that should continually raise questions concerning the appropriateness of both the existing situation, and our actions and proposals. Power is also integral to all three worlds, and is a facet of even our most minute and intimate action. Power has a dual nature—it is constraining and enabling—and is thus what we fight against, and what we use, in bringing about change.

Knowledge, including our methodologies and meta-methodologies, is inevitably linked to power. Knowledge is generally suppressed and distorted, constituted so as to maintain prevailing constraints and structures, yet at the same time, just as with power, it has a positive side for it is knowledge and critical reflection that has the power to assist us in bringing about change. We must recognise that the different methodologies that we might employ are all embedded in their own paradigms, embodying particular and partial views of the world. With critical reflection, we must be aware of the underpinning paradigm in order to properly appreciate the methodology, but we do not simply accept this. We should always reinterpret the methodology or technique within a critical framework. Thus, for example, statistical analysis is generally wedded upon objectivistic assumptions. But statistics can still be used very effectively within a critical engagement, for example to highlight the extent of inequality, provided that we have an awareness of their contentious nature (Mingers 2006).

Interventions in situations should be made so as to provide the conditions for rationality and discourse, not the final judgements. This should aim towards maximum participation in real, open debate amongst all those affected by decisions; encouragement for participants genuinely to try to put themselves in the place of the other; and discourse about both general norms and agreements as well as their application in particular situations.

The actual *process* of critical multimethodology will be a continual cycle of reflection, judgement and action. It will bring in and knit together methodologies and techniques as seems appropriate to assist action. Such choices depend on both the stage of the intervention and the particular domain of interest at the time as well as the wider context of relationships discussed above.

We must not expect change to come about easily. The social world is constituted and structured through the micro-operation of power, and individually our structural coupling within varied domains is strongly conservative and resistant to change (Brocklesby 1997).

# Chapter 11: Reprise

In this book we have traversed much terrain, from the nature of biological organisms to practical intervention in companies and organisations. In this final chapter I do not want to try to reiterate or summarise all that; I just want to pull out some of the major themes that I see running through these diverse areas.

The first theme that will hopefully be apparent in all the material that has been presented is the fundamental ideas of systems thinking. I would argue that all the main authors whose work I have drawn on are systems thinkers even though not all of them would see themselves explicitly as part of the systems movement. Clearly people such as Maturana, Varela, Luhmann and Checkland do acknowledge systems thinking but others such as Giddens, Bhaskar and Habermas do not draw on this literature explicitly. Nevertheless, it seems to me to be self-evident that their theoretical work clearly embodies an essentially holistic viewpoint.

Moreover, I would claim that all these writers are paradigm examples of excellent systems work. Unfortunately, there have in the past been many poor examples of systems applications. Because systems thinking can be applied across the disciplines it has often been the case that systems ideas have been applied to a particular domain by people who are not themselves expert in that area. The result of this is often weak and superficial, and contributes to a poor reputation for systems. It is much better when people who are already expert in their own discipline use systems concepts to develop their own ideas. This is true for all those mentioned above in their respective domains of biology, neuroscience, sociology, philosophy and management science.

The second theme is the importance of philosophy for academic activity. Much research within universities, particularly in the hard sciences (including much of hard OR) but even in the social sciences and humanities, is carried on with little attention to, or even awareness of, the issues that philosophy raises—especially issues of epistemology, ontology, methodology, and ethics. This seems to me inexcusable. These fundamental issues must be addressed by every discipline and underpin any scholarly research occurring within a discipline. This does not mean that every researcher has to have a philosophical section in ever paper, or that they need to see themselves as contributing to the philophical debates, but they do need to be aware of the deep questions posed in these areas and their own responses to them.

Systems thinking brings these issues to the fore with its recognition of the importance of the observer or researcher in any analysis. "Everything said is said by an observer" as Maturana observed; "the systems approach begins when first you view the world through the eyes of another" as Churchman (1968) put it. Positivism saw the efacement of the observer as one of its main planks of objectivity until Heisenberg demonstrated the inseparability of the observed and the observer even in the depth of quantum physics. Systems thinking, especially in its later $2^{nd}$ order cybernetics or soft systems modes, reinstates the inescapability of researchers, analysts, agents and practitioners interacting with and influencing the objects of their activity. But we should not see this as the loss of, what has now been shown to be an illusory, objectivity. Rather we should follow Ackoff in recognising that objectivity results from "the open interaction of a wide variety of individual subjectivities" (Ackoff 1974).

The third theme is the intimate connection between knowledge and action or, its complementarity, between mind and body. Against the thrust of thought since Descartes, I have tried to show how we cannot separate off knowledge from action or mind from body. Maturana has shown through the theory of autopoiesis that with living systems "cognition *is* effective action," while Merleau-Ponty, amazingly perhaps for a phenomenologist, argued that it is the body that knows and the body that acts. The Cartesian split between body and mind is particularly clear within both information systems and management science. Within IS, and especially artificial intelligence, the "information processing" model of human cognition has had its limitations revealed in the failure of such fads as expert systems and knowledge management. While within management science the move to soft systems recognised the importance of the varied "Weltanschauungen" of participants within an organisation but failed to apply this to the agent using the methodology, or see the importance of their embodiment.

The fourth theme is that of pluralism: of ontology, epistemology and methodology. It seems to me that one of the things the succeeding waves of critique within the philosophy of science (positivism, interpretivism, post-positivism, constructivism, post-modernism) has brought is a refutation of any form of monism. We have to recognise a plurality of types of systems—material, social, psychological, conceptual; of epistemological relations to these systems; and of methodologies for generating knowledge(s) about them. This should not be seen as some sort of slide into relativism, but rather a recognition of the amazing complexity of the world that we are trying to understand and ultimately shape. No one said it was going to be easy!

The final theme I wish to pull out is that of "being critical." We have talked about "critical realism," "critical systems," "critical pluralism," "Critical Theory": what if anything do all these have in common? One approach is to look at the antonym for critical, that is being "uncritical," which Encarta defines as "accepting or approving something without analyzing or questioning it or discriminating between good and bad." So, in being critical, in whatever area or domain, we need to constantly reveal the constraints, assumptions and conditions that are in force and then test and challenge their strength and validity. This may be in terms of knowledge: recognising that it is partial, limited and fallible; of methodologies: understanding their assumptions and limitations; of organisational practices: challenging the taken-for-granted traditions and structures; of society: not accepting undesirable constraints and unnecessary absences; and finally of ourselves: recognising our own desires, competances and limitations and struggling to transcend them.

# Sources

In writing this book I have drawn on much of my previously published work. Sometimes I have incorporated it more or less unchanged, elsewhere I have knitted in particular extracts or developed what I had already written. The following shows the main sources and I am grateful to the publishers for permission to reproduce them.

Mingers, J. (2005). Can social systems be autopoietic? Bhaskar's and Giddens' social theories. *J. Theory of Social Behaviour* 34, 4, 403–428, Blackwell

Mingers J (2003). Real-izing information systems. In *Social Theory and Philosophy for Information Systems* (Mingers, J and Willcocks, L, Eds), Wiley.

Mingers, J. (2003). "Observing organisations: an evaluation of Luhmann's theory of organisations." in: T. Hernes and T. Bakken (eds.), *Autopoietic Organisation Theory: Drawing on Niklas Luhmann's Social Systems Perspective.* Copenhagen Business School Press.

Mingers, J. (2003). A classification of the philosophical assumptions of management science methods. *Journal of the Operational Research Society*, 54, 559–570, Palgrave Press.

Mingers, J. (2002). Can social systems be autopoietic? Assessing Luhman's social theory. *Sociological Review* 50, 2 278–299, Blackwell.

Mingers, J. (2001). Embodying information systems: the contribution of phenomenology. *Information and Organisation* 11, 2 103–128, Elsevier.

Mingers, J. (2001). Multimethodology: mixing and matching methods. In: J. Rosenhead and J. Mingers (eds) *Rational Analysis for a Problematic World Revisited: Problem Structuring Methods for Complexity, Uncertainty and Conflict*, 289–310, Wiley.

Mingers, J. (2000). What is it to be critical? Teaching a critical approach to management undergraduates. *Management Learning* 31, 2, 219–237, Sage Publications.

Mingers, J. (2000) The contribution of critical realism as an underpinning philosophy for OR/MS and systems. *Journal of the Operational Research Society*, 51, 1256–1270, Palgrave Press.

Mingers J (2000). The contribution of critical realism as an underpinning philosophy for OR/MS and systems. *Journal of the Operational Research Society* 51, 11, 1256–1270. Palgrave Press.

Mingers, J. (1999). Information, meaning and communication: an autopoietic approach to linking the social and individual. *Cybernetics and Human Knowing* 6, 4 25–42, Imprint Academic.

Mingers, J. (1997) Multi-Paradigm Multimethodology. In: *Multimethodology: Theory and Practice of Combining Management Science Methodologies*, Mingers, J. & Gill, A. (eds), 1–20. Wiley.

Mingers, J. (1997) Towards critical pluralism. In: Multimethodology: *Theory and Practice of Combining Management Science Methodologies*, Mingers, J. & Gill, A. (eds), 407–440. Wiley.

Mingers, J. (1997). Systems typologies in the light of autopoiesis: a reconceptualization of Boulding's hierarchy, and a typology of self-referential systems. *Systems Research and Behavioural Science*, 14, 303–313, Wiley

Mingers, J. (1996), An evaluation of theories of information with regard to the semantic and pragmatic aspects of information systems. *Systems Practice* 9, 3 187–209, Kluwer/Plenum.

Mingers J (1995). *Self-Producing Systems: Implications and Applications of Autopoiesis*. Plenum Press, New York, Chapter 3.

Mingers, J. (1995). Information and meaning: foundations for an intersubjective account. *Information Systems Journal* 5, 285–306, Blackwell.

# References

Ackerman, F., C. Eden, et al. (1997). "Modeling for litigation: mixing qualitative and quantitative approaches." *Interfaces* **27**(2): 48-65.

Ackoff, R. (1974). "The social responsibility of operational research." *Operational Research Quarterly* **25**: 361–371.

Ackoff, R. (1977). "Optimization + objectivity = opt out." *European Journal of Operational Research* **1**(1): 1–7.

Ackoff, R. (1979). "The future of operational research is past." *Journal of the Operational Research Society* **30**: 93–104.

Ackoff, R. and F. Emery (1972). *On Purposeful Systems*. London, Tavistock.

Ackroyd, S. and S. Fleetwood (2000). *Realist Perspectives on Management and Organisations*. London, Routledge.

Alberts, B., Bray, D., et al (1989). *Molecular Biology of the Cell*. New York, Garland.

Alvesson, M. and D. Karreman (2001). "Odd Couple: Making Sense of the Curious Concept of Knowledge Management." *J Management Studies* **38**(7): 995–1018.

Alvesson, M. and H. Willmott, Eds. (1992). *Critical Management Studies*. London, SAGE Publications.

Andrew, A. M. (1979). "Autopoiesis and self-organisation." *J. Cybernetics* **9**: 359.

Angel, I. (1997). Welcome to the 'brave new world'. *Information Systems: An Emerging Discipline?* J. Mingers and F. Stowell. London, McGraw Hill: 363–384.

Applegate, L. and J. King (1999). "Rigor and relevance: careers on the line." *MISQ* **23**(1): 18–19.

Archer, M. (1990). Human agency and social structure: a critique of Giddens. *Anthony Giddens: Consensus and Controversy*. J. Clark, C. Modgil and S. Modgil. Cambridge, CUP: 47–56.

Archer, M. (1995). *Realist Social Theory: the Morphogenetic Approach*. Cambridge, Cambridge U. P.

Archer, M. (1996). "Social integration and system integration: developing the distinction." *Sociology* **30**(4): 679–699.

Archer, M. (1998). Realism and morphogenesis. *Critical Realism: Essential Readings*. M. Archer, R. Bhaskar, A. Collier, T. Lawson and A. Norrie. London, Routledge: 356–382.

Archer, M. (2000). *Being Human: The Problem of Agency*. Cambridge, Cambridge University Press.

Archer, M. (2000). "For structure: its properties and powers: a reply to Anthony King." *Sociological Review* **48**: 464–472.

Archer, M., R. Bhaskar, et al., Eds. (1998). *Critical Realism: Essential Readings*. London, Routledge.

Artandi, S. (1973). "Information concepts and their utility." *J. of the American Society for Information Science* **24**: 242–245.

Ashby, W. R. (1956). *An Introduction to Cybernetics*. London, Chapman Hall.

Ashenden, S. and D. Owen, Eds. (1999). *Foucault contra Habermas*. London, Sage.

Avison, D. and M. Myers (1995). "Information systems and anthropology: an anthropological perspective on IT and organisational culture." *Information Technology and People* **8**(3): 43–56.

Bachmann, P., P. Luisi, et al. (1991). "Self-replicating reverse micelles." *Chimia* **45**(9): 266–268.

Bachmann, P., P. Walde, et al. (1990). "Self-replicating reverse micelles and chemical autopoiesis." *J. Am. Chem. Soc.* **112**(22): 8200–8201.

Bachmann, P., P. Walde, et al. (1991). "Self-replicating micelles—aqueous micelles and enzymatically driven reactions in reverse micelles." *J. Am. Chem. Soc.* **113**(22): 8204–8209.

Baert, P. (1996). "Realist philosophy of the social sciences and economics : a critique." *Cambridge J. of Economics* **20**: 513–522.

Bahm, A. (1981). "Five types of systems philosophy." *Int. J. of General Systems* **6**: 233–237.

Bar-Hillel, Y. and R. Carnap (1952). An outline of a theory of semantic information. Cambridge, MA, Research Laboratory of Electronics, MIT.

Bar-Hillel, Y. and R. Carnap, Eds. (1964). *Language and Information: Selected Essays on their Theory and Application*. Reading, Mass., Addison-Wesley.

Barnes, S. (1977). *Interests and the Growth of Knowledge*. London, Routledge.

Bartlett, S. and P. Suber (1987). *Self Reference: Reflections on Reflexivity*. Dordrecht, Martinus Nijhoff.

Bateson, G. (1973). Form, substance and difference. *Steps to an Ecology of Mind*. London, Paladin: 423–440.

Bateson, G. (1973). *Steps to an Ecology of Mind*. Hertfordshire, Granada Publishing.

Beer, S. (1966). *Decision and Control*. London, Wiley.

Beer, S. (1985). *Diagnosing the System for Organisations*. Chichester, Wiley.

Belkin, N. and S. Robertson (1976). "Information science and the phenomenon of information." *J. of the American Society for Information Science* **27**: 197–204.

Bell, D. (1999). The axial age of technology. Foreword 1999. *The Coming of the Post-Industrial Society*. D. Bell. New York, Basic Books: ix-lxxxv.

Benbasat, I. and R. Weber (1996). "Rethinking "diversity" in information systems research." *Information Systems Research* **7**(4): 389–399.

Benhabib, S. (1992). *Situating the Self: Gender, Community and Postmodernism in Contemporary Ethics*. Cambridge, Polity Press.

Bennett, P., F. Ackerman, et al. (1997). Analysing litigation and negotiation: using a combined methodology. *Multimethodology: The Theory and Practice of Combining Management Science Methodologies*. J. Mingers and A. Gill. Chichester, Wiley: 59–88.

Benson, S. and C. Standing (2001). "Effective knowledge management: knowledge, thinking and the personal-corporate knowledge nexus problem." *Information Systems Frontiers* **3**(2): 227–238.

Berger, P. and T. Luckman (1967). *The Social Construction of Reality*. London, Penguin.

Bergson, H. (1911). *Creative Evolution*. London, MacMillan.

Berkeley, G. (1995). *A Treatise Concerning the Principles of Human Knowledge*. Indianapolis, Hackett Pub. Co.

Bernstein, R. (1992). Foucault: critique as philosophical ethos. *Philosophical Interventions in the Unfinished Project of Enlightenment*. A. Honneth, T. McCarthy, C. Offe and A. Wellmer. Cambridge, MIT Press: 280–310.

Best, S. and D. Kellner (1991). *Postmodern Theory: Critical Interrogations*. New York, Guilford Press.

Beynon-Davies, P. (1995). "Information systems 'failure': the case of the London Ambulance Service's Computer Aided Despatch project." *European Journal of Information Systems* **4**: 171–184.

Bhaskar, R. (1978). *A Realist Theory of Science*. Hemel Hempstead, Harvester.

Bhaskar, R. (1979). *The Possibility of Naturalism*. Sussex, Harvester Press.

Bhaskar, R. (1986). *Scientific Realism and Human Emancipation*. London, Verso.

Bhaskar, R. (1989). *Reclaiming Reality*. London, Verso.

Bhaskar, R. (1993). *Dialectic: the Pulse of Freedom*. London, Verso.

Bhaskar, R. (1994). *Plato Etc*. London, Verso.

Bhaskar, R. (1997). "On the ontological status of ideas." *J. for the Theory of Social Behaviour* **27**(2/3): 139–147.

Bhaskar, R. (2002). Critical realism and ethnomethodology: debate with Rom Harre. *From Science to Emancipation*. R. Bhaskar. London, Sage: 96–124.

Bijker, W., T. Hughes, et al., Eds. (1987). *The Social Construction of Technological Systems*. Cambridge, MIT Press.

Blackler, F. (1995). "Knowledge, knowledge work and organisations: an overview and interpretation." *Organisation Studies* **16**(6): 16–36.

Blaycock, P. and P. Rees (1984). "Cognitive style and the usefulness of information." *Decision Sciences* **15**: 74–91.

Bleicher, J. (1980). *Contemporary Hermeneutics*. London, Routledge.

Bloor, D. (1976). *Knowledge and Social Imagery*. London, Routledge.

Boisot, M. (1995). *Information Space: a Framework for Learning in Organisations*. London, Routledge.

Boland, R. (1991). Information systemsuse as a hermeneutic process. *Information Systems Research: Contemporary Approaches and Emergent Traditions*. H.-E. Nissen, H. Klein and R. Hirscheim. Amsterdam, North Holland: 439–458.

Booth, W. (1979). *Critical Understanding: the Powers and Limits of Pluralism*. Chicago, University of Chicago Press.

Boulding, K. (1956). "General systems theory—the skeleton of science." *Management Science* 2(3): 197–208.

Bradley, F. (1914). *Essays on Truth and Reality*. Oxford, Oxford University Press.

Brocklesby, J. (1994). "Let the jury decide: assessing the cultural feasibility of total systems intervention." *Systems Practice* 7(1): 75—86.

Brocklesby, J. (1995). "Intervening in the cultural constitution of systems—methodological complementarism and other visions for systems science." *Journal of the Operational Research Society* 46(11): 1285–1298.

Brocklesby, J. (1997). Becoming multimethodology literature: an assessment of the cognitive difficulties of working across paradigms. *Multimethodology: The Theory and Practice of Combining Management Science Methodologies*. J. Mingers and A. Gill. Chichester, Wiley: 189–216.

Brocklesby, J. and S. Cummings (1995). "Combining hard, soft and critical methodologies in systems research: the cultural constraints." *Systems Research* 12(1): 239–245.

Brocklesby, J. and S. Cummings (1996). "Foucault plays Habermas: an alternative philosophical underpinning for critical systems thinking." *Journal of the Operational Research Society* 47(6): 741–754.

Brown, A., S. Fleetwood, et al., Eds. (2002). *Critical Realism and Marxism*. London, Routledge.

Brown, C. (1988). "A new interdisciplinary impulse and the anthropology of the 1990s." *International Social Science Journal* 40(2): 211–220.

Bryant, G. (1995). *Practical Sociology*. Cambridge, Polity Press.

Bryant, J. (1988). "Frameworks of inquiry: OR practice across the hard-soft divide." *Journal of the Operational Research Society* 39(5): 423–435.

Bryant, J. (1993). "OR enactment: the theatrical metaphor as an analytic framework." *Journal of the Operational Research Society* 44(6): 551–561.

Buckley, W. (1967). *Sociology and Modern Systems Theory*. Englewood Cliffs, Prentice Hall.

Buckley, W., Ed. (1968). *Modern Systems Research for the Behavioural Scientist*. Chicago, Aldine.

Bühler, K. (1982). *Karl Bühler: Semiotic Foundations of Language Theory*. New York, Plenum Press.

Bunge, M. (1977). "General systems and holism." *General Systems* **22**: 87–90.

Bunge, M. (1992). "System boundary." *Int. J. of General Systems* **20**: 215–229.

Burrell, G. and G. Morgan (1979). *Sociological Paradigms and Organisational Analysis*. London, Heinemann.

Byrne, D. (1998). *Complexity Theory and the Social Sciences*. London, Routledge.

Callaos, N. and B. Callaos (2002). "Towards a systemic notion of information: practical consequences." *Informing Science* **5**(1): 1–11.

Callinicos, A. (1995). Critical realism and beyond: Roy Bhaskar's dialectic. York, University of York, Dept. of Politics.

Cannon, W. (1939). *The Wisdom of the Body.* New York, Norton.

Castells, M. (1996). *The Rise of the Networked Society*. Oxford, Basil Blackwell.

Chalmers, A. (1988). "Is Bhaskar's realism realistic?" *Radical Philosophy* **49**(Summer): 18–23.

Checkland, P. (1981). *Systems Thinking, Systems Practice*. Chichester, Wiley.

Checkland, P. (1983). "OR and the systems movement—mappings and conflicts." *Journal of the Operational Research Society* **34**(8): 661–675.

Checkland, P. (1985). "From optimizing to learning: a development of systems thinking for the 1990s." *Journal of the Operational Research Society* **36**(9): 757–768.

Checkland, P. (1989). *OR and social science: fundamental thoughts*. Operational Research and the Social Sciences, Cambridge, Plenum Press.

Checkland, P. (1999). Soft systems methodology: a 30-year retrospective. *Systems Thinking, Systems Practice (2nd ed.)*. P. Checkland. Chichester, Wiley: A1–A66.

Checkland, P. and S. Holwell (1998). "Action research: Its nature and validity." *Systemic Practice and Action Research* **11**(1): 9–21.

Checkland, P. and J. Scholes (1990). *Soft Systems Methodology in Action.* Chichester, Wiley.

Cheon, M., V. Grover, et al. (1993). "The evolution of empirical research in IS: A study in IS maturity." *Information & Management* **24**: 107–119.

Chomsky, N. (1957). *Syntactic Structures.* The Hague, Mouton.

Churchman, C. W. (1968). *The Systems Approach.* New York, Dell Publishing.

Churchman, C. W. (1970). "Operations Research as a profession." *Management Science* **17**: B37–53.

Churchman, C. W. (1971). *The Design of Enquiring Systems.* New York, Basic Books.

Churchman, C. W. (1979). *The Systems Approach and its Enemies.* New York, Basic Books.

Ciborra, C. (1998). "Crisis and foundations: an inquiry into the nature and limits of models and methods in the information systems discipline." *J. Strategic Information Systems* **7**: 5–16.

Cicourel, A. (1973). *Cognitive Sociology: Language and meaning in Social Interaction.* London, Penguin.

Cohen, I. (1989). *Structuration Theory: Anthony Giddens and the Constitution of Social Life.* London, Macmillan.

Collins, H. (1985). *Changing Order: Replication and Induction in Scientific Practice.* Beverly Hills, Sage.

Collins, H. (1993). "The structure of knowledge." *Social Research* **60**: 95–116.

Cornelius, I. (2002). Theorizing information for information science. *Annual Review of Information Science and Technology.* B. Cronin. Medford NJ, Information Today Inc: 393–425.

Coyne, R. (1995). *Designing Information Technology in the Postmodern Age.* Cambridge, MIT Press.

Craib, I. (1992). *Anthony Giddens.* London, Routledge.

Crossley, N. (1994). *The Politics of Subjectivity.* Aldershot, Avebury.

Dando, M. and R. Sharp (1978). "Operational Research in the UK in 1977: causes and consequences of a myth." *Journal of the Operational Research Society* **29**: 939–949.

Danermark, B., M. Ekstrom, et al. (2002). *Explaining Society: Critical Realism in the Social Sciences.* London, Routledge.

Davenport, T. and L. Prusak (1998). *Working Knowledge.* Cambridge, MA, Harvard University Press.

Dawkins, R. (1978). *The Selfish Gene.* London, Granada.

Deetz, S. (1996). "Describing differences in approach to organisation science: rethinking Burrell and Morgan and their legacy." *Organisation Science* **7**(2): 191–207.

Derrida, J. (1978). *Writing and Difference.* London, RKP.

Dery, R., M. Landry, et al. (1993). "Revisiting the issue of model validation in OR: an epistemological view." *EJOR* **66**: 168–183.

Dewey, J. (1938). *Logic: the Theory of Inquiry.* New York, Holt.

Dretske, F. (1981). *Knowledge and the Flow of Information.* Oxford, Blackwell.

Dreyfus, H. (1992). *What Computers Still Can't Do: a Critique of Artificial Reason.* Cambridge, MA, MIT Press.

Dreyfus, H. (1996). "The current relevance of Merleau-Ponty's phenomenology of embodiment." *Electronic Journal of Analytic Philosophy* **4**(Spring).

Driesch, H. (1908). *The Science and Philosophy of the Organism.* London, Black.

Drummond, H. (1996). "The politics of risk: trials and tribulations of the Taurus project." *Journal of Information Technology* **11**: 347–357.

Earl, M. (1994). Knowledge as strategy: reflections on Skandia International and Shorko Films. *Strategic Information Systems: a European Perspective.* C. Ciborra and T. Jelassi. Chichester, Wiley.

Eden, C. (1989). Operational research as negotiation. *Operational Research and the Social Sciences.* M. Jackson, P. Keys and S. Cropper. London, Plenum: 43–50.

Eden, C. (1989). Using cognitive mapping for strategic options development and analysis. *Rational Analysis for a Problematic World.* J. Rosenhead. Chichester, Wiley: 21–42.

Eden, C. (1993). "From the playpen to the bombsite—the changing nature of management science." *Omega-International Journal of Management Science* **21**(2): 139–154.

Eden, C. (1994). Cognitive mapping and problem structuring for systems dynamics model building, Dept. of Management Science, Strathclyde University.

Eden, C. and F. Ackerman (1998). *Making Strategy: The Journey of Strategic Management*. London, Sage.

Eden, C. and F. Ackermann (2001). SODA—the principles. *Rational Analysis for a Problematic World Revisited: Problem Structuring Methods for Complexity, Uncertainty and Conflict*. J. Rosenhead and J. Mingers. Chichester, Wiley: 21–42.

Eilon, S. (1975). "Seven faces of research." *Opl. Res. Q.* **26**:359–367.

Ewald, F. (1987). The law of law. *Autopoiesis and the Law*. G. Teubner. Berlin, de Gruyter: 36–50.

Farradane, J. (1976). "Towards a truer information science." *Information Science* **10**(3): 91–101.

Featherstone, M., B. Turner, et al., Eds. (1991). *The Body: Social Process and Cultural Theory*. London, Sage.

Fildes, R. and J. Ranyard (1997). "Success and survival of operational reserach groups—a review." *Journal of the Operational Research Society* **48**: 336–360.

Fine, B. (2002). Addressing the critical and the real in critical realism, Dialogues in Economics: a Postautistic Economics Forum. **2003**.

Fleck, J. (1997). "Contingent knowledge and technology development." *Technology Analysis and Strategic Management* **9**(4): 383–397.

Fleetwood, S., Ed. (1999). *Critical Realism in Economics: Development and Debate*. London, Routledge.

Fleetwood, S. (2001). "Causal laws, functional relations and tendencies." *Review of Political Economy* **13**(2): 201–220.

Fleetwood, S. (2002). "Boylan and O'Gorman's causal holism: a critical realist evaluation." *Cambridge Journal of Economics* **26**(1): 27–45.

Flegg, G. (1974). *From Geometry to Topology*. London, English Universities Press.

Fleischaker, G. (1988). "Autopoiesis: the status of its system logic." *Biosystems* **22**: 37–49.

Fleischaker, G. (1990). "Origins of life; an operational definition." *Origins of Life and Evolution of the Biosphere* **20**: 127–137.

Fleischaker, G. (1991). "The myth of the putative 'organism'." *Uroboros* **1**(2): 23–43.

Fleischaker, G. (1992a). "Are osmotic or social systems autopoietic? A reply in the negative." *Int. J. General Systems* **21**: 163–173.

Fleischaker, G. (1992b). "Its not mine and its not a dictum." *Int. J. General Systems* **21**(2): 257–258.

Flood, R. and M. Jackson (1991). *Creative Problem Solving: Total Systems Intervention*. London, Wiley.

Flood, R. and N. Romm (1995). "Enhancing the process of methodology choice in total systems intervention (TSI) and improving chances of tackling coercion." *Systems Practice* **8**(4): 377–408.

Floridi, L. (2002). Is information meaningful data? Oxford, Philosophy and Computing Laboratory.

Floridi, L. (2002). "What is the philosophy of information?" *Metaphilosophy* **33**(1/2): 123–145.

Foucault, M. (1980). *The History of Sexuality—an Introduction*. New York, Random House.

Foucault, M. (1980). *Power/Knowledge: Selected Interviews and Other Writings 1972–1977*. Brighton, Harvester Press.

Foucault, M. (1982). Afterword: The Subject and Power. *Foucault: Beyond Structuralism and Hermeneutics*. H. Dreyfus and P. Rabinow. Chicago, University of Chicago Press: 208–226.

Foucault, M. (1988a). *Politics, Philosophy, Culture*. London, Routledge.

Foucault, M. (1988b). Technologies of the Self. *Technologies of the Self: An Interview with Michel Foucault*. L. Martin, H. Gutman and P. Hutton. Amherst, University of Massachusetts Press: 16–49.

Foucault, M. (1988c). Truth, Power, Self: an Interview with Michel Foucault. *Technologies of the Self: An Interview with Michel Foucault*. L. Martin, H. Gutman and P. Hutton. Amherst, University of Massachusetts Press: 9–15.

Foucault, M. (1988d). What is Enlightenment? *The Foucault Reader*. P. Rabinow. London, Penguin: 32–50.

Freeman, L. (2001). "Information systems knowledge: foundations, definitions and applications." *Information Systems Frontiers* **3**(2): 249–266.

Frege, G. (1952). *Translations from the philosophical writings of Gottlob Frege*. Oxford, Blackwell.

Freifelder, D. (1983). *Molecular Biology*. Boston, Science Books International.

Friend, J. (2001). The strategic choice approach. *Rational Analysis for a Problematic World Revisited: Problem Structuring Methods for Complexity, Uncertainty and Conflict*. J. Rosenhead and J. Mingers. Chichester, Wiley: 115–150.

Friend, J. and A. Hickling (1987). *Planning Under Pressure: The Strategic Choice Approach*. Oxford, Pergamon.

Fuenmayor, R. (1991). "Truth and openness: an epistemology for interpretative systemology." **4**: 473–490.

Galliers, R., Ed. (1992). *Information Systems Research: Issues, Methods and Practical Guidelines*. Oxford, Blackwell.

Galliers, R., N. Mylonopoulos, et al. (1997). *IS research agendas and practices in the UK*. 2nd UKAIS Conference, University of Southampton, McGraw Hill.

Gergen, K. (1999). *An invitation to social construction*. London, Sage.

Gettier, E. (1963). "Is justified true belief knowledge?" *Synthesis* **23**: 121–123.

Giddens, A., Ed. (1974). *Positivism and Sociology*. London, Heineman.

Giddens, A. (1976). *New Rules of Sociological Method*. London, Hutchinson.

Giddens, A. (1979). *Central Problems in Social Theory: Action Structure and Contradiction in Social Analysis*. London, Macmillan.

Giddens, A. (1981). *A Contemporary Critique of Historical Materialism*. London, Macmillan Press.

Giddens, A. (1984). *The Constitution of Society*. Cambridge, Polity Press.

Giddens, A. (1987). *Social Theory and Modern Sociology*. Cambridge, Polity Press.

Giddens, A. (1989). A reply to my critics. *Social Theory of Modern Societies: Anthony Giddens and his Critics*. D. Held and J. Thompson. Cambridge, Cambridge University Press: 249–301.

Giddens, A. (1990a). *The Consequences of Modernity*. Cambridge, Polity Press.

Giddens, A. (1990b). Structuration theory and sociological analysis. *Anthony Giddens: Consensus and Controversy*. J. Clark, C. Modgil and S. Modgil. London, Falmer Press: 297–315.

Giddens, A. (1992). *The Transformation of Intimacy: Sexuality, Love and Eroticism in Modern Society*. Cambridge, Polity.

Gioia, D. and E. Pitre (1990). "Multiparadigm perspectives on theory building." *Academy of Management Review* **15**(4): 584–602.

Goldkuhl, G. and K. Lyytinen (1982). A language action view of information systems. *Proc. of 3rd International Conference on Information Systems*. M. Ginzberg and K. Ross. Ann Arbour: 13–29.

Goldratt, E. (1997). *Critical Chain*. Great Barrington, MA, North River Press.

Goldratt, E. and J. Cox (1984). *The Goal*. NY, North River Press.

Goles, T. and R. Hirschheim (2000). "The paradigm is dead, the paradigm is dead ... long live the paradigm: the legacy of Burrell and Morgan." *Omega* **28**(3): 249–268.

Greenhill, A. (2001). *Managerial subjectivity and information systems: a discussion paper*. Eighth Americas Conference on Information Systems, Boston.

Gregory, R. (1972). *Eye and Brain*. London, Weidenfeld.

Gregory, W. (1996). "Discordant pluralism: a new strategy for critical systems thinking?" *Systems Practice* **9**: 605–620.

Groff, R. (2000). "The truth of the matter—Roy Bhaskar's critical realism and the concept of alethic truth." *Philosophy of the Social Sciences* **30**(3): 407–435.

Grosz, E. (1994). *Volatile Bodies: Towards a Corporeal Feminism*. Bloomington, Indiana University Press.

Grover, V. and T. Davenport (2001). "General perspectives on knowledge management: fostering a research agenda." *J. Management Information Systems* **18**(1): 5–21.

Guba, E. (1990). The alternative paradigm dialog. *The Paradigm Dialog*. E. Guba. California, Sage Publications.

Habermas, J. (1974). *Theory and Practice*. London, Heinemann.

Habermas, J. (1978). *Knowledge and Human Interests*. London, Heinemann.

Habermas, J. (1979). *Communication and the Evolution of Society*. London, Heinemann.

Habermas, J. (1984). *The Theory of Communicative Action Vol. 1: Reason and the Rationalization of Society*. London, Heinemann.

Habermas, J. (1985). Excursus on Luhmann's appropriation of the philosophy of the subject through systems theory. *The Philosophical Discourse of Modernity*. Cambridge, Polity Press: 368–385.

Habermas, J. (1987). *The Theory of Communicative Action Vol. 2: Lifeworld and System: a Critique of Functionalist Reason*. Oxford, Polity Press.

Habermas, J. (1990a). "Jurgen Habermas: Morality, Society and Ethics." *Acta Sociologica* 33(2): 93–114.

Habermas, J. (1990b). *Moral Consciousness and Communicative Action*. Cambridge, Polity Press.

Habermas, J. (1992). Discourse ethics: notes on a programme of philosophical justification. *Moral Consciousness and Communicative Action*. J. Habermas. Cambridge, Polity Press: 43–115.

Habermas, J. (1993). *Justification and Application*. Cambridge, Polity Press.

Habermas, J. (1993). On the pragmatic, the ethical, and the moral employments of practical reason. *Justification and Application*. Cambridge, Polity Press: 1–17.

Habermas, J. (1994). What theories can accomplish—and what they can't. *The Past as Future: Jurgen Habermas Interviewed by Michael Haller*. M. Haller. Cambridge, Polity Press: 99–120.

Habermas, J. (2003). *Truth and Justification*. Cambridge, Polity Press.

Hall, A. D. (1962). *A methodology for systems engineering*. N.Y., Van Nostrand Reinhold.

Hammond, M., J. Howarth, et al. (1991). *Understanding Phenomenology*. Oxford, Blackwell.

Hansen, N. (1958). *Patterns of Discovery*. New York, Cambridge University Press.

Harnden, R. (1989). *Outside and then: an interpretive approach to the VSM. The Viable Systems Model: Interpretations and Applications of Stafford Beer's VSM.* R. Espejo and R. Harnden. Chichester, Wiley: 383-404.

Harnden, R. (1990). "The languaging of models: the understanding and communication of models with particular reference to Stafford Beer's cybernetic model of organisation structure." *Systems Practice* **3**(3): 289–302.

Hartley, R. (1928). "Transmission of information." *Bell Systems Technical Journal* **7**: 535–563.

Harvey, D. L. (2002). "Agency and community: A critical realist paradigm." *Journal for the Theory of Social Behaviour* **32**(2): 163–194.

Harvey, L. and M. Myers (1995). "Scholarship and practice: the contribution of ethnographic research methods to bridging the gap." *Information Technology and People* **8**(3): 13–27.

Hassard, J. (1990). Ethnomethodology and organisational research: an introduction. *The Theory and Philosophy of Organisations.* J. Hassard and D. Pym. London, Routledge.

Hassard, J. and M. Parker, Eds. (1993). *Postmodernism and Organisations*. London, Sage.

Hayles, N. (1992). "The materiality of informatics." *Configurations* **1**: 147–170.

Hayles, N. K. (1999). The second wave of cybernetics: from reflexivity to self-organisation. *How We Became Posthuman: Virtual Bodies in Cybernetics, Literature, and Informatics.* Chicago, University of Chicago Press: 131–159.

Heidegger, M. (1962). *Being and Time*. Oxford, Blackwell.

Heims, S. (1993). *Constructing a Social Science for Postwar America: The Cybernetics Group 1946–1953.* Massachusetts, MIT Press.

Held, R. and A. Hein (1958). "Adaption of disarranged hand-eye coordination contingent upon reafferent stimulation." *Perceptual-Motor Skills* **8**: 87–90.

Hempel, C. (1965). *Aspects of Scientific Explanation*. New York, Free Press.

Hesse, M. (1974). *The Structure of Scientific Inference*. Berkeley, U. of California Press.

Hintikka, J. (1968). The varieties of information and scientific explanation. *Logic, Methodology and Philosophy of Science III*. B. van Rootselar and J. Staal. Amsterdam, North Holland: 311–331.

Horwich, P. (1991). *Truth*. Oxford, Blackwell.

Hughes, P. and G. Brecht (1978). *Vicious Circles and Infinity*. Harmondsworth, Penguin.

Hughes, W. (1996). *Critical Thinking*. Ontario, Broadview Press.

Hume, D. (1967). *Enquiries Concerning Human Understanding and the Principles of Morals*. Oxford, Clarendon Press.

Husserl, E. (1970). *The Crisis of European Sciences and Transcendental Phenomenology*. Chicago, Northwestern U. Press.

Husserl, E. (1977). *Cartesian Meditations*. The Hague, Martinus Nijhoff.

Hutchins, E. (1995). *Cognition in the Wild*. Cambridge, MIT Press.

Ingram, D. (1994). Foucault and Habermas on the subject of reason. *Cambridge Companion to Foucault*. G. Gutting. Cambridge, Cambridge University Press: 215–261.

Jackson, M. (1982). "The nature of soft systems thinking: the work of Churchman, Ackoff, and Checkland." *J. Applied Systems Analysis* **9**: 17–27.

Jackson, M. (1989a). Evaluating the managerial significance of the VSM. *Harnden, R.* R. Espejo and R. Harnden. London, Wiley: 407-440.

Jackson, M. (1989b). Which systems methodology when? Initial results from a research program. *Systems Prospects: the Next Ten Years of Systems Research*. R. Flood, M. Jackson and P. Keys. New York, Plenum.

Jackson, M. (1990). "Beyond a system of systems methodologies." *Journal of the Operational Research Society* **41**(8): 657–668.

Jackson, M. (1999). "Towards coherent pluralism in management science." *Journal of the Operational Research Society* **50**(1): 12–22.

Jackson, M. (2000). *Systems Approaches to Management*. Dordrecht, Kluwer Academic.

Jackson, M. and P. Keys (1984). "Towards a system of system methodologies." *Journal of the Operational Research Society* **35**(6): 473–486.

Jakobson, R. and M. Halle (1956). *Fundamentals of Language*. The Hague, Mouton.

James, W. (1976). *The meaning of truth*. Cambridge, Mass., Harvard University Press.

Jumarie, G. (1987). "Towards a mathematical theory of autopoiesis." *Cybernetica* **30**(3): 59–89.

Kaufmann, S. (1995). *At Home in the Universe: the search for the Laws of Complexity*. London, Penguin.

Keat, R. and J. Urry (1981). *Social Theory as Science*. London, RKP.

Kelly, M. (1994). Foucault, Habermas, and the self-referentiality of critique. *Critique and Power: Recasting the Foucault/Habermas Debate*. Massachusets, MIT Press: 365–400.

Keys, P. (1991). "A technologist's response to Miser." *Journal of the Operational Research Society* **42**(5): 431–433.

Keys, P. (1997). "Approaches to understanding the process of OR: Review, critique and extension." *Omega-International Journal of Management Science* **25**(1): 1–13.

Keys, P. (1998). "OR as technology revisited." *Journal of the Operational Research Society* **49**(2): 99–108.

Kickert, W. (1993). "Autopoiesis and the science of public administration: essence, sense and nonsense." *Organisation Studies* **14**(2): 261–278.

King, A. (1999a). "Against structure: A critique of morphogenetic social theory." *Sociological Review* **47**(2): 199–227.

King, A. (1999b). "The impossibility of naturalism: The antinomies of Bhaskar's realism." *J. for the Theory of Social Behaviour* **29**(3): 267–290.

King, A. (2000). "The accidental derogation of the lay actor: a critique of Giddens's concept of structure." *Philosophy of the Social Sciences* **30**(3): 362–383.

King, G. (1991). "'Truth is stranger than prediction, more questionable than causal inference." *American J. Political Science* **35**(4): 1047–1053.

Klein, H. and M. Huynh (2004). The critical social theory of Jurgen Habermas and its implications for IS research. *Social Theory and Philosophy for Information Systems*. J. Mingers and L. Willcocks. Chichester, Wiley.

Klir, G. J. (1969). *An approach to general systems theory.* New York, Van Nostrand Reinhold Co.

Klir, G. J. (1991). *Facets of systems science.* New York, Plenum Press.

Knorr-Cetina, K. and M. Mulkay, Eds. (1983). *Science Observed.* London, Sage.

Korzybski, I. (1933). *Science and Sanity: An Introduction to Non-Aristotelian Systems and General Semantics.* Fort Worth, Institute of General Semantics.

Kotidiatis, K. and Mingers, J. (2005). Combining PSMs with hard OR methods: the philosophical and practical challenges. KBS working paper 98, Canterbury, Kent Business School.

Krull, M., Luhmann, N. and Maturana, H. (1989). "Basic concepts of the theory of autopoietic systems." *Systemic Studies* **1**: 79–104.

Kuhn, T. (1970). *The Structure of Scientific Revolutions.* Chicago, Chicago University Press.

Kuhn, T. (1977). *The Essential Tension : Selected Studies in Scientific Tradition and Change.* Chicago, University of Chicago Press.

Lacan, J. (1970). The insistence of the letter in the unconsciousness. *Structuralism.* J. Ehrmann. New York, Anchor.

Lakoff, G. and M. Johnson (1987). *Women, Fire and Dangerous Things: What Categories Reveal About the Mind.* Chicago, U. Chicago Press.

Lambert, D. and A. Hughes (1988). "Key words and concepts in structuralist and functionalist biology." *J. of Theoretical Biology* **133**: 133–145.

Landry, M. and C. Banville (1992). "A disciplined methodological pluralism for MIS research." *Accounting, Management & Information Technology* **2**(2): 77–97.

Lane, D. (1998). "Can we have confidence in generic structures*?" Journal of the Operational Research Society* **49**(9): 936-947.

Lane, D. (1999). "Social theory and system dynamics practice." *European Journal of Operational Research* **113**: 501–527.

Lane, D. (2000). "Should system dynamics be described as a 'hard' or 'deterministic' systems approach?" *Systems Research and Behavioural Science* **17**: 3–22.

Lash, S. (2002). *Critique of Information.* London, Sage.

Laszlo, E. (1972a). Introduction to systems philosophy : toward a new paradigm of contemporary thought. N.Y., Gordon and Breach.

Laszlo, E. (1972b). The systems view of the world : the natural philosophy of the new developments in the sciences. New York, G. Braziller.

Latour, B. (1987). *Science in Action*. Milton Keynes, OU Press.

Lawson, T. (1996). "Developments in economics as a realist social theory." *Review of Social Economy* **54**(4): 405–422.

Lawson, T. (1997). *Economics and Reality*. London, Routledge.

Lawson, T. (1999). "Connections and distinctions: Post Keynesianism and critical realism." *Journal of Post Keynesian Economics* **22**(1): 3–14.

Layder, D. (1985). "Power, structure and agency." *J. for the Theory of Social Behaviour* **15**(2): 131–149.

Layder, D. (1987). "Key issues in structuration theory: Some critical remarks." *Current Perspectives in Social Theory* **8**: 25–46.

Layder, D. (1989). "The macro/micro distinction, social relations and methodological bracketing: Unresolved issues in structuration theory." *Current Perspectives in Social Theory* **9**: 123–141.

Layder, D. (1993). *New Strategies in Social Research*. Cambridge, Polity Press.

Layder, D. (1994). *Understanding Social Theory*. London, Sage.

Lee, H. (1961). *Symbolic Logic*. New York, Random House.

Levine, D. and S. Lippman, Eds. (1995). *The Economics of Information*. London, Edward Elgar.

Levi-Strauss, C. (1963). *Structural Anthropology*. New York, basic Books.

Lewis, M. and A. Grimes (1999). "Metatriangulation: building theory from multiple paradigms." *Academy of Management Review* **24**(4): 672–690.

Lewis, P. (1991). "The decision-making basis for information systems: the contribution of Vickers' concept of appreciation to a soft systems perspective." *European J. Information Systems* **1**: 33–43.

Lewis, P. (1993). "Linking soft systems methodology with data-focussed information systems developments." *J. Information Systems* **3**: 169–186.

Lewis, P. (2000). "Realism, causality and the problem of social structure." *Journal for the Theory of Social Behaviour* **30**(3): 249–268.

Luhmann, N. (1982a). *The Differentiation of Society*. NY, Columbia University Press.

Luhmann, N. (1982b). "The world society as a social system." *Int. J. General Systems* **8**: 131–138.

Luhmann, N. (1984). *Soziale Systeme*. Frankfurt, Suhrkamp.

Luhmann, N. (1985). "Society, meaning, religion—based on self-reference." *Sociological Analysis* **46**(1): 5–20.

Luhmann, N. (1986). The autopoiesis of social systems. *Sociocybernetic Paradoxes*. F. Geyer and J. van der Zouwen. London, SAGE Publications.

Luhmann, N. (1987). Closure and openness: on reality in the world of law. *Autopoiesis and the Law*. G. Teubner. Berlin, de Gruyter: 335–348.

Luhmann, N. (1989a). *Ecological Communication*. Cambridge, Polity Press.

Luhmann, N. (1989b). "Law as a social system." *Northwestern University Law Review* **83**: 136–150.

Luhmann, N. (1990a). *Essays in Self-Reference*. NY, Columbia University Press.

Luhmann, N. (1990b). Meaning as sociology's basic concept. *Essays in Self-Reference*. N. Luhmann. NY, Columbia University Press.

Luhmann, N. (1995). *Social Systems*. Stanford, Stanford University Press.

Luhmann, N. (1996). "Membership and motives in social systems." *Systems Research* **13**(3): 341–348.

Luhmann, N. (2000a). *Organisation und Entscheidung*. Opladen, Verlag.

Luhmann, N. (2000b). *The Reality of the Mass Media*. Cambridge, Polity Press.

Luisi, P. and Varela, F. (1989). "Self-replicating micelles—a chemical version of a minimal autopoietic system." *Origins of Life and Evolution of the Biosphere* **19**: 633–643.

Lyytinen, K. and H. Klein (1985). The critical theory of Jurgen Habermas as a basis for a theory of information systems. *Research Methods in Information Systems*. E. Mumford, R. Hirscheim, G. Fitzgerald and T. Wood-Harper. Amsterdam, Elsevier: 219–236.

Lyytinen, K., R. Klein, et al. (1991). "The effectiveness of office information systems: a social action perspective." *J. Information Systems* **1**: 41–60.

Mabin, V. and S. Balderstone (2003). "The performance of the theory of constraints methodology." *International Journal of Operations and Production Management* **23**(6): 568–595.

Mabin, V., J. Davies, et al. (2005). "The theory of constraints: a methodology apart?—a comparison with selected OR/MS methodologies." *Omega—The International Journal of Management Science* **forthcoming**.

Mabin, V., S. Forgeson, et al. (2001). "harnessing resistance: using the theory of constraints to assist change management." *J. European Industrial Training* **25**(2): 168–191.

MacIntyre, A. (1985). *After Virtue*. London, Duckworth.

Mackay, D. (1956). The place of "meaning" in the theory of information. *Information Theory: Third London Symposium*. C. Cherry. London, Butterworth: 215–225.

Mackay, D. (1969). *Information, Mechanism and Meaning*. Cambridge MA, MIT Press.

Madison, G. (1981). *The Phenomenology of Merleau-Ponty*. Athens, Ohio U. Press.

Mandelbrot, B. (1982). *The Fractal Geometry of Nature*. New York, W.H. Freeman.

Margulis, L. (1993). *Symbiosis in Cell Evolution: Microbial Communities in the Archean and Proterozoic Eons*. New York, Freeman.

Marquis, J.-P. (1996). "A critical note on Bunge's 'System Boundary' and a new proposal." *Int. J. of General Systems* **24**(3): 245–255.

Marsden, R. (1993). "The Politics of Organisational Analysis." *Organisation Studies* **14**(1): 93–124.

Marshall, N. and J. Sapsed (2000). *The limits of disembodied knowledge: challenges of inter-project learning in the production of complex products and systems*. Knowledge Management: Concepts and Controversies, University of Warwick.

Mason, R. and I. Mitroff (1981). *Challenging Strategic Planning Assumptions*. New York, Wiley.

Maturana, H. (1970). Biology of Cognition. Urbana, Univ of Illinois.

References                                                                        281

Maturana, H. (1970). The Neurophysiology of Cognition. *Cognition: a Multiple View*. P. Garvin. NY, Spartan Books: 3–23.

Maturana, H. (1974). Cognitive strategies. *Cybernetics of Cybernetics*. H. Von Foester. 457–469, Biological Computer Laboratory, University of Illinois.

Maturana, H. (1975). Communication and representation functions. *Encyclopedie de la Pleiade, Series Methodique*. J. Piaget. Paris, Gallimard.

Maturana, H. (1978a). Biology of language: the epistemology of reality. *Psychology and Biology of Language and Thought: Essays in Honour of Eric Lenneberg*. M. G. and E. Lenneberg. New York, Academic Press: 27–63.

Maturana, H. (1978b). Cognition. *Wahrnehmung und Kommunikation*. P. Hejl, Kock, W. and Roth, G. Frankfurt, Peter Lang: 29–49.

Maturana, H. (1980a). Autopoiesis: reproduction, heredity and evolution. *Autopoiesis, Dissipative Structures and Spontaneous Social Orders AAAS Selected Symposium 55*. M. Zeleny. Boulder, Westview Press: 45–79.

Maturana, H. (1980b). Man and society. *Autopoietic Systems in the Social Sciences*. F. Benseler, P. Hejl and W. Kock. Frankfurt, Campus Verlag: 11–31.

Maturana, H. (1981). Autopoiesis. *Autopoiesis: A Theory of Living Organisation*. M. Zeleny. New York, Elsevier-North Holland: 21–33.

Maturana, H. (1983). "What is it to see?" *Arch. Biol. Med. Exp.* **16**: 255–269.

Maturana, H. (1987a). The biological foundations of self-consciousness and the physical domain of existence. *Physics of Cognitive Processes*. E. Caianiello. Singapore, World Scientific: 324–379.

Maturana, H. (1987b). Everything is said by an observer. *Gaia: a Way of Knowing*. W. Thompson. Barmington.**, Lindisfarne Press.

Maturana, H. (1988). "Reality: the search for objectivity or the quest for a compelling argument." *Irish Journal of Psychology* **9**: 25–82.

Maturana, H. (1990). Science and daily life: the ontology of scientific explanations. *Selforganisation: Portrait of a Scientific Revolution*. W. Krohn, G. Kuers and H. Nowotny. Dordrecht, Kluwer Academic Publishers: 12–35.

Maturana, H. (1991a). "Response to Berman's critique of "The Tree of Knowledge."" *J. Human Psychology* **31**(2): 88–97.

Maturana, H. (1991b). "Response to Jim Birch." *J. Family Therapy* **13**(375–393.): autopoiesis.

Maturana, H. (1993). The origin of the theory of autopoiesis. *Autopoiesis: Eine Theorie im Brennpunkt Kritik.* H. Fischer. Heidelberg, Carl-Auer-Systeme: 121–123.

Maturana, H. (1995). Biology of self-consciousness. *Consciousness: Distinction and Reflection.* G. Trautteur. Naples, Bibliopolis.

Maturana, H. and G. Guiloff (1980). "The quest for the intelligence of intelligence." *J. Social Biol. Struct.* **3**: 135–148.

Maturana, H., Lettvin, J., McCulloch, S. and Pitts, W. (1960). "Anatomy and physiology of vision in the frog." *Journal of General Physiology* **43**: 129–175.

Maturana, H., Mpodozis, J. and Letelier, J. (1995). "Brain, language and the origin of human mental functions." *Biology Research* **28**: 15–26.

Maturana, H., Uribe, G. and Frenk, S. (1968). "A biological theory of relativistic colour coding in the primate retina." *Archiva de Biologia y Medicina Experimentales* Suplemento 1: 1–30.

Maturana, H. and F. Varela (1975). Autopoietic systems—a characterization of the living organisation. Urbana, Univ of Illinois.

Maturana, H. and F. Varela (1980). *Autopoiesis and Cognition: The Realization of the Living.* Dordrecht, Reidel.

Maturana, H. and F. Varela (1980). Autopoiesis: the organisation of the living. *Autopoiesis and Cognition: The Realization of the Living.* H. Maturana and F. Varela. Dordrecht, Reidel: 63–134.

Maturana, H. and F. Varela (1987). *The Tree of Knowledge.* Boston, Shambhala.

McCarthy, T. (1991). The critique of impure reason: Foucault and the Frankfurt School. *Ideals and Illusions: On Reconstruction and Deconstruction in Contemporary Critical Theory.* T. McCarthy. Massachusets, MIT Press: 43–75.

McMullin, B. and F. Varela (1997). *Rediscovering Computational Autopoiesis.* Sante Fe, Santa Fe Institute.

McPeck, J. (1981). *Critical Thinking and Education.* Oxford, Martin Robertson.

Mead, G. (1934). *Mind, Self and Society.* Chicago, University of Chicago Press.

Mendoza, J. (1997). The duality of structure. *Anthony Giddens: Critical Assessments.* G. Bryant and D. Jary. London, Routledge. **2**: 219–270.

Merleau-Ponty, M. (1962). *Phenomenology of Perception.* London, Routledge.

Merleau-Ponty, M. (1963). *The Structure of Behaviour.* Boston, Beacon Press.

Merleau-Ponty, M. (1964). *Signs.* Evanston, Northwestern U. Press.

Merleau-Ponty, M. (1969). *The Visible and the Invisible.* Evanston, Northwestern University Press.

Meynen, H. T. (1992). The bringing forth of dialogue: Latour versus Maturana. *New Perspectives on Cybernetics: Self-organisation, Autonomy and Connectionism.* G. van de Vijver. Dordrecht, Kluwer Academic: 157–174.

Midgley, G. (2000). *Systemic Intervention: Philosophy, Methodology, and Practice.* New York, Kluwer. Plenum.

Miller, J. (1978). *Living Systems.* New York, McGraw Hill.

Miller, J., A. Dermaid, et al. (1997). "Trans-organisational innovation:a framework for research." *Technology Analysis and Strategic Management* **9**(4): 399–418.

Mingers, J. (1984). "Subjectivism and soft systems methodology—a critique." *J. Applied Systems Analysis* **11**: 85–103.

Mingers, J. (1989). Problems of measurement. *Operational Research and the Social Sciences.* M. Jackson, P. Keys and S. Cropper. New York, Plenum Press: 471–477.

Mingers, J. (1992). "Recent developments in critical management science." *Journal of the Operational Research Society* **43**(1): 1–10.

Mingers, J. (1993a). "The system of systems methodologies—a reply to Schecter." *Journal of the Operational Research Society* **44**(2): 206–208.

Mingers, J. (1993b). "Systems methodologies and critical management science— some comments." *Journal of the Operational Research Society* **44**(8): 849–850.

Mingers, J. (1995). *Self-Producing Systems: Implications and Applications of Autopoiesis.* New York, Plenum Press.

Mingers, J. (1995). Using Soft Systems Methodology in the design of information systems. Information *Systems Provision: The Contribution of Soft Systems Methodology.* F. Stowell. London, McGraw-Hill: 18-50.

Mingers, J. (1996a). "A comparison of Maturana's autopoietic social theory and Giddens' theory of structuration." *Systems Research* **13**(4): 469–482.

Mingers, J. (1996b). "An evaluation of theories of information with regard to the semantic and pragmatic aspects of information systems." *Systems Practice* **9**(3): 187–209.

Mingers, J. (1997a). "Systems typologies in the light of autopoiesis: a reconceptualization of Boulding's hierarchy, and a typology of self-referential systems." *Systems Research and Behavioural Science* **14**: 303–313.

Mingers, J. (1997b). Towards critical pluralism. *Multimethodology: Theory and Practice of Combining Management Science Methodologies*. J. Mingers and A. Gill. Chichester, Wiley: 407–440.

Mingers, J. (2000a). "The contribution of critical realism as an underpinning philosophy for OR/MS and systems." *Journal of the Operational Research Society* **51**(11): 1256–1270.

Mingers, J. (2000b). "An idea ahead of its time: the history and development of soft systems methodology." *Systemic Practice and Action Research* **13**(6): 733–756.

Mingers, J. (2000c). "Variety is the spice of life: combining soft and hard OR/MS methods." *International Transactions in Operational Research* **7**: 673–691.

Mingers, J. (2000d). "What is it to be critical? Teaching a critical approach to management undergraduates." *Management Learning* **31**(2): 219–237.

Mingers, J. (2001a). "Combining IS research methods: towards a pluralist methodology." *Information Systems Research* **12**(3): 240–259.

Mingers, J. (2001b). "Embodying information systems: the contribution of phenomenology." *Information and Organisation* **11**(2): 103–128.

Mingers, J. (2003a). Observing organisations: An evaluation of Luhmann's theory of organisations. *Autopoietic Organisation Theory: Drawing on Niklas Luhmann's Social Systems Perspective*. T. Hernes and T. Bakken. Copenhagen, Copenhagen Business School Press: 103–122.

Mingers, J. (2003b). "The paucity of multimethod research: A survey of the IS literature." *Information Systems Journal* **13**: 233–249.

Mingers, J. (2004). Future directions in management science modeling: critical realism and multimethodology. *Critical Realism in Action in Organisations and Management Studies*. S. Fleetwood and S. Ackroyd. London, Routledge.

Mingers, J. (2005). "Classifying philosophical assumptions: a reply to Ormerod." *J. Operational Research Society* **56**(4): 465–467.

Mingers, J. (2005). "A critique of statistical modelling in management science from a critical realist perspective: its role within multimethodology." *J. Operational Research Society* **56**(in press).

Mingers, J. and J. Brocklesby (1997). "Multimethodology: towards a framework for mixing methodologies." *Omega* **25**(5): 489–509.

Mingers, J. and A. Gill, Eds. (1997). *Multimethodology: Theory and Practice of Combining Management Science Methodologies*. Chichester, Wiley.

Mingers, J. and L. Willcocks, Eds. (2004). *Social Theory and Philosophy for Information Systems*. Chichester, Wiley.

Miser, H. (1991). "Comments on 'OR as technology'." *Journal of the Operational Research Society* **42**(5): 429–433.

Miser, H. (1996). "Comments prompted by 'On the nature of OR—entering the fray." *Journal of the Operational Research Society* **47**: 1322–1323.

Monod, J. (1974). *Chance and Necessity*. London, Fontana.

Morgan, G. (1986). *Images of Organisation*. Newbury Park, Sage.

Morris, C. (1938). Foundations of the theory of signs. *International Encyclopedia of Unified Science*. O. Neurath. Chicago, University of Chicago Press. **1**.

Muller-Mehrbach, H. (1994). "A system of systems approaches." *Interfaces* **24**(4): 16–25.

Munro, I. (1996). The question of ethics in OR and systems thinking: an exploration of three emancipatory themes. Coventry, Warwick Business School Research Bureau.

Munro, I. and J. Mingers (2002). "The use of multimethodology in practice—results of a survey of practitioners." *Journal of the Operational Research Society* **59**(4): 369–378.

Mutch, A. (1999). Information: a critical realist approach. *Proceedings of the 2nd Information Seeking in Context*. T. Wilson and D. Allen. London, Taylor Graham: 535–551.

Myers, M. (1994). "Dialectical hermeneutics: a theoretical framework for the implementation of information systems." *Information Systems Journal* **5**: 51–70.

Nandhakumar, J. and M. Jones (1997). "Too close for comfort? Distance and engagement in interpretive information systems research." *Information Systems Journal* **7**: 109–131.

Nauta, D. (1972). *The Meaning of Information*. The Hague, Mouton.

Nellhaus, T. (1998). "Signs, social ontology, and critical realism." *Journal For the Theory of Social Behaviour* **28**(1): 1–+.

Neurath, O. and B. McGuinness (1987). *Unified science : the Vienna circle monograph series originally edited by Otto Neurath*. Dordrecht, D. Reidel Pub. Co.

New, C. (1994). "Structure, agency and social transformation." *Journal for the Theory of Social Behaviour* **24**(3): 187–205.

New, C. (1995). "Sociology and the Case For Realism." *Sociological Review* **43**(4): 808–827.

Newman, J. (2001). "Some observations on the semantics of "information."" *Information Systems Frontiers* **3**(2): 155–167.

Ngwenyama, O. (1991). The critical social theory approach to information systems: problems and challenges. *Information Systems Research: Contemporary Approaches and Emergent Traditions*. H.-E. Nissen, H. Klein and R. Hirscheim. Amsterdam, North Holland: 267–280.

Ngwenyama, O. and A. Lee (1997). "Communication richness in electronic mail: critical social theory and the contextuality of meaning." *MIS Quarterly* **21**(June): 145–167.

Nissen, H.-E., H. Klein, et al., Eds. (1991). *Information Systems Research: Contemporary Approaches and Emergent Traditions*. Amsterdam, North Holland.

Norris, C. (1997). *New Idols of the Cave: On the Limits of Anti-Realism*. Manchester, Manchester University Press.

Nutt, P. (1979). "Influence of Decision Styles on Use of Decision Models." *Technological Forecasting and Social Change* **14**: 77–93.

Nutt, P. (1986). "Decision Style and its Impact on Managers and Management." *Technological Forecasting and Social Change* **29**: 341–366.

Olsen, W. (1999). *Developing open-systems interpretations of path analysis: fragility analysis using farm data from India*. Critical Realism: Implications for Practice, Örebro University Sweden, Centre for Critical Realism.

Orlikowski, W. and J. Baroudi (1991). "Studying information technology in organisations: research approaches and assumptions." *Information Systems Research* **2**(1): 1–28.

Orlikowski, W. and D. Robey (1991). "Information technology and the structuring of organisations." *Information Systems Research* **2**(2): 143–169.

Ormerod, R. (1995). "Putting soft OR methods to work: information systems strategy development at Sainsbury's." *Journal of the Operational Research Society* **46**(3): 277–293.

Ormerod, R. (1996a). "On the nature of OR—entering the fray." *Journal of the Operational Research Society* **47**(1): 1–17.

Ormerod, R. (1996b). "Putting soft OR methods to work—information systems strategy development at Richards Bay." *Journal of the Operational Research Society* **47**(9): 1083–1097.

Ormerod, R. (1996c). "Response to Miser: the objects and objectives of operational research." *Journal of the Operational Research Society* **47**: 1323–1326.

Ormerod, R. (1997). Mixing methods in practice: a transformation-competence perspective. *Multimethodology: Theory and Practice of Combining Management Science Methodologies*. J. Mingers and A. Gill. Chichester, Wiley: 29–58.

Ormerod, R. J. (2001). Mixing methods in practice. *Rational Analysis for a Problematic World Revisited: Problem Structuring Methods for Complexity, Uncertainty and Conflict*. J. Rosenhead and J. Mingers. Chichester, Wiley: 289–310.

Ormerod, R. J. (2005). "Comments on the classification of management science methods by Mingers." *J. Operational Research Society* **56**(4): 463–465.

Otten, K. (1978). Information and communication. *Perspectives in Information Science*. A. Debbons and W. Cameron. Leyden, Noordhof: 127–148.

Outhwaite, W. (1987). *New Philosophies of Social Science: Realism, Hermeneutics and Critical Theory*. London, Macmillan.

Parker, M. and G. McHugh (1991). "Five texts in search of an author: a response to John Hassard's 'Multiple Paradigms and Organisational Analysis'." *Organisation Studies* **12**(3): 451–456.

Parsons, T. (1951). *The Social System*, Glencoe.

Paterson, J. and G. Teubner (1998). "Changing maps: Empirical legal autopoiesis." *Social & Legal Studies* **7**(4): 451–486.

Paul, R. (1990). *Critical Thinking*. Santa Rosa, Foundation for Critical Thinking.

Peirce, C. (1878). "How to make our ideas clear." *Popular Science Monthly* (January).

Peirce, C. (1965). *Collected Papers of Charles Sanders Peirce (8 Volumes)*. Cambridge, Harvard University Press.

Pfeffer, J. (1993). "Barriers to the advance of organisational science: paradigm development as a dependent variable." *Academy of Management Review* **18**(4): 599–620.

Piaget, J. (1969). *The Mechanisms of Perception*. New York, Basic Books.

Plato (2004). *Theaetetus,* Harmondsworth, Penguin.

Polanyi, M. (1958). *Personal Knowledge: Towards a Post-Critical Philosophy*. London, Routledge.

Popper, K. (1959). *The Logic of Scientific Discovery*. London, Hutchinson.

Popper, K. (1962). *The Open Society and its Enemies*. London, RKP.

Popper, K. (1969). *Conjectures and Refutations*. London, Routledge and Kegan Paul.

Popper, K. (1972). *Objective Knowledge: an Evolutionary Approach.* London, Oxford University Press.

Porpora, D. (1989). "Four Concepts of Social Structure." *J. for the Theory of Social Behaviour* **19**(2): 195–211.

Porpora, D. (1998a). *Do realist run regressions?* 2nd International Centre for Critical Realism Conference, University of Essex.

Porpora, D. (1998b). Four Concepts of Social Structure. *Critical Realism: Essential Readings*. M. Archer, R. Bhaskar, A. Collier, T. Lawson and A. Norrie. London, Routledge: 339–355.

Poster, M. (1990). *The Mode of Information*. Cambridge, Polity.

Poster, M. (1995). *The Second Media Age*. Cambridge, Polity Press.

Pratt, A. (1977). "The information of the image: A model of the communication process." *Libri* **27**(3): 204–220.

Pratt, A. (1995). "Putting critical realism to work: the practical implications for geographical research." *Progress in Human Geography* **19**(1): 61–74.

Priban, I. (1968). "Models in medicine." *Science Journal* **6**: 61–67.

Probert, S. (1996). *Is Total Systems Intervention compelling?* 40th Annual Meeting of ISSS, International Society for the Systems Sciences.

Putnam, H. (1981). *Reason, truth, and history*. Cambridge, Cambridge University Press.

Quine, W. (1992). *Pursuit of Truth*. Boston, Harvard University Press.

Ramsey, F. (1927). "Facts and propositions." *Proc. of the Aristotelian Society* **7**.

Rapoport, A. (1986). *General system theory : essential concepts & applications.* Tunbridge Wells, Kent, Abacus.

Raven, P. and C. Johnson (1991). *Understanding Biology*. St Louis, Mosby-Year Book.

Ravetz, G. (1971). *Scientific Knowledge and its Social Problems*. Oxford, Oxford University Press.

Reed, M. (1997). "In praise of duality and dualism: rethinking agency and structure in organisational analysis." *Organisation Studies* **18**(1): 21–42.

Reed, M. (2001). "Organisation, trust and control: a realist analysis." *Organisation Studies* **22**(2): 201–228.

Robb, F. (1991). "Accounting—a virtual autopoietic system?" *Systems Practice* **4**(3): 215–235.

Robb, F. (1992). "Autopoiesis and supra-human systems." *Int. Journal of Gen. Sys.* **21**(2): 197–206.

Roberts, D. (1973). *The Existential Graphs of C.S. Peirce*. The Hague, Mouton.

Robey, D. (1996). "Diversity in information systems research: threat, promise and responsibility." *Information Systems Research* **7**(4): 400–408.

Robinson, H., P. Hall, et al. (1998). "Postmodern software development." *The Computer Journal* **41**(6): 363–375.

Robinson, S. (2001). "Soft with a Hard Centre: Discrete Event Simulation in Facilitation." *Journal of the Operational Research Society* **52**(8): 905–915.

Ron, A. (1999). *Regression analysis and the philosophy of social sciences—a critical realist view*. Critical Realism: Implications for Practice, Örebro University Sweden, Centre for Critical Realism.

Rorty, R. (1980). *Philosophy and the Mirror of Nature*. Oxford, Blackwell.

Rorty, R. (1982). *Consequences of Pragmatism*. Minnesota, Minnesota University Press.

Rorty, R. (1989). *Contingency, Irony and Solidarity*. Cambridge, Cambridge U. P.

Rosenau, P. (1992). *Post-Modernism and the Social Sciences*. Princeton, Princeton University Press.

Rosseel, E. and G. van der Linden (1990). "Self-monitoring and self-steering in social interaction: Theoretical comments and an empirical investigation." *Kybernetes* **1991**(1): 18–33.

Russell, B. (1912). *The Problems of Philosophy*. Oxford, Oxford University Press.

Ryle, G. (1963). *The Concept of Mind*. London, Peregrine Books.

Saussure, F. (1960). *Course in General Linguistics*. London, Peter Owen.

Savage, A. and J. Mingers (1996). "A framework for linking Soft Systems Methodology (SSM) and Jackson Systems Development (JSD)." *Information Systems Journal* **6**: 109-129.

Sayer, A. (1992). *Method in Social Science*. London, Routledge.

Sayer, A. (1997). "Critical realism and the limits to critical social science." *Journal For the Theory of Social Behaviour* **27**(4): 473–+.

Sayer, A. (2000). *Realism and Social Science*. London, Sage.

Schlick, M., H. L. Mulder, et al. (1979). *Philosophical papers : Edited by Henk L. Mulder and Barbara F.B. van de Velde-Schlick; translated by Peter Heath*. Dordrecht, Holland, D. Reidel.

Schultze, U. and D. Leidner (2002). "Studying knowledge management in information systems research: discourses and theoretical assumptions." *MIS Quarterly* **26**(3): 213–242.

Schutz, A. (1972). *The Phenomenology of the Social World*. London, Heinemann.

Searle, J. (1996). *The Construction of Social Reality*. London, Penguin Books.

Sewell, W. (1992). "A theory of structure: duality, agency, and transformation." *American Journal of Sociology* **98**(1): 1–29.

Shannon, C. and W. Weaver (1949). *The Mathematical Theory of Communication.* Illinois, University of Illinois Press.

Sheffer, H. (1913). "Five independent postulates for Boolean algebra." *Transactions of the American Mathematics Society* **14**: 481–488.

Shilling, C. (1993). *The Body and Social Theory.* London, Sage.

Simons, P. (1987). *Parts: a Study in Ontology.* Oxford, Clarendon Press.

Slocum, J. (1978). "Does Cognitive Style Affect Diagnosis and Interventions Strategies of Change Agents?" *Group and Organisation Studies* **3**(2): 199–210.

Smaling, A. (1994). "The pragmatic dimension: paradigmatic and pragmatic aspects of choosing a qualitative or quantitative method." *Quality and Quantity* **28**: 233–249.

Spaul, M. (1995). An ethical basis for critical systems thinking: communicative or communitarian? *Critical Issues in Systems Theory and Practice.* K. Ellis. New York, Plenum Press: 511–516.

Spencer-Brown, G. (1972). *Laws of Form.* NY, Julien Press.

Stamper, R. (1991). The semiotic framework for information systems research. *Information Systems Research: Contemporary Approaches and Emergent Traditions.* H.-E. Nissen, H. Klein and R. Hirscheim. Amsterdam, North Holland.

Stamper, R. (1997). Organisational semiotics. *Information Systems: an Emerging Discipline?* J. Mingers and F. Stowell. London, McGraw-Hill: 267–284.

Stokes, P. (1990). Socio-cybernetics and the project of scientificisation of sociology. *Self-Steering and Cognition in Complex Systems: Towards a New Cybernetics.* E. Heylighen, E. Rosseel and F. Demeyere. London, Gordon and Breech.

Stowell, F., Ed. (1995). *Information Systems Provision: the Contribution of Soft Systems Methodology.* London, McGraw Hill.

Strawson, P. (1950). "Truth." *Proc. of the Aristotelian Society* **24**.

Stumph, S. and R. Dunbar (1991). "The effects of personality type on choices made in strategic decision situations." *Decision Sciences* **22**: 1047–1069.

Suber, P. (1990). *Paradox of Self-Amendment*. New York, P. Lang Publishers.

Swan, J. and H. Scarbrough (2001). "Knowledge management: concepts and controversies." *J Management Studies* **38**(7): 913–921.

Synnott, A. (1993). *The Body Social: Symbolism, Self and Society*. London, Routledge.

Tabary, J. (1991). "Hierarchy and autonomy." *Int. Journal of General Systems* **18**: 241–250.

Taket, A. and L. White (1993). "After OR: An Agenda for Postmodernism and Poststructuralism in OR." *Journal of the Opertations Research Society* **44**: 9.

Taket, A. and L. White (1994). "Postmodernism—Why Bother?" *Systemist* **16**(3): 175–186.

Tarski, A. (1944). "The semantic conception of truth." *Philosophy and Phenomenological Research* **4**: 341–375.

Tashakkori, A. and C. Teddlie (1998). *Mixed Methodology: Combining Qualitative and Quantitative Approaches*. London, SAGE Publications.

Teubner, G. (1990). *And God laughed ... indeterminancy, self-reference and paradox in law*. European University Institute, Florence.

Teubner, G. (1993). *Law as an Autopoietic System*. Oxford, Blackwell.

Thompson, E., Palacios, A. and Varela, F. (1992). "Ways of coloring." *comparative color vision as a case study for cognitive science* **Behavioral and Brain Sciences**(15).

Thompson, J. (1989). The theory of structuration. *Social Theory of Modern Societies: Anthony Giddens and his Critics*. D. Held and J. Thompson. Cambridge, Cambridge University Press: 56–76.

Trefethen, F. (1995). A history of Operations Research. *Understanding the Process of Operational Research*. P. Keys. Chichester, Wiley: 47–76.

Tsang, E. and K. Kwan (1999). "Replication and theory development in organisational science: a critical realist perspective." *Academy of Management Review* **24**(4): 759–780.

Tsoukas, H. and D. Papoulias (1996). "Creativity in OR/MS: from technique to epistemology." *Interfaces* **26**(2): 73–79.

Tuomi, I. (1999). "Data is more than knowledge: implications of the reversed knowledge hierarchy for knowledge management and knowledge memory." *J. Management Information Systems* **16**(3): 103–117.

Turner, B. (1984). *The Body and Society*. Oxford, Blackwell.

Ulrich, W. (1991). Critical heuristics of social systems design. *Critical Systems Thinking: Directed Readings*. R. Flood and M. Jackson. Chichester, Wiley: 103–115.

Ulrich, W. (1994). *Critical Heuristics of Social Planning: a New Approach to Practical Philosophy*. Chichester, Wiley.

Ulrich, W. (2000). "Reflective practice in the Civil Society: the contribution of critically systemic thinking." *Reflective Practice* **1**(2): 247–268.

van der Spek, R. and A. Spijkervet (1997). Knowledge management: dealing intelligently with knowledge. *Knowledge Management and its Integrative Elements*. J. Liebowitz and L. Wilcox. New York, CRC Press: 31–59.

Van Maanen, J. (1995). "Fear and loathing in organisation studies." *Organisation Science* **6**(6): 687–692.

Van Maanen, J. (1995). "Style as theory." *Organisation Science* **6**(1): 133–143.

Varela, C. (1999). "Determinism and the recovery of human agency: the embodying of persons." *J. for the Theory of Social Behaviour* **29**(4): 385–402.

Varela, C. (2002). "The impossibility of which naturalism? A response and a reply." *J. for the Theory of Social Behaviour* **32**(1): 105–111.

Varela, C. and R. Harre (1996). "Conflicting varieties of realism: Causal powers and the problems of social structure." *Journal For the Theory of Social Behaviour* **26**(3): 313 (14 pages).

Varela, F. (1977). On being autonomous: the lessons of natural history for systems theory. *Applied Systems Research*. G. Klir. NY, Plenum Press: 77–85.

Varela, F. (1979). *Principles of Biological Autonomy*. New York, Elsevier-North Holland.

Varela, F. (1981a). Autonomy and autopoiesis. *Self-Organising Systems—an Interdisciplinary Approach*. G. Roth and H. Schwegler. Frankfurt, Campus Verlag: 14–24.

Varela, F. (1981b). Describing the logic of the living. The adequacy and limitations of the idea of autopoiesis. *Autopoiesis: A Theory of the Living Organisation.* M. Zeleny. New York, Elsevier-North Holland: 36–48.

Varela, F. (1984). Living ways of sense-making: a middle path for neuroscience. *Order and Disorder: Proceedings of the Stanford International Symposium.* P. Livingstone. Stanford, Anma Libri: 208–224.

Varela, F. (1991). "Making it concrete: before, during and after breakdowns." *Revue Internationale de Psychopathologie* **4**: 435–450.

Varela, F. (1992). Whence perceptual meaning? A cartography of current ideas. *Understanding Origins: Contemporary Views on the Origin of Life, Mind and Society.* F. V. a. J. Dupuy. Dordrecht, Kluwer Academic: 235–263.

Varela, F. and A. Coutinho (1991). "Second generation immune networks." *Immunology Today* **12**(5): 159–167.

Varela, F., A. Coutinho, et al. (1988). Cognitive networks: immune, neural, and otherwise. *Theoretical Immunology: SFI Series on the Science of Complexity.* A. Perelson. New Jersey, Addison Wesley: 359–375.

Varela, F., Maturana, H. and Uribe, R. (1974). "Autopoiesis: the organisation of living systems, its characterization and a model." *Biosystems* **5**(4): 187–196.

Varela, F., Thompson, E. and Rosch, E. (1991). *The Embodied Mind.* Cambridge, MIT Press.

Veld, R. J., L. Schaap, et al. (1991). *Autopoiesis and Configuration Theory: New Approaches to Societal Steering.* Dordrecht, Kluwer.

Vennix, J. (1996). *Group Model Building: Facilitating Team Learning Using Systems Dynamics.* London, Wiley.

von Bertalanffy, L. (1971). *General Systems Theory.* London, Penguin.

Von Foerster, H. (1984). *Observing Systems.* CA, Intersystems Publications.

Von Foerster, H. (1984). On constructing a reality. *Observing Systems.* H. V. Foerster. CA, Intersystems Publications: 287–309.

Von Glasersfeld, E. (1984). An introduction to radical constructivism … *The Invented Reality.* P. Watzlawick. New York, Norton.

Walsham, G. (1995). "The emergence of interpretivism in IS research." *Information Systems Research* **6**(4): 376–394.

Walsham, G. (1997). Actor-network theory and IS research: current status and future prospects. *Information Systems and Qualitative Research*. A. Lee, J. Liebenau and J. DeGross. London, Chapman Hall: 466–480.

Weaver, G. and D. Gioia (1994). "Paradigms lost: incommensurability vs structurationist inquiry." *Organisational Studies 15* **4**(565–590).

Weinberg, G. M. (1975). *An introduction to general systems thinking.* N.Y., Wiley.

Weiner, N. (1948). *Cybernetics: or Communication and Control in the Animal and the Machine.* Cambridge, MIT Press.

White, L. (1994). "The death of the expert." *Journal of the Operational Research Society* **45**(7): 733–748.

White, L. and A. Taket (1996). "The end of theory?" *Omega, Int. J. Mgmt. Sci.* **24**(1): 47–56.

White, L. and A. Taket (1997). Critiquing multimethodology as metamethodology: Working towards pragmatic pluralism. *Multimethodology: The Theory and Practice of Combining Management Science Methodologies.* J. Mingers and A. Gill. Chichester, Wiley: 379–407.

Whitehead, A. N. and B. Russell (1925). *Principia mathematica.* Cambridge, The University Press.

Whittington, R. (1992). "Putting Giddens into action—social systems and managerial agency." *J. Management Studies* **29**(6): 693–712.

Wiig, K. (1993). *Knowledge Management Foundations: Thinking about Thinking— How People and Organisations Create, Represent, and Use Knowledge.* Arlington, TX, Schema Press.

Wilden, A. (1977). *System and Structure.* London, Tavistock.

Winograd, T. and F. Flores (1987). *Understanding Computers and Cognition.* New York, Addison Wesley.

Winter, S. (1987). Knowledge and competence as strategic assets. *The Competitive Challenge.* D. Teece. Cambridge, MA, Ballinger: 159–184.

Wittgenstein, L. (1958). *Philosophical Investigations.* Oxford, Blackwell.

Wittgenstein, L. (1974). *Tractatus logico-philosophicus.* London, Routledge and Kegan Paul.

Wolstenholme, E. (1993). "A case study in community care using systems thinking." *Journal of the Operational Research Society* **44**(9): 925-934.

Wolstenholme, E. and R. Coyle (1983). "The development of systems dynamics as a methodology for system description and qualitative analysis." *Journal of the Operational Research Society* **34**: 569-581.

Woolgar, S., Ed. (1988). Knowledge and Reflexivity: New frontiers in the Sociology of Knowledge. Beverly Hills, Sage.

Wright, C. (1999). "They shoot dead horses don't they? Locating agency in the agent-structure problematique." *European J. of International Relations* **5**(1): 109–142.

Yeung, H. (1997). "Critical realism and realist research in human geography." *Progress in Human Geography* **21**(1): 51–74.

Young, I. (1990). *Justice and the Politics of Difference*. Princeton, Princeton University Press.

Zadeh, L. (1996). Fuzzy sets, fuzzy logic and fuzzy systems. NJ, World Scientific Publishing.

Zeleny, M. and C. Hufford (1992). "The application of autopoiesis in systems analysis: Are autopoietic systems also social systems?" *Int. J. Gen. Sys.* **21**(2): 145–160.

Zeleny, M. and C. Hufford (1992). "The ordering of the unknown by causing it to order itself." *Int. J. Gen. Sys.* **21**(2): 239–253.

# Names Index

Figures are denoted by *f*. Tables are denoted by *t*.

300 *Real*ising Systems Thinking: Knowledge and Action in Management Science

Uribe, G. 57
Urry, J. 18, 19

van der Linden, G. 56
van ders Spek, R. 133
Van Maanen, J. 13
Varela, F. 1, 3, 5, 6, 7, 33–40, 42–4, 47–53,
    57, 70, 84, 85, 94, 96, 97, 105, 113, 137,
    151, 152, 156, 157, 167, 171, 174, 179,
    190, 192, 193, 257
Veld, R. J. 170
Vennix, J. 237
von Bertalanffy, L. 1, 11, 66, 90
Von Foerster, H. 55, 91
Von Glasersfeld, E. 12

Walde, P. 49
Walsham, G. 4, 13
Weaver, G. 204
Weaver, W. 107, 113
Weber, R. 13
Weinberg, G. M. 66

Weiner, N. 1, 11
White, L. 12, 13, 208, 242, 245
Whitehead, A. N. 15, 74
Whittington, R. 214
Wiig, K. 133
Wilden, A. 56, 79, 122
Willcocks, L. 13
Wilmott, H. 246
Winograd, T. 62
Winter, S. 133
Wittgenstein, L. 15, 25, 77, 81, 118, 126,
    140, 148
Wolstenholme, E. 237
Woolgar, S. 18
Wright, C. 20, 181

Yeung, H. 20
Young, I. 241, 245, 246

Zadek, L. 75
Zeleny, M. 41, 49, 167

# Subject Index

Figures are denoted by *f*. Tables are denoted by *t*.